INTERNATIONAL LITIGATION AND ARBITRATION

SELECTED TREATIES, STATUTES AND RULES

Third Edition

By

Andreas F. Lowenfeld

Herbert and Rose Rubin Professor of International Law
New York University School of Law

AMERICAN CASEBOOK SERIES®

Mat #40335921

American Casebook Series and West Group are trademarks
registered in the U.S. Patent and Trademark Office.

COPYRIGHT © 1993 WEST PUBLISHING CO.
© West, a Thomson business, 2001
© 2005 Thomson/West
      610 Opperman Drive
      P.O. Box 64526
      St. Paul, MN 55164–0526
      1–800–328–9352

Printed in the United States of America

ISBN 0–314–15914–2

TEXT IS PRINTED ON 10% POST CONSUMER RECYCLED PAPER

Preface

The documents here collected range from those easily found in any law library, such as excerpts from the Federal Rules of Civil Procedure, the Uniform Foreign Money-Judgments Act, and the Federal Arbitration Act, to documents available only in specialist libraries, such as the rules of various arbitral institutions, excerpts from British statutes and rules dealing with jurisdiction and judgments, and the confidential documents laws of the United Kingdom, France, and Switzerland.

The booklet contains the most important international treaties concerning international litigation, including the New York Convention on the Recognition and Enforcement of Foreign Arbitral Awards, the Brussels Convention on Jurisdiction and the Enforcement of Judgments and the successor EU Regulation, and the Hague Service and Evidence Conventions. For this Third Edition, the so-called ICSID Convention, providing for arbitration between foreign investors and host states, has been added to the arbitration documents, along with a typical Bilateral Investment Treaty. The Vienna Consular Convention has been added to the documents concerning litigation involving foreign governments.

The booklet contains not only the United States Foreign Sovereign Immunities Act, but also the comparable British statue and European Convention on State Immunity. It also contains the Alien Tort Statute of 1789, as well as several recent legislative efforts to provide civil remedies to persons injured by inhumane acts.

It is not surprising in view of the increasing volume of international litigation that many of the documents reproduced in the previous editions have been amended. The effort here is to present all of the documents as they read at year-end 2004.

It is clear to me that no one can make progress as a lawyer in the international arena without becoming familiar and comfortable with the relevant documents—statutes, treaties, and rules—national and multinational. While the booklet was prepared for use with my book on International Litigation and Arbitration, it may well be useful for teachers who prefer to use other books or their own materials.

Practitioners may also find that this Documents Supplement saves many hours of searching, not only when preparing for litigation, but when drafting contracts, particularly in choosing between litigation and arbitration clauses, and if the latter, in choosing a situs and an arbitral institution. If some of the documents here reproduced seem baffling, the practitioner is invited to sample the principal book. The book is written for students, but I am convinced after some forty years working in the field that we all remain students—probing, doubting, questioning—even as we serve as negotiators, advocates, judges, or arbitrators.

I am grateful to Katrina Szakal and Kristina Medic for twice bringing the collection of documents up to date and guiding me in the electronic age.

A.F.L.

July 2005

Table of Contents

LITIGATION INVOLVING FOREIGN GOVERNMENTS

DISCOVERY AND FOREIGN GOVERNMENT COMPULSION

INTERNATIONAL LITIGATION AND ARBITRATION

SELECTED TREATIES, STATUTES AND RULES

Third Edition

*

JURISDICTIONAL STATUTES AND RULES

NEW YORK STATUTES ON JURISDICTION OF COURTS

(Excerpts)

CIVIL PRACTICE LAW AND RULES

§ 301. Jurisdiction over persons, property or status

A court may exercise such jurisdiction over persons, property, or status as might have been exercised heretofore.

§ 302. Personal jurisdiction by acts of non-domiciliaries

(a) Acts which are the basis of jurisdiction. As to a cause of action arising from any of the acts enumerated in this section, a court may exercise personal jurisdiction over any non-domiciliary, or his executor or administrator, who in person or through an agent:

1. transacts any business within the state or contracts anywhere to supply goods or services in the state; or

2. commits a tortious act within the state, except as to a cause of action for defamation of character arising from the act; or

3. commits a tortious act without the state causing injury to person or property within the state, except as to a cause of action for defamation of character arising from the act, if he

    (i) regularly does or solicits business, or engages in any other persistent course of conduct, or derives substantial revenue from goods used or consumed or services rendered, in the state, or

    (ii) expects or should reasonably expect the act to have consequences in the state and derives substantial revenue from interstate or international commerce; or

4. owns, uses or possesses any real property situated within the state.

(b) Personal jurisdiction over non-resident defendant in matrimonial actions or family court proceedings. A court in any matrimonial action or family court proceeding involving a demand for support, alimony, maintenance, distributive awards or special relief in matrimonial actions may exercise personal jurisdiction over the respondent or defendant notwithstanding the fact that he or she no longer is a resident or domiciliary of this state, or over his or her executor or administrator, if the party seeking support is a resident of or domiciled in this state at the time such demand is made, provided that this state was the matrimonial domicile of the parties before their separation, or the defendant abandoned the plaintiff in this state, or the claim for support, alimony, maintenance, distributive awards or special relief in matrimonial actions accrued under the laws of this state or under an agreement executed in this state. The family court may exercise personal jurisdiction over a non-resident respondent to the extent provided in sections one hundred fifty-four and one thousand thirty-six of the family court act.

(c) **Effect of appearance.** Where personal jurisdiction is based solely upon this section, an appearance does not confer such jurisdiction with respect to causes of action not arising from an act enumerated in this section.

NEW YORK CHOICE OF LAW AND CHOICE OF FORUM STATUTES

BUSINESS CORPORATION LAW

§ 1314. Actions or special proceedings against foreign corporations

(a) An action or special proceeding against a foreign corporation may be maintained by a resident of this state or by a domestic corporation of any type or kind for any cause of action.

(b) Except as otherwise provided in this article, an action or special proceeding against a foreign corporation may be maintained by another foreign corporation of any type or kind or by a non-resident in the following cases only:

(1) Where it is brought to recover damages for the breach of a contract made or to be performed within this state, or relating to property situated within this state at the time of the making of the contract.

(2) Where the subject matter of the litigation is situated within this state.

(3) Where the cause of action arose within this state, except where the object of the action or special proceeding is to affect the title of real property situated outside this state.

(4) Where, in any case not included in the preceding subparagraphs, a non-domiciliary would be subject to the personal jurisdiction of the courts of this state under section 302 of the civil practice law and rules.

(5) Where the defendant is a foreign corporation doing business or authorized to do business in this state.

(c) Paragraph (b) does not apply to a corporation which was formed under the laws of the United States and which maintains an office in this state.

GENERAL OBLIGATIONS LAW

§ 5–1401. Choice of law

1. The parties to any contract, agreement or undertaking, contingent or otherwise, in consideration of, or relating to any obligation arising out of a transaction covering in the aggregate not less than two hundred fifty thousand dollars, including a transaction otherwise covered by subsection one of section 1–105 of the uniform commercial code, may agree that the law of this state shall govern their rights and duties in whole or in part, whether or not such contract, agreement or undertaking bears a reasonable relation to this state. This section shall not apply to any contract, agreement or undertaking (a) for labor or personal services, (b) relating to any transaction for personal, family or household services, or (c) to the extent provided to the contrary in subsection two of section 1–105 of the uniform commercial code.

2. Nothing contained in this section shall be construed to limit or deny the enforcement of any provision respecting choice of law in any other contract, agreement or undertaking.

(Added L.1984, c. 421, § 1.)

§ 5–1402. Choice of forum

1. Notwithstanding any act which limits or affects the right of a person to maintain an action or proceeding, including, but not limited to, paragraph (b) of section thirteen hundred fourteen of the business corporation law and subdivision two of section two hundred-b of the banking law, any person may maintain an action or proceeding against a foreign corporation, non-resident, or foreign state where the action or proceeding arises out of or relates to any contract, agreement or undertaking for which a choice of New York law has been made in whole or in part pursuant to section 5–1401 and which (a) is a contract, agreement or undertaking, contingent or otherwise, in consideration of, or relating to any obligation arising out of a transaction covering in the aggregate, not less than one million dollars, and (b) which contains a provision or provisions whereby such foreign corporation or non-resident agrees to submit to the jurisdiction of the courts of this state.

2. Nothing contained in this section shall be construed to affect the enforcement of any provision respecting choice of forum in any other contract, agreement or undertaking.

(Added L.1984, c. 421, § 1.)

ALI RESTATEMENT (THIRD) OF FOREIGN RELATIONS LAW

§ 402. Bases of Jurisdiction to Prescribe

Subject to § 403, a state has jurisdiction to prescribe law with respect to

(1)(a) conduct that, wholly or in substantial part, takes place within its territory;

(b) the status of persons, or interests in things, present within its territory;

(c) conduct outside its territory that has or is intended to have substantial effect within its territory;

(2) the activities, interests, status, or relations of its nationals outside as well as within its territory; and

(3) certain conduct outside its territory by persons not its nationals that is directed against the security of the state or against a limited class of other state interests.

§ 403. Limitations on Jurisdiction to Prescribe

(1) Even when one of the bases for jurisdiction under § 402 is present, a state may not exercise jurisdiction to prescribe law with respect to a person or activity having connections with another state when the exercise of such jurisdiction is unreasonable.

(2) Whether exercise of jurisdiction over a person or activity is unreasonable is determined by evaluating all relevant factors, including, where appropriate:

(a) the link of the activity to the territory of the regulating state, *i.e.,* the extent to which the activity takes place within the territory, or has substantial, direct, and foreseeable effect upon or in the territory;

(b) the connections, such as nationality, residence, or economic activity, between the regulating state and the person principally responsible for the activity to be regulated, or between that state and those whom the regulation is designed to protect;

(c) the character of the activity to be regulated, the importance of regulation to the regulating state, the extent to which other states regulate such activities, and the degree to which the desirability of such regulation is generally accepted;

(d) the existence of justified expectations that might be protected or hurt by the regulation;

(e) the importance of the regulation to the international political, legal, or economic system;

(f) the extent to which the regulation is consistent with the traditions of the international system;

(g) the extent to which another state may have an interest in regulating the activity; and

(h) the likelihood of conflict with regulation by another state.

(3) When it would not be unreasonable for each of two states to exercise jurisdiction over a person or activity, but the prescriptions by the two states are in conflict, each state has an obligation to evaluate its own as well as the other state's interest in exercising jurisdiction, in light of all the relevant factors, including those set out in Subsection (2); a state should defer to the other state if that state's interest is clearly greater.

UNITED KINGDOM: RULES OF THE SUPREME COURT

ORDER 11

(through 1999)

Principal cases in which service of writ out of jurisdiction is permissible (O.11, r.1)

1. (1) Provided that the writ does not contain any claim mentioned in Order 75, r.2(1) and is not a writ to which paragraph (2) of this rule applies, service of a writ out of the jurisdiction is permissible with the leave of the Court if in the action begun by the writ—

(a) relief is sought against a person domiciled within the jurisdiction;

(b) an injunction is sought ordering the defendant to do or refrain from doing anything within the jurisdiction (whether or not damages are also claimed in respect of a failure to do or the doing of that thing);

(c) the claim is brought against a person duly served within or out of the jurisdiction and a person out of the jurisdiction is a necessary or proper party thereto;

(d) the claim is brought to enforce, rescind, dissolve, annul or otherwise affect a contract, or to recover damages or obtain other relief in respect of the breach of a contract, being (in either case) a contract which—

(i) was made within the jurisdiction, or

(ii) was made by or through an agent trading or residing within the jurisdiction on behalf of a principal trading or residing out of the jurisdiction, or

(iii) is by its terms, or by implication, governed by English law, or

(iv) contains a term to the effect that the High Court shall have jurisdiction to hear and determine any action in respect of the contract;

(e) the claim is brought in respect of a breach committed within the jurisdiction of a contract made within or out of the jurisdiction, and irrespective of the fact, if such be the case, that the breach was preceded or accompanied by a breach committed out of the jurisdiction that rendered impossible the performance of so much of the contract as ought to have been performed within the jurisdiction;

(f) the claim is founded on a tort and the damage was sustained, or resulted from an act committed, within the jurisdiction;

(g) the whole subject-matter of the action is land situate within the jurisdiction (with or without rents or profits) or the perpetuation of testimony relating to land so situate;

(h) the claim is brought to construe, rectify, set aside or enforce an act, deed, will, contract, obligation or liability affecting land situate within the jurisdiction;

(i) the claim is made for a debt secured on immovable property or is made to assert, declare or determine proprietary or possessory rights, or rights of security, in or over movable property, or to obtain authority to dispose of movable property, situate within the jurisdiction;

(j) the claim is brought to execute the trusts of a written instrument being trusts that ought to be executed according to English law and of which the person to be served with the writ is a trustee, or for any relief or remedy which might be obtained in any such action;

(k) the claim is made for the administration of the estate of a person who died domiciled within the jurisdiction or for any relief or remedy which might be obtained in any such action;

(l) the claim is brought in a probate action within the meaning of Order 76;

(m) the claim is brought to enforce any judgment or arbitral award;

(n) the claim is brought against a defendant not domiciled in Scotland or Northern Ireland in respect of a claim by the Commissioners of Inland Revenue for or in relation to any of the duties or taxes which have been, or are for the time being, placed under their care and management;

(o) the claim is brought under the Nuclear Installations Act 1965 or in respect of contributions under the Social Security Act 1975;

(p) the claim is made for a sum to which the Directive of the Council of the European Communities dated 15th March 1976 No. 76/308/EEC applies, and service is to be effected in a country which is a member State of the European Economic Community.

(q) the claim is made under the Drug Trafficking Offences Act 1986;

(r) the claim is made under the Banking Act 1987;

(s) the claim is made under Part VI of the Criminal Justice Act 1988.

(t) the claim is brought for money had and received or for an account or other relief against the defendant as constructive trustee, and the defendant's alleged liability arises out of acts committed, whether by him or otherwise, within the jurisdiction.

(2) Service of a writ out of the jurisdiction is permissible without the leave of the Court provided that each claim made by the writ is either:—

(a) a claim which by virtue of the Civil Jurisdiction and Judgments Act 1982 the Court has power to hear and determine, made in proceedings to which the following conditions apply—

(i) no proceedings between the parties concerning the same cause of action are pending in the courts of any other part of the United Kingdom or of any other Convention territory, and

(ii) either—

the defendant is domiciled in any part of the United Kingdom or in any other Convention territory, or the proceedings begun by the writ are proceedings to which Article 16 of Schedule 1 or of Schedule 4 refers, or the defendant is a party to an agreement conferring jurisdiction to which Article 17 of Schedule 1 or of Schedule 4 to that Act applies,

or

(b) a claim which by virtue of any other enactment the High Court has power to hear and determine notwithstanding that the person against whom the claim is made is not within the jurisdiction of the Court or that the wrongful act, neglect or default giving rise to the claim did not take place within its jurisdiction.

(3) Where a writ is to be served out of the jurisdiction under paragraph (2), the time to be inserted in the writ within which the defendant served therewith must acknowledge service shall be—

(a) 21 days where the writ is to be served out of the jurisdiction under paragraph (2)(a) in Scotland, Northern Ireland or in the European territory of another Contracting State, or

(b) 31 days where the writ is to be served under paragraph (2)(a) in any other territory of a Contracting State, or

(c) limited in accordance with the practice adopted under r.4(4) where the writ is to be served under paragraph (2)(a) in a country not referred to in sub-paragraphs (a) or (b) or under paragraph (2)(b).

(4) For the purposes of this rule, and of r.9 of this Order, domicile is to be determined in accordance with the provisions of sections 41 to 46 of the Civil Jurisdictions and Judgments Act 1982 and "Convention territory" means the territory or territories of any Contracting State, as defined by s.1(3) of that Act, to which the Conventions as defined in s.1(1) of that Act apply.

Application for, and grant of, leave to serve writ out of jurisdiction (O.11, r.4)

4. (1) An application for the grant of leave under rule 1(1) must be supported by an affidavit stating—

(a) the grounds on which the application is made,

(b) that in the deponent's belief the plaintiff has a good cause of action,

(c) in what place or country the defendant is, or probably may be found, and

(d) where the application is made under rule 1(1)(c), the grounds for the deponent's belief that there is between the plaintiff and the person on whom a writ has been served a real issue which the plaintiff may reasonably ask the Court to try.

(2) No such leave shall be granted unless it shall be made sufficiently to appear to the Court that the case is a proper one for service out of the jurisdiction under this Order.

(3) Where the application is for the grant of leave under rule 1 to serve a writ in Scotland or Northern Ireland, if it appears to the Court that there may be a concurrent remedy there, the Court, in deciding whether to grant leave shall have regard to the comparative cost and convenience of proceeding there or in England, and (where that is relevant) to the powers and jurisdiction of the sheriff court in Scotland or the county courts or courts of summary jurisdiction in Northern Ireland.

(4) An order granting under rules 1 or 2 leave to serve a writ, out of the jurisdiction must limit a time within which the defendant to be served must acknowledge service.

Service of writ abroad: general (O.11, r.5)

5.   (1) Subject to the following provisions of this rule, Order 10, rule 1(1), (4), (5) and (6) and Order 65, rule 4, shall apply in relation to the service of a writ, notwithstanding that the writ is to be served out of the jurisdiction, save that the accompanying form of acknowledgement of service shall be modified in such manner as may be appropriate.

(2) Nothing in this rule or in any order or direction of the Court made by virtue of it shall authorize or require the doing of anything in a country in which service is to be effected which is contrary to the law of that country.

(3) A writ which is to be served out of the jurisdiction—

(a) need not be served personally on the person required to be served so long as it is served on him in accordance with the law of the country in which service is effected; and

(b) need not be served by the plaintiff or his agent if it is served by a method provided for by rule 6 or rule 7.

(4) *[Deleted by R.S.C. (Amendment No. 2) 1979 (S.I. 1979 No. 402).]*

(5) An official certificate stating that a writ as regards which rule 6 has been complied with has been served on a person personally, or in accordance with the law of the country in which service was effected, on a specified date, being a certificate—

(a) by a British consular authority in that country, or

(b) by the government or judicial authorities of that country, or

(c) by any other authority designated in respect of that country under the Hague Convention,

shall be evidence of the facts so stated.

(6) An official certificate by the Secretary of State stating that a writ has been duly served on a specified date in accordance with a request made under rule 7 shall be evidence of that fact.

(7) A document purporting to be such a certificate as is mentioned in paragraph (5) or (6) shall, until the contrary is proved, be deemed to be such a certificate.

(8) In this rule and rule 6 "the Hague Convention" means the Convention on the service abroad of judicial and extra-judicial documents in civil or commercial matters signed at the Hague on November 15, 1965.

Service of process on a foreign State (O.11, r.7)

7. (1) Subject to paragraph (4) where a person to whom leave has been granted under rule 1 to serve a writ on a State, as defined in section 14 of the State Immunity Act 1978, wishes to have the writ served on that State, he must lodge in the Central Office—

(a) a request for service to be arranged by the Secretary of State; and

(b) a copy of the writ; and

(c) except where the official language of the State is, or the official languages of that party include, English, a translation of the writ in the official language or one of the official languages of the State.

(2) Rule 6(6) shall apply in relation to a translation lodged under paragraph (1) of this rule as it applies in relation to a translation lodged under paragraph (5) of that rule.

(3) Documents duly lodged under this Rule shall be sent by the Senior Master to the Secretary of State with a request that the Secretary of State arrange for the writ to be served on the State or the government in question, as the case may be.

(4) Where section 12(6) of the State Immunity Act 1978 applies and the State has agreed to a method of service other than that provided by the preceding paragraphs, the writ may be served either by the method agreed or in accordance with the preceding paragraphs of this rule.

UNITED KINGDOM: THE CIVIL PROCEDURE (AMENDMENT) RULES 2000*

SPECIAL PROVISIONS ABOUT SERVICE OUT OF THE JURISDICTION

Scope of this Section

6.17   This Section contains rules about—

(a) service out of the jurisdiction;

(b) how to obtain the permission of the court to serve out of the jurisdiction; and

(c) the procedure for serving out of the jurisdiction.

(Rule 2.3 defines "jurisdiction")

Definitions

6.18   For the purposes of this Part—

(a) "the 1982 Act" means the Civil Jurisdiction and Judgments Act 1982;

(b) "the Hague Convention" means the Convention on the service abroad of judicial and extra-judicial documents in civil or commercial matters signed at the Hague on November 15, 1965;

(c) "Contracting State" has the meaning given by section 1(3) of the 1982 Act;

(d) "Convention territory" means the territory or territories of any Contracting State to which the Brussels or Lugano Conventions (as defined in section 1(1) of the 1982 Act) apply;

(e) "Civil Procedure Convention" means the Brussels and Lugano Conventions and any other Convention entered into by the United Kingdom regarding service outside the jurisdiction;

(f) "United Kingdom Overseas Territory" means those territories as set out in the relevant practice direction.

(g) "domicile" is to be determined in accordance with sections 41 to 46 of the 1982 Act;

(h) "claim form" includes petition and application notice; and

(i) "claim" includes petition and application.

(Rule 6.30 provides that where an application notice is to be served out of the jurisdiction under this Part, rules 6.21(4), 6.22 and 6.23 do not apply)

Service out of the jurisdiction where the permission of the court is not required

6.19—(1) A claim form may be served on a defendant out of the jurisdiction where each claim included in the claim form made against

---

* Statutory Instrument 2000 No. 221
(L.1).

the defendant to be served is a claim which the court has power to determine under the 1982 Act and—

(a) no proceedings between the parties concerning the same claim are pending in the courts of any part of the United Kingdom or any other Convention territory; and

(b)

(i) the defendant is domiciled in the United Kingdom or in any Convention territory;

(ii) Article 16 of Schedule 1, 3C or 4 to the 1982 Act refers to the proceedings; or

(iii) the defendant is a party to an agreement conferring jurisdiction to which Article 17 of Schedule 1, 3C or 4 to the 1982 Act refers.

(2) A claim form may be served on a defendant out of the jurisdiction where each claim included in the claim form made against the defendant to be served is a claim which, under any other enactment, the court has power to determine, although—

(a) the person against whom the claim is made is not within the jurisdiction; or

(b) the facts giving rise to the claim did not occur within the jurisdiction.

(3) Where a claim form is to be served out of the jurisdiction under this rule, it must contain a statement of the grounds on which the claimant is entitled to serve it out of the jurisdiction.

Service out of the jurisdiction where the permission of the court is required

6.20 In any proceedings to which rule 6.19 does not apply, a claim form may be served out of the jurisdiction with the permission of the court if—

General grounds

(1) a claim is made for a remedy against a person domiciled within the jurisdiction;

(2) a claim is made for an injunction ordering the defendant to do or refrain from doing an act within the jurisdiction;

(3) a claim is made against someone on whom the claim form has been or will be served and—

(a) there is between the claimant and that person a real issue which it is reasonable for the court to try; and

(b) the claimant wishes to serve the claim form on another person who is a necessary or proper party to that claim;

Claims for interim remedies

(4) a claim is made for an interim remedy under section 25(1) of the 1982 Act;

Claims in relation to contracts

(5) a claim is made in respect of a contract where the contract—

(a) was made within the jurisdiction;

(b) was made by or through an agent trading or residing within the jurisdiction;

(c) is governed by English law; or

(d) contains a term to the effect that the court shall have jurisdiction to determine any claim in respect of the contract;

(6) a claim is made in respect of a breach of contract committed within the jurisdiction;

(7) a claim is made for a declaration that no contract exists where, if the contract was found to exist, it would comply with the conditions set out in paragraph (5);

Claims in tort

(8) a claim is made in tort where—

(a) damage was sustained within the jurisdiction; or

(b) the damage sustained resulted from an act committed within the jurisdiction;

Enforcement

(9) a claim is made to enforce any judgment or arbitral award;

Claims about property within the jurisdiction

(10) the whole subject matter of a claim relates to property located within the jurisdiction;

Claims about trusts etc.

(11) a claim is made for any remedy which might be obtained in proceedings to execute the trusts of a written instrument where—

(a) the trusts ought to be executed according to English law; and

(b) the person on whom the claim form is to be served is a trustee of the trusts;

(12) a claim is made for any remedy which might be obtained in proceedings for the administration of the estate of a person who died domiciled within the jurisdiction;

(13) a claim is made in probate proceedings which includes a claim for the rectification of a will;

(14) a claim is made for a remedy against the defendant as constructive trustee where the defendant's alleged liability arises out of acts committed within the jurisdiction;

(15) a claim is made for restitution where the defendant's alleged liability arises out of acts committed within the jurisdiction;

(Probate proceedings are defined in the Contentious Probate Proceedings practice direction supplementing Part 49)

Claims by the Inland Revenue

(16) a claim is made by the Commissioners of the Inland Revenue relating to duties or taxes against a defendant not domiciled in Scotland or Northern Ireland;

Claim for costs order in favour of or against third parties

(17) a claim is made by a party to proceedings for an order that the court exercise its power under section 51 of the Supreme Court Act 1981 to make a costs order in favour of or against a person who is not a party to those proceedings;

(Rule 48.2 sets out the procedure where the court is considering whether to exercise its discretion to make a costs order in favour of or against a non-party)

Claims under various enactments

(18) a claim made under an enactment specified in the relevant practice direction.

Application for permission to serve claim form out of jurisdiction

6.21—(1) An application for permission under rule 6.20 must be supported by written evidence stating—

(a) the grounds on which the application is made and the paragraph or paragraphs of rule 6.20 relied on;

(b) that the claimant believes that his claim has a reasonable prospect of success; and

(c) the defendant's address or, if not known, in what place or country the defendant is, or is likely, to be found.

(2) Where the application is made in respect of a claim referred to in rule 6.20(3), the written evidence must also state the grounds on which the witness believes that there is between the claimant and the person on whom the claim form has been, or will be served, a real issue which it is reasonable for the court to try.

(3) Where—

(a) the application is for permission to serve a claim form in Scotland or Northern Ireland; and

(b) it appears to the court that the claimant may also be entitled to a remedy there, the court, in deciding whether to give permission, shall—

(i) compare the cost and convenience of proceeding there or in the jurisdiction; and

(ii) (where relevant) have regard to the powers and jurisdiction of the Sheriff court in Scotland or the county courts or courts of summary jurisdiction in Northern Ireland.

(4) An order giving permission to serve a claim form out of the jurisdiction must specify the periods within which the defendant may—

(a) file an acknowledgment of service;

(b) file or serve an admission; and

(c) file a defence.

(Part 11 sets out the procedure by which a defendant may dispute the court's jurisdiction)

Period for acknowledging service or admitting the claim where the claim form is served out of the jurisdiction under rule 6.19

6.22—(1) This rule sets out the period for filing an acknowledgment of service or filing or serving an admission where a claim form has been served out of the jurisdiction under rule 6.19.

(Part 10 contains rules about the acknowledgment of service and Part 14 contains rules about admissions)

(2) If the claim form is to be served under rule 6.19(1) in Scotland, Northern Ireland or in the European territory of another Contracting State the period is—

(a) where the defendant is served with a claim form which states that particulars of claim are to follow, 21 days after the service of the particulars of claim; and

(b) in any other case, 21 days after service of the claim form.

(3) If the claim form is to be served under rule 6.19(1) in any other territory of a Contracting State the period is—

(a) where the defendant is served with a claim form which states that particulars of claim are to follow, 31 days after the service of the particulars of claim; and

(b) in any other case, 31 days after service of the claim form.

(4) If the claim form is to be served under—

(a) rule 6.19(1) in a country not referred to in paragraphs (2) or (3); or

(b) rule 6.19(2),

the period is set out in the relevant practice direction.

Period for filing a defence where the claim form is served out of the jurisdiction under rule 6.19

6.23—(1) This rule sets out the period for filing a defence where a claim form has been served out of the jurisdiction under rule 6.19.

(Part 15 contains rules about the defence)

(2) If the claim form is to be served under rule 6.19(1) in Scotland, Northern Ireland or in the European territory of another Contracting State the period is—

(a) 21 days after service of the particulars of claim; or

(b) if the defendant files an acknowledgment of service, 35 days after service of the particulars of claim.

(3) If the claim form is to be served under rule 6.19(1) in any other territory of a Contracting State the period is—

(a) 31 days after service of the particulars of claim; or

(b) if the defendant files an acknowledgment of service, 45 days after service of the particulars of claim.

(4) If the claim form is to be served under—

(a) rule 6.19(1) in a country not referred to in paragraphs (2) or (3); or

(b) rule 6.19(2),

the period is set out in the relevant practice direction.

Method of service—general provisions

6.24—(1) Where a claim form is to be served out of the jurisdiction, it may be served by any method—

(a) permitted by the law of the country in which it is to be served;

(b) provided for by—

(i) rule 6.25 (service through foreign governments, judicial authorities and British Consular authorities); or

(ii) rule 6.26 (service on a State); or

(c) permitted by a Civil Procedure Convention.

(2) Nothing in this rule or in any court order shall authorise or require any person to do anything in the country where the claim form is to be served which is against the law of that country.

Service through foreign governments, judicial authorities and British Consular authorities

6.25—(1) Where a claim form is to be served on a defendant in any country which is a party to the Hague Convention, the claim form may be served—

(a) through the authority designated under the Hague Convention in respect of that country; or

(b) if the law of that country permits—

(i) through the judicial authorities of that country, or

(ii) through a British Consular authority in that country.

(2) Where—

(a) paragraph (4) (service in Scotland etc., other than under the Hague Convention) does not apply; and

(b) a claim form is to be served on a defendant in any country which is a party to a Civil Procedure Convention (other than the Hague Convention) providing for service in that country, the claim form may be served, if the law of that country permits—

(i) through the judicial authorities of that country; or

(ii) through a British Consular authority in that country (subject to any provisions of the applicable convention about the nationality of persons who may be served by such a method).

(3) Where—

(a) paragraph (4) (service in Scotland etc., other than under the Hague Convention) does not apply; and

(b) a claim form is to be served on a defendant in any country with respect to which there is no Civil Procedure Convention providing for service in that country,

the claim form may be served, if the law of that country so permits—

(i) through the government of that country, where that government is willing to serve it;

or

(ii) through a British Consular authority in that country.

(4) Except where a claim form is to be served in accordance with paragraph (1) (service under the Hague Convention), the methods of service permitted by this rule are not available where the claim form is to be served in—

(a) Scotland, Northern Ireland, the Isle of Man or the Channel Islands;

(b) any Commonwealth State;

(c) any United Kingdom Overseas Territory; or

(d) the Republic of Ireland.

Procedure where service is to be through foreign governments, judicial authorities and British Consular authorities

6.26—(1) This rule applies where the claimant wishes to serve the claim form through—

(a) the judicial authorities of the country where the claim form is to be served;

(b) a British Consular authority in that country;

(c) the authority designated under the Hague Convention in respect of that country; or

(d) the government of that country.

(2) Where this rule applies, the claimant must file—

(a) a request for service of the claim form by the method in paragraph (1) that he has chosen;

(b) a copy of the claim form;

(c) any translation required under rule 6.28; and

(d) any other documents, copies of documents or translations required by the relevant practice direction.

(3) When the claimant files the documents specified in paragraph (2), the court officer will—

(a) seal the copy of the claim form; and

(b) forward the documents to the Senior Master.

(4) The Senior Master will send documents forwarded under this rule—

(a) where the claim form is being served through the authority designated under the Hague Convention, to that authority; or

(b) in any other case, to the Foreign and Commonwealth Office with a request that it arranges for the claim to be served by the method indicated in the request for service filed under paragraph (2) or, where that request indicates alternative methods, by the most convenient method.

(5) An official certificate which—

(a) states that the claim form has been served in accordance with this rule either personally, or in accordance with the law of the country in which service was effected;

(b) specifies the date on which the claim form was served; and

(c) is made by

(i) a British Consular authority in the country where the claim form was served;

(ii) the government or judicial authorities in that country; or

(iii) any other authority designated in respect of that country under the Hague Convention,

shall be evidence of the facts stated in the certificate.

(6) A document purporting to be an official certificate under paragraph (5) shall be treated as such a certificate, unless it is proved not to be.

Service of claim form on State where court permits service out of the jurisdiction

6.27—(1) This rule applies where a claimant wishes to serve the claim form on a State.

(2) The claimant must file in the Central Office of the Royal Courts of Justice—

(a) a request for service to be arranged by the Foreign and Commonwealth Office;

(b) a copy of the claim form; and

(c) any translation required under rule 6.28.

(3) The Senior Master will send documents filed under this rule to the Foreign and Commonwealth Office with a request that it arranges for the claim form to be served.

(4) An official certificate by the Foreign and Commonwealth Office stating that a claim form has been duly served on a specified date in accordance with a request made under this rule shall be evidence of that fact.

(5) A document purporting to be such a certificate shall be treated as such a certificate, unless it is proved not to be.

(6) Where—

(a) section 12(6) of the State Immunity Act 1978 applies; and

(b) the State has agreed to a method of service other than through the Foreign and Commonwealth Office,

the claim may be served either by the method agreed or in accordance with this rule.

(Section 12(6) of the State Immunity Act 1978 provides that section 12(1) of that Act, which prescribes a method for serving documents on a State, does not prevent the service of a claim form or other document in a manner to which the State has agreed)

(7) In this rule "State" has the meaning given by section 14 of the State Immunity Act 1978.

Translation of claim form

6.28—(1) Except where paragraph (4) or (5) applies, every copy of the claim form filed under rule 6.26 (service through judicial authorities, foreign governments etc.) or 6.27 (service on State) must be accompanied by a translation of the claim form.

(2) The translation must be—

(a) in the official language of the country in which it is to be served; or

(b) if there is more than one official language of that country, in any official language which is appropriate to the place in the country where the claim form is to be served.

(3) Every translation filed under this rule must be accompanied by a statement by the person making it that it is a correct translation, and the statement must include—

(a) the name of the person making the translation;

(b) his address; and

(c) his qualifications for making a translation.

(4) The claimant is not required to file a translation of a claim form filed under rule 6.26 (service through judicial authorities, foreign governments etc.) where the claim form is to be served—

(a) in a country of which English is an official language; or

(b) on a British subject,

unless a Civil Procedure Convention expressly requires a translation.

(5) The claimant is not required to file a translation of a claim form filed under rule 6.27 (service on State) where English is an official language of the State where the claim form is to be served.

Undertaking to be responsible for expenses of the Foreign and Commonwealth Office

6.29 Every request for service filed under rule 6.26 (service through judicial authorities, foreign governments etc.) or rule 6.27 (service on State) must contain an undertaking by the person making the request—

(a) to be responsible for all expenses incurred by the Foreign and Commonwealth Office or foreign judicial authority; and

(b) to pay those expenses to the Foreign and Commonwealth Office or foreign judicial authority on being informed of the amount.

Service of documents other than the claim form

6.30—(1) Where an application notice is to be served out of the jurisdiction under this Section of this Part—

(a) rules 6.21(4), 6.22 and 6.23 do not apply; and

(b) where the person on whom the application notice has been served is not a party to proceedings in the jurisdiction in which the application is made, that person may make an application to the court under rule 11(1) as if he were a defendant and rule 11(2) does not apply.

(Rule 6.21(4) provides that an order giving permission to serve a claim form out of the jurisdiction must specify the periods within which the defendant may (a) file an acknowledgment of service, (b) file or serve an admission, and (c) file a defence)

(Rule 6.22 provides rules for the period for acknowledging service or admitting the claim where the claim form is served out of the jurisdiction under rule 6.19)

(Rule 6.23 provides rules for the period for filing a defence where the claim form is served out of the jurisdiction under rule 6.19)

(The practice direction supplementing this Section of this Part provides that where an application notice is to be served out of the jurisdiction in accordance with this Section of this Part, the court must have regard to the country in which the application notice is to be served in setting the date for the hearing of the application and giving any direction about service of the respondent's evidence)

(Rule 11(1) provides that a defendant may make an application to the court to dispute the court's jurisdiction to try the claim or argue that the court should not exercise its jurisdiction. Rule 11(2) provides that a defendant who wishes to make such an application must first file an acknowledgment of service in accordance with Part 10)

(2) Unless paragraph (3) applies, where the permission of the court is required for a claim form to be served out of the jurisdiction the permission of the court must also be obtained for service out of the jurisdiction of any other document to be served in the proceedings.

(3) Where—

(a) the court gives permission for a claim form to be served out of the jurisdiction; and

(b) the claim form states that particulars of claim are to follow, the permission of the court is not required to serve the particulars of claim out of the jurisdiction.

Proof of service

6.31   Where—

(a) a hearing is fixed when the claim is issued;

(b) the claim form is served on a defendant out of the jurisdiction; and

(c) that defendant does not appear at the hearing,

the claimant may take no further steps against that defendant until the claimant files written evidence showing that the claim form has been duly served.

FEDERAL RULES PERTAINING TO SERVICE

RULES PERTAINING TO SERVICE

(as of 2005)

(Excerpts)

Rule 3—Commencement of Action

A civil action is commenced by filing a complaint with the court.

Rule 4—Summons

(a) Form. The summons shall be signed by the clerk, bear the seal of the court, identify the court and the parties, be directed to the defendant, and state the name and address of the plaintiff's attorney or, if unrepresented, of the plaintiff. It shall also state the time within which the defendant must appear and defend, and notify the defendant that failure to do so will result in a judgment by default against the defendant for the relief demanded in the complaint. The court may allow a summons to be amended.

(b) Issuance. Upon or after filing the complaint, the plaintiff may present a summons to the clerk for signature and seal. If the summons is in proper form, the clerk shall sign, seal, and issue it to the plaintiff for service on the defendant. A summons, or a copy of the summons if addressed to multiple defendants, shall be issued for each defendant to be served.

(c) Service with Complaint; by Whom Made.

(1) A summons shall be served together with a copy of the complaint. The plaintiff is responsible for service of a summons and complaint within the time allowed under subdivision (m) and shall furnish the person effecting service with the necessary copies of the summons and complaint.

(2) Service may be effected by any person who is not a party and who is at least 18 years of age. At the request of the plaintiff, however, the court may direct that service be effected by a United States marshal, deputy United States marshal, or other person or officer specially appointed by the court for that purpose. Such an appointment must be made when the plaintiff is authorized to proceed in forma pauperis pursuant to 28 U.S.C. § 1915 or is authorized to proceed as a seaman under 28 U.S.C. § 1916.

(d) Waiver of Service; Duty to Save Costs of Service; Request to Waive.

(1) A defendant who waives service of a summons does not thereby waive any objection to the venue or to the jurisdiction of the court over the person of the defendant.

(2) An individual, corporation, or association that is subject to service under subdivision (e), (f), or (h) and that receives notice of an action in the manner provided in this paragraph has a duty to avoid

unnecessary costs of serving the summons. To avoid costs, the plaintiff may notify such a defendant of the commencement of the action and request that the defendant waive service of a summons. The notice and request

(A) shall be in writing and shall be addressed directly to the defendant, if an individual, or else to an officer or managing or general agent (or other agent authorized by appointment or law to receive service of process) of a defendant subject to service under subdivision (h);

(B) shall be dispatched through first-class mail or other reliable means;

(C) shall be accompanied by a copy of the complaint and shall identify the court in which it has been filed;

(D) shall inform the defendant, by means of a text prescribed in an official form promulgated pursuant to Rule 84, of the consequences of compliance and of a failure to comply with the request;

(E) shall set forth the date on which the request is sent;

(F) shall allow the defendant a reasonable time to return the waiver, which shall be at least 30 days from the date on which the request is sent, or 60 days from that date if the defendant is addressed outside any judicial district of the United States; and

(G) shall provide the defendant with an extra copy of the notice and request, as well as a prepaid means of compliance in writing.

If a defendant located within the United States fails to comply with a request for waiver made by a plaintiff located within the United States, the court shall impose the costs subsequently incurred in effecting service on the defendant unless good cause for the failure be shown.

(3) A defendant that, before being served with process, timely returns a waiver so requested is not required to serve an answer to the complaint until 60 days after the date on which the request for waiver of service was sent, or 90 days after that date if the defendant was addressed outside any judicial district of the United States.

(4) When the plaintiff files a waiver of service with the court, the action shall proceed, except as provided in paragraph (3), as if a summons and complaint had been served at the time of filing the waiver, and no proof of service shall be required.

(5) The costs to be imposed on a defendant under paragraph (2) for failure to comply with a request to waive service of a summons shall include the costs subsequently incurred in effecting service under subdivision (e), (f), or (h), together with the costs, including a reasonable attorney's fee, of any motion required to collect the costs of service.

(e) Service Upon Individuals Within a Judicial District of the United States. Unless otherwise provided by federal law, service upon an individual from whom a waiver has not been obtained and filed, other than an infant or an incompetent person, may be effected in any judicial district of the United States:

(1) pursuant to the law of the state in which the district court is located, or in which service is effected, for the service of a summons upon the defendant in an action brought in the courts of general jurisdiction of the State; or

(2) by delivering a copy of the summons and of the complaint to the individual personally or by leaving copies thereof at the individual's dwelling house or usual place of abode with some person of suitable age and discretion then residing therein or by delivering a copy of the summons and of the complaint to an agent authorized by appointment or by law to receive service of process.

(f) Service Upon Individuals in a Foreign Country. Unless otherwise provided by federal law, service upon an individual from whom a waiver has not been obtained and filed, other than an infant or an incompetent person, may be effected in a place not within any judicial district of the United States:

(1) by any internationally agreed means reasonably calculated to give notice, such as those means authorized by the Hague Convention on the Service Abroad of Judicial and Extrajudicial Documents; or

(2) if there is no internationally agreed means of service or the applicable international agreement allows other means of service, provided that service is reasonably calculated to give notice:

(A) in the manner prescribed by the law of the foreign country for service in that country in an action in any of its courts of general jurisdiction; or

(B) as directed by the foreign authority in response to a letter rogatory or letter of request; or

(C) unless prohibited by the law of the foreign country, by

(i) delivery to the individual personally of a copy of the summons and the complaint; or

(ii) any form of mail requiring a signed receipt, to be addressed and dispatched by the clerk of the court to the party to be served; or

(3) by other means not prohibited by international agreement as may be directed by the court.

(g) Service Upon Infants and Incompetent Persons. Service upon an infant or an incompetent person in a judicial district of the United States shall be effected in the manner prescribed by the law of the state in which the service is made for the service of summons or other like process upon any such defendant in an action brought in the courts of general jurisdiction of that state. Service upon an infant or an incompetent person in a place not within any judicial district of the United States shall be effected in the manner prescribed by paragraph (2)(A) or (2)(B) of subdivision (f) or by such means as the court may direct.

(h) Service Upon Corporations and Associations. Unless otherwise provided by federal law, service upon a domestic or foreign corporation or upon a partnership or other unincorporated association that is subject to suit under a common name, and from which a waiver of service has not been obtained and filed, shall be effected:

(1) in a judicial district of the United States in the manner prescribed for individuals by subdivision (e)(1), or by delivering a copy of the summons and of the complaint to an officer, a managing or general agent, or to any other agent authorized by appointment or by law to receive service of process and, if the agent is one authorized by statute to receive service and the statute so requires, by also mailing a copy to the defendant, or

(2) in a place not within any judicial district of the United States in any manner prescribed for individuals by subdivision (f) except personal delivery as provided in paragraph (2)(C)(i) thereof.

(i) Service Upon the United States, Its Agencies, Corporations, Officers, or Employees.

(1) Service upon the United States shall be effected

(A) by delivering a copy of the summons and of the complaint to the United States attorney for the district in which the action is brought or to an assistant United States attorney or clerical employee designated by the United States attorney in a writing filed with the clerk of the court or by sending a copy of the summons and of the complaint by registered or certified mail addressed to the civil process clerk at the office of the United States attorney and

(B) by also sending a copy of the summons and of the complaint by registered or certified mail to the Attorney General of the United States at Washington, District of Columbia, and

(C) in any action attacking the validity of an order of an order of an officer or agency of the United States not made a party, by also sending a copy of the summons and of the complaint by registered or certified mail to the officer or agency.

(2) (A) Service on an agency or corporation of the United States, or an officer or employee of the United States sued only in an official capacity, is effected by serving the United States in the manner prescribed by Rule 4(i)(1) and by also sending a copy of the summons and complaint by registered or certified mail to the officer, employee, agency, or corporation.

(B) Service on an officer or employee of the United States sued in an individual capacity for acts or omissions occurring in connection with the performance of duties on behalf of the United States–whether or not the officer or employee is sued also in an official capacity–is effected by serving the United States in the manner prescribed by Rule 4(i)(1) and by serving the officer or employee in the manner prescribed by Rule 4 (e), (f), or (g).

(3) The court shall allow a reasonable time to serve process under Rule 4(i) for the purpose of curing the failure to serve:

(A) all persons required to be served in an action governed by Rule 4(i)(2)(A), if the plaintiff has served either the United States attorney or the Attorney General of the United States, or

(B) the United States in an action governed by Rule 4(i)(2)(B), if the plaintiff has served an officer or employee of the United States sued in an individual capacity. Service upon an officer, agency, or corporation of the United States shall be effected by serving the United States in the manner prescribed by paragraph (1) of this subdivision and by also sending a copy of the summons and of the complaint by registered or certified mail to the officer, agency, or corporation.

(3) The court shall allow a reasonable time for service of process under this subdivision for the purpose of curing the failure to serve multiple officers, agencies, or corporations of the United States if the plaintiff has effected service on either the United States attorney or the Attorney General of the United States.

(j) Service Upon Foreign, State, or Local Governments.

(1) Service upon a foreign state or a political subdivision, agency, or instrumentality thereof shall be effected pursuant to 28 U.S.C. 1608.

(2) Service upon a state, municipal corporation, or other governmental organization subject to suit shall be effected by delivering a copy of the summons and of the complaint to its chief executive officer or by serving the summons and complaint in the manner prescribed by the law of that state for the service of summons or other like process upon any such defendant.

(k) Territorial Limits of Effective Service.

(1) Service of a summons or filing a waiver of service is effective to establish jurisdiction over the person of a defendant

(A) who could be subjected to the jurisdiction of a court of general jurisdiction in the state in which the district court is located, or

(B) who is a party joined under Rule 14 or Rule 19 and is served at a place within a judicial district of the United States and not more than 100 miles from the place from which the summons issues, or

(C) who is a subject to the federal interpleader jurisdiction under 28 U.S.C. 1335, or

(D) when authorized by a statute of the United States.

(2) If the exercise of jurisdiction is consistent with the Constitution and laws of the United States, serving a summons or filing a waiver of service is also effective, with respect to claims arising under federal law, to establish personal jurisdiction over the person of any defendant who is not subject to the jurisdiction of the courts of general jurisdiction of any state.

(l) Proof of Service. If service is not waived, the person effecting service shall make proof thereof to the court. If service is made by a person other than a United States marshal or deputy United States marshal, the person shall make affidavit thereof. Proof of service in a place not within any judicial district of the United States shall, if effected under paragraph (1) of subdivision (f), be made pursuant to the applicable treaty or convention, and shall, if effected under paragraph (2) or (3) thereof, include a receipt signed by the addressee or other evidence of delivery to the addressee satisfactory to the court. Failure to make proof of service does not affect the validity of the service. The court may allow a proof of service to be amended.

(m) Time Limit for Service. If service of the summons and complaint is not made upon a defendant within 120 days after the filing of the complaint, the court, upon motion or on its own initiative after notice to the plaintiff, shall dismiss the action without prejudice as to that defendant or direct that service be effected within a specified time; provided that if the plaintiff shows good cause for the failure, the court shall extend the time for service for an appropriate period. This subdivision does not apply to service in a foreign country pursuant to subdivision (f) or (j)(1).

(n) Seizure of Property; Service of Summons Not Feasible.

(1) If a statute of the United States so provides, the court may assert jurisdiction over property. Notice to claimants of the property shall then be sent in the manner provided by the statute or by service of a summons under this rule.

(2) Upon a showing that personal jurisdiction over a defendant cannot, in the district where the action is brought, be obtained with reasonable efforts by service of summons in any manner authorized by this rule, the court may assert jurisdiction over any of the defendant's assets found within the district by seizing the assets under the circumstances and in the manner provided by the law of the state in which the district court is located.

THE HAGUE SERVICE CONVENTION

CONVENTION ON THE SERVICE ABROAD OF JUDICIAL AND EXTRAJUDICIAL DOCUMENTS IN CIVIL OR COMMERCIAL MATTERS

The States signatory to the present Convention,

Desiring to create appropriate means to ensure that judicial and extrajudicial documents to be served abroad shall be brought to the notice of the addressee in sufficient time,

Desiring to improve the organization of mutual judicial assistance for that purpose by simplifying and expediting the procedure,

Have resolved to conclude a Convention to this effect and have agreed upon the following provisions:

Article 1

The present Convention shall apply in all cases, in civil or commercial matters, where there is occasion to transmit a judicial or extrajudicial document for service abroad.

This Convention shall not apply where the address of the person to be served with the document is not known.

CHAPTER I—JUDICIAL DOCUMENTS

Article 2

Each contracting State shall designate a Central Authority which will undertake to receive requests for service coming from other contracting States and to proceed in conformity with the provisions of articles 3 to 6.

Each State shall organize the Central Authority in conformity with its own law.

Article 3

The authority or judicial officer competent under the law of the State in which the documents originate shall forward to the Central Authority of the State addressed a request conforming to the model annexed to the present Convention, without any requirement of legalization or other equivalent formality.

The document to be served or a copy thereof shall be annexed to the request. The request and the document shall both be furnished in duplicate.

Article 4

If the Central Authority considers that the request does not comply with the provisions of the present Convention it shall promptly inform the applicant and specify its objections to the request.

Article 5

The Central Authority of the State addressed shall itself serve the document or shall arrange to have it served by an appropriate agency, either—

(a) by a method prescribed by its internal law for the service of documents in domestic actions upon persons who are within its territory, or

(b) by a particular method requested by the applicant, unless such a method is incompatible with the law of the State addressed.

Subject to sub-paragraph (b) of the first paragraph of this article, the document may always be served by delivery to an addressee who accepts it voluntarily.

If the document is to be served under the first paragraph above, the Central Authority may require the document to be written in, or translated into, the official language or one of the official languages of the State addressed.

That part of the request, in the form attached to the present Convention, which contains a summary of the document to be served, shall be served with the document.

Article 6

The Central Authority of the State addressed or any authority which it may have designated for that purpose, shall complete a certificate in the form of the model annexed to the present Convention.

The certificate shall state that the document has been served and shall include the method, the place and the date of service and the person to whom the document was delivered. If the document has not been served, the certificate shall set out the reasons which have prevented service.

The applicant may require that a certificate not completed by a Central Authority or by a judicial authority shall be countersigned by one of these authorities.

The certificate shall be forwarded directly to the applicant.

Article 7

The standard terms in the model annexed to the present Convention shall in all cases be written either in French or in English. They may also be written in the official language, or in one of the official languages, of the State in which the documents originate.

The corresponding blanks shall be completed either in the language of the State addressed or in French or in English.

Article 8

Each contracting State shall be free to effect service of judicial documents upon persons abroad, without application of any compulsion, directly through its diplomatic or consular agents.

Any State may declare that it is opposed to such service within its territory, unless the document is to be served upon a national of the State in which the documents originate.

Article 9

Each contracting State shall be free, in addition, to use consular channels to forward documents, for the purpose of service, to those authorities of another contracting State which are designated by the latter for this purpose.

Each contracting State may, if exceptional circumstances so require, use diplomatic channels for the same purpose.

Article 10

Provided the State of destination does not object, the present Convention shall not interfere with—

(a) the freedom to send judicial documents, by postal channels, directly to persons abroad,

(b) the freedom of judicial officers, officials or other competent persons of the State of origin to effect service of judicial documents directly through the judicial officers, officials or other competent persons of the State of destination.

(c) the freedom of any person interested in a judicial proceeding to effect service of judicial documents directly through the judicial officers, officials or other competent persons of the State of destination.

Article 11

The present Convention shall not prevent two or more contracting States from agreeing to permit, for the purpose of service of judicial documents, channels of transmission other than those provided for in the preceding articles and, in particular, direct communication between their respective authorities.

Article 12

The service of judicial documents coming from a contracting State shall not give rise to any payment or reimbursement of taxes or costs for the services rendered by the State addressed.

The applicant shall pay or reimburse the costs occasioned by—

(a) the employment of a judicial officer or of a person competent under the law of the State of destination,

(b) the use of a particular method of service.

Article 13

Where a request for service complies with the terms of the present Convention, the State addressed may refuse to comply therewith only if it deems that compliance would infringe its sovereignty or security.

It may not refuse to comply solely on the ground that, under its internal law, it claims exclusive jurisdiction over the subject-matter of the action or that its internal law would not permit the action upon which the application is based.

The Central Authority shall, in case of refusal, promptly inform the applicant and state the reasons for the refusal.

Article 14

Difficulties which may arise in connection with the transmission of judicial documents for service shall be settled through diplomatic channels.

Article 15

Where a writ of summons or an equivalent document had to be transmitted abroad for the purpose of service, under the provisions of the present Convention, and the defendant has not appeared, judgment shall not be given until it is established that—

(a) the document was served by a method prescribed by the internal law of the State addressed for the service of documents in domestic actions upon persons who are within its territory, or

(b) the document was actually delivered to the defendant or to his residence by another method provided for by this Convention,

and that in either of these cases the service or the delivery was effected in sufficient time to enable the defendant to defend.

Each contracting State shall be free to declare that the judge, notwithstanding the provisions of the first paragraph of this article, may give judgment even if no certificate of service or delivery has been received, if all the following conditions are fulfilled—

(a) the document was transmitted by one of the methods provided for in this Convention,

(b) a period of time of not less than six months, considered adequate by the judge in the particular case, has elapsed since the date of the transmission of the document,

(c) no certificate of any kind has been received, even though every reasonable effort has been made to obtain it through the competent authorities of the State addressed.

Notwithstanding the provisions of the preceding paragraphs the judge may order, in case of urgency, any provisional or protective measures.

Article 16

When a writ of summons or an equivalent document had to be transmitted abroad for the purpose of service, under the provisions of the present Convention, and a judgment has been entered against a defendant who has not appeared, the judge shall have the power to relieve the defendant from the effects of the expiration of the time for appeal from the judgment if the following conditions are fulfilled—

(a) the defendant, without any fault on his part, did not have knowledge of the document in sufficient time to defend, or knowledge of the judgment in sufficient time to appeal, and

(b) the defendant has disclosed a *prima facie* defense to the action on the merits.

An application for relief may be filed only within a reasonable time after the defendant has knowledge of the judgment.

Each contracting State may declare that the application will not be entertained if it is filed after the expiration of a time to be stated in the declaration, but which shall in no case be less than one year following the date of the judgment.

This article shall not apply to judgments concerning status or capacity of persons.

CHAPTER II—EXTRAJUDICIAL DOCUMENTS
Article 17

Extrajudicial documents emanating from authorities and judicial officers of a contracting State may be transmitted for the purpose of service in another contracting State by the methods and under the provisions of the present Convention.

CHAPTER III—GENERAL CLAUSES
Article 18

Each contracting State may designate other authorities in addition to the Central Authority and shall determine the extent of their compe tence.

The applicant shall, however, in all cases, have the right to address a request directly to the Central Authority.

Federal States shall be free to designate more than one Central Authority.

Article 19

To the extent that the internal law of a contracting State permits methods of transmission, other than those provided for in the preceding articles, of documents coming from abroad, for service within its territory, the present Convention shall not affect such provisions.

Article 20

The present Convention shall not prevent an agreement between any two or more contracting States to dispense with—

(a) the necessity for duplicate copies of transmitted documents as required by the second paragraph of article 3,

(b) the language requirements of the third paragraph of article 5 and article 7,

(c) the provisions of the fourth paragraph of article 5,

(d) the provisions of the second paragraph of article 12.

Article 21

Each contracting State shall, at the time of the deposit of its instrument of ratification or accession, or at a later date, inform the Ministry of Foreign Affairs of the Netherlands of the following—

(a) the designation of authorities, pursuant to articles 2 and 18,

(b) the designation of the authority competent to complete the certificate pursuant to article 6,

(c) the designation of the authority competent to receive documents transmitted by consular channels, pursuant to article 9.

Each contracting State shall similarly inform the Ministry, where appropriate, of—

(a) opposition to the use of methods of transmission pursuant to articles 8 and 10,

(b) declarations pursuant to the second paragraph of article 15 and the third paragraph of article 16,

(c) all modifications of the above designations, oppositions and declarations.

Article 22

Where Parties to the present Convention are also Parties to one or both of the Conventions on civil procedure signed at The Hague on 17th July 1905 [99 BFSP 990], and on 1st March 1954 [286 UNTS 265], this Convention shall replace as between them articles 1 to 7 of the earlier Conventions.

Article 23

The present Convention shall not affect the application of article 23 of the Convention on civil procedure signed at The Hague on 17th July 1905, or of article 24 of the Convention on civil procedure signed at The Hague on 1st March 1954.

These articles shall, however, apply only if methods of communication, identical to those provided for in these Conventions, are used.

Article 24

Supplementary agreements between parties to the Conventions of 1905 and 1954 shall be considered as equally applicable to the present Convention, unless the Parties have otherwise agreed.

Article 25

Without prejudice to the provisions of articles 22 and 24, the present Convention shall not derogate from Conventions containing provisions on the matters governed by this Convention to which the contracting States are, or shall become, Parties.

Article 26

The present Convention shall be open for signature by the States represented at the Tenth Session of the Hague Conference on Private International Law.

It shall be ratified, and the instruments of ratification shall be deposited with the Ministry of Foreign Affairs of the Netherlands.

Article 27

The present Convention shall enter into force on the sixtieth day after the deposit of the third instrument of ratification referred to in the second paragraph of article 26.

The Convention shall enter into force for each signatory State which ratifies subsequently on the sixtieth day after the deposit of its instrument of ratification.

Article 28

Any State not represented at the Tenth Session of the Hague Conference on Private International Law may accede to the present Convention after it has entered into force in accordance with the first paragraph of article 27. The instrument of accession shall be deposited with the Ministry of Foreign Affairs of the Netherlands.

The Convention shall enter into force for such a State in the absence of any objection from a State, which has ratified the Convention before such deposit, notified to the Ministry of Foreign Affairs of the Netherlands within a period of six months after the date on which the said Ministry has notified it of such accession.

In the absence of any such objection, the Convention shall enter into force for the acceding State on the first day of the month following the expiration of the last of the periods referred to in the preceding paragraph.

Article 29

Any State may, at the time of signature, ratification or accession, declare that the present Convention shall extend to all the territories for the international relations of which it is responsible, or to one or more of them. Such a declaration shall take effect on the date of entry into force of the Convention for the State concerned.

At any time thereafter, such extensions shall be notified to the Ministry of Foreign Affairs of the Netherlands.

The Convention shall enter into force for the territories mentioned in such an extension on the sixtieth day after the notification referred to in the preceding paragraph.

Article 30

The present Convention shall remain in force for five years from the date of its entry into force in accordance with the first paragraph of article 27, even for States which have ratified it or acceded to it subsequently.

If there has been no denunciation, it shall be renewed tacitly every five years.

Any denunciation shall be notified to the Ministry of Foreign Affairs of the Netherlands at least six months before the end of the five year period.

It may be limited to certain of the territories to which the Convention applies.

The denunciation shall have effect only as regards the State which has notified it. The Convention shall remain in force for the other contracting States.

Article 31

The Ministry of Foreign Affairs of the Netherlands shall give notice to the States referred to in article 26, and to the States which have acceded in accordance with article 28, of the following—

(a) the signatures and ratifications referred to in article 26;

(b) the date of which the present Convention enters into force in accordance with the first paragraph of article 27;

(c) the accessions referred to in article 28 and the dates on which they take effect;

(d) the extensions referred to in article 29 and the dates on which they take effect;

(e) the designations, oppositions and declarations referred to in article 21;

(f) the denunciations referred to in the third paragraph of article 30.

IN WITNESS WHEREOF the undersigned, being duly authorised thereto have signed the present Convention.

DONE at The Hague, on the 15th day of November, 1965, in the English and French languages, both texts being equally authentic, in a single copy which shall be deposited in the archives of the Government of the Netherlands, and of which a certified copy shall be sent, through the diplomatic channel, to each of the States represented at the Tenth Session of the Hague Conference on Private International Law.

ANNEX TO THE CONVENTION

Forms

REQUEST

FOR SERVICE ABROAD OF JUDICIAL OR EXTRAJUDICIAL DOCUMENTS

Convention on the service abroad of judicial and extrajudicial documents in civil or commercial matters, signed at The Hague, 15th of November, 1965.

Identity and address of the applicant   Address of receiving authority

The undersigned applicant has the honour to transmit—in duplicate—the documents listed below and, in conformity with article 5 of the above-mentioned Convention, requests prompt service of one copy thereof on the addressee, i.e., (identity and address) _____

(*a*) in accordance with the provisions of sub-paragraph (a) of the first paragraph of article 5 of the Convention*.

(*b*) in accordance with the following particular method (sub-paragraph (b) of the first paragraph of article 5)*:

_____
_____
_____

(*c*) by delivery to the addressee, if he accepts it voluntarily (second paragraph of article 5)*.

The authority is requested to return or have returned to the applicant a copy of the documents—and of the annexes*—with a certificate as provided on the reverse side.

List of documents

_____
_____
_____
_____
_____
_____   Done at _____, the _____
_____
_____   Signature and/or stamp.
_____
* Delete if inappropriate.

Reverse of the request

CERTIFICATE

The undersigned authority has the honour to certify, in conformity with article 6 of the Convention,

1) that the document has been served*
   — the (date) _____
   — at (place, street, number) _____

   — in one of the following methods authorised by article 5—
     (*a*) in accordance with the provisions of sub-paragraph (a) of the first paragraph of article 5 of the Convention*.
     (*b*) in accordance with the following particular method*:
     _____

     (*c*) by delivery to the addressee, who accepted it voluntarily*.
   The documents referred to in the request have been delivered to:
   — (identity and description of person) _____

   — relationship to the addressee (family, business or other):
   _____

2) that the document has not been served, by reason of the following facts*:
   _____
   _____
   _____

In conformity with the second paragraph of article 12 of the Convention, the applicant is requested to pay or reimburse the expenses detailed in the attached statement*:

Annexes
Documents returned: _____
_____
_____

Done at _____, the _____

In appropriate cases, documents establishing the service:
_____
_____   Signature and/or stamp.
_____

* Delete if inappropriate.

SUMMARY OF THE DOCUMENT TO BE 39

Convention on the service abroad of judicial and
extrajudicial documents in civil or commercial matter
signed at The Hague, the 15th of November, 1965.

(article 5, fourth paragraph)

Name and address of the requesting authority: _____
_____
_____

Particulars of the parties*: _____
_____
_____

JUDICIAL DOCUMENT**

Nature and purpose of the document: _____
_____
_____

Nature and purpose of the proceedings and, where appropriate, the
amount in dispute: _____
_____
_____

Date and place for entering appearance**: _____
_____

Court which has given judgment**: _____

Date of judgment**: _____
Time limits stated in the document**: _____
_____

EXTRAJUDICIAL DOCUMENT**

Nature and purpose of the document: _____
_____

Time limits stated in the document**: _____
_____
_____

* If appropriate, identity and address of the person interested in the
transmission of the document.
** Delete if inappropriate.

Parties to the Convention

(as of 2004)

...ua and Barbuda	Lithuania
...ntina	Luxembourg
...amas	Malawi
...rbados	Mexico
...elarus	Netherlands
Belgium	Norway
Botswana	Pakistan
Bulgaria	Poland
Canada	Portugal
China (People's Republic of)	Republic of Korea
Cyprus	Romania
Czech Republic	Russian Federation
Denmark	San Marino
Egypto	Seychelles
Estonia	Slovak Republic
Finland	Slovenia
France	Spain
Germany	Sri Lanka
Greece	Sweden
Hungary	Switzerland
Ireland	Turkey
Israel	Ukraine
Italy	United Kingdom of Great Britain and Northern Ireland
Japan	United States of America
Kuwait	Venezuela
Latvia	

ENFORCEMENT OF FOREIGN JUDGMENTS

Great Benefit Procedurally

UNIFORM FOREIGN MONEY–JUDGMENTS RECOGNITION ACT*

§ 1. [Definitions]

As used in this Act:

(1) "foreign state" means any governmental unit other than the United States, or any state, district, commonwealth, territory, insular possession thereof, or the Panama Canal Zone, the Trust Territory of the Pacific Islands, or the Ryukyu Islands;

(2) "foreign judgment" means any judgment of a foreign state granting or denying recovery of a sum of money, other than a judgment for taxes, a fine or other penalty, or a judgment for support in matrimonial or family matters. *] Not in FL Act*

§ 2. [Applicability]

This Act applies to any foreign judgment that is final and conclusive and enforceable where rendered even though an appeal therefrom is pending or it is subject to appeal.

§ 3. [Recognition and Enforcement]

Except as provided in section 4, a foreign judgment meeting the requirements of section 2 is conclusive between the parties to the extent that it grants or denies recovery of a sum of money. The foreign judgment is enforceable in the same manner as the judgment of a sister state which is entitled to full faith and credit.

§ 4. [Grounds for Non-recognition]

(a) A foreign judgment is not conclusive if *mandatory*

(1) the judgment was rendered under a system which does not provide impartial tribunals or procedures compatible with the requirements of due process of law;

(2) the foreign court did not have personal jurisdiction over the defendant; or

---

* As of 2004, the Act was in effect in the following states: Alaska, California, Colorado, Connecticut, Delaware, the District of Columbia, Florida, Georgia, Hawaii, Idaho, Illinois, Iowa, Maine, Maryland, Massachusetts, Michigan, Minnesota, Missouri, Montana, New Jersey, New Mexico, New York, North Carolina, North Dakota, Ohio, Oklahoma, Oregon, Pennsylvania, Texas, U.S. Virgin Islands, Virginia, and Washington.

(3) the foreign court did not have jurisdiction over the subject matter.**

(b) A foreign judgment need not be recognized if

Pemissive

(1) the defendant in the proceedings in the foreign court did not receive notice of the proceedings in sufficient time to enable him to defend;

(2) the judgment was obtained by fraud;

(3) the [cause of action] [claim for relief] on which the judgment is based is repugnant to the public policy of this state;

(4) the judgment conflicts with another final and conclusive judgment;

(5) the proceeding in the foreign court was contrary to an agreement between the parties under which the dispute in question was to be settled otherwise than by proceedings in that court; or

(6) in the case of jurisdiction based only on personal service, the foreign court was a seriously inconvenient forum for the trial of the action.

§ 5.   [Personal Jurisdiction]

(a) The foreign judgment shall not be refused recognition for lack of personal jurisdiction if

(1) the defendant was served personally in the foreign state;

(2) the defendant voluntarily appeared in the proceedings, other than for the purpose of protecting property seized or threatened with seizure in the proceedings or of contesting the jurisdiction of the court over him;

(3) the defendant prior to the commencement of the proceedings had agreed to submit to the jurisdiction of the foreign court with respect to the subject matter involved;

(4) the defendant was domiciled in the foreign state when the proceedings were instituted or, being a body corporate had its principal place of business, was incorporated, or had otherwise acquired corporate status, in the foreign state;

(5) the defendant had a business office in the foreign state and the proceedings in the foreign court involved a [cause of action] [claim for relief] arising out of business done by the defendant through that office in the foreign state; or

(6) the defendant operated a motor vehicle or airplane in the foreign state and the proceedings involved a [cause of action] [claim for relief] arising out of such operation.

(b) The courts of this state may recognize other bases of jurisdiction.

** In the New York version, this section appears in paragraph (b), i.e., under discre- tionary grounds for refusal of recognition (CPLR § 5304(b)(1)).

§ 6.   [Stay in Case of Appeal]

If the defendant satisfies the court either that an appeal is pending or that he is entitled and intends to appeal from the foreign judgment, the court may stay the proceedings until the appeal has been determined or until the expiration of a period of time sufficient to enable the defendant to prosecute the appeal.

§ 7.   [Saving Clause]

This Act does not prevent the recognition of a foreign judgment in situations not covered by this Act.

§ 8.   [Uniformity of Interpretation]

This Act shall be so construed as to effectuate its general purpose to make uniform the law of those states which enact it.

§ 9.   [Short Title]

This Act may be cited as the Uniform Foreign Money–Judgments Recognition Act.

NEW YORK AMENDMENT ON FOREIGN CURRENCY JUDGMENTS

JUDICIARY LAW

§ 27. In all judgments or decrees rendered by any court for any debt, damages or costs, in all executions issued thereupon, and in all accounts arising from proceedings in courts the amount shall be computed, as near as may be, in dollars and cents, rejecting lesser fractions; and no judgment, or other proceeding, shall be considered erroneous for such omissions.

(b) In any case in which the cause of action is based upon an obligation denominated in a currency other than currency of the United States, a court shall render or enter a judgment or decree in the foreign currency of the underlying obligation. Such judgment or decree shall be converted into currency of the United States at the rate of exchange prevailing on the date of entry of the judgment or decree.

(As amended L.1987, c. 326, § 1.)

UNITED KINGDOM CIVIL JURISDICTION AND JUDGMENTS ACT 1982*

(Excerpts)

Provisions relating to recognition and enforcement of judgments

31. (1) A judgment given by a court of an overseas country against a state other than the United Kingdom or the state to which that court belongs shall be recognised and enforced in the United Kingdom if, and only if—

(a) it would be so recognised and enforced if it had not been given against a state; and

(b) that court would have had jurisdiction in the matter if it had applied rules corresponding to those applicable to such matters in the United Kingdom in accordance with sections 2 to 11 of the State Immunity Act 1978.

. . .

32. (1) Subject to the following provisions of this section, a judgment given by a court of an overseas country in any proceedings shall not be recognised or enforced in the United Kingdom if—

(a) the bringing of those proceedings in that court was contrary to an agreement under which the dispute in question was to be settled otherwise than by proceedings in the courts of that country; and

(b) those proceedings were not brought in that court by, or with the agreement of, the person against whom the judgment was given; and

(c) that person did not counterclaim in the proceedings or otherwise submit to the jurisdiction of that court.

(2) Subsection (1) does not apply where the agreement referred to in paragraph (a) of that subsection was illegal, void or unenforceable or was incapable of being performed for reasons not attributable to the fault of the party bringing the proceedings in which the judgment was given.

(3) In determining whether a judgment given by a court of an overseas country should be recognised or enforced in the United Kingdom, a court in the United Kingdom shall not be bound by any decision of the overseas court relating to any of the matters mentioned in subsection (1) or (2).

(4) Nothing in subsection (1) shall affect the recognition or enforcement in the United Kingdom of—

(a) a judgment which is required to be recognised or enforced there under the 1968 Convention;

. . .

* c. 27. 22 Halsbury's Statutes 531–33
(4th ed. 1995 Reissue).

33. (1) For the purposes of determining whether a judgment given by a court of an overseas country should be recognised or enforced in England and Wales or Northern Ireland, the person against whom the judgment was given shall not be regarded as having submitted to the jurisdiction of the court by reason only of the fact that he appeared (conditionally or otherwise) in the proceedings for all or any one or more of the following purposes, namely—

(a) to contest the jurisdiction of the court;

(b) to ask the court to dismiss or stay the proceedings on the ground that the dispute in question should be submitted to arbitration or to the determination of the courts of another country;

(c) to protect, or obtain the release of, property seized or threatened with seizure in the proceedings.

(2) Nothing in this section shall affect the recognition or enforcement in England and Wales or Northern Ireland of a judgment which is required to be recognised or enforced there under the 1968 Convention.

34. No proceedings may be brought by a person in England and Wales or Northern Ireland on a cause of action in respect of which a judgment has been given in his favor in proceedings between the same parties, or their privies, in a court in another part of the United Kingdom or in a court of an overseas country, unless that judgment is not enforceable or entitled to recognition in England and Wales or, as the case may be, in Northern Ireland.

EUROPEAN COMMUNITIES: CONVENTION ON JURISDICTION AND ENFORCEMENT OF JUDGMENTS IN CIVIL AND COMMERCIAL MATTERS

Consolidated and updated version of the Brussels Convention of 1968 and the Protocol of 1971, following the accession of Austria, Finland, and Sweden[1]

PREAMBLE

THE HIGH CONTRACTING PARTIES TO THE TREATY ESTABLISHING THE EUROPEAN ECONOMIC COMMUNITY,

DESIRING to implement the provisions of Article 220 of that Treaty by virtue of which they undertook to secure the simplification of formalities governing the reciprocal recognition and enforcement of judgments of courts or tribunals;

ANXIOUS to strengthen in the Community the legal protection of persons therein established;

CONSIDERING that it is necessary for this purpose to determine the international jurisdiction of their courts, to facilitate recognition and to introduce an expeditious procedure for securing the enforcement of judgments, authentic instruments and court settlements;[2]

HAVE DECIDED to conclude this Convention and to this end have designated as their Plenipotentiaries:

HIS MAJESTY THE KING OF THE BELGIANS:

   Mr. Pierre HARMEL, Minister for Foreign Affairs;

THE PRESIDENT OF THE FEDERAL REPUBLIC OF GERMANY:

   Mr. Willy BRANDT, Vice-Chancellor, Minister for Foreign Affairs;

THE PRESIDENT OF THE FRENCH REPUBLIC:

   Mr. Michel DEBRE, Minister for Foreign Affairs;

THE PRESIDENT OF THE ITALIAN REPUBLIC:

   Mr. Giuseppe MEDICI, Minister for Foreign Affairs;

---

1. Text as amended by the Convention of 9 October 1978 on the accession of the Kingdom of Denmark, Ireland and the United Kingdom of Great Britain and Northern Ireland—hereafter referred to as the "1978 Accession Convention"—by the Convention of 25 October 1982 on the accession of the Hellenic Republic—hereafter referred to as the "1982 Accession Convention"—by the Convention of 26 May 1989 on the accession of the Kingdom of Spain and the Portuguese Republic—hereafter referred to as the "1989 Accession Convention"—and by the 1997 Convention on the accession of the Republic of Austria, the Republic of Finland and the Kingdom of Sweden—hereinafter referred to as the "1997 Accession Convention".

2. The Preamble of the 1989 Accession Convention contained the following text: "MINDFUL that on 16 September 1988 the Member States of the Community and the Member States of the European Free Trade Association concluded in Lugano the Convention on jurisdiction and the enforcement of judgments in civil and commercial matters, which extends the principles of the Brussels Convention to the States becoming parties to that Convention".

HIS ROYAL HIGHNESS THE GRAND DUKE OF LUXEMBOURG:

Mr. Pierre GREGOIRE, Minister for Foreign Affairs;

HER MAJESTY THE QUEEN OF THE NETHERLANDS:

Mr. J. M. A. H. LUNS, Minister for Foreign Affairs;

WHO, meeting within the Council, having exchanged their Full Powers, found in good and due form,

HAVE AGREED AS FOLLOWS:

TITLE I. SCOPE

Article 1

This Convention shall apply in civil and commercial matters whatever the nature of the court or tribunal. It shall not extend, in particular, to revenue, customs or administrative matters.[3]

The Convention shall not apply to:

1.   the status or legal capacity of natural persons, rights in property arising out of a matrimonial relationship, wills and succession;

2.   bankruptcy, proceedings relating to the winding-up of insolvent companies or other legal persons, judicial arrangements, compositions and analogous proceedings;

3.   social security;

4.   arbitration.

TITLE II. JURISDICTION
Section 1: General provisions

Article 2

Subject to the provisions of this Convention, persons domiciled in a Contracting State shall, whatever their nationality, be sued in the courts of that State.

Persons who are not nationals of the State in which they are domiciled shall be governed by the rules of jurisdiction applicable to nationals of that State.

Article 3

Persons domiciled in a Contracting State may be sued in the courts of another Contracting State only by virtue of the rules set out in Sections 2 to 6 of this Title.

In particular the following provisions shall not be applicable as against them:

— in Belgium: Article 15 of the civil code (Code civil—Burgerlijk Wetboek) and Article 638 of the judicial code (Code judiciaire—Gerechtelijk Wetboek),

---

3. Second sentence added by Article 3 of the 1978 Accession Convention.

— in Denmark: Article 246 (2) and (3) of the law on civil procedure (Lov om rettens pleje),[4]

— in the Federal Republic of Germany: Article 23 of the code of civil procedure (Zivilprozessiordnung),

– in Greece, Article 40 of the code of civil procedure (Κώδικας Πολιτικῆς Δικονομίας),

— in France: Articles 14 and 15 of the civil code (Code civil),

— in Ireland: the rules which enable jurisdiction to be founded on the document instituting the proceedings having been served on the defendant during his temporary presence in Ireland,

— in Italy: Articles 2 and 4, Nos 1 and 2 of the code of civil procedure (Codice di procedura civile),

— in Luxembourg: Articles 14 and 15 of the civil code (Code civil),

— in the Netherlands: Articles 126 (3) and 127 of the code of civil procedure (Wetboek van Burgerlijke Rechtsvordering),

— in Austria: Article 99 of the Law on Court Jurisdiction (Jurisdiktions- norm),

— in Portugal: Articles 65 and 65A of the code of civil procedure (Código de Processo Civil) and Article 11 of the code of labour procedure (Código de Processo de Trabalho),[5]

— in Finland: the second, third and fourth sentences of the first paragraph of Section 1 of Chapter 10 of the Code of Judicial Procedure (oikeudenkäymiskaari/rätteg angsbalken),

— in Sweden: the first sentence of the first paragraph of Section 3 of Chapter 10 of the Code of Judicial Procedure (rätteg angsbalken),

— in the United Kingdom: the rules which enable jurisdiction to be founded on:

  (a) the document instituting the proceedings having been served on the defendant during his temporary presence in the United Kingdom; or

  (b) the presence within the United Kingdom of property belonging to the defendant; or

  (c) the seizure by the plaintiff of property situated in the United Kingdom.[6]

Article 4

If the defendant is not domiciled in a Contracting State, the jurisdiction of the courts of each Contracting State shall, subject to the provisions of Article 16, be determined by the law of that State.

4. As amended by a Communication of 8 February 1988 made in accordance with Article VI of the annexed Protocol, and confirmed by Annex I(d)(1) to the 1989 Accession Convention.

5. As amended by a Communication of 8 June 2000 made in accordance with Article VI of the annexed Protocol.

6. Second subparagraph as amended by Article 4 of the 1978 Accession Convention, by Article 3 of the 1982 Accession Convention, by Article 3 of the 1989 Accession Convention and by Article 2 of the 1997 Accession Convention.

As against such a defendant, any person domiciled in a Contracting State may, whatever his nationality, avail himself in that State of the rules of jurisdiction there in force, and in particular those specified in the second paragraph of Article 3, in the same way as the nationals of that State.

Section 2: Special jurisdiction

Article 5

A person domiciled in a Contracting State may, in another Contracting State, be sued:

1. in matters relating to a contract, in the courts for the place of performance of the obligation in question; in matters relating to individual contracts of employment, this place is that where the employee habitually carries out his work, or if the employee does not habitually carry out his work in any one country, the employer may also be sued in the courts for the place where the business which engaged the employee was or is now situated;[7]

2. in matters relating to maintenance, in the courts for the place where the maintenance creditor is domiciled or habitually resident or, if the matter is ancillary to proceedings concerning the status of a person, in the court which, according to its own law, has jurisdiction to entertain those proceedings, unless that jurisdiction is based solely on the nationality of one of the parties;[8]

3. in matters relating to tort, delict or quasi-delict, in the courts for the place where the harmful event occurred;

4. as regards a civil claim for damages or restitution which is based on an act giving rise to criminal proceedings, in the court seised of those proceedings, to the extent that that court has jurisdiction under its own law to entertain civil proceedings;

5. as regards a dispute arising out of the operations of a branch, agency or other establishment, in the courts for the place in which the branch, agency or other establishment is situated;

6. as settlor, trustee or beneficiary of a trust created by the operation of a statute, or by a written instrument, or created orally and evidenced in writing, in the courts of the Contracting State in which the trust is domiciled;[9]

7. Point 1 as amended by Article 4 of the 1989 Accession Convention.

8. Point 2 as amended by Article 5(3) of the 1978 Accession Convention.

9. Point 6 added by Article 5(4) of the 1978 Accession Convention.

7. as regards a dispute concerning the payment of remuneration claimed in respect of the salvage of a cargo or freight, in the court under the authority of which the cargo or freight in question:

(a) has been arrested to secure such payment, or

(b) could have been so arrested, but bail or other security has been given;

provided that this provision shall apply only if it is claimed that the defendant has an interest in the cargo or freight or had such an interest at the time of salvage.[10]

Article 6

A person domiciled in a Contracting State may also be sued:

1. where he is one of a number of defendants, in the courts for the place where any one of them is domiciled;

2. as a third party in an action on a warranty or guarantee or in any other third party proceedings, in the court seised of the original proceedings, unless these were instituted solely with the object of removing him from the jurisdiction of the court which would be competent in his case;

3. on a counter-claim arising from the same contract or facts on which the original claim was based, in the court in which the original claim is pending;

4. in matters relating to a contract, if the action may be combined with an action against the same defendant in matters relating to rights in rem in immovable property, in the court of the Contracting State in which the property is situated.[11]

Article 6a[12]

Where by virtue of this Convention a court of a Contracting State has jurisdiction in actions relating to liability from the use or operation of a ship, that court, or any other court substituted for this purpose by the internal law of that State, shall also have jurisdiction over claims for limitation of such liability.

Section 3: Jurisdiction in matters relating to insurance

Article 7

In matters relating to insurance, jurisdiction shall be determined by this Section, without prejudice to the provisions of Articles 4 and 5 point 5.

Article 8[13]

An insurer domiciled in a Contracting State may be sued:

1. in the courts of the State where he is domiciled, or

2. in another Contracting State, in the courts for the place where the policy-holder is domiciled, or

10. Point 7 added by Article 5(4) of the 1978 Accession Convention.

11. Point 4 added by Article 5 of the 1989 Accession Convention.

12. Article added by Article 6 of the 1978 Accession Convention.

13. Text as amended by Article 7 of the 1978 Accession Convention.

3. if he is a co-insurer, in the courts of a Contracting State in which proceedings are brought against the leading insurer.

An insurer who is not domiciled in a Contracting State but has a branch, agency or other establishment in one of the Contracting States shall, in disputes arising out of the operations of the branch, agency or establishment, be deemed to be domiciled in that State.

Article 9

In respect of liability insurance or insurance of immovable property, the insurer may in addition be sued in the courts for the place where the harmful event occurred. The same applies if movable and immovable property are covered by the same insurance policy and both are adversely affected by the same contingency.

Article 10

In respect of liability insurance, the insurer may also, if the law of the court permits it, be joined in proceedings which the injured party had brought against the insured.

The provisions of Articles 7, 8 and 9 shall apply to actions brought by the injured party directly against the insurer, where such direct actions are permitted.

If the law governing such direct actions provides that the policy-holder or the insured may be joined as a party to the action, the same court shall have jurisdiction over them.

Article 11

Without prejudice to the provisions of the third paragraph of Article 10, an insurer may bring proceedings only in the courts of the Contracting State in which the defendant is domiciled, irrespective of whether he is the policy-holder, the insured or a beneficiary.

The provisions of this Section shall not affect the right to bring a counterclaim in the court in which, in accordance with this Section, the original claim is pending.

Article 12[14]

The provisions of this Section may be departed from only by an agreement on jurisdiction:

1. which is entered into after the dispute has arisen, or

2. which allows the policy-holder, the insured or a beneficiary to bring proceedings in courts other than those indicated in this Section, or

14. Text as amended by Article 8 of the 1978 Accession Convention.

3.   which is concluded between a policy-holder and an insurer, both of whom are domiciled in the same Contracting State, and which has the effect of conferring jurisdiction on the courts of that State even if the harmful event were to occur abroad, provided that such an agreement is not contrary to the law of that State, or

4.   which is concluded with a policy-holder who is not domiciled in a Contracting State, except in so far as the insurance is compulsory or relates to immovable property in a Contracting State, or

5.   which relates to a contract of insurance in so far as it covers one or more of the risks set out in Article 12a.

Article 12a[15]

The following are the risks referred to in point 5 of Article 12:

1.   Any loss of or damage to:

(a) sea-going ships, installations situated offshore or on the high seas, or aircraft, arising from perils which relate to their use for commercial purposes;

(b) goods in transit other than passengers' baggage where the transit consists of or includes carriage by such ships or aircraft;

2.   Any liability, other than for bodily injury to passengers or loss of or damage to their baggage:

(a) arising out of the use or operation of ships, installations or aircraft as referred to in point 1 (a) above in so far as the law of the Contracting State in which such aircraft are registered does not prohibit agreements on jurisdiction regarding insurance of such risks;

(b) for loss or damage caused by goods in transit as described in point 1 (b) above;

3.   Any financial loss connected with the use or operation of ships, installations or aircraft as referred to in point 1 (a) above, in particular loss of freight or charter-hire;

4.   Any risk or interest connected with any of those referred to in points 1 to 3 above.

Section 4: Jurisdiction over consumer contracts[16]

Article 13

In proceedings concerning a contract concluded by a person for a purpose which can be regarded as being outside his trade or profession, hereinafter called "the consumer", jurisdiction shall be determined by this Section, without prejudice to the provisions of point 5 of Articles 4 and 5, if it is:

1.   a contract for the sale of goods on instalment credit terms; or

15. Article added by Article 9 of the 1978 Accession Convention.

16. Text as amended by Article 10 of the 1978 Accession Convention.

2.   a contract for a loan repayable by instalments, or for any other form of credit, made to finance the sale of goods; or

3.   any other contract for the supply of goods or a contract for the supply of services, and

(a) in the State of the consumer's domicile the conclusion of the contract was preceded by a specific invitation addressed to him or by advertising; and

(b) the consumer took in that State the steps necessary for the conclusion of the contract.

Where a consumer enters into a contract with a party who is not domiciled in a Contracting State but has a branch, agency or other establishment in one of the Contracting States, that party shall, in disputes arising out of the operations of the branch, agency or establishment, be deemed to be domiciled in that State.

This Section shall not apply to contracts of transport.

Article 14

A consumer may bring proceedings against the other party to a contract either in the courts of the Contracting State in which that party is domiciled or in the courts of the Contracting State in which he is himself domiciled.

Proceedings may be brought against a consumer by the other party to the contract only in the courts of the Contracting State in which the consumer is domiciled.

These provisions shall not affect the right to bring a counter-claim in the court in which, in accordance with this Section, the original claim is pending.

Article 15

The provisions of this Section may be departed from only by an agreement:

1.   which is entered into after the dispute has arisen; or

2.   which allows the consumer to bring proceedings in courts other than those indicated in this Section; or

3.   which is entered into by the consumer and the other party to the contract, both of whom are at the time of conclusion of the contract domiciled or habitually resident in the same Contracting State, and which confers jurisdiction on the courts of that State, provided that such an agreement is not contrary to the law of that State.

Section 5: Exclusive jurisdiction

Article 16

The following courts shall have exclusive jurisdiction, regardless of domicile:

1.   (a) in proceedings which have as their object rights in rem in immovable property or tenancies of immovable property, the courts of the Contracting State in which the property is situated;

   (b) however, in proceedings which have as their object tenancies of immovable property concluded for temporary private use for a maximum period of six consecutive months, the courts of the Contracting State in which the defendant is domiciled shall also have jurisdiction, provided that the landlord and the tenant are natural persons and are domiciled in the same Contracting State;[17]

2.   in proceedings which have as their object the validity of the constitution, the nullity or the dissolution of companies or other legal persons or associations of natural or legal persons, or the decisions of their organs, the courts of the Contracting State in which the company, legal person or association has its seat;

3.   in proceedings which have as their object the validity of entries in public registers, the courts of the Contracting State in which the register is kept;

4.   in proceedings concerned with the registration or validity of patents, trade marks, designs, or other similar rights required to be deposited or registered, the courts of the Contracting State in which the deposit or registration has been applied for, has taken place or is under the terms of an international convention deemed to have taken place;

5.   in proceedings concerned with the enforcement of judgments, the courts of the Contracting State in which the judgment has been or is to be enforced.

Section 6: Prorogation of jurisdiction

Article 17[18]

If the parties, one or more of whom is domiciled in a Contracting State, have agreed that a court or the courts of a Contracting State are to have jurisdiction to settle any disputes which have arisen or which may arise in connection with a particular legal relationship, that court or those courts shall have exclusive jurisdiction. Such an agreement conferring jurisdiction shall be either:

   (a) in writing or evidenced in writing; or

   (b) in a form which accords with practices which the parties have established between themselves; or

   (c) in international trade or commerce, in a form which accords with a usage of which the parties are or ought to have been aware and which in such trade or commerce is widely known to, and regularly observed by, parties to contracts of the type involved in the particular trade or commerce concerned.

---

17. Point 1 as amended by Article 6 of the 1989 Accession Convention.

18. Text as amended by Article 11 of the 1978 Accession Convention and by Article 7 of the 1989 Accession Convention.

Where such an agreement is concluded by parties, none of whom is domiciled in a Contracting State, the courts of other Contracting States shall have no jurisdiction over their disputes unless the court or courts chosen have declined jurisdiction.

The court or courts of a Contracting State on which a trust instrument has conferred jurisdiction shall have exclusive jurisdiction in any proceedings brought against a settlor, trustee or beneficiary, if relations between these persons or their rights or obligations under the trust are involved.

Agreements or provisions of a trust instrument conferring jurisdiction shall have no legal force if they are contrary to the provisions of Articles 12 or 15, or if the courts whose jurisdiction they purport to exclude have exclusive jurisdiction by virtue of Article 16.

If an agreement conferring jurisdiction was concluded for the benefit of only one of the parties, that party shall retain the right to bring proceedings in any other court which has jurisdiction by virtue of this Convention.

In matters relating to individual contracts of employment an agreement conferring jurisdiction shall have legal force only if it is entered into after the dispute has arisen or if the employee invokes it to seise courts other than those for the defendant's domicile or those specified in Article 5(1).

Article 18

Apart from jurisdiction derived from other provisions of this Convention, a court of a Contracting State before whom a defendant enters an appearance shall have jurisdiction. This rule shall not apply where appearance was entered solely to contest the jurisdiction, or where another court has exclusive jurisdiction by virtue of Article 16.

Section 7: Examination as to jurisdiction and admissibility

Article 19

Where a court of a Contracting State is seised of a claim which is principally concerned with a matter over which the courts of another Contracting State have exclusive jurisdiction by virtue of Article 16, it shall declare of its own motion that it has no jurisdiction.

Article 20

Where a defendant domiciled in one Contracting State is sued in a court of another Contracting State and does not enter an appearance, the court shall declare of its own motion that it has no jurisdiction unless its jurisdiction is derived from the provisions of the Convention.

The court shall stay the proceedings so long as it is not shown that the defendant has been able to receive the document instituting the proceedings or an equivalent document in sufficient time to enable him to arrange for his defence, or that all necessary steps have been taken to this end.[19]

The provisions of the foregoing paragraph shall be replaced by those of Article 15 of the Hague Convention of 15 November 1965 on the service abroad of judicial and extrajudicial documents in civil or commercial matters, if the document instituting the proceedings or notice thereof had to be transmitted abroad in accordance with that Convention.

Section 8: Lis pendens—related actions

Article 21[20]

Where proceedings involving the same cause of action and between the same parties are brought in the courts of different Contracting States, any court other than the court first seised shall of its own motion stay its proceedings until such time as the jurisdiction of the court first seised is established.

Where the jurisdiction of the court first seised is established, any court other than the court first seised shall decline jurisdiction in favour of that court.

Article 22

Where related actions are brought in the courts of different Contracting States, any court other than the court first seised may, while the actions are pending at first instance, stay its proceedings.

A court other than the court first seised may also, on the application of one of the parties, decline jurisdiction if the law of that court permits the consolidation of related actions and the court first seised has jurisdiction over both actions.

For the purposes of this Article, actions are deemed to be related where they are so closely connected that it is expedient to hear and determine them together to avoid the risk of irreconcilable judgments resulting from separate proceedings.

Article 23

Where actions come within the exclusive jurisdiction of several courts, any court other than the court first seised shall decline jurisdiction in favour of that court.

Section 9: Provisional, including protective, measures

Article 24

Application may be made to the courts of a Contracting State for such provisional, including protective, measures as may be available under the law of that State, even if, under this Convention, the courts of another Contracting State have jurisdiction as to the substance of the matter.

---

19. Second subparagraph as amended by Article 12 of the 1978 Accession Convention.

20. Text as amended by Article 8 of the 1989 Accession Convention.

TITLE III. RECOGNITION AND ENFORCEMENT

Article 25

For the purposes of this Convention, "judgment" means any judgment given by a court or tribunal of a Contracting State, whatever the judgment may be called, including a decree, order, decision or writ of execution, as well as the determination of costs or expenses by an officer of the court.

Section 1: Recognition

Article 26

A judgment given in a Contracting State shall be recognized in the other Contracting States without any special procedure being required.

Any interested party who raises the recognition of a judgment as the principal issue in a dispute may, in accordance with the procedures provided for in Sections 2 and 3 of this Title, apply for a decision that the judgment be recognized.

If the outcome of proceedings in a court of a Contracting State depends on the determination of an incidental question of recognition that court shall have jurisdiction over that question.

Article 27

A judgment shall not be recognized:

1. if such recognition is contrary to public policy in the State in which recognition is sought;

2. where it was given in default of appearance, if the defendant was not duly served with the document which instituted the proceedings or with an equivalent document in sufficient time to enable him to arrange for his defence[21];

3. if the judgment is irreconcilable with a judgment given in a dispute between the same parties in the State in which recognition is sought;

4. if the court of the State of origin, in order to arrive at its judgment, has decided a preliminary question concerning the status or legal capacity of natural persons, rights in property arising out of a matrimonial relationship, wills or succession in a way that conflicts with a rule of the private international law of the State in which the recognition is sought, unless the same result would have been reached by the application of the rules of private international law of that State[22];

5. if the judgment is irreconcilable with an earlier judgment given in a non-contracting State involving the same cause of action and

---

21. Point 2 as amended by Article 13 (1) of the 1978 Accession Convention.

22. Point 4 as amended by Annex I (a) (2) first subparagraph to the 1989 Accession Convention.

between the same parties, provided that this latter judgment fulfils the conditions necessary for its recognition in the state addressed.[23]

Article 28

Moreover, a judgment shall not be recognized if it conflicts with the provisions of Sections 3, 4 or 5 of Title II, or in a case provided for in Article 59.

In its examination of the grounds of jurisdiction referred to in the foregoing paragraph, the court or authority applied to shall be bound by the findings of fact on which the court of the State of origin based its jurisdiction.[24]

Subject to the provisions of the first paragraph, the jurisdiction of the court of the State of origin may not be reviewed; the test of public policy referred to in point 1 of Article 27 may not be applied to the rules relating to jurisdiction.[25]

Article 29

Under no circumstances may a foreign judgment be reviewed as to its substance.

Article 30

A court of a Contracting State in which recognition is sought of a judgment given in another Contracting State may stay the proceedings if an ordinary appeal against the judgment has been lodged.

A court of a Contracting State in which recognition is sought of a judgment given in Ireland or the United Kingdom may stay the proceedings if enforcement is suspended in the State of origin, by reason of an appeal.[26]

Section 2: Enforcement

Article 31

A judgment given in a Contracting State and enforceable in that State shall be enforced in another Contracting State when, on the application of any interested party, it has been declared enforceable there.[27]

However, in the United Kingdom, such a judgment shall be enforced in England and Wales, in Scotland, or in Northern Ireland when, on the

23. Point 5 added by Article 13 (2) of the 1978 Accession Convention and amended by Annex I (d) (2) second subparagraph to the 1989 Accession Convention.

24. As amended by Annex I (d) (3) first subparagraph to the 1989 Accession Convention.

25. As amended by Annex I (d) (3) second subparagraph to the 1989 Accession Convention.

26. Second subparagraph added by Article 14 of the 1978 Accession Convention and amended by Annex I (d) (4) to the 1989 Accession Convention.

27. Text as amended by Article 9 of the 1989 Accession Convention.

application of any interested party, it has been registered for enforcement in that part of the United Kingdom.[28]

Article 32

1.   The application shall be submitted:

— in Belgium, to the tribunal de première instance or rechtbank van eerste aanleg,

— in Denmark, to the byret,[29]

— in the Federal Republic of Germany, to the presiding judge of a chamber of the Landgericht,

— in Greece, to the Μονομελές Πρωτοδικείο,

— in Spain, to the Juzgado de Primera Instancia,

— in France, to the presiding judge of the tribunal de grande instance,

— in Ireland, to the High Court,

— in Italy, to the corte d'appello,

— in Luxembourg, to the presiding judge of the tribunal d'arrondissement,

— in the Netherlands, to the presiding judge of the arrondissements-rechtbank,

— in Austria, to the Bezirksgericht,

— in Portugal, to the Tribunal de Comarca,[30]

— in Finland, to the kaeraejaeoikeus/tingsraett,

— in Sweden, to the Svea hovraett,

— in the United Kingdom:

　　1.   in England and Wales, to the High Court of Justice, or in the case of maintenance judgment to the Magistrates' Court on transmission by the Secretary of State;

　　2.   in Scotland, to the Court of Session, or in the case of a maintenance judgment to the Sheriff Court on transmission by the Secretary of State;

　　3.   in Northern Ireland, to the High Court of Justice, or in the case of a maintenance judgment to the Magistrates' Court on transmission by the Secretary of State.[31]

28. Second subparagraph added by Article 15 of the 1978 Accession Convention.

29. As amended by a Communication of 8 February 1988 made in accordance with Article VI of the annexed Protocol, and confirmed by Annex I (d) (5) to the 1989 Accession Convention.

30. As amended by a Communication of 8 June 2000 made in accordance with Article VI of the annexed Protocol.

31. First subparagraph as amended by Article 16 of the 1978 Accession Convention, by Article 4 of the 1982 Accession Convention, by Article 10 of the 1989 Acces-

2.   The jurisdiction of local courts shall be determined by reference to the place of domicile of the party against whom enforcement is sought. If he is not domiciled in the State in which enforcement is sought, it shall be determined by reference to the place of enforcement.

Article 33

The procedure for making the application shall be governed by the law of the State in which enforcement is sought. The applicant must give an address for service of process within the area of jurisdiction of the court applied to. However, if the law of the State in which enforcement is sought does not provide for the furnishing of such an address, the applicant shall appoint a representative ad litem.

The documents referred to in Articles 46 and 47 shall be attached to the application.

Article 34

The court applied to shall give its decision without delay; the party against whom enforcement is sought shall not at this stage of the proceedings be entitled to make any submissions on the application.

The application may be refused only for one of the reasons specified in Articles 27 and 28.

Under no circumstances may the foreign judgment be reviewed as to its substance.

Article 35

The appropriate officer of the court shall without delay bring the decision given on the application to the notice of the applicant in accordance with the procedure laid down by the law of the State in which enforcement is sought.

Article 36

If enforcement is authorized, the party against whom enforcement is sought may appeal against the decision within one month of service thereof.

If that party is domiciled in a Contracting State other than that in which the decision authorizing enforcement was given, the time for appealing shall be two months and shall run from the date of service, either on him in person or at his residence. No extension of time may be granted on account of distance.

Article 37[32]

1.   An appeal against the decision authorizing enforcement shall be lodged in accordance with the rules governing procedure in contentious matters:

sion Convention and by Article 3 of the 1997 Accession Convention.

32.   Text as amended by Article 17 of the 1978 Accession Convention, by Article 5

— in Belgium, with the tribunal de première instance or rechtbank van eerste aanleg,

— in Denmark, with the landsret,

— in the Federal Republic of Germany, with the Oberlandesgericht,

— in Greece, with the Εφετειο,

— in Spain, with the Audiencia Provincial,

— in France, with the cour d'appel,

— in Ireland, with the High Court,

— in Italy, with the corte d'appello,

— in Luxembourg, with the Cour supérieure de justice sitting as a court of civil appeal,

— in the Netherlands, with the arrondissementsrechtbank,

— in Austria, with the Bezirksgericht,

— in Portugal, with the Tribunal de Relação,

— in Finland, with the hovioikeus/hovraett,

— in Sweden, with the Svea hovraett,

— in the United Kingdom:

(a) in England and Wales, with the High Court of Justice, or in the case of a maintenance judgment with the Magistrates' Court;

(b) in Scotland, with the Court of Session, or in the case of a maintenance judgment with the Sheriff Court;

(c) in Northern Ireland, with the High Court of Justice, or in the case of a maintenance judgment with the Magistrates' Court.

2.   The judgment given on the appeal may be contested only:

— in Belgium, Greece, Spain, France, Italy, Luxembourg and in the Netherlands, by an appeal in cassation,

— in Denmark, by an appeal to the hoojesteret, with the leave of the Minister of Justice,

— in the Federal Republic of Germany, by a Rechtsbeschwerde,

— in Ireland, by an appeal on a point of law to the Supreme Court,

— in Austria, in the case of an appeal, by a Revisionrekurs and, in the case of opposition proceedings, by a Berufung with the possibility of a revision,

— in Portugal, by an appeal on a point of law,

— in Finland, by an appeal to korkein oikeushoegsta domstolen,

of the 1982 Accession Convention, by Article 11 of the 1989 Accession Convention and by Article 4 of the 1997 Accession Convention.

— in Sweden, by an appeal to Hoegsta domstolen,

— in the United Kingdom, by a single further appeal on a point of law.

Article 38

The court with which the appeal under Article 37(1) is lodged may, on the application of the appellant, stay the proceedings if an ordinary appeal has been lodged against the judgment in the State of origin or if the time for such an appeal has not yet expired; in the latter case, the court may specify the time within which such an appeal is to be lodged.[33]

Where the judgment was given in Ireland or the United Kingdom, any form of appeal available in the State of origin shall be treated as an ordinary appeal for the purposes of the first paragraph.[34]

The court may also make enforcement conditional on the provision of such security as it shall determine.

Article 39

During the time specified for an appeal pursuant to Article 36 and until any such appeal has been determined, no measures of enforcement may be taken other than protective measures taken against the property of the party against whom enforcement is sought.

The decision authorizing enforcement shall carry with it the power to proceed to any such protective measures.

Article 40

If the application for enforcement is refused, the applicant may appeal:

— in Belgium, to the cour d'appel or hof van beroep,

— in Denmark, to the landsret,

— in the Federal Republic of Germany, to the Oberlandesgericht,

— in Greece, to the Εφετείο,

— in Spain, to the Audiencia Provincial,

— in France, to the court d'appel,

— in Ireland, to the High Court,

— in Italy, to the corte d'appello,

— in Luxembourg, to the Cour supérieure de justice sitting as a court of civil appeal,

— in the Netherlands, to the gerechtshof,

— in Austria, to the Bezirksgericht,

— in Portugal, to the Tribunal da Relação,

---

33. As amended by Annex I (d) (6) first subparagraph to the 1989 Accession Convention.

34. Second subparagraph added by Article 18 of the 1978 Accession Convention and amended by Annex I (d) (6) second subparagraph to the 1989 Accession Convention.

— in Finland, to hovioikeus/hovraetten,

— in Sweden, to the Svea hovraett,

— in the United Kingdom:

   (a) in England and Wales, to the High Court of Justice, or in the case of a maintenance judgment to the Magistrates' Court;

   (b) in Scotland, to the Court of Session, or in the case of a maintenance judgment to the Sheriff Court;

   (c) in Northern Ireland, to the High Court of Justice, or in the case of a maintenance judgment to the Magistrates' Court.[35]

2.   The party against whom enforcement is sought shall be summoned to appear before the appellate court. If he fails to appear, the provisions of the second and third paragraphs of Article 20 shall apply even where he is not domiciled in any of the Contracting States.

Article 41[36]

A judgment given on an appeal provided for in Article 40 may be contested only:

— in Belgium, Greece, Spain, France, Italy, Luxembourg and in the Netherlands, by an appeal in cassation,

— in Denmark, by an appeal to the hojesteret, with the leave of the Minister of Justice,

— in the Federal Republic of Germany, by a Rechtsbeschwerde,

— in Ireland, by an appeal on a point of law to the Supreme Court,

— in Austria, by a Revisionsrekurs,

— in Portugal, by an appeal on a point of law,

— in Finland, by an appeal to korkein oikeus/hoegsta domstolen,

— in Sweden, by an appeal to Hoegsta domstolen,

—in the United Kingdom, by a single further appeal on a point of law.

Article 42

Where a foreign judgment has been given in respect of several matters and enforcement cannot be authorized for all of them, the court shall authorize enforcement for one or more of them.

An applicant may request partial enforcement of a judgment.

Article 43

A foreign judgment which orders a periodic payment by way of a penalty shall be enforceable in the State in which enforcement is sought only if

35. First subparagraph as amended by Article 19 of the 1978 Accession Convention, by Article 6 of the 1982 Accession Convention, by Article 12 of the 1989 Accession Convention and by Article 5 of the 1997 Accession Convention.

36. Text as amended by Article 20 of the 1978 Accession Convention, by Article 7 of the 1982 Accession Convention, by Article 13 of the 1989 Accession Convention and by Article 6 of the 1997 Accession Convention.

the amount of the payment has been finally determined by the courts of the State of origin.[37]

Article 44[38]

An applicant who, in the State of origin has benefited from complete or partial legal aid or exemption from costs or expenses, shall be entitled, in the procedures provided for in Articles 32 to 35, to benefit from the most favourable legal aid or the most extensive exemption from costs or expenses provided for by the law of the State addressed.

However, an applicant who requests the enforcement of a decision given by an administrative authority in Denmark in respect of a maintenance order may, in the State addressed, claim the benefits referred to in the first paragraph if he presents a statement from the Danish Ministry of Justice to the effect that he fulfils the economic requirements to qualify for the grant of complete or partial legal aid or exemption from costs or expenses.

Article 45

No security, bond or deposit, however described, shall be required of a party who in one Contracting State applies for enforcement of a judgment given in another Contracting State on the ground that he is a foreign national or that he is not domiciled or resident in the State in which enforcement is sought.

Section 3: Common provisions

Article 46

A party seeking recognition or applying for enforcement of a judgment shall produce:

    1.   a copy of the judgment which satisfies the conditions necessary to establish its authenticity;

    2.   in the case of a judgment given in default, the original or a certified true copy of the document which establishes that the party in default was served with the document instituting the proceedings or with an equivalent document.[39]

Article 47[40]

A party applying for enforcement shall also produce:

    1.   documents which establish that, according to the law of the State of origin the judgment is enforceable and has been served;

37. As amended by Annex I (d) (7) to the 1989 Accession Convention.

38. Text as amended by Article 21 of the 1978 Accession Convention and by Annex I (d) (8) to the 1989 Accession Convention.

39. Point 2 as amended by Article 22 of the 1978 Accession Convention.

40. As amended by Annex I (d) (9) to the 1989 Accession Convention.

2.   where appropriate, a document showing that the applicant is in receipt of legal aid in the State of origin.

Article 48

If the documents specified in point 2 of Articles 46 and 47 are not produced, the court may specify a time for their production, accept equivalent documents or, if it considers that it has sufficient information before it, dispense with their production.

If the court so requires, a translation of the documents shall be produced; the translation shall be certified by a person qualified to do so in one of the Contracting States.

Article 49

No legalization or other similar formality shall be required in respect of the documents referred to in Articles 46 or 47 or the second paragraph of Article 48, or in respect of a document appointing a representative *ad litem*.

TITLE IV. AUTHENTIC INSTRUMENTS AND COURT SETTLEMENTS

Article 50

A document which has been formally drawn up or registered as an authentic instrument and is enforceable in one Contracting State shall, in another Contracting State, be declared enforceable there, on application made in accordance with the procedures provided for in Article 31 *et seq*. The application may be refused only if enforcement of the instrument is contrary to public policy in the State addressed.[41]

The instrument produced must satisfy the conditions necessary to establish its authenticity in the State of origin.

The provisions of Section 3 of Title III shall apply as appropriate.

Article 51

A settlement which has been approved by a court in the course of proceedings and is enforceable in the State in which it was concluded shall be enforceable in the State addressed under the same conditions as authentic instruments.[42]

TITLE V. GENERAL PROVISIONS

Article 52

In order to determine whether a party is domiciled in the Contracting State whose courts are seised of a matter, the Court shall apply its internal law.

41. First paragraph as amended by Article 14 of the 1989 Accession Convention.

42. As amended by Annex I (d) (10) to the 1989 Accession Convention.

If a party is not domiciled in the State whose courts are seised of the matter, then, in order to determine whether the party is domiciled in another Contracting State, the court shall apply the law of that State.[43]

Article 53

For the purposes of this Convention, the seat of a company or other legal person or association of natural or legal persons shall be treated as its domicile. However, in order to determine that seat, the court shall apply its rules of private international law.

In order to determine whether a trust is domiciled in the Contracting State whose courts are seised of the matter, the court shall apply its rules of private international law.[44]

TITLE VI. TRANSITIONAL PROVISIONS

Article 54[45]

The provisions of the Convention shall apply only to legal proceedings instituted and to documents formally drawn up or registered as authentic instruments after its entry into force in the State of origin and, where recognition or enforcement of a judgment or authentic instruments is sought, in the State addressed.

However, judgments given after the date of entry into force of this Convention between the State of origin and the State addressed in proceedings instituted before that date shall be recognized and enforced in accordance with the provisions of Title III if jurisdiction was founded upon rules which accorded with those provided for either in Title II of this Convention or in a convention concluded between the State of origin and the State addressed which was in force when the proceedings were instituted.[46]

---

43. Third paragraph deleted by Article 15 of the 1989 Accession Convention.

44. Second subparagraph added by Article 23 of the 1978 Accession Convention.

45. Text as replaced by Article 16 of the 1989 Accession Convention.

46. Title V of the 1978 Accession Convention contains the following transitional provisions:

"Article 34

1. The 1968 Convention and the 1971 Protocol, with the amendments made by this Convention, shall apply only to legal proceedings instituted and to authentic instruments formally drawn up or registered after the entry into force of this Convention in the State of origin and, where recognition or enforcement of a judgment or authentic instrument is sought, in the State addressed.

2. However, as between the six Contracting States to the 1968 Convention, judgments given after the date of entry into force of this Convention in proceedings instituted before that date shall be recognized and enforced in accordance with the provisions of Title III of the 1968 Convention as amended.

3. Moreover, as between the six Contracting States to the 1968 Convention and the three States mentioned in Article 1 of this Convention, and as between those three States, judgments given after the date of entry into force of this Convention between the State of origin and the State addressed in proceedings instituted before that date shall also be recognized and enforced in accordance with the provisions of Title III of the 1968 Convention as amended if jurisdiction was founded upon rules which accorded with the provisions of Title II, as amended, or with provisions of a convention concluded between the State of origin and the State addressed which was in force when the proceedings were instituted."

If the parties to a dispute concerning a contract had agreed in writing before 1 June 1988 for Ireland or before 1 January 1987 for the United Kingdom that the contract was to be governed by the law of Ireland or of a part of the United Kingdom, the courts of Ireland or of that part of the United Kingdom shall retain the right to exercise jurisdiction in the dispute.[47]

Article 54a[48]

For a period of three years from 1 November 1986 for Denmark and from 1 June 1988 for Ireland, jurisdiction in maritime matters shall be determined in these States not only in accordance with the provisions of Title II, but also in accordance with the provisions of paragraphs 1 to 6 following. However, upon the entry into force of the International Convention relating to the arrest of sea-going ships, signed at Brussels on 10 May 1952, for one of these States, these provisions shall cease to have effect for that State.

1.   A person who is domiciled in a Contracting State may be sued in the courts of one of the States mentioned above in respect of a maritime claim if the ship to which the claim relates or any other ship owned by

Title V of the 1982 Accession Convention contains the following transitional provisions:

"Article 12

1. The 1968 Convention and the 1971 Protocol, as amended by the 1978 Convention, shall apply only to legal proceedings instituted and to authentic instruments formally drawn up or registered after the entry into force of this Convention in the State of origin and, where recognition or enforcement of a judgment or authentic instrument is sought, in the State addressed.

2. However, as between the State of origin and the State addressed, judgments given after the date of entry into force of this Convention in proceedings instituted before that date shall be recognized and enforced in accordance with the provisions of Title III of the 1968 Convention, as amended by the 1978 Convention, and by this Convention if jurisdiction was founded upon rules which accorded with the provisions of Title II, as amended by the 1968 Convention or with provisions of a convention concluded between the State of origin and the State addressed which was in force when the proceedings were instituted."

Title VI of the 1989 Accession Convention contains the following transitional provisions:

"Article 29

1. The 1968 Convention and the 1971 Protocol, as amended by the 1978 Convention, the 1982 Convention and this Convention, shall apply only to legal proceedings instituted and to authentic instruments formally drawn up or registered after the entry into force of this Convention in the State of origin and, where recognition or enforcement of a judgment or authentic instrument is sought, in the State addressed.

2. However, judgments given after the date of entry into force of this Convention between the State of origin and the State addressed in proceedings instituted before that date shall be recognized and enforced in accordance with the provisions of Title III of the 1968 Convention, as amended by the 1978 Convention, the 1982 Convention and this Convention, if jurisdiction was founded upon rules which accorded with the provisions of Title II of the 1968 Convention, as amended, or with the provisions of a convention which was in force between the State of origin and the State addressed when the proceedings were instituted."

47. This paragraph replaces Article 35 of Title V of the 1978 Accession Convention which was extended to the Hellenic Republic by Article 1 (2) of the 1982 Accession Convention. Article 28 of the 1989 Accession Convention provided for the deletion of both these provisions.

48. Article added by Article 17 of the 1989 Accession Convention. It corresponds to Article 36 of Title V of the 1978 Accession Convention which was extended to the Hellenic Republic by Article 1(2) of the 1982 Accession Convention. Article 28 of the 1989 Accession Convention provided for the deletion of both these provisions.

him has been arrested by judicial process within the territory of the latter State to secure the claim, or could have been so arrested there but bail or other security has been given, and either:

(a) the claimant is domiciled in the latter State; or

(b) the claim arose in the latter State; or

(c) the claim concerns the voyage during which the arrest was made or could have been made; or

(d) the claim arises out of a collision or out of damage caused by a ship to another ship or to goods or persons on board either ship, either by the execution or non-execution of a manoeuvre or by the non-observance of regulations; or

(e) the claim is for salvage; or

(f) the claim is in respect of a mortgage or hypothecation of the ship arrested.

2. A claimant may arrest either the particular ship to which the maritime claim relates, or any other ship which is owned by the person who was, at the time when the maritime claim arose, the owner of the particular ship. However, only the particular ship to which the maritime claim relates may be arrested in respect of the maritime claims set out in (5) (*o*), (p) or (q) of this Article.

3. Ships shall be deemed to be in the same ownership when all the shares therein are owned by the same person or persons.

4. When in the case of a charter by demise of a ship the charterer alone is liable in respect of a maritime claim relating to that ship, the claimant may arrest that ship or any other ship owned by the charterer, but no other ship owned by the owner may be arrested in respect of such claim. The same shall apply to any case in which a person other than the owner of a ship is liable in respect of a maritime claim relating to that ship.

5. The expression "maritime claim" means a claim arising out of one or more of the following:

(a) damage caused by any ship either in collision or otherwise;

(b) loss of life or personal injury caused by any ship or occurring in connection with the operation on any ship;

(c) salvage;

(d) agreement relating to the use or hire of any ship whether by charterparty or otherwise;

(e) agreement relating to the carriage of goods in any ship whether by charterparty or otherwise;

(f) loss of or damage to goods including baggage carried in any ship;

(g) general average;

(h) bottomry;

(i) towage;

(j) pilotage;

(k) goods or materials wherever supplied to a ship for her operation or maintenance;

(l) construction, repair or equipment of any ship or dock charges and dues;

(m) wages of masters, officers or crew;

(n) master's disbursements, including disbursements made by shippers, charterers or agents on behalf of a ship or her owner;

(o) dispute as to the title to or ownership of any ship;

(p) disputes between co-owners of any ship as to the ownership, possession, employment or earnings of that ship;

(q) the mortgage or hypothecation of any ship.

6.   In Denmark, the expression "arrest" shall be deemed as regards the maritime claims referred to in 5 (o) and (p) of this Article, to include a "forbud", where that is the only procedure allowed in respect of such a claim under Articles 646 to 653 of the law on civil procedure (lov om rettens pleje).

TITLE VII. RELATIONSHIP TO OTHER CONVENTIONS

Article 55

Subject to the provisions of the second subparagraph of Article 54, and of Article 56, this Convention shall, for the States which are parties to it, supersede the following conventions concluded between two or more of them:

— the Convention between Belgium and France on jurisdiction and the validity and enforcement of judgments, arbitration awards and authentic instruments, signed at Paris on 8 July 1899,

— the Convention between Belgium and the Netherlands on jurisdiction, bankruptcy, and the validity and enforcement of judgments, arbitration awards and authentic instruments, signed at Brussels on 28 March 1925,

— the Convention between France and Italy on the enforcement of judgments in civil and commercial matters, signed at Rome on 3 June 1930,

— the Convention between the United Kingdom and the French Republic providing for the reciprocal enforcement of judgments in civil and commercial matters, with Protocol, signed at Paris on 18 January 1934,[49]

49. Fourth and fifth indents added by Article 24 of the 1978 Accession Convention.

— the Convention between the United Kingdom and the Kingdom of Belgium providing for the reciprocal enforcement of judgments in civil and commercial matters, with Protocol, signed at Brussels on 2 May 1934,[50]

— the Convention between Germany and Italy on the recognition and enforcement of judgments in civil and commercial matters, signed at Rome on 9 March 1936,

— the Convention between the Kingdom of Belgium and Austria on the reciprocal recognition and enforcement of judgments and authentic instruments relating to maintenance obligations, signed at Vienna on 25 October 1957,[51]

— the Convention between the Federal Republic of Germany and the Kingdom of Belgium on the mutual recognition and enforcement of judgments, arbitration awards and authentic instruments in civil and commercial matters, signed at Bonn on 30 June 1958,

— the Convention between the Kingdom of the Netherlands and the Italian Republic on the recognition and enforcement of judgments in civil and commercial matters, signed at Rome on 17 April 1959,

— the Convention between the Federal Republic of Germany and Austria on the reciprocal recognition and enforcement of judgments, settlements and authentic instruments in civil and commercial matters, signed at Vienna on 6 June 1959,[52]

— the Convention between the Kingdom of Belgium and Austria on the reciprocal recognition and enforcement of judgments, arbitral awards and authentic instruments in civil and commercial matters, signed at Vienna on 16 June 1959,[53]

— the Convention between the United Kingdom and the Federal Republic of Germany for the reciprocal recognition and enforcement of judgments in civil and commercial matters, signed at Bonn on 14 July 1960,[54]

— the Convention between the United Kingdom and Austria providing for the reciprocal recognition and enforcement of judgments in civil and commercial matters, signed at Vienna on 14 July 1961, with amending Protocol signed at London on 6 March 1970,[55]

— the Convention between the Kingdom of Greece and the Federal Republic of Germany for the reciprocal recognition and enforcement of judgments, settlements and authentic instruments in civil and commercial matters, signed in Athens on 4 November 1961,[56]

50. Fourth and fifth indents added by Article 24 of the 1978 Accession Convention.

51. Seventh indent added by Article 7 of the 1997 Accession Convention.

52. 10th indent added by Article 7 of the 1997 Accession Convention.

53. 11th indent added by Article 7 of the 1997 Accession Convention.

54. 12th indent added by Article 24 of the 1978 Accession Convention.

55. 13th indent added by Article 7 of the 1997 Accession Convention.

56. 14th indent added by Article 8 of the 1982 Accession Convention.

— the Convention between the Kingdom of Belgium and the Italian Republic on the recognition and enforcement of judgments and other enforceable instruments in civil and commercial matters, signed at Rome on 6 April 1962,

— the Convention between the Kingdom of the Netherlands and the Federal Republic of Germany on the mutual recognition and enforcement of judgments and other enforceable instruments in civil and commercial matters, signed at The Hague on 30 August 1962,

— the Convention between the Kingdom of the Netherlands and Austria on the reciprocal recognition and enforcement of judgments and authentic instruments in civil and commercial matters, signed at The Hague on 6 February 1963,[57]

— the Convention between the United Kingdom and the Republic of Italy for the reciprocal recognition and enforcement of judgments in civil and commercial matters, signed at Rome on 7 February 1964, with amending Protocol signed at Rome on 14 July 1970,[58]

— the Convention between France and Austria on the recognition and enforcement of judgments and authentic instruments in civil and commercial matters, signed at Vienna on 15 July 1966,[59]

— the Convention between the United Kingdom and the Kingdom of the Netherlands providing for the reciprocal recognition and enforcement of judgments in civil matters, signed at The Hague on 17 November 1967,[60]

— the Convention between Spain and France on the recognition and enforcement of judgment arbitration awards in civil and commercial matters, signed at Paris on 28 May 1969,[61]

— the Convention between Luxembourg and Austria on the recognition and enforcement of judgments and authentic instruments in civil and commercial matters, signed at Luxembourg on 29 July 1971,[62]

— the Convention between Italy and Austria on the recognition and enforcement of judgments in civil and commercial matters, of judicial settlements and of authentic instruments, signed at Rome on 16 November 1971,[63]

— the Convention between Spain and Italy regarding legal aid and the recognition and enforcement of judgments in civil and commercial matters, signed at Madrid on 22 May 1973,[64]

57. 17th indent added by Article 7 of the 1997 Accession Convention.

58. 18th indent added by Article 24 of the 1978 Accession Convention.

59. 19th indent added by Article 7 of the 1997 Accession Convention.

60. 20th indent added by Article 24 of the 1978 Accession Convention.

61. 21st indent added by Article 18 of the 1989 Accession Convention.

62. 22nd indent added by Article 7 of the 1997 Accession Convention.

63. 23rd indent added by Article 7 of the 1997 Accession Convention.

64. 24th indent added by Article 18 of the 1989 Accession Convention.

— the Convention between Finland, Iceland, Norway, Sweden and Denmark on the recognition and enforcement of judgments in civil matters, signed at Copenhagen on 11 October 1977,[65]

— the Convention between Austria and Sweden on the recognition and enforcement of judgments in civil matters, signed at Stockholm on 16 September 1982,[66]

— the Convention between Spain and the Federal Republic of Germany on the recognition and enforcement of judgments, settlements and enforceable authentic instruments in civil and commercial matters, signed at Bonn on 14 November 1983,[67]

— the Convention between Austria and Spain on the recognition and enforcement of judgments, settlements and enforceable authentic instruments in civil and commercial matters, signed at Vienna on 17 February 1984,[68]

— the Convention between Finland and Austria on the recognition and enforcement of judgments in civil matters, signed at Vienna on 17 November 1986,[69] and, in so far as it is in force:

— the Treaty between Belgium, the Netherlands and Luxembourg on jurisdiction, bankruptcy, and the validity and enforcement of judgments, arbitration awards and authentic instruments, signed at Brussels on 24 November 1961.

Article 56

The Treaty and the conventions referred to in Article 55 shall continue to have effect in relation to matters to which this Convention does not apply.

They shall continue to have effect in respect of judgments given and documents formally drawn up or registered as authentic instruments before the entry into force of this Convention.

Article 57

1. This Convention shall not affect any conventions to which the Contracting States are or will be parties and which in relation to particular matters, govern jurisdiction or the recognition or enforcement of judgments.[70]

2. With a view to its uniform interpretation, paragraph 1 shall be applied in the following manner:

65. 25th indent added by Article 7 of the 1997 Accession Convention.

66. 26th indent added by Article 7 of the 1997 Accession Convention.

67. 27th indent added by Article 18 of the 1989 Accession Convention.

68. 28th indent added by Article 7 of the 1997 Accession Convention.

69. 29th indent added by Article 7 of the 1997 Accession Convention.

70. First paragraph as amended by Article 25 (1) of the 1978 Accession Convention and by Article 19 of the 1989 Accession Convention.

(a) this Convention shall not prevent a court of a Contracting State which is a party to a convention on a particular matter from assuming jurisdiction in accordance with that Convention, even where the defendant is domiciled in another Contracting State which is not a party to that Convention. The court hearing the action shall, in any event, apply Article 20 of this Convention;

(b) judgments given in a Contracting State by a court in the exercise of jurisdiction provided for in a convention on a particular matter shall be recognized and enforced in the other Contracting State in accordance with this Convention. Where a convention on a particular matter to which both the State of origin and the State addressed are parties lays down conditions for the recognition or enforcement of judgments, those conditions shall apply. In any event, the provisions of this Convention which concern the procedure for recognition and enforcement of judgments may be applied.[71]

3.   This Convention shall not affect the application of provisions which, in relation to particular matters, govern jurisdiction or the recognition or enforcement of judgments and which are or will be contained in acts of the institutions of the European Communities or in national laws harmonized in implementation of such acts.[72]

Article 58[73]

Until such time as the Convention on jurisdiction and the enforcement of judgments in civil and commercial matters, signed at Lugano on 16 September 1988, takes effect with regard to France and the Swiss Confederation, this Convention shall not affect the rights granted to Swiss nationals by the Convention between France and the Swiss Confederation on jurisdiction and enforcement of judgments in civil matters, signed at Paris on 15 June 1869.

Article 59

This Convention shall not prevent a Contracting State from assuming, in a convention on the recognition and enforcement of judgments, an obligation towards a third State not to recognize judgments given in other Contracting States against defendants domiciled or habitually resident in the third State where, in cases provided for in Article 4, the judgments could only be founded on a ground of jurisdiction specified in the second paragraph of Article 3.

However, a Contracting State may not assume an obligation towards a third State not to recognize a judgment given in another Contracting State by a court basing its jurisdiction on the presence within that State

71. Paragraph 2 added by Article 19 of the 1989 Accession Convention. This paragraph corresponds to Article 25 (2) of the 1978 Accession Convention which was extended to the Hellenic Republic by Article 1 (2) of the 1982 Accession Convention. Article 28 of the 1989 Accession Convention provided for the deletion of both these provision.

72. Paragraph added by Article 25 (1) of the 1978 Accession Convention.

73. Text as amended by Article 20 of the 1989 Accession Convention.

of property belonging to the defendant, or the seizure by the plaintiff of property situated there:

1. if the action is brought to assert or declare proprietary or possessory rights in that property, seeks to obtain authority to dispose of it, or arises from another issue relating to such property; or

2. if the property constitutes the security for a debt which is the subject-matter of the action.[74]

TITLE VIII. FINAL PROVISIONS

Article 60[75]

Article 61[76]

This Convention shall be ratified by the signatory States. The instruments of ratification shall be deposited with the Secretary–General of the Council of the European Communities.

Article 62[77]

This Convention shall enter into force on the first day of the third month following the deposit of the instrument of ratification by the last signatory State to take this step.

Article 63

The Contracting States recognize that any State which becomes a member of the European Economic Community shall be required to accept this Convention as a basis for the negotiations between the Contracting States and that State necessary to ensure the implementation of the last paragraph of Article 220 of the Treaty establishing the European Economic Community.

The necessary adjustments may be the subject of a special convention between the Contracting States of the one part and the new Member States of the other part.

74. Second subparagraph added by Article 26 of the 1978 Accession Convention.

75. Article 21 of the 1989 Accession Convention provides for the deletion of Article 60 as amended by Article 27 of the 1978 Convention.

76. Ratification of the 1978 and 1982 Accession Conventions was governed by Articles 38 and 14 of those Conventions. The ratification of the 1989 Accession Convention is governed by Article 31 of that Convention, which reads as follows:

"Article 31: This Convention shall be ratified by the signatory States. The instruments of ratification shall be deposited with the Secretary–General of the Council of the European Communities."

77. The entry into force of the 1978 and 1982 Accession Conventions was governed by Articles 39 and 15 of those Conventions. The entry into force of the 1989 Accession Convention is governed by Article 32 of that Convention, which reads as follows:

"Article 32

1. This Convention shall enter into force on the first day of the third month following the date on which two signatory States, of which one is the Kingdom of Spain or the Portuguese Republic, deposit their instruments of ratification.

2. This Convention shall take effect in relation to any other signatory State on the first day of the third month following the deposit of its instrument of ratification."

Article 64[78]

The Secretary–General of the Council of the European Communities shall notify the signatory States of:

   (a) the deposit of each instrument of ratification;

   (b) the date of entry into force of this Convention;

   (c) ... ;[79]

   (d) any declaration received pursuant to Article IV of the Protocol;

   (e) any communication made pursuant to Article VI of the Protocol.

Article 65

The Protocol annexed to this Convention by common accord of the Contracting States shall form an integral part thereof.

Article 66

This Convention is concluded for an unlimited period.

Article 67

Any Contracting State may request the revision of this Convention. In this event, a revision conference shall be convened by the President of the Council of the European Communities.

Article 68[80]

This Convention, drawn up in a single original in the Dutch, French, German and Italian languages, all four texts being equally authentic, shall be deposited in the archives of the Secretariat of the Council of the

---

78. Notification concerning the 1978 and 1982 Accession Conventions is governed by Articles 40 and 16 of those Conventions. Notification concerning the 1989 Accession Convention is governed by Article 33 of that Convention, which reads as follows:

"Article 33 The Secretary–General of the Council of the European Communities shall notify the signatory States of:

   (a) the deposit of each instrument of ratification;

   (b) the dates of entry into force of this Convention for the Contracting States."

79. Article 22 of the 1989 Accession Convention provides for the deletion of letter (c) as amended by Article 28 of the 1978 Accession Convention.

80. An indication of the authentic texts of the Accession Conventions is to be found in the following provisions:

— with regard to the 1978 Accession Convention, in Article 41 of that Convention, which reads as follows: "Article 41. This Convention, drawn up in a single original in the Danish, Dutch, English, French, German, Irish and Italian languages, all seven texts being equally authentic, shall be deposited in the archives of the Secretariat of the Council of the European Communities. The Secretary–General shall transmit a certified copy to the Government of each signatory State."

— with regard to the 1982 Accession Convention, in Article 17 of that Convention, which reads as follows: "Article 17. This Convention, drawn up in a single original in the Danish, Dutch, English, French, German, Greek, Irish and Italian languages, all eight texts being equally authentic, shall be deposited in the archives of the General Secretariat of the Council of the European Communities. The Secretary–General shall transmit a certified copy to the Government of each signatory State."

— with regard to the 1989 Accession Convention, in Article 34 of that Convention, which reads as follows: "Article 34. This Convention, drawn up in a single original in the Danish, Dutch, English, French, German, Greek, Irish, Italian, Portuguese and Spanish languages, all 10 texts being equally authentic, shall be deposited in the

European Communities. The Secretary–General shall transmit a certified copy to the Government of each signatory State.[81]

PROTOCOL[82]

The High Contracting Parties have agreed upon the following provisions, which shall be annexed to the Convention:

Article I

Any person domiciled in Luxembourg who is sued in a court of another Contracting State pursuant to Article 5 (1) may refuse to submit to the jurisdiction of that court. If the defendant does not enter an appearance the court shall declare of its own motion that it has no jurisdiction.

An agreement conferring jurisdiction, within the meaning of Article 17, shall be valid with respect to a person domiciled in Luxembourg only if that person has expressly and specifically so agreed.

Article II

Without prejudice to any more favourable provisions of national laws, persons domiciled in a Contracting State who are being prosecuted in the

archives of the General Secretariat of the Council of the European Communities. The Secretary–General shall transmit a certified copy to the Government of each signatory State.''

81. Legal backing for the drawing-up of the authentic texts of the 1968 Convention in the official languages of the acceding Member States is to be found:

— with regard to the 1978 Accession Convention, in Article 37 of that Convention, which reads as follows: "Article 37. The Secretary–General of the Council of the European Communities shall transmit a certified copy of the 1968 Convention and of the 1971 Protocol in the Dutch, French, German and Italian languages to the Governments of the Kingdom of Denmark, Ireland and the United Kingdom of Great Britain and Northern Ireland. The texts of the 1968 Convention and the 1971 Protocol, drawn up in the Danish, English and Irish languages, shall be annexed to this Convention. The texts drawn up in the Danish, English and irish languages shall be authentic under the same conditions as the original texts of the 1968 Convention and the 1971 Protocol.''

— with regard to the 1982 Accession Convention, in Article 13 of that Convention, which reads as follows: "Article 13. The Secretary–General of the Council of the European Communities shall transmit a certified copy of the 1968 Convention, of the 1971 Protocol and of the 1978 Convention in the Danish, Dutch, English, French,

German, Irish and Italian languages to the Government of the Hellenic Republic. The texts of the 1968 Convention, of the 1971 Protocol and of the 1978 Convention, drawn up in the Greek language, shall be annexed to this Convention. The texts drawn up in the Greek language shall be authentic under the same conditions as the other texts of the 1968 Convention, the 1971 Protocol and the 1978 Convention.''

— with regard to the 1989 Accession Convention, in Article 30 of that Convention, which reads as follows: "Article 30. 1. The Secretary–General of the Council of the European Communities shall transmit a certified copy of the 1968 Convention, of the 1971 Protocol, of the 1978 Convention and of the 1982 Convention in the Danish, Dutch, English, French, German, Greek, Irish and Italian languages to the Governments of the Kingdom of Spain and of the Portuguese Republic. 2. The texts of the 1968 Convention, of the 1971 Protocol, of the 1978 Convention and of the 1982 Convention, drawn up in the Portuguese and Spanish languages, are set out in Annexes II, III, IV and V to this Convention. The texts drawn up in the Portuguese and Spanish languages shall be authentic under the same conditions as the other texts of the 1968 Convention, the 1971 Protocol, the 1978 Convention and the 1982 Convention.''

82. Text as amended by the 1978 Accession Convention, the 1982 Accession Convention and the 1989 Accession Convention.

criminal courts of another Contracting State of which they are not nationals for an offence which was not intentionally committed may be defended by persons qualified to do so, even if they do not appear in person.

However, the court seised of the matter may order appearance in person; in the case of failure to appear, a judgment given in the civil action without the person concerned having had the opportunity to arrange for his defence need not be recognized or enforced in the other Contracting States.

Article III

In proceedings for the issue of an order for enforcement, no charge, duty or fee calculated by reference to the value of the matter in issue may be levied in the State in which enforcement is sought.

Article IV

Judicial and extrajudicial documents drawn up in one Contracting State which have to be served on persons in another Contracting State shall be transmitted in accordance with the procedures laid down in the conventions and agreements concluded between the Contracting States.

Unless the State in which service is to take place objects by declaration to the Secretary–General of the Council of the European Communities, such documents may also be sent by the appropriate public officers of the State in which the document has been drawn up directly to the appropriate public officers of the State in which the addressee is to be found. In this case the officer of the State of origin shall send a copy of the document to the officer of the State applied to who is competent to forward it to the addressee. The document shall be forwarded in the manner specified by the law of the State applied to. The forwarding shall be recorded by a certificate sent directly to the officer of the State of origin.

Article V[83]

The jurisdiction specified in Articles 6(2) and 10 in actions on a warranty or guarantee or in any other third party proceedings may not be resorted to in the Federal Republic of Germany or in Austria. Any person domiciled in another Contracting State may be sued in the courts:

— of the Federal Republic of Germany, pursuant to Articles 68, 72, 73 and 74 of the code of civil procedure (*Zivilprozessordnung*) concerning third-party notices,

— in Austria, pursuant to Article 21 of the code of civil procedure (*Zivilprozessordnung*) concerning third-party notices.

Judgments given in the other Contracting States by virtue of point 2 of Article 6 or Article 10 shall be recognized and enforced in the Federal Republic of Germany and in Austria in accordance with Title III. Any

83. Article amended by Article 8 of the 1997 Accession Convention.

effects which judgments given in those States may have on third parties by application of provisions in the preceding paragraph shall also be recognized in the other Contracting States.

Article Va[84]

In matters relating to maintenance, the expression "court" includes the Danish administrative authorities.

In Sweden, in summary proceedings concerning orders to pay (*betal-ningsfoeralaeggande*) and assistance (*handraeckning*), the expression "court" includes the "Swedish enforcement service" (*kronofogdemyndighet*).

Article Vb[85]

In proceedings involving a dispute between the master and a member of the crew of a sea-going ship registered in Denmark, in Greece, in Ireland or in Portugal, concerning remuneration or other conditions of service, a court in a Contracting State shall establish whether the diplomatic or consular officer responsible for the ship has been notified of the dispute. It shall stay the proceedings so long as he has not been notified. It shall of its own motion decline jurisdiction if the officer, having been duly notified, has exercised the powers accorded to him in the matter by a consular convention, or in the absence of such a convention has, within the time allowed, raised any objection to the exercise of such jurisdiction.

Article Vc[86]

Articles 52 and 53 of this Convention shall, when applied by Article 69 (5) of the Convention for the European patent for the common market, signed at Luxembourg on 15 December 1975, to the provisions relating to "residence" in the English text of that Convention, operate as if "residence" in that text were the same as "domicile" in Articles 52 and 53.

Article Vd[87]

Without prejudice to the jurisdiction of the European Patent Office under the Convention on the grant of European patents, signed at Munich on 5 October 1973, the courts of each Contracting State shall have exclusive jurisdiction, regardless of domicile, in proceedings concerned with the registration or validity of any European patent granted for that State which is not a Community patent by virtue of the provisions of Article 86 of the Convention for the European patent for the common market, signed at Luxembourg on 15 December 1975.

84. Article added by Article 29 of the 1978 Accession Convention and amended by Article 9 of the 1997 Accession Convention.

85. Article added by Article 29 of the 1978 Accession Convention, amended by Article 9 of the 1982 Accession Convention and by Article 23 of the 1989 Accession Convention.

86. Article added by Article 29 of the 1978 Accession Convention.

87. Article added by Article 29 of the 1978 Accession Convention.

Article Ve[88]

Arrangements relating to maintenance obligations concluded with administrative authorities or authenticated by them shall also be regarded as authentic instruments within the meaning of the first paragraph of Article 50 of the Convention.

Article VI

The Contracting States shall communicate to the Secretary–General of the Council of the European Communities the text of any provisions of their laws which amend either those articles of their laws mentioned in the Convention or the lists of courts specified in Section 2 of Title III of the Convention.

JOINT DECLARATION

The Governments of the Kingdom of Belgium, the Federal Republic of Germany, the French Republic, the Italian Republic, the Grand Duchy of Luxembourg and the Kingdom of the Netherlands,

On signing the Convention on jurisdiction and the enforcement of judgments in civil and commercial matters,

Desiring to ensure that the Convention is applied as effectively as possible,

Anxious to prevent differences of interpretation of the Convention from impairing its unifying effect,

Recognizing that claims and disclaimers of jurisdiction may arise in the application of the Convention,

Declare themselves ready:

　　1.　to study these questions and in particular to examine the possibility of conferring jurisdiction in certain matters on the Court of Justice of the European Communities and, if necessary, to negotiate an agreement to this effect;

　　2.　to arrange meetings at regular intervals between their representatives.

PROTOCOL

on the interpretation by the Court of Justice of the Convention of 27 September 1968 on jurisdiction and the enforcement of judgments in civil and commercial matters.[89]

---

88. Article added by Article 10 of the 1997 Accession Convention.

89. Text as amended by the Convention of 9 October 1978 on the accession of the Kingdom of Denmark, Ireland and the United Kingdom of Great Britain and Northern Ireland—hereafter referred to as the "1978 Accession Convention"—by the Convention of 25 October 1982 on the accession of the Hellenic Republic—hereafter referred to as the "1982 Accession Convention", and by the Convention of 26 May 1989 on the accession of the Kingdom of Spain and the Portuguese Republic—hereafter referred to as the "1989 Accession Convention".

THE HIGH CONTRACTING PARTIES TO THE TREATY ESTAB-
LISHING THE EUROPEAN ECONOMIC COMMUNITY,

Having regard to the Declaration annexed to the Convention on jurisdiction and the enforcement of judgments in civil and commercial matters,
signed at Brussels on 27 September 1968,

Have decided to conclude a Protocol conferring jurisdiction on the Court
of Justice of the European Communities to interpret that Convention,
and to this end have designated as their Plenipotentiaries:

HIS MAJESTY THE KING OF THE BELGIANS:

Mr. Alfons VRANCKX, Minister of Justice;

THE PRESIDENT OF THE FEDERAL REPUBLIC OF GERMANY:

Mr. Gerhard JAHN, Federal Minister of Justice;

THE PRESIDENT OF THE FRENCH REPUBLIC:

Mr. Rene PLEVEN, Keeper of the Seals, Minister of Justice;

THE PRESIDENT OF THE ITALIAN REPUBLIC:

Mr. Erminio PENNACCHINI, Under Secretary of State in the
Ministry of Justice;

HIS ROYAL HIGHNESS THE GRAND DUKE OF LUXEMBOURG:

Mr. Eugene SCHAUS, Minister of Justice, Deputy Prime Minister;

HER MAJESTY THE QUEEN OF THE NETHERLANDS:

Mr. C. H. F. POLAK, Minister of Justice;

WHO, meeting within the Council, having exchanged their Full Powers,
found in good and due form,

HAVE AGREED AS FOLLOWS:

Article 1

The Court of Justice of the European Communities shall have jurisdiction to give rulings on the interpretation of the Convention on jurisdiction and the enforcement of judgments in civil and commercial matters
and of the Protocol annexed to that Convention, signed at Brussels on 27
September 1968, and also on the interpretation of the present Protocol.

The Court of Justice of the European Communities shall also have
jurisdiction to give rulings on the interpretation of the Convention on
the accession of the Kingdom of Denmark, Ireland and the United
Kingdom of Great Britain and Northern Ireland to the Convention of 27
September 1968 and to this Protocol.[90]

The Court of Justice of the European Communities shall also have
jurisdiction to give rulings on the interpretation of the Convention on
the accession of the Hellenic Republic to the Convention of 27 September
1968 and to this Protocol, as adjusted by the 1978 Convention.[91]

90. Second paragraph added by Article
30 of the 1978 Accession Convention.

91. Third paragraph added by Article 10
of the 1982 Accession Convention.

The Court of Justice of the European Communities shall also have jurisdiction to give rulings on the interpretation of the Convention on the accession of the Kingdom of Spain and the Portuguese Republic to the Convention of 27 September 1968 and to this Protocol, as adjusted by the 1978 Convention and the 1982 Convention.[92]

The Court of Justice of the European Communities shall also have jurisdiction to give rulings on the interpretation of the Convention on the accession of the Republic of Austria, the Republic of Finland and the Kingdom of Sweden to the Convention of 27 September 1968 and to this Protocol, as adjusted by the 1978 Convention, the 1982 Convention and the 1989 Convention.[93]

Article 2

The following courts may request the Court of Justice to give preliminary rulings on questions of interpretation:

1.

— in Belgium: la Cour de Cassation—het Hof van Cassatie and le Conseil d'État—de Raad van State,

— in Denmark: hojesteret,

— in the Federal Republic of Germany: die obersten Gerichtshofe des Bundes,

— in Greece: the ανωτατα δικαστήρια,

— in Spain: el Tribunal Supremo,

— in France: la Cour de Cassation and le Conseil d'État,

— in Ireland: the Supreme Court,

— in Italy: la Corte Suprema di Cassazione,

— in Luxembourg: la Cour supérieure de Justice when sitting as Cour de Cassation,

— in Austria, the Oberste Gerichshof, the Verwaltungsgerichtshof and the Verfassungsgerichtshof,

— in the Netherlands: de Hoge Raad,

— in Finland, korkein oikeus/hoegsta domstolen and korkein hallintooikeus/hoegsta foervaltningsdomstolen,

— in Sweden, Hoegsta domstolen, Regeringsraetten, Arbetsdomstolen and Marknadsdomstolen,

— in Portugal: o Supremo Tribunal de Justiça and o Supremo Tribunal Administrativo,

92. Fourth paragraph added by Article 24 of the 1989 Accession Convention.

93. Fifth paragraph added by Article 11 of the 1997 Accession Convention.

— in the United Kingdom: the House of Lords and courts to which application has been made under the second paragraph of Article 37 or under Article 41 of the Convention;[94]

2. the courts of the Contracting States when they are sitting in an appellate capacity;

3. in the cases provided for in Article 37 of the Convention, the courts referred to in that Article.

Article 3

1. Where a question of interpretation of the Convention or of one of the other instruments referred to in Article 1 is raised in a case pending before one of the courts listed in point 1 of Article 2, that court shall, if it considers that a decision on the question is necessary to enable it to give judgment, request the Court of Justice to give a ruling thereon.

2. Where such a question is raised before any court referred to in point 2 or 3 of Article 2, that court may, under the conditions laid down in paragraph 1, request the Court of Justice to give a ruling thereon.

Article 4

1. The competent authority of a Contracting State may request the Court of Justice to give a ruling on a question of interpretation of the Convention or of one of the other instruments referred to in Article 1 if judgments given by courts of that State conflict with the interpretation given either by the Court of Justice or in a judgment of one of the courts of another Contracting State referred to in point 1 or 2 of Article 2. The provisions of this paragraph shall apply only to judgments which have become *res judicata*.

2. The interpretation given by the Court of Justice in response to such a request shall not affect the judgments which gave rise to the request for interpretation.

3. The Procurators–General of the Courts of Cassation of the Contracting States, or any other authority designated by a Contracting State, shall be entitled to request the Court of Justice for a ruling on interpretation in accordance with paragraph 1.

4. The Registrar of the Court of Justice shall give notice of the request to the Contracting States, to the Commission and to the Council of the European Communities; they shall then be entitled within two months of the notification to submit statements of case or written observations to the Court.

5. No fees shall be levied or any costs or expenses awarded in respect of the proceedings provided for in this Article.

94. Point 1 as amended by Article 31 of the 1978 Accession Convention, by Article 11 of the 1982 Accession Convention, by Article 25 of the 1989 Accession Convention and by Article 12 of the 1997 Accession Convention.

Article 5

1.   Except where this Protocol otherwise provides, the provisions of the Treaty establishing the European Economic Community and those of the Protocol on the Statute of the Court of Justice annexed thereto, which are applicable when the Court is requested to give a preliminary ruling, shall also apply to any proceedings for the interpretation of the Convention and the other instruments referred to in Article 1.

2.   The Rules of Procedure of the Court of Justice shall, if necessary, be adjusted and supplemented in accordance with Article 188 of the Treaty establishing the European Economic Community.

Article 6[95]

Article 7[96]

This Protocol shall be ratified by the signatory States. The instruments of ratification shall be deposited with the Secretary–General of the Council of the European Communities.

Article 8[97]

This Protocol shall enter into force on the first day of the third month following the deposit of the instrument of ratification by the last signatory State to take this step; provided that it shall at the earliest enter into force at the same time as the Convention of 27 September 1968 on jurisdiction and the enforcement of judgments in civil and commercial matters.

Article 9

The Contracting States recognize that any State which becomes a member of the European Economic Community, and to which Article 63 of the Convention on jurisdiction and the enforcement of judgments in civil and commercial matters applies, must accept the provisions of this Protocol, subject to such adjustments as may be required.

Article 10

The Secretary–General of the Council of the European Communities shall notify the signatory States of:

   (a) the deposit of each instrument of ratification;

   (b) the date of entry into force of this Protocol;

   (c) any designation received pursuant to Article 4(3);

   (d) . . . . [98]

95. Article 26 of the 1989 Accession Convention provides for the deletion of Article 6 as amended by Article 32 of the 1978 Accession Convention.

96. See Footnote 76 on page 75.

97. See Footnote 77 on page 75.

98. Article 27 of the 1989 Accession Convention provides for the deletion of (d) as amended by Article 33 of the 1978 Accession Convention.

Article 11

The Contracting States shall communicate to the Secretary–General of the Council of the European Communities the texts of any provisions of their laws which necessitate an amendment to the list of courts in point 1 of Article 2.

Article 12

This Protocol is concluded for an unlimited period.

Article 13

Any Contracting State may request the revision of this Protocol. In this event, a revision conference shall be convened by the President of the Council of the European Communities.

Article 14

This Protocol, drawn up in a single original in the Dutch, French, German and Italian languages, all four texts being equally authentic, shall be deposited in the archives of the Secretariat of the Council of the European Communities. The Secretary–General shall transmit a certified copy to the Government of each signatory State.

JOINT DECLARATION

The Governments of the Kingdom of Belgium, the Federal Republic of Germany, the French Republic, the Italian Republic, the Grand Duchy of Luxembourg and the Kingdom of the Netherlands,

On signing the Protocol on the interpretation by the Court of Justice of the Convention of 27 September 1968 on jurisdiction and the enforcement of judgments in civil and commercial matters,

Desiring to ensure that the provisions of that Protocol are applied as effectively and as uniformly as possible,

Declare themselves ready to organize, in cooperation with the Court of Justice, an exchange of information on the judgments given by the courts referred to in Article 2(1) of that Protocol in application of the Convention and the Protocol of 27 September 1968.

JOINT DECLARATION

9 October 1978

THE REPRESENTATIVES OF THE GOVERNMENTS OF THE MEMBER STATES OF THE EUROPEAN ECONOMIC COMMUNITY, MEETING WITHIN THE COUNCIL,

Desiring to ensure that in the spirit of the Convention of 27 September 1968 uniformity of jurisdiction should also be achieved as widely as possible in maritime matters,

Considering that the International Convention relating to the arrest of sea-going ships, signed at Brussels on 10 May 1952, contains provisions relating to such jurisdiction,

Considering that all of the Member States are not parties to the said Convention,

Express the wish that Member States which are coastal States and have not already become parties to the Convention of 10 May 1952 should do so as soon as possible.

JOINT DECLARATION

26 May 1989

concerning the ratification of the Convention on the accession of the Kingdom of Spain and the Portuguese Republic to the 1968 Brussels Convention

Upon signature of the Convention on the accession of the Kingdom of Spain and the Portuguese Republic to the 1968 Brussels Convention, done at Donostia—San Sebastian on 26 May 1989,

THE REPRESENTATIVES OF THE GOVERNMENTS OF THE MEMBER STATES OF THE EUROPEAN COMMUNITIES, MEETING WITHIN THE COUNCIL,

DESIROUS that, in particular with a view to the completion of the internal market, application of the Brussels Convention and of the 1971 Protocol should be rapidly extended to the entire Community,

WELCOMING the conclusion on 16 September 1988 of the Lugano Convention which extends the principles of the Brussels Convention to those States becoming parties to the Lugano Convention, designed principally to govern relations between the Member States of the European Economic Community (EEC) and those of the European Free Trade Association (EFTA) with regard to the legal protection of persons established in any of those States and to the simplification of formalities for the reciprocal recognition and enforcement of judgments,

CONSIDERING that the Brussels Convention has as its legal basis Article 220 of the Treaty of Rome and is interpreted by the Court of Justice of the European Communities,

MINDFUL that the Lugano Convention does not affect the application of the Brussels Convention as regards relations between Member States of the European Economic Community, since such relations must be governed by the Brussels Convention,

NOTING that the Lugano Convention is to enter into force after two States, of which one is a member of the European Communities and the other a member of the European Free Trade Association, have deposited their instruments of ratification,

DECLARE THEMSELVES READY to take every appropriate measure with a view to ensuring that national procedures for the ratification of the Convention on the accession of the Kingdom of Spain and the Portuguese Republic to the Brussels Convention, signed today, are completed as soon as possible and, if possible, by 31 December 1992 at the latest.

COUNCIL REGULATION (EC) NO. 44/2001 ON JURISDICTION AND THE RECOGNITION AND ENFORCEMENT OF JUDGMENTS IN CIVIL AND COMMERCIAL MATTERS

22 December 2000

THE COUNCIL OF THE EUROPEAN UNION,

Having regard to the Treaty establishing the European Community, and in particular Article 61(c) and Article 67(1) thereof,

Having regard to the proposal from the Commission[1],

Having regard to the opinion of the European Parliament[2],

Having regard to the opinion of the Economic and Social Committee[3],

Whereas:

(1) The Community has set itself the objective of maintaining and developing an area of freedom, security and justice, in which the free movement of persons is ensured. In order to establish progressively such an area, the Community should adopt, amongst other things, the measures relating to judicial cooperation in civil matters which are necessary for the sound operation of the internal market.

(2) Certain differences between national rules governing jurisdiction and recognition of judgments hamper the sound operation of the internal market. Provisions to unify the rules of conflict of jurisdiction in civil and commercial matters and to simplify the formalities with a view to rapid and simple recognition and enforcement of judgments from Member States bound by this Regulation are essential.

(3) This area is within the field of judicial cooperation in civil matters within the meaning of Article 65 of the Treaty.

(4) In accordance with the principles of subsidiarity and proportionality as set out in Article 5 of the Treaty, the objectives of this Regulation cannot be sufficiently achieved by the Member States and can therefore be better achieved by the Community. This Regulation confines itself to the minimum required in order to achieve those objectives and does not go beyond what is necessary for that purpose.

(5) On 27 September 1968 the Member States, acting under Article 293, fourth indent, of the Treaty, concluded the Brussels Convention on Jurisdiction and the Enforcement of Judgments in Civil and Commercial Matters, as amended by Conventions on the Accession of the New Member States to that Convention (hereinafter referred to as the "Brus-

---

1. OJ C 376, 28.12.1999, p. 1.

2. Opinion delivered on 21 September 2000 (not yet published in the Official Journal).

3. OJ C 117, 26.4.2000, p. 6.

sels Convention'')[4]. On 16 September 1988 Member States and EFTA States concluded the Lugano Convention on Jurisdiction and the Enforcement of Judgments in Civil and Commercial Matters, which is a parallel Convention to the 1968 Brussels Convention. Work has been undertaken for the revision of those Conventions, and the Council has approved the content of the revised texts. Continuity in the results achieved in that revision should be ensured.

(6) In order to attain the objective of free movement of judgments in civil and commercial matters, it is necessary and appropriate that the rules governing jurisdiction and the recognition and enforcement of judgments be governed by a Community legal instrument which is binding and directly applicable.

(7) The scope of this Regulation must cover all the main civil and commercial matters apart from certain well-defined matters.

(8) There must be a link between proceedings to which this Regulation applies and the territory of the Member States bound by this Regulation. Accordingly common rules on jurisdiction should, in principle, apply when the defendant is domiciled in one of those Member States.

(9) A defendant not domiciled in a Member State is in general subject to national rules of jurisdiction applicable in the territory of the Member State of the court seised, and a defendant domiciled in a Member State not bound by this Regulation must remain subject to the Brussels Convention.

(10) For the purposes of the free movement of judgments, judgments given in a Member State bound by this Regulation should be recognised and enforced in another Member State bound by this Regulation, even if the judgment debtor is domiciled in a third State.

(11) The rules of jurisdiction must be highly predictable and founded on the principle that jurisdiction is generally based on the defendant's domicile and jurisdiction must always be available on this ground save in a few well-defined situations in which the subject-matter of the litigation or the autonomy of the parties warrants a different linking factor. The domicile of a legal person must be defined autonomously so as to make the common rules more transparent and avoid conflicts of jurisdiction.

(12) In addition to the defendant's domicile, there should be alternative grounds of jurisdiction based on a close link between the court and the action or in order to facilitate the sound administration of justice.

(13) In relation to insurance, consumer contracts and employment, the weaker party should be protected by rules of jurisdiction more favourable to his interests than the general rules provide for.

4. OJ L 299, 31.12.1972, p. 32. OJ L 304, 30.10.1978, p. 1. OJ L 388, 31.12.1982, p. 1. OJ L 285, 3.10.1989, p. 1. OJ C 15, 15.1.1997, p. 1. For a consolidated text, see OJ C 27, 26.1.1998, p. 1.

(14) The autonomy of the parties to a contract, other than an insurance, consumer or employment contract, where only limited autonomy to determine the courts having jurisdiction is allowed, must be respected subject to the exclusive grounds of jurisdiction laid down in this Regulation.

(15) In the interests of the harmonious administration of justice it is necessary to minimise the possibility of concurrent proceedings and to ensure that irreconcilable judgments will not be given in two Member States. There must be a clear and effective mechanism for resolving cases of lis pendens and related actions and for obviating problems flowing from national differences as to the determination of the time when a case is regarded as pending. For the purposes of this Regulation that time should be defined autonomously.

(16) Mutual trust in the administration of justice in the Community justifies judgments given in a Member State being recognised automatically without the need for any procedure except in cases of dispute.

(17) By virtue of the same principle of mutual trust, the procedure for making enforceable in one Member State a judgment given in another must be efficient and rapid. To that end, the declaration that a judgment is enforceable should be issued virtually automatically after purely formal checks of the documents supplied, without there being any possibility for the court to raise of its own motion any of the grounds for non-enforcement provided for by this Regulation.

(18) However, respect for the rights of the defence means that the defendant should be able to appeal in an adversarial procedure, against the declaration of enforceability, if he considers one of the grounds for non-enforcement to be present. Redress procedures should also be available to the claimant where his application for a declaration of enforceability has been rejected.

(19) Continuity between the Brussels Convention and this Regulation should be ensured, and transitional provisions should be laid down to that end. The same need for continuity applies as regards the interpretation of the Brussels Convention by the Court of Justice of the European Communities and the 1971 Protocol[5] should remain applicable also to cases already pending when this Regulation enters into force.

(20) The United Kingdom and Ireland, in accordance with Article 3 of the Protocol on the position of the United Kingdom and Ireland annexed to the Treaty on European Union and to the Treaty establishing the European Community, have given notice of their wish to take part in the adoption and application of this Regulation.

(21) Denmark, in accordance with Articles 1 and 2 of the Protocol on the position of Denmark annexed to the Treaty on European Union and to the Treaty establishing the European Community, is not partici-

5. OJ L 204, 2.8.1975, p. 28. OJ L 304, 30.10.1978, p. 1. OJ L 388, 31.12.1982, p. 1. OJ L 285, 3.10.1989, p. 1. OJ C 15, 15.1.1997, p. 1. For a consolidated text see OJ C 27, 26.1.1998, p. 28.

pating in the adoption of this Regulation, and is therefore not bound by it nor subject to its application.

(22) Since the Brussels Convention remains in force in relations between Denmark and the Member States that are bound by this Regulation, both the Convention and the 1971 Protocol continue to apply between Denmark and the Member States bound by this Regulation.

(23) The Brussels Convention also continues to apply to the territories of the Member States which fall within the territorial scope of that Convention and which are excluded from this Regulation pursuant to Article 299 of the Treaty.

(24) Likewise for the sake of consistency, this Regulation should not affect rules governing jurisdiction and the recognition of judgments contained in specific Community instruments.

(25) Respect for international commitments entered into by the Member States means that this Regulation should not affect conventions relating to specific matters to which the Member States are parties.

(26) The necessary flexibility should be provided for in the basic rules of this Regulation in order to take account of the specific procedural rules of certain Member States. Certain provisions of the Protocol annexed to the Brussels Convention should accordingly be incorporated in this Regulation.

(27) In order to allow a harmonious transition in certain areas which were the subject of special provisions in the Protocol annexed to the Brussels Convention, this Regulation lays down, for a transitional period, provisions taking into consideration the specific situation in certain Member States.

(28) No later than five years after entry into force of this Regulation the Commission will present a report on its application and, if need be, submit proposals for adaptations.

(29) The Commission will have to adjust Annexes I to IV on the rules of national jurisdiction, the courts or competent authorities and redress procedures available on the basis of the amendments forwarded by the Member State concerned; amendments made to Annexes V and VI should be adopted in accordance with Council Decision 1999/468/EC of 28 June 1999 laying down the procedures for the exercise of implementing powers conferred on the Commission[6],

HAS ADOPTED THIS REGULATION:

CHAPTER I
SCOPE

Article 1

1. This Regulation shall apply in civil and commercial matters whatever the nature of the court or tribunal. It shall not extend, in particular, to revenue, customs or administrative matters.

---

6. OJ L 184, 17.7.1999, p. 23.

2. The Regulation shall not apply to:

(a) the status or legal capacity of natural persons, rights in property arising out of a matrimonial relationship, wills and succession;

(b) bankruptcy, proceedings relating to the winding-up of insolvent companies or other legal persons, judicial arrangements, compositions and analogous proceedings;

(c) social security;

(d) arbitration.

3. In this Regulation, the term "Member State" shall mean Member States with the exception of Denmark.

CHAPTER II
JURISDICTION
Section 1
General provisions
Article 2

1. Subject to this Regulation, persons domiciled in a Member State shall, whatever their nationality, be sued in the courts of that Member State.

2. Persons who are not nationals of the Member State in which they are domiciled shall be governed by the rules of jurisdiction applicable to nationals of that State.

Article 3

1. Persons domiciled in a Member State may be sued in the courts of another Member State only by virtue of the rules set out in Sections 2 to 7 of this Chapter.

2. In particular the rules of national jurisdiction set out in Annex I shall not be applicable as against them.

Article 4

1. If the defendant is not domiciled in a Member State, the jurisdiction of the courts of each Member State shall, subject to Articles 22 and 23, be determined by the law of that Member State.

2. As against such a defendant, any person domiciled in a Member State may, whatever his nationality, avail himself in that State of the rules of jurisdiction there in force, and in particular those specified in Annex I, in the same way as the nationals of that State.

Section 2
Special jurisdiction
Article 5

A person domiciled in a Member State may, in another Member State, be sued:

1. (a) in matters relating to a contract, in the courts for the place of performance of the obligation in question;

(b) for the purpose of this provision and unless otherwise agreed, the place of performance of the obligation in question shall be:

— in the case of the sale of goods, the place in a Member State where, under the contract, the goods were delivered or should have been delivered,

— in the case of the provision of services, the place in a Member State where, under the contract, the services were provided or should have been provided,

(c) if subparagraph (b) does not apply then subparagraph (a) applies;

2. in matters relating to maintenance, in the courts for the place where the maintenance creditor is domiciled or habitually resident or, if the matter is ancillary to proceedings concerning the status of a person, in the court which, according to its own law, has jurisdiction to entertain those proceedings, unless that jurisdiction is based solely on the nationality of one of the parties;

3. in matters relating to tort, delict or quasi-delict, in the courts for the place where the harmful event occurred or may occur;

4. as regards a civil claim for damages or restitution which is based on an act giving rise to criminal proceedings, in the court seised of those proceedings, to the extent that that court has jurisdiction under its own law to entertain civil proceedings;

5. as regards a dispute arising out of the operations of a branch, agency or other establishment, in the courts for the place in which the branch, agency or other establishment is situated;

6. as settlor, trustee or beneficiary of a trust created by the operation of a statute, or by a written instrument, or created orally and evidenced in writing, in the courts of the Member State in which the trust is domiciled;

7. as regards a dispute concerning the payment of remuneration claimed in respect of the salvage of a cargo or freight, in the court under the authority of which the cargo or freight in question:

(a) has been arrested to secure such payment, or

(b) could have been so arrested, but bail or other security has been given;

provided that this provision shall apply only if it is claimed that the defendant has an interest in the cargo or freight or had such an interest at the time of salvage.

Article 6

A person domiciled in a Member State may also be sued:

1. where he is one of a number of defendants, in the courts for the place where any one of them is domiciled, provided the claims are so

closely connected that it is expedient to hear and determine them together to avoid the risk of irreconcilable judgments resulting from separate proceedings;

2.   as a third party in an action on a warranty or guarantee or in any other third party proceedings, in the court seised of the original proceedings, unless these were instituted solely with the object of removing him from the jurisdiction of the court which would be competent in his case;

3.   on a counter-claim arising from the same contract or facts on which the original claim was based, in the court in which the original claim is pending;

4.   in matters relating to a contract, if the action may be combined with an action against the same defendant in matters relating to rights in rem in immovable property, in the court of the Member State in which the property is situated.

Article 7

Where by virtue of this Regulation a court of a Member State has jurisdiction in actions relating to liability from the use or operation of a ship, that court, or any other court substituted for this purpose by the internal law of that Member State, shall also have jurisdiction over claims for limitation of such liability.

Section 3

Jurisdiction in matters relating to insurance

Article 8

In matters relating to insurance, jurisdiction shall be determined by this Section, without prejudice to Article 4 and point 5 of Article 5.

Article 9

1.   An insurer domiciled in a Member State may be sued:

(a) in the courts of the Member State where he is domiciled, or

(b) in another Member State, in the case of actions brought by the policyholder, the insured or a beneficiary, in the courts for the place where the plaintiff is domiciled,

(c) if he is a co-insurer, in the courts of a Member State in which proceedings are brought against the leading insurer.

2.   An insurer who is not domiciled in a Member State but has a branch, agency or other establishment in one of the Member States shall, in disputes arising out of the operations of the branch, agency or establishment, be deemed to be domiciled in that Member State.

Article 10

In respect of liability insurance or insurance of immovable property, the insurer may in addition be sued in the courts for the place where the harmful event occurred. The same applies if movable and immovable property are covered by the same insurance policy and both are adversely affected by the same contingency.

Article 11

1. In respect of liability insurance, the insurer may also, if the law of the court permits it, be joined in proceedings which the injured party has brought against the insured.

2. Articles 8, 9 and 10 shall apply to actions brought by the injured party directly against the insurer, where such direct actions are permitted.

3. If the law governing such direct actions provides that the policyholder or the insured may be joined as a party to the action, the same court shall have jurisdiction over them.

Article 12

1. Without prejudice to Article 11(3), an insurer may bring proceedings only in the courts of the Member State in which the defendant is domiciled, irrespective of whether he is the policyholder, the insured or a beneficiary.

2. The provisions of this Section shall not affect the right to bring a counter-claim in the court in which, in accordance with this Section, the original claim is pending.

Article 13

The provisions of this Section may be departed from only by an agreement:

1. which is entered into after the dispute has arisen, or

2. which allows the policyholder, the insured or a beneficiary to bring proceedings in courts other than those indicated in this Section, or

3. which is concluded between a policyholder and an insurer, both of whom are at the time of conclusion of the contract domiciled or habitually resident in the same Member State, and which has the effect of conferring jurisdiction on the courts of that State even if the harmful event were to occur abroad, provided that such an agreement is not contrary to the law of that State, or

4. which is concluded with a policyholder who is not domiciled in a Member State, except in so far as the insurance is compulsory or relates to immovable property in a Member State, or

5. which relates to a contract of insurance in so far as it covers one or more of the risks set out in Article 14.

Article 14

The following are the risks referred to in Article 13(5):

1.   any loss of or damage to:

(a) seagoing ships, installations situated offshore or on the high seas, or aircraft, arising from perils which relate to their use for commercial purposes;

(b) goods in transit other than passengers' baggage where the transit consists of or includes carriage by such ships or aircraft;

2.   any liability, other than for bodily injury to passengers or loss of or damage to their baggage:

(a) arising out of the use or operation of ships, installations or aircraft as referred to in point 1(a) in so far as, in respect of the latter, the law of the Member State in which such aircraft are registered does not prohibit agreements on jurisdiction regarding insurance of such risks;

(b) for loss or damage caused by goods in transit as described in point 1(b);

3.   any financial loss connected with the use or operation of ships, installations or aircraft as referred to in point 1(a), in particular loss of freight or charter-hire;

4.   any risk or interest connected with any of those referred to in points 1 to 3;

5.   notwithstanding points 1 to 4, all "large risks" as defined in Council Directive 73/239/EEC[7], as amended by Council Directives 88/357/EEC[8] and 90/618/EEC[9], as they may be amended[10].

Section 4

Jurisdiction over consumer contracts

Article 15

1.   In matters relating to a contract concluded by a person, the consumer, for a purpose which can be regarded as being outside his trade or profession, jurisdiction shall be determined by this Section, without prejudice to Article 4 and point 5 of Article 5, if:

(a) it is a contract for the sale of goods on instalment credit terms; or

(b) it is a contract for a loan repayable by instalments, or for any other form of credit, made to finance the sale of goods; or

(c) in all other cases, the contract has been concluded with a person who pursues commercial or professional activities in the Member State

---

7.   OJ L 228, 16.8.1973, p. 3. Directive as last amended by Directive 2000/26/EC of the European Parliament and of the Council (OJ L 181, 20.7.2000, p. 65).

8.   OJ L 172, 4.7.1988, p. 1. Directive as last amended by Directive 2000/26/EC.

9.   OJ L 330, 29.11.1990, p. 44.

10.   OJ L 160, 30.6.2000, p. 37.

of the consumer's domicile or, by any means, directs such activities to that Member State or to several States including that Member State, and the contract falls within the scope of such activities.

2. Where a consumer enters into a contract with a party who is not domiciled in the Member State but has a branch, agency or other establishment in one of the Member States, that party shall, in disputes arising out of the operations of the branch, agency or establishment, be deemed to be domiciled in that State.

3. This Section shall not apply to a contract of transport other than a contract which, for an inclusive price, provides for a combination of travel and accommodation.

Article 16

1. A consumer may bring proceedings against the other party to a contract either in the courts of the Member State in which that party is domiciled or in the courts for the place where the consumer is domiciled.

2. Proceedings may be brought against a consumer by the other party to the contract only in the courts of the Member State in which the consumer is domiciled.

3. This Article shall not affect the right to bring a counter-claim in the court in which, in accordance with this Section, the original claim is pending.

Article 17

The provisions of this Section may be departed from only by an agreement:

1. which is entered into after the dispute has arisen; or

2. which allows the consumer to bring proceedings in courts other than those indicated in this Section; or

3. which is entered into by the consumer and the other party to the contract, both of whom are at the time of conclusion of the contract domiciled or habitually resident in the same Member State, and which confers jurisdiction on the courts of that Member State, provided that such an agreement is not contrary to the law of that Member State.

Section 5

Jurisdiction over individual contracts of employment

Article 18

1. In matters relating to individual contracts of employment, jurisdiction shall be determined by this Section, without prejudice to Article 4 and point 5 of Article 5.

2. Where an employee enters into an individual contract of employment with an employer who is not domiciled in a Member State but has a branch, agency or other establishment in one of the Member States, the employer shall, in disputes arising out of the operations of the

branch, agency or establishment, be deemed to be domiciled in that Member State.

Article 19

An employer domiciled in a Member State may be sued:

1. in the courts of the Member State where he is domiciled; or

2. in another Member State:

(a) in the courts for the place where the employee habitually carries out his work or in the courts for the last place where he did so, or

(b) if the employee does not or did not habitually carry out his work in any one country, in the courts for the place where the business which engaged the employee is or was situated.

Article 20

1. An employer may bring proceedings only in the courts of the Member State in which the employee is domiciled.

2. The provisions of this Section shall not affect the right to bring a counter-claim in the court in which, in accordance with this Section, the original claim is pending.

Article 21

The provisions of this Section may be departed from only by an agreement on jurisdiction:

1. which is entered into after the dispute has arisen; or

2. which allows the employee to bring proceedings in courts other than those indicated in this Section.

Section 6

Exclusive jurisdiction

Article 22

The following courts shall have exclusive jurisdiction, regardless of domicile:

1. in proceedings which have as their object rights in rem in immovable property or tenancies of immovable property, the courts of the Member State in which the property is situated.

However, in proceedings which have as their object tenancies of immovable property concluded for temporary private use for a maximum period of six consecutive months, the courts of the Member State in which the defendant is domiciled shall also have jurisdiction, provided that the tenant is a natural person and that the landlord and the tenant are domiciled in the same Member State;

2. in proceedings which have as their object the validity of the constitution, the nullity or the dissolution of companies or other legal persons or associations of natural or legal persons, or of the validity of

the decisions of their organs, the courts of the Member State in which the company, legal person or association has its seat. In order to determine that seat, the court shall apply its rules of private international law;

3. in proceedings which have as their object the validity of entries in public registers, the courts of the Member State in which the register is kept;

4. in proceedings concerned with the registration or validity of patents, trade marks, designs, or other similar rights required to be deposited or registered, the courts of the Member State in which the deposit or registration has been applied for, has taken place or is under the terms of a Community instrument or an international convention deemed to have taken place.

Without prejudice to the jurisdiction of the European Patent Office under the Convention on the Grant of European Patents, signed at Munich on 5 October 1973, the courts of each Member State shall have exclusive jurisdiction, regardless of domicile, in proceedings concerned with the registration or validity of any European patent granted for that State;

5. in proceedings concerned with the enforcement of judgments, the courts of the Member State in which the judgment has been or is to be enforced.

Section 7

Prorogation of jurisdiction

Article 23

1. If the parties, one or more of whom is domiciled in a Member State, have agreed that a court or the courts of a Member State are to have jurisdiction to settle any disputes which have arisen or which may arise in connection with a particular legal relationship, that court or those courts shall have jurisdiction. Such jurisdiction shall be exclusive unless the parties have agreed otherwise. Such an agreement conferring jurisdiction shall be either:

(a) in writing or evidenced in writing; or

(b) in a form which accords with practices which the parties have established between themselves; or

(c) in international trade or commerce, in a form which accords with a usage of which the parties are or ought to have been aware and which in such trade or commerce is widely known to, and regularly observed by, parties to contracts of the type involved in the particular trade or commerce concerned.

2. Any communication by electronic means which provides a durable record of the agreement shall be equivalent to "writing".

3. Where such an agreement is concluded by parties, none of whom is domiciled in a Member State, the courts of other Member States shall

have no jurisdiction over their disputes unless the court or courts chosen have declined jurisdiction.

4.   The court or courts of a Member State on which a trust instrument has conferred jurisdiction shall have exclusive jurisdiction in any proceedings brought against a settlor, trustee or beneficiary, if relations between these persons or their rights or obligations under the trust are involved.

5.   Agreements or provisions of a trust instrument conferring jurisdiction shall have no legal force if they are contrary to Articles 13, 17 or 21, or if the courts whose jurisdiction they purport to exclude have exclusive jurisdiction by virtue of Article 22.

Article 24

Apart from jurisdiction derived from other provisions of this Regulation, a court of a Member State before which a defendant enters an appearance shall have jurisdiction. This rule shall not apply where appearance was entered to contest the jurisdiction, or where another court has exclusive jurisdiction by virtue of Article 22.

Section 8
Examination as to jurisdiction and admissibility

Article 25

Where a court of a Member State is seised of a claim which is principally concerned with a matter over which the courts of another Member State have exclusive jurisdiction by virtue of Article 22, it shall declare of its own motion that it has no jurisdiction.

Article 26

1.   Where a defendant domiciled in one Member State is sued in a court of another Member State and does not enter an appearance, the court shall declare of its own motion that it has no jurisdiction unless its jurisdiction is derived from the provisions of this Regulation.

2.   The court shall stay the proceedings so long as it is not shown that the defendant has been able to receive the document instituting the proceedings or an equivalent document in sufficient time to enable him to arrange for his defence, or that all necessary steps have been taken to this end.

3.   Article 19 of Council Regulation (EC) No 1348/2000 of 29 May 2000 on the service in the Member States of judicial and extrajudicial documents in civil or commercial matters (10) shall apply instead of the provisions of paragraph 2 if the document instituting the proceedings or an equivalent document had to be transmitted from one Member State to another pursuant to this Regulation.

4.   Where the provisions of Regulation (EC) No 1348/2000 are not applicable, Article 15 of the Hague Convention of 15 November 1965 on the Service Abroad of Judicial and Extrajudicial Documents in Civil or

Commercial Matters shall apply if the document instituting the proceedings or an equivalent document had to be transmitted pursuant to that Convention.

Section 9

Lis pendens—related actions

Article 27

1. Where proceedings involving the same cause of action and between the same parties are brought in the courts of different Member States, any court other than the court first seised shall of its own motion stay its proceedings until such time as the jurisdiction of the court first seised is established.

2. Where the jurisdiction of the court first seised is established, any court other than the court first seised shall decline jurisdiction in favour of that court.

Article 28

1. Where related actions are pending in the courts of different Member States, any court other than the court first seised may stay its proceedings.

2. Where these actions are pending at first instance, any court other than the court first seised may also, on the application of one of the parties, decline jurisdiction if the court first seised has jurisdiction over the actions in question and its law permits the consolidation thereof.

3. For the purposes of this Article, actions are deemed to be related where they are so closely connected that it is expedient to hear and determine them together to avoid the risk of irreconcilable judgments resulting from separate proceedings.

Article 29

Where actions come within the exclusive jurisdiction of several courts, any court other than the court first seised shall decline jurisdiction in favour of that court.

Article 30

For the purposes of this Section, a court shall be deemed to be seised:

1. at the time when the document instituting the proceedings or an equivalent document is lodged with the court, provided that the plaintiff has not subsequently failed to take the steps he was required to take to have service effected on the defendant, or

2. if the document has to be served before being lodged with the court, at the time when it is received by the authority responsible for service, provided that the plaintiff has not subsequently failed to take the steps he was required to take to have the document lodged with the court.

Section 10

Provisional, including protective, measures

Article 31

Application may be made to the courts of a Member State for such provisional, including protective, measures as may be available under the law of that State, even if, under this Regulation, the courts of another Member State have jurisdiction as to the substance of the matter.

CHAPTER III

RECOGNITION AND ENFORCEMENT

Article 32

For the purposes of this Regulation, "judgment" means any judgment given by a court or tribunal of a Member State, whatever the judgment may be called, including a decree, order, decision or writ of execution, as well as the determination of costs or expenses by an officer of the court.

Section 1

Recognition

Article 33

1.   A judgment given in a Member State shall be recognised in the other Member States without any special procedure being required.

2.   Any interested party who raises the recognition of a judgment as the principal issue in a dispute may, in accordance with the procedures provided for in Sections 2 and 3 of this Chapter, apply for a decision that the judgment be recognised.

3.   If the outcome of proceedings in a court of a Member State depends on the determination of an incidental question of recognition that court shall have jurisdiction over that question.

Article 34

A judgment shall not be recognised:

1.   if such recognition is manifestly contrary to public policy in the Member State in which recognition is sought;

2.   where it was given in default of appearance, if the defendant was not served with the document which instituted the proceedings or with an equivalent document in sufficient time and in such a way as to enable him to arrange for his defence, unless the defendant failed to commence proceedings to challenge the judgment when it was possible for him to do so;

3.   if it is irreconcilable with a judgment given in a dispute between the same parties in the Member State in which recognition is sought;

4.   if it is irreconcilable with an earlier judgment given in another Member State or in a third State involving the same cause of action and

between the same parties, provided that the earlier judgment fulfils the conditions necessary for its recognition in the Member State addressed.

Article 35

1. Moreover, a judgment shall not be recognised if it conflicts with Sections 3, 4 or 6 of Chapter II, or in a case provided for in Article 72.

2. In its examination of the grounds of jurisdiction referred to in the foregoing paragraph, the court or authority applied to shall be bound by the findings of fact on which the court of the Member State of origin based its jurisdiction.

3. Subject to the paragraph 1, the jurisdiction of the court of the Member State of origin may not be reviewed. The test of public policy referred to in point 1 of Article 34 may not be applied to the rules relating to jurisdiction.

Article 36

Under no circumstances may a foreign judgment be reviewed as to its substance.

Article 37

1. A court of a Member State in which recognition is sought of a judgment given in another Member State may stay the proceedings if an ordinary appeal against the judgment has been lodged.

2. A court of a Member State in which recognition is sought of a judgment given in Ireland or the United Kingdom may stay the proceedings if enforcement is suspended in the State of origin, by reason of an appeal.

Section 2

Enforcement

Article 38

1. A judgment given in a Member State and enforceable in that State shall be enforced in another Member State when, on the application of any interested party, it has been declared enforceable there.

2. However, in the United Kingdom, such a judgment shall be enforced in England and Wales, in Scotland, or in Northern Ireland when, on the application of any interested party, it has been registered for enforcement in that part of the United Kingdom.

Article 39

1. The application shall be submitted to the court or competent authority indicated in the list in Annex II.

2. The local jurisdiction shall be determined by reference to the place of domicile of the party against whom enforcement is sought, or to the place of enforcement.

Article 40

1.   The procedure for making the application shall be governed by the law of the Member State in which enforcement is sought.

2.   The applicant must give an address for service of process within the area of jurisdiction of the court applied to. However, if the law of the Member State in which enforcement is sought does not provide for the furnishing of such an address, the applicant shall appoint a representative ad litem.

3.   The documents referred to in Article 53 shall be attached to the application.

Article 41

The judgment shall be declared enforceable immediately on completion of the formalities in Article 53 without any review under Articles 34 and 35. The party against whom enforcement is sought shall not at this stage of the proceedings be entitled to make any submissions on the application.

Article 42

1.   The decision on the application for a declaration of enforceability shall forthwith be brought to the notice of the applicant in accordance with the procedure laid down by the law of the Member State in which enforcement is sought.

2.   The declaration of enforceability shall be served on the party against whom enforcement is sought, accompanied by the judgment, if not already served on that party.

Article 43

1.   The decision on the application for a declaration of enforceability may be appealed against by either party.

2.   The appeal is to be lodged with the court indicated in the list in Annex III.

3.   The appeal shall be dealt with in accordance with the rules governing procedure in contradictory matters.

4.   If the party against whom enforcement is sought fails to appear before the appellate court in proceedings concerning an appeal brought by the applicant, Article 26(2) to (4) shall apply even where the party against whom enforcement is sought is not domiciled in any of the Member States.

5.   An appeal against the declaration of enforceability is to be lodged within one month of service thereof. If the party against whom enforcement is sought is domiciled in a Member State other than that in which the declaration of enforceability was given, the time for appealing shall be two months and shall run from the date of service, either on him

in person or at his residence. No extension of time may be granted on account of distance.

Article 44

The judgment given on the appeal may be contested only by the appeal referred to in Annex IV.

Article 45

1.   The court with which an appeal is lodged under Article 43 or Article 44 shall refuse or revoke a declaration of enforceability only on one of the grounds specified in Articles 34 and 35. It shall give its decision without delay.

2.   Under no circumstances may the foreign judgment be reviewed as to its substance.

Article 46

1.   The court with which an appeal is lodged under Article 43 or Article 44 may, on the application of the party against whom enforcement is sought, stay the proceedings if an ordinary appeal has been lodged against the judgment in the Member State of origin or if the time for such an appeal has not yet expired; in the latter case, the court may specify the time within which such an appeal is to be lodged.

2.   Where the judgment was given in Ireland or the United Kingdom, any form of appeal available in the Member State of origin shall be treated as an ordinary appeal for the purposes of paragraph 1.

3.   The court may also make enforcement conditional on the provision of such security as it shall determine.

Article 47

1.   When a judgment must be recognised in accordance with this Regulation, nothing shall prevent the applicant from availing himself of provisional, including protective, measures in accordance with the law of the Member State requested without a declaration of enforceability under Article 41 being required.

2.   The declaration of enforceability shall carry with it the power to proceed to any protective measures.

3.   During the time specified for an appeal pursuant to Article 43(5) against the declaration of enforceability and until any such appeal has been determined, no measures of enforcement may be taken other than protective measures against the property of the party against whom enforcement is sought.

Article 48

1.   Where a foreign judgment has been given in respect of several matters and the declaration of enforceability cannot be given for all of

them, the court or competent authority shall give it for one or more of them.

2. An applicant may request a declaration of enforceability limited to parts of a judgment.

Article 49

A foreign judgment which orders a periodic payment by way of a penalty shall be enforceable in the Member State in which enforcement is sought only if the amount of the payment has been finally determined by the courts of the Member State of origin.

Article 50

An applicant who, in the Member State of origin has benefited from complete or partial legal aid or exemption from costs or expenses, shall be entitled, in the procedure provided for in this Section, to benefit from the most favourable legal aid or the most extensive exemption from costs or expenses provided for by the law of the Member State addressed.

Article 51

No security, bond or deposit, however described, shall be required of a party who in one Member State applies for enforcement of a judgment given in another Member State on the ground that he is a foreign national or that he is not domiciled or resident in the State in which enforcement is sought.

Article 52

In proceedings for the issue of a declaration of enforceability, no charge, duty or fee calculated by reference to the value of the matter at issue may be levied in the Member State in which enforcement is sought.

Section 3

Common provisions

Article 53

1. A party seeking recognition or applying for a declaration of enforceability shall produce a copy of the judgment which satisfies the conditions necessary to establish its authenticity.

2. A party applying for a declaration of enforceability shall also produce the certificate referred to in Article 54, without prejudice to Article 55.

Article 54

The court or competent authority of a Member State where a judgment was given shall issue, at the request of any interested party, a certificate using the standard form in Annex V to this Regulation.

Article 55

1. If the certificate referred to in Article 54 is not produced, the court or competent authority may specify a time for its production or accept an equivalent document or, if it considers that it has sufficient information before it, dispense with its production.

2. If the court or competent authority so requires, a translation of the documents shall be produced. The translation shall be certified by a person qualified to do so in one of the Member States.

Article 56

No legalisation or other similar formality shall be required in respect of the documents referred to in Article 53 or Article 55(2), or in respect of a document appointing a representative ad litem.

CHAPTER IV
AUTHENTIC INSTRUMENTS AND COURT SETTLEMENTS

Article 57

1. A document which has been formally drawn up or registered as an authentic instrument and is enforceable in one Member State shall, in another Member State, be declared enforceable there, on application made in accordance with the procedures provided for in Articles 38, et seq. The court with which an appeal is lodged under Article 43 or Article 44 shall refuse or revoke a declaration of enforceability only if enforcement of the instrument is manifestly contrary to public policy in the Member State addressed.

2. Arrangements relating to maintenance obligations concluded with administrative authorities or authenticated by them shall also be regarded as authentic instruments within the meaning of paragraph 1.

3. The instrument produced must satisfy the conditions necessary to establish its authenticity in the Member State of origin.

4. Section 3 of Chapter III shall apply as appropriate. The competent authority of a Member State where an authentic instrument was drawn up or registered shall issue, at the request of any interested party, a certificate using the standard form in Annex VI to this Regulation.

Article 58

A settlement which has been approved by a court in the course of proceedings and is enforceable in the Member State in which it was concluded shall be enforceable in the State addressed under the same conditions as authentic instruments. The court or competent authority of a Member State where a court settlement was approved shall issue, at the request of any interested party, a certificate using the standard form in Annex V to this Regulation.

CHAPTER V

GENERAL PROVISIONS

Article 59

1. In order to determine whether a party is domiciled in the Member State whose courts are seised of a matter, the court shall apply its internal law.

2. If a party is not domiciled in the Member State whose courts are seised of the matter, then, in order to determine whether the party is domiciled in another Member State, the court shall apply the law of that Member State.

Article 60

1. For the purposes of this Regulation, a company or other legal person or association of natural or legal persons is domiciled at the place where it has its:

(a) statutory seat, or

(b) central administration, or

(c) principal place of business.

2. For the purposes of the United Kingdom and Ireland "statutory seat" means the registered office or, where there is no such office anywhere, the place of incorporation or, where there is no such place anywhere, the place under the law of which the formation took place.

3. In order to determine whether a trust is domiciled in the Member State whose courts are seised of the matter, the court shall apply its rules of private international law.

Article 61

Without prejudice to any more favourable provisions of national laws, persons domiciled in a Member State who are being prosecuted in the criminal courts of another Member State of which they are not nationals for an offence which was not intentionally committed may be defended by persons qualified to do so, even if they do not appear in person. However, the court seised of the matter may order appearance in person; in the case of failure to appear, a judgment given in the civil action without the person concerned having had the opportunity to arrange for his defence need not be recognised or enforced in the other Member States.

Article 62

In Sweden, in summary proceedings concerning orders to pay (*betalningsföreläggande*) and assistance (*handräckning*), the expression "court" includes the "Swedish enforcement service" (*kronofogdemyndighet*).

Article 63

1. A person domiciled in the territory of the Grand Duchy of Luxembourg and sued in the court of another Member State pursuant to Article 5(1) may refuse to submit to the jurisdiction of that court if the final place of delivery of the goods or provision of the services is in Luxembourg.

2. Where, under paragraph 1, the final place of delivery of the goods or provision of the services is in Luxembourg, any agreement conferring jurisdiction must, in order to be valid, be accepted in writing or evidenced in writing within the meaning of Article 23(1)(a).

3. The provisions of this Article shall not apply to contracts for the provision of financial services.

4. The provisions of this Article shall apply for a period of six years from entry into force of this Regulation.

Article 64

1. In proceedings involving a dispute between the master and a member of the crew of a seagoing ship registered in Greece or in Portugal, concerning remuneration or other conditions of service, a court in a Member State shall establish whether the diplomatic or consular officer responsible for the ship has been notified of the dispute. It may act as soon as that officer has been notified.

2. The provisions of this Article shall apply for a period of six years from entry into force of this Regulation.

Article 65

1. The jurisdiction specified in Article 6(2), and Article 11 in actions on a warranty of guarantee or in any other third party proceedings may not be resorted to in Germany and Austria. Any person domiciled in another Member State may be sued in the courts:

(a) of Germany, pursuant to Articles 68 and 72 to 74 of the Code of Civil Procedure (*Zivilprozessordnung*) concerning third-party notices,

(b) of Austria, pursuant to Article 21 of the Code of Civil Procedure (*Zivilprozessordnung*) concerning third-party notices.

2. Judgments given in other Member States by virtue of Article 6(2), or Article 11 shall be recognised and enforced in Germany and Austria in accordance with Chapter III. Any effects which judgments given in these States may have on third parties by application of the provisions in paragraph 1 shall also be recognised in the other Member States.

CHAPTER VI
TRANSITIONAL PROVISIONS

Article 66

1. This Regulation shall apply only to legal proceedings instituted and to documents formally drawn up or registered as authentic instruments after the entry into force thereof.

2.   However, if the proceedings in the Member State of origin were instituted before the entry into force of this Regulation, judgments given after that date shall be recognised and enforced in accordance with Chapter III,

(a) if the proceedings in the Member State of origin were instituted after the entry into force of the Brussels or the Lugano Convention both in the Member State or origin and in the Member State addressed;

(b) in all other cases, if jurisdiction was founded upon rules which accorded with those provided for either in Chapter II or in a convention concluded between the Member State of origin and the Member State addressed which was in force when the proceedings were instituted.

CHAPTER VII

RELATIONS WITH OTHER INSTRUMENTS

Article 67

This Regulation shall not prejudice the application of provisions governing jurisdiction and the recognition and enforcement of judgments in specific matters which are contained in Community instruments or in national legislation harmonised pursuant to such instruments.

Article 68

1.   This Regulation shall, as between the Member States, supersede the Brussels Convention, except as regards the territories of the Member States which fall within the territorial scope of that Convention and which are excluded from this Regulation pursuant to Article 299 of the Treaty.

2.   In so far as this Regulation replaces the provisions of the Brussels Convention between Member States, any reference to the Convention shall be understood as a reference to this Regulation.

Article 69

Subject to Article 66(2) and Article 70, this Regulation shall, as between Member States, supersede the following conventions and treaty concluded between two or more of them:

— the Convention between Belgium and France on Jurisdiction and the Validity and Enforcement of Judgments, Arbitration Awards and Authentic Instruments, signed at Paris on 8 July 1899,

— the Convention between Belgium and the Netherlands on Jurisdiction, Bankruptcy, and the Validity and Enforcement of Judgments, Arbitration Awards and Authentic Instruments, signed at Brussels on 28 March 1925,

— the Convention between France and Italy on the Enforcement of Judgments in Civil and Commercial Matters, signed at Rome on 3 June 1930,

— the Convention between the United Kingdom and the French Republic providing for the reciprocal enforcement of judgments in civil and commercial matters, with Protocol, signed at Paris on 18 January 1934,

— the Convention between the United Kingdom and the Kingdom of Belgium providing for the reciprocal enforcement of judgments in civil and commercial matters, with Protocol, signed at Brussels on 2 May 1934,

— the Convention between Germany and Italy on the Recognition and Enforcement of Judgments in Civil and Commercial Matters, signed at Rome on 9 March 1936,

— the Convention between Belgium and Austria on the Reciprocal Recognition and Enforcement of Judgments and Authentic Instruments relating to Maintenance Obligations, signed at Vienna on 25 October 1957,

— the Convention between Germany and Belgium on the Mutual Recognition and Enforcement of Judgments, Arbitration Awards and Authentic Instruments in Civil and Commercial Matters, signed at Bonn on 30 June 1958,

— the Convention between the Netherlands and Italy on the Recognition and Enforcement of Judgments in Civil and Commercial Matters, signed at Rome on 17 April 1959,

— the Convention between Germany and Austria on the Reciprocal Recognition and Enforcement of Judgments, Settlements and Authentic Instruments in Civil and Commercial Matters, signed at Vienna on 6 June 1959,

— the Convention between Belgium and Austria on the Reciprocal Recognition and Enforcement of Judgments, Arbitral Awards and Authentic Instruments in Civil and Commercial Matters, signed at Vienna on 16 June 1959,

— the Convention between the United Kingdom and the Federal Republic of Germany for the reciprocal recognition and enforcement of judgments in civil and commercial matters, signed at Bonn on 14 July 1960,

— the Convention between the United Kingdom and Austria providing for the reciprocal recognition and enforcement of judgments in civil and commercial matters, signed at Vienna on 14 July 1961, with amending Protocol signed at London on 6 March 1970,

— the Convention between Greece and Germany for the Reciprocal Recognition and Enforcement of Judgments, Settlements and Authentic Instruments in Civil and Commercial Matters, signed in Athens on 4 November 1961,

— the Convention between Belgium and Italy on the Recognition and Enforcement of Judgments and other Enforceable Instruments in Civil and Commercial Matters, signed at Rome on 6 April 1962,

— the Convention between the Netherlands and Germany on the Mutual Recognition and Enforcement of Judgments and Other Enforceable Instruments in Civil and Commercial Matters, signed at The Hague on 30 August 1962,

— the Convention between the Netherlands and Austria on the Reciprocal Recognition and Enforcement of Judgments and Authentic Instruments in Civil and Commercial Matters, signed at The Hague on 6 February 1963,

— the Convention between the United Kingdom and the Republic of Italy for the reciprocal recognition and enforcement of judgments in civil and commercial matters, signed at Rome on 7 February 1964, with amending Protocol signed at Rome on 14 July 1970,

— the Convention between France and Austria on the Recognition and Enforcement of Judgments and Authentic Instruments in Civil and Commercial Matters, signed at Vienna on 15 July 1966,

— the Convention between the United Kingdom and the Kingdom of the Netherlands providing for the reciprocal recognition and enforcement of judgments in civil matters, signed at The Hague on 17 November 1967,

— the Convention between Spain and France on the Recognition and Enforcement of Judgment Arbitration Awards in Civil and Commercial Matters, signed at Paris on 28 May 1969,

— the Convention between Luxembourg and Austria on the Recognition and Enforcement of Judgments and Authentic Instruments in Civil and Commercial Matters, signed at Luxembourg on 29 July 1971,

— the Convention between Italy and Austria on the Recognition and Enforcement of Judgments in Civil and Commercial Matters, of Judicial Settlements and of Authentic Instruments, signed at Rome on 16 November 1971,

— the Convention between Spain and Italy regarding Legal Aid and the Recognition and Enforcement of Judgments in Civil and Commercial Matters, signed at Madrid on 22 May 1973,

— the Convention between Finland, Iceland, Norway, Sweden and Denmark on the Recognition and Enforcement of Judgments in Civil Matters, signed at Copenhagen on 11 October 1977,

— the Convention between Austria and Sweden on the Recognition and Enforcement of Judgments in Civil Matters, signed at Stockholm on 16 September 1982,

— the Convention between Spain and the Federal Republic of Germany on the Recognition and Enforcement of Judgments, Settlements and Enforceable Authentic Instruments in Civil and Commercial Matters, signed at Bonn on 14 November 1983,

— the Convention between Austria and Spain on the Recognition and Enforcement of Judgments, Settlements and Enforceable Authentic

Instruments in Civil and Commercial Matters, signed at Vienna on 17 February 1984,

— the Convention between Finland and Austria on the Recognition and Enforcement of Judgments in Civil Matters, signed at Vienna on 17 November 1986, and

— the Treaty between Belgium, the Netherlands and Luxembourg in Jurisdiction, Bankruptcy, and the Validity and Enforcement of Judgments, Arbitration Awards and Authentic Instruments, signed at Brussels on 24 November 1961, in so far as it is in force.

Article 70

1.   The Treaty and the Conventions referred to in Article 69 shall continue to have effect in relation to matters to which this Regulation does not apply.

2.   They shall continue to have effect in respect of judgments given and documents formally drawn up or registered as authentic instruments before the entry into force of this Regulation.

Article 71

1.   This Regulation shall not affect any conventions to which the Member States are parties and which in relation to particular matters, govern jurisdiction or the recognition or enforcement of judgments.

2.   With a view to its uniform interpretation, paragraph 1 shall be applied in the following manner:

(a) this Regulation shall not prevent a court of a Member State, which is a party to a convention on a particular matter, from assuming jurisdiction in accordance with that convention, even where the defendant is domiciled in another Member State which is not a party to that convention. The court hearing the action shall, in any event, apply Article 26 of this Regulation;

(b) judgments given in a Member State by a court in the exercise of jurisdiction provided for in a convention on a particular matter shall be recognised and enforced in the other Member States in accordance with this Regulation.

Where a convention on a particular matter to which both the Member State of origin and the Member State addressed are parties lays down conditions for the recognition or enforcement of judgments, those conditions shall apply. In any event, the provisions of this Regulation which concern the procedure for recognition and enforcement of judgments may be applied.

Article 72

This Regulation shall not affect agreements by which Member States undertook, prior to the entry into force of this Regulation pursuant to Article 59 of the Brussels Convention, not to recognise judgments given, in particular in other Contracting States to that Convention, against defendants domiciled or habitually resident in a third country where, in cases provided for in Article 4 of that Convention, the judgment could only be founded on a ground of jurisdiction specified in the second paragraph of Article 3 of that Convention.

CHAPTER VIII

FINAL PROVISIONS

Article 73

No later than five years after the entry into force of this Regulation, the Commission shall present to the European Parliament, the Council and the Economic and Social Committee a report on the application of this Regulation. The report shall be accompanied, if need be, by proposals for adaptations to this Regulation.

Article 74

1.   The Member States shall notify the Commission of the texts amending the lists set out in Annexes I to IV. The Commission shall adapt the Annexes concerned accordingly.

2.   The updating or technical adjustment of the forms, specimens of which appear in Annexes V and VI, shall be adopted in accordance with the advisory procedure referred to in Article 75(2).

Article 75

1.   The Commission shall be assisted by a committee.

2.   Where reference is made to this paragraph, Articles 3 and 7 of Decision 1999/468/EC shall apply.

3.   The Committee shall adopt its rules of procedure.

Article 76

This Regulation shall enter into force on 1 March 2002.

This Regulation is binding in its entirety and directly applicable in the Member States in accordance with the Treaty establishing the European Community.

Done at Brussels, 22 December 2000.

For the Council

The President

C.   PIERRET

ANNEX I

Rules of jurisdiction referred to in Article 3(2) and Article 4(2)

The rules of jurisdiction referred to in Article 3(2) and Article 4(2) are the following:

— in Belgium: Article 15 of the Civil Code (*Code civil/Burgerlijk Wetboek*) and Article 638 of the Judicial Code (*Code judiciaire/Gerechtelijk Wetboek*);

— in the Czech Republic: Article 86 of Act No 99/1963 Coll., the Code of Civil Procedure (*občanský soudní řád*), as amended,

— in Germany: Article 23 of the Code of Civil Procedure (*Zivilprozessordnung*),

— in Estonia: Article 139, paragraph 2 of the Code of Civil Procedure (*tsiviilkohtumenetluseseadustik*),

– in Greece, Article 40 of the code of civil procedure (Κώδικας Πολιτικής Δικονομίας),

— in France: Articles 14 and 15 of the Civil Code (*Code civil*),

— in Ireland: the rules which enable jurisdiction to be founded on the document instituting the proceedings having been served on the defendant during his temporary presence in Ireland,

— in Italy: Articles 3 and 4 of Act 218 of 31 May 1995,

— in Cyprus: section 21(2) of the Courts of Justice Law No 14 of 1960, as amended,

— in Latvia: Articles 7 to 25 of the Civil Law (*Civillikums*),

— in Lithuania: Article 31 of the Code of Civil Procedure (*Civilinio proceso kodeksas*),

— in Luxembourg: Articles 14 and 15 of the Civil Code (*Code civil*),

— in Hungary: Article 57 of Law Decree No. 13 of 1979 on International Private Law (*a nemzetközi magánjogról szóló 1979. évi 13. törvényerej"urendelet*),

— in Malta: Articles 742, 743 and 744 of the Code of Organisation and Civil Procedure—Cap. 12 (*Kodici ta' Organizzazzjoni u Procedura Civili—Kap. 12*) and Article 549 of the Commercial Code—Cap. 13 (*Kodici talkummerc-Kap. 13*),

— in Austria: Article 99 of the Court Jurisdiction Act (*Jurisdiktionsnorm*),

— in Poland: Articles 1103 and 1110 of the Code of Civil Procedure (*Kodeks postępowania cywilnego*),

— in Portugal: Articles 65 and 65A of the Code of Civil Procedure (*Código de Processo Civil*) and Article 11 of the Code of Labour Procedure (*Código de Processo de Trabalho*),

— in Slovenia: Articles 48(2) and 58 of the Private International Law and Procedure Act (*Zakon o mednarodnem zasebnem pravu in postopku*),

— in Slovakia: sections 37, 39 (*only as regards maintenance*) and 46 of Act No 97/1963 Zb. on Private International Law and Rules of Procedure relating thereto,

— in Finland: the second, third and fourth sentences of the first paragraph of Section 1 of Chapter 10 of the Code of Judicial Procedure (*oikeudenkäymiskaari/ rättegangsbalken*),

— in Sweden: the first sentence of the first paragraph of Section 3 of Chapter 10 of the Code of Judicial Procedure (*rättegangsbalken*),

— in the United Kingdom: rules which enable jurisdiction to be founded on:

(a) the document instituting the proceedings having been served on the defendant during his temporary presence in the United Kingdom; or

(b) the presence within the United Kingdom of property belonging to the defendant; or

(c) the seizure by the plaintiff of property situated in the United Kingdom.

ANNEX II

The courts or competent authorities to which the application referred to in Article 39 may be submitted are the following:

— in Belgium, the *"tribunal de première instance"* or *"rechtbank van eerste aanleg"* or *"erstinstanzliches Gericht"*,

— in the Czech Republic, the *"okresní soud"* or *"soudní exekutor"*,

— in Germany:

(a) the presiding Judge of a chamber of the *"Landgericht"*;

(b) a notary ("...") in a procedure of declaration of enforceability of an authentic instrument,

— in Estonia, the *"maakohus"* or the *"linnakohus"*,

— in Greece, to the Μονομελές Πρωτοδικείο,

— in Spain, the *"Juzgado de Primera Instancia"*,

— in France, the presiding judge of the *"tribunal de grande instance"*,

— in Ireland, the High Court,

— in Italy, the *"Corte d'appello"*,

— in Cyprus, the '*Επαρχιακό .ικαστήριο*' or in the case of a maintenance judgment the '*Οικογενειακό.ικαστήριο*',

— in Latvia, the *"rajona (pilsetas) tiesa"*,

— in Lithuania, the *"Lietuvos apeliacinis teismas"*,

— in Luxembourg, the presiding judge of the *"tribunal d'arrondissement"*,

— in Hungary, the *"megyei bíróság székhelyén m"uköd helyi bíróság"*, and in Budapest the *"Budai Központi Kerületi Bíróság"*,

— in Malta, the *"Prim" "Awla tal-Qorti Civili"* or *"Qorti tal-Magistrati ta" "Ghawdex fil-gurisdizzjoni superjuri taghha"*, or, in the case of a maintenance judgment, the *"Registratur tal-Qorti"* on transmission by the *"Ministru responsabbli ghall-Gustizzja"*,

— in the Netherlands, the *"voorzieningenrechter van de rechtbank"*,

— in Austria, the *"Bezirksgericht"*,

— in Poland, the *"Sąd Okrgowy"*,

— in Portugal, the *"Tribunal de Comarca"*,

— in Slovenia, the *"Okrajno sodišče"*,

— in Slovakia, the *"okresný súd"* or *"exekútor"*,

— in Finland, the *"käräjäoikeus/tingsrätt"*,

— in Sweden, the *"Svea hovrätt"*,

— in the United Kingdom:

(a) in England and Wales, the High Court of Justice, or in the case of a maintenance judgment, the Magistrate's Court on transmission by the Secretary of State;

(b) in Scotland, the Court of Session, or in the case of a maintenance judgment, the Sheriff Court on transmission by the Secretary of State;

(c) in Northern Ireland, the High Court of Justice, or in the case of a maintenance judgment, the Magistrate's Court on transmission by the Secretary of State;

(d) in Gibraltar, the Supreme Court of Gibraltar, or in the case of a maintenance judgment, the Magistrates' Court on transmission by the Attorney General of Gibraltar.

ANNEX III

The courts with which appeals referred to in Article 43(2) may be lodged are the following:

— in Belgium,

(a) as regards appeal by the defendant: the *'tribunal de première instance'* or *"rechtbank van eerste aanleg"* or *"erstinstanzliches Gericht"*,

(b) as regards appeal by the applicant: the *"Cour d'appel"* or *"hof van beroep"*,

— in the Czech Republic, the *"okresní soud"*,

— in the Federal Republic of Germany, the *"Oberlandesgericht"*,

— in Estonia, the *"ringkonnakohus"*,

— in Greece, to the Εφετείο,

— in Spain, the *"Audiencia Provincial"*,

— in France, the *"cour d'appel"*,

— in Ireland, the High Court,

— in Italy, the *"corte d'appello"*,

— in Cyprus, the '*Επαρχιακό .ικαστήριο*' or in the case of a maintenance judgment the '*Οικογενειακό .ικαστήριο*',

— in Latvia, the *"Apgabaltiesa"*,

— in Lithuania, the *"Lietuvos Aukščiausiasis Teismas"*,

— in Luxembourg, the *"Cour supérieure de Justice"* sitting as a court of civil appeal,

— in Hungary, the *"megyei bíróság"*; in Budapest, the*"Fvárosi Bíróság"*,

— in Malta, the *"Qorti ta' l-Appell"* in accordance with the procedure laid down for appeals in the Kodi.i ta' Organizzazzjoni u Pro.edura .ivili—Kap.12 or in the case of a maintenance judgment by '*citazzjoni*' before the '*Prim' Awla tal-Qorti ivili jew il-Qorti tal-Magistrati ta' Ghawdex fil-gurisdizzjoni superjuri taghha*",

— in the Netherlands:

    (a) for the defendant: the *"arrondissementsrechtbank"*,

    (b) for the applicant: the *"gerechtshof"*,

— in Austria, the *"Bezirksgericht"*,

— in Poland, the *"Sąd Apelacyjny"*,

— in Portugal, the *"Tribunal de Relação"*,

— in Slovenia, the *"Višje sodišče"*,

— in Slovakia, *"odvolanie"* to the *"krajský súd"* or *"námietka"* to the *"okresný súd"* in cases of execution ordered by the *"exekútor"*,

— in Finland, the *"hovioikeus/hovrätt"*,

— in Sweden, the *"Svea hovrätt"*,

— in the United Kingdom:

    (a) in England and Wales, the High Court of Justice, or in the case of a maintenance judgment, the Magistrate's Court;

    (b) in Scotland, the Court of Session, or in the case of a maintenance judgment, the Sheriff Court;

    (c) in Northern Ireland, the High Court of Justice, or in the case of a maintenance judgment, the Magistrate's Court;

    (d) in Gibraltar, the Supreme Court of Gibraltar, or in the case of a maintenance judgment, the Magistrates' Court.

ANNEX IV

The appeals which may be lodged pursuant to Article 44 are the following:

— in Belgium, Greece, Spain, France, Italy, Luxembourg and the Netherlands, an appeal in cassation,

— in the Czech Republic, a *"dovolání"* and a *"žaloba pro zmatečnost"*,

— in Germany, a *"Rechtsbeschwerde"*,

— in Estonia, a *"kassatsioonkaebus"*,

— in Ireland, an appeal on a point of law to the Supreme Court,

— in Cyprus, an appeal to the Supreme Court,

— in Latvia, an appeal to the *"Augstaka tiesa"*,

— in Lithuania, by a retrial, only in cases prescribed by statute,

— in Hungary, *"felülvizsgálati kérelem"*,

— in Malta, no further appeal lies to any other court; in the case of a maintenance judgment the *"Qorti ta' l-Appell"* in accordance with the procedure laid down for appeal in the *"kodici ta' Organizzazzjoni u Procedura Civili—Kap. 12"*,

— in Austria, a *"Revisionsrekurs"*,

— in Poland, by an appeal in cassation to the *"Sąd Najwys.zy"*,

— in Portugal, an appeal on a point of law,

— in Slovenia, the *"retrial, only in cases prescribed by statute"*,

— in Slovakia *"odvolanie"* in cases of execution ordered by the *"exekútor"* to the *"Krajský súd"*,

— in Finland, an appeal to the *"korkein oikeus/högsta domstolen"*,

— in Sweden, an appeal to the *"Högsta domstolen"*,

— in the United Kingdom, a single further appeal on a point of law.

ANNEX V

Certificate referred to in Articles 54 and 58 of the Regulation on judgments and court settlements (English, inglés, anglais, inglese, ...)

1.   Member State of origin

2.   Court or competent authority issuing the certificate

2.1. Name

2.2. Address

2.3. Tel./fax/e-mail

3.   Court which delivered the judgment/approved the court settlement (*)

3.1.   Type of court

3.2.   Place of court

4.   Judgment/court settlement (*)

4.1.   Date

4.2.   Reference number

4.3.   The parties to the judgment/court settlement (*)

4.3.1.   Name(s) of plaintiff(s)

4.3.2.   Name(s) of defendant(s)

4.3.3.   Name(s) of other party(ies), if any

4.4.   Date of service of the document instituting the proceedings where judgment was given in default of appearance

4.5.   Text of the judgment/court settlement (*) as annexed to this certificate

5.   Names of parties to whom legal aid has been granted The judgment/court settlement (*) is enforceable in the Member State of origin (Articles 38 and 58 of the Regulation) against: Name:

Done at ... , date ...

Signature and/or stamp ...

(*) Delete as appropriate.

ANNEX VI

Certificate referred to in Article 57(4) of the Regulation on authentic instruments (English, ingles, anglais, inglese ...)

1.   Member State of origin

2.   Competent authority issuing the certificate

2.1.   Name

2.2.   Address

2.3.   Tel./fax/e-mail

3.   Authority which has given authenticity to the instrument

3.1.   Authority involved in the drawing up of the authentic instrument (if applicable)

3.1.1.   Name and designation of authority

3.1.2.   Place of authority

3.2.   Authority which has registered the authentic instrument (if applicable)

3.2.1.   Type of authority

3.2.2.   Place of authority

4.   Authentic instrument

4.1.   Description of the instrument

4.2.   Date

4.2.1.   on which the instrument was drawn up

4.2.2.   if different: on which the instrument was registered

4.3.   Reference number

4.4.   Parties to the instrument

4.4.1.   Name of the creditor

4.4.2.   Name of the debtor

5.   Text of the enforceable obligation as annexed to this certificate. The authentic instrument is enforceable against the debtor in the Member State of origin (Article 57(1) of the Regulation)

Done at . . . , date . . .

Signature and/or stamp . . .

CONVENTION BETWEEN THE UNITED KINGDOM OF GREAT BRITAIN AND NORTHERN IRELAND AND CANADA PROVIDING FOR THE RECIPROCAL RECOGNITION AND ENFORCEMENT OF JUDGMENTS IN CIVIL AND COMMERCIAL MATTERS

The United Kingdom of Great Britain and Northern Ireland, and Canada,

Desiring to provide on the basis of reciprocity for the recognition and enforcement of judgments in civil and commercial matters;

Have agreed as follows:

PART I

Definitions

ARTICLE 1

In this Convention

(a) "appeal" includes any proceeding by way of discharging or setting aside a judgment or an application for a new trial or a stay of execution;

(b) "the 1968 Convention" means the Convention of 27th September 1968 on Jurisdiction and the Enforcement of Judgments in Civil and Commercial Matters as amended[1];

(c) "court of a Contracting State" means

(i) in relation to the United Kingdom, any court of the United Kingdom or of any territory to which this Convention extends pursuant to Article XIII;

(ii) in relation to Canada, the Federal Court of Canada or any court of a province or territory to which this Convention extends pursuant to Article XII,

and the expressions "court of the United Kingdom" and "court of Canada" shall be construed accordingly;

(d) "judgment" means any decision, however described (judgment, order and the like), given by a court in a civil or commercial matter, and includes an award in proceedings on an arbitration if the award has become enforceable in the territory of origin in the same manner as a judgment given by a court in that territory;

(e) "judgment creditor" means the person in whose favour the judgment was given, and includes his executors, administrators, successors and assigns;

---

1. Treaty Series No. 10 (1988). Cm 306.

(f) "judgment debtor" means the person against whom the judgment was given and includes any person against whom the judgment is enforceable under the law of the territory of origin;

(g) "original court" in relation to any judgment means the court by which the judgment was given;

(h) "registering court" means a court to which an application for the registration of a judgment is made;

(i) "territory of origin" means the territory for which the original court was exercising jurisdiction.

PART II

Scope of the Convention

ARTICLE II

1.   Subject to the provisions of this Article, this Convention shall apply to any judgment given by a court of a Contracting State after the Convention enters into force and, for the purposes of Article IX, to any judgment given by a court of a third State which is party to the 1968 Convention.

2.   This Convention shall not apply to

(a) orders for the periodic payment of maintenance;

(b) the recovery of taxes, duties or charges of a like nature or the recovery of a fine or penalty;

(c) judgments given on appeal from decisions of tribunals other than courts;

(d) judgments which determine

(i) the status or legal capacity of natural persons;

(ii) custody or guardianship of infants;

(iii) matrimonial matters;

(iv) succession to or the administration of the estates of deceased persons;

(v) bankruptcy, insolvency or the winding up of companies or other legal persons;

(vi) the management of the affairs of a person not capable of managing his own affairs.

3.   Part III of this Convention shall apply only to a judgment whereby a sum of money is made payable.

4.   This Convention is without prejudice to any other remedy available to a judgment creditor for the recognition and enforcement in one Contracting State of a judgment given by a court of the other Contracting State.

PART III

Enforcement of Judgments

ARTICLE III

1. Where a judgment has been given by a court of one Contracting State, the judgment creditor may apply in accordance with Article VI to a court of the other Contracting State at any time within a period of six years after the date of the judgment (or, where there have been proceedings by way of appeal against the judgment, after the date of the last judgment given in those proceedings) to have the judgment registered, and on any such application the registering court shall, subject to such simple and rapid procedures as each Contracting State may prescribe and to the other provisions of this Convention, order the judgment to be registered.

2. In addition to the sum of money payable under the judgment of the original court including interest accrued to the date of registration, the judgment shall be registered for the reasonable costs of and incidental to registration, if any, including the costs of obtaining a certified copy of the judgment from the original court.

3. If, on an application for the registration of a judgment, it appears to the registering court that the judgment is in respect of different matters and that some, but not all, of the provisions of the judgment are such that if those provisions had been contained in separate judgments those judgments could properly have been registered, the judgment may be registered in respect of the provisions aforesaid but not in respect of any other provisions contained therein.

4. Subject to the other provisions of this Convention

     (a) a registered judgment shall, for the purposes of enforcement, be of the same force and effect;

     (b) proceedings may be taken on it; and

     (c) the registering court shall have the same control over its enforcement, as if it had been a judgment originally given in the registering court with effect from the date of registration.

ARTICLE IV

1. Registration of a judgment shall be refused or set aside if

     (a) the judgment has been satisfied;

     (b) the judgment is not enforceable in the territory of origin;

     (c) the original court is not regarded by the registering court as having jurisdiction;

     (d) the judgment was obtained by fraud;

     (e) enforcement of the judgment would be contrary to public policy in the territory of the registering court;

(f) the judgment is a judgment of a country or territory other than the territory of origin which has been registered in the original court or has become enforceable in the territory of origin in the same manner as a judgment of that court; or

(g) in the view of the registering court the judgment debtor either is entitled to immunity from the jurisdiction of that court or was entitled to immunity in the original court and did not submit to its jurisdiction.

2.   The law of the registering court may provide that registration of a judgment may or shall be set aside if

(a) the judgment debtor, being the defendant in the original proceedings, either was not served with the process of the original court or did not receive notice of those proceedings in sufficient time to enable him to defend the proceedings and, in either case, did not appear;

(b) another judgment has been given by a court having jurisdiction in the matter in dispute prior to the date of judgment in the original court; or

(c) the judgment is not final or an appeal is pending or the judgment debtor is entitled to appeal or to apply for leave to appeal against the judgment in the territory of origin.

3.   If at the date of the application for registration the judgment of the original court has been partly satisfied, the judgment shall be registered only in respect of the balance remaining payable at that date.

4.   A judgment shall not be enforced so long as, in accordance with the provisions of this Convention and the law of the registering court, it is competent for any party to make an application to have the registration of the judgment set aside or, where such an application is made, until the application has been finally determined.

Article V

1.   For the purposes of Article IV(1)(c) the original court shall be regarded as having jurisdiction if

(a) the judgment debtor, being a defendant in the original court, submitted to the jurisdiction of that court by voluntarily appearing in the proceedings;

(b) the judgment debtor was plaintiff in, or counterclaimed in, the proceedings in the original court;

(c) the judgment debtor, being a defendant in the original court, had before the commencement of the proceedings agreed, in respect of the subject matter of the proceedings, to submit to the jurisdiction of that court or of the courts of the territory of origin;

(d) the judgment debtor, being a defendant in the original court, was at the time when the proceedings were instituted habitually resident in, or being a body corporate had its principal place of business in, the territory of origin;

(e) the judgment debtor, being a defendant in the original court, had an office or place of business in the territory of origin and the proceedings were in respect of a transaction effected through or at that office or place; or

(f) the jurisdiction of the original court is otherwise recognized by the registering court.

2. Notwithstanding anything in sub-paragraphs (d), (e) and (f) of paragraph (1), the original court shall not be regarded as having jurisdiction if

(a) the subject matter of the proceedings was immovable property outside the territory of origin; or

(b) the bringing of the proceedings in the original court was contrary to an agreement under which the dispute in question was to be settled otherwise than by proceedings in the courts of the territory of origin.

PART IV

Procedures

ARTICLE VI

1. Any application for the registration in the United Kingdom of a judgment of a court of Canada shall be made

(a) in England and Wales, to the High Court of Justice;

(b) in Scotland, to the Court of Session;

(c) in Northern Ireland, to the High Court of Justice.

2. Any application for the registration in Canada of a judgment of a court of the United Kingdom shall be made

(a) in the case of a judgment relating to a matter within the competence of the Federal Court of Canada, to the Federal Court of Canada;

(b) in the case of any other judgment, to a court of a province or territory designated by Canada pursuant to Article XII.

3. The practice and procedure governing registration (including notice to the judgment debtor and applications to set registration aside) shall, except as otherwise provided in this Convention, be governed by the law of the registering Court.

4. The registering court may require that an application for registration be accompanied by

(a) the judgment of the original court or a certified copy thereof;

(b) a certified translation of the judgment, if given in a language other than the language of the territory of the registering court;

(c) proof of the notice given to the defendant in the original proceedings, unless this appears from the judgment; and

(d) particulars of such other matters as may be required by the rules of the registering court.

ARTICLE VII

All matters concerning

(a) the conversion of the sum payable under a registered judgment into the currency of the territory of the registering court; and

(b) the interest payable on the judgment with respect to the period following its registration.

shall be determined by the law of the registering court.

PART V

Recognition of Judgments

ARTICLE VIII

Any judgment given by a court of one Contracting State for the payment of a sum of money which could be registered under this Convention, whether or not the judgment has been registered, and any other judgment given by such a court, which if it were a judgment for the payment of a sum of money could be registered under this Convention, shall, unless registration has been or would be refused or set aside on any ground other than that the judgment has been satisfied or could not be enforced in the territory of origin, be recognised in a court of the other Contracting State as conclusive between the parties thereto in all proceedings founded on the same cause of action.

PART VI

Recognition and Enforcement of Third State Judgments

ARTICLE IX

1. The United Kingdom undertakes, in the circumstances permitted by Article 59 of the 1968 Convention, not to recognise or enforce under that Convention any judgment given in a third State which is a Party to that Convention against a person domiciled or habitually resident in Canada.

2. For the purposes of paragraph (1)

(a) an individual shall be treated as domiciled in Canada if and only if he is resident in Canada and the nature and circumstances of his residence indicate that he has a substantial connection with Canada; and

(b) a corporation or association shall be treated as domiciled in Canada if and only if it is incorporated or formed under a law in force in Canada and has a registered office there, or its central management and control is exercised in Canada.

PART VII

Final Provisions

ARTICLE X

This Convention shall not affect any conventions, international instruments or reciprocal arrangements to which both Contracting States are or will be parties and which, in relation to particular matters, govern the recognition or enforcement of judgments.

ARTICLE XI

Either Contracting State may, on the exchange of instruments of ratification or at any time thereafter, declare that it will not apply the Convention to a judgment that imposes a liability which that State is under a treaty obligation toward any other State not to recognise or enforce. Any such declaration shall specify the treaty containing the obligation.

ARTICLE XII

1. On the exchange of instruments of ratification, Canada shall designate the provinces or territories to which this Convention shall extend[1] and the courts of the provinces and territories concerned to which application for the registration of a judgment given by a court of the United Kingdom may be made.

2. The designation by Canada may be modified by a further designation given at any time thereafter[2].

3. Any designation shall take effect three months after the date on which it is given.

ARTICLE XIII

1. The United Kingdom may at any time while this Convention is in force declare that this Convention shall extend to the Isle of Man, any of the Channel Islands, Gibraltar or the Sovereign Base Areas of Akrotiri and Dhekelia (being territories to which the 1968 Convention may be applied pursuant to Article 60 of that Convention).

2. Any declaration pursuant to paragraph (1) shall specify the courts of the territories to which application for the registration of a judgment given by a court of Canada shall be made.

1. On ratifying the Government of Canada declared that the Convention should extend to the provinces of British Columbia, Manitoba, New Brunswick, Nova Scotia and Ontario.

2. By later declarations the Convention was extended to the Yukon Territory with effect from 21 October 1987 and to the province of Prince Edward Island with effect from 17 September 1988.

3. Any declaration made by the United Kingdom pursuant to this Article may be modified by a further declaration given at any time thereafter.

4. Any declaration pursuant to this Article shall take effect three months after the date on which it is given.

ARTICLE XIV

1. This Convention shall be ratified; instruments of ratification shall be exchanged at London.

2. This Convention shall enter into force three months after the date on which instruments of ratification are exchanged.

3. This Convention may be terminated by notice in writing by either Contracting State and it shall terminate three months after the date of such notice.

In witness whereof, the undersigned, duly authorized thereto by their respective Governments, have signed this Convention.

Done in duplicate at Ottawa, this 24th day of April 1984 in the English and French languages, each version being equally authentic.

For the Government of the United Kingdom of Great Britain and Northern Ireland:
R.H. BAKER

For the Government of Canada:

JOHN C. TAIT

INTERNATIONAL ARBITRATION: RULES AND STATUTES

AMERICAN ARBITRATION ASSOCIATION COMMERCIAL ARBITRATION RULES

As amended July 1, 2003

R–1. Agreement of Parties* **

(a) The parties shall be deemed to have made these rules a part of their arbitration agreement whenever they have provided for arbitration by the American Arbitration Association (hereinafter AAA) under its Commercial Arbitration Rules or for arbitration by the AAA of a domestic commercial dispute without specifying particular rules. These rules and any amendment of them shall apply in the form in effect at the time the administrative requirements are met for a demand for arbitration or submission agreement received by the AAA. The parties, by written agreement, may vary the procedures set forth in these rules. After appointment of the arbitrator, such modifications may be made only with the consent of the arbitrator.

(b) Unless the parties or the AAA determines otherwise, the Expedited Procedures shall apply in any case in which no disclosed claim or counterclaim exceeds $75,000, exclusive of interest and arbitration fees and costs. Parties may also agree to use these procedures in larger cases. Unless the parties agree otherwise, these procedures will not apply in cases involving more than two parties. The Expedited Procedures shall be applied as described in Sections E–1 through E–10 of these rules, in

---

* The AAA applies the Supplementary Procedures for Consumer–Related Disputes to arbitration clauses in agreements between individual consumers and businesses where the business has a standardized, systematic application of arbitration clauses with customers and where the terms and conditions of the purchase of standardized, consumable goods or services are nonnegotiable or primarily non-negotiable in most or all of its terms, conditions, features, or choices. The product or service must be for personal or household use. The AAA will have the discretion to apply or not to apply the Supplementary Procedures and the parties will be able to bring any disputes concerning the application or non-application to the attention of the arbitrator. Consumers are not prohibited from seeking relief in a small claims court for disputes or claims within the scope of its jurisdiction, even in consumer arbitration cases filed by the business.

** A dispute arising out of an employer promulgated plan will be administered under the AAA's National Rules for the Resolution of Employment Disputes.

addition to any other portion of these rules that is not in conflict with the Expedited Procedures.

(c) Unless the parties agree otherwise, the Procedures for Large, Complex Commercial Disputes shall apply to all cases in which the disclosed claim or counterclaim of any party is at least $500,000, exclusive of claimed interest, arbitration fees and costs. Parties may also agree to use the Procedures in cases involving claims or counterclaims under $500,000, or in nonmonetary cases. The Procedures for Large, Complex Commercial Disputes shall be applied as described in Sections L–1 through L–4 of these rules, in addition to any other portion of these rules that is not in conflict with the Procedures for Large, Complex Commercial Disputes.

(d) All other cases shall be administered in accordance with Sections R–1 through R–54 of these rules.

R–2. AAA and Delegation of Duties

When parties agree to arbitrate under these rules, or when they provide for arbitration by the AAA and an arbitration is initiated under these rules, they thereby authorize the AAA to administer the arbitration. The authority and duties of the AAA are prescribed in the agreement of the parties and in these rules, and may be carried out through such of the AAA's representatives as it may direct. The AAA may, in its discretion, assign the administration of an arbitration to any of its offices.

R–3. National Roster of Arbitrators

The AAA shall establish and maintain a National Roster of Commercial Arbitrators ("National Roster") and shall appoint arbitrators as provided in these rules. The term "arbitrator" in these rules refers to the arbitration panel, constituted for a particular case, whether composed of one or more arbitrators, or to an individual arbitrator, as the context requires.

R–4. Initiation Under an Arbitration Provision in a Contract

(a) Arbitration under an arbitration provision in a contract shall be initiated in the following manner:

(i) The initiating party (the "claimant") shall, within the time period, if any, specified in the contract(s), give to the other party (the "respondent") written notice of its intention to arbitrate (the "demand"), which demand shall contain a statement setting forth the nature of the dispute, the names and addresses of all other parties, the amount involved, if any, the remedy sought, and the hearing locale requested.

(ii) The claimant shall file at any office of the AAA two copies of the demand and two copies of the arbitration provisions of the contract, together with the appropriate filing fee as provided in the schedule included with these rules.

(iii) The AAA shall confirm notice of such filing to the parties.

(b) A respondent may file an answering statement in duplicate with the AAA within 15 days after confirmation of notice of filing of the demand is sent by the AAA. The respondent shall, at the time of any such filing, send a copy of the answering statement to the claimant. If a counterclaim is asserted, it shall contain a statement setting forth the nature of the counterclaim, the amount involved, if any, and the remedy sought. If a counterclaim is made, the party making the counterclaim shall forward to the AAA with the answering statement the appropriate fee provided in the schedule included with these rules.

(c) If no answering statement is filed within the stated time, respondent will be deemed to deny the claim. Failure to file an answering statement shall not operate to delay the arbitration.

(d) When filing any statement pursuant to this section, the parties are encouraged to provide descriptions of their claims in sufficient detail to make the circumstances of the dispute clear to the arbitrator.

R–5. Initiation Under a Submission

Parties to any existing dispute may commence an arbitration under these rules by filing at any office of the AAA two copies of a written submission to arbitrate under these rules, signed by the parties. It shall contain a statement of the nature of the dispute, the names and addresses of all parties, any claims and counterclaims, the amount involved, if any, the remedy sought, and the hearing locale requested, together with the appropriate filing fee as provided in the schedule included with these rules. Unless the parties state otherwise in the submission, all claims and counterclaims will be deemed to be denied by the other party.

R–6. Changes of Claim

After filing of a claim, if either party desires to make any new or different claim or counterclaim, it shall be made in writing and filed with the AAA. The party asserting such a claim or counterclaim shall provide a copy to the other party, who shall have 15 days from the date of such transmission within which to file an answering statement with the AAA. After the arbitrator is appointed, however, no new or different claim may be submitted except with the arbitrator's consent.

R–7. Jurisdiction

(a) The arbitrator shall have the power to rule on his or her own jurisdiction, including any objections with respect to the existence, scope or validity of the arbitration agreement.

(b) The arbitrator shall have the power to determine the existence or validity of a contract of which an arbitration clause forms a part. Such an arbitration clause shall be treated as an agreement independent of the other terms of the contract. A decision by the arbitrator that the contract is null and void shall not for that reason alone render invalid the arbitration clause.

(c) A party must object to the jurisdiction of the arbitrator or to the arbitrability of a claim or counterclaim no later than the filing of the answering statement to the claim or counterclaim that gives rise to the objection. The arbitrator may rule on such objections as a preliminary matter or as part of the final award.

R–8. Mediation

At any stage of the proceedings, the parties may agree to conduct a mediation conference under the Commercial Mediation Procedures in order to facilitate settlement. The mediator shall not be an arbitrator appointed to the case. Where the parties to a pending arbitration agree to mediate under the AAA's rules, no additional administrative fee is required to initiate the mediation.

R–9. Administrative Conference

At the request of any party or upon the AAA's own initiative, the AAA may conduct an administrative conference, in person or by telephone, with the parties and/or their representatives. The conference may address such issues as arbitrator selection, potential mediation of the dispute, potential exchange of information, a timetable for hearings and any other administrative matters.

R–10. Fixing of Locale

The parties may mutually agree on the locale where the arbitration is to be held. If any party requests that the hearing be held in a specific locale and the other party files no objection thereto within 15 days after notice of the request has been sent to it by the AAA, the locale shall be the one requested. If a party objects to the locale requested by the other party, the AAA shall have the power to determine the locale, and its decision shall be final and binding.

R–11. Appointment from National Roster

If the parties have not appointed an arbitrator and have not provided any other method of appointment, the arbitrator shall be appointed in the following manner:

(a) Immediately after the filing of the submission or the answering statement or the expiration of the time within which the answering statement is to be filed, the AAA shall send simultaneously to each party to the dispute an identical list of 10 (unless the AAA decides that a different number is appropriate) names of persons chosen from the National Roster. The parties are encouraged to agree to an arbitrator from the submitted list and to advise the AAA of their agreement.

(b) If the parties are unable to agree upon an arbitrator, each party to the dispute shall have 15 days from the transmittal date in which to strike names objected to, number the remaining names in order of preference, and return the list to the AAA. If a party does not return the list within the time specified, all persons named therein shall be deemed acceptable. From among the persons who have been approved on both lists, and in accordance with the designated order of mutual preference, the AAA shall invite the acceptance of an arbitrator to serve. If the parties fail to agree on any of the persons named, or if acceptable arbitrators are unable to act, or if for any other reason the appointment cannot be made from the submitted lists, the AAA shall have the power to make the appointment from among other members of the National Roster without the submission of additional lists.

(c) Unless the parties agree otherwise when there are two or more claimants or two or more respondents, the AAA may appoint all the arbitrators.

R–12.   Direct Appointment by a Party

(a) If the agreement of the parties names an arbitrator or specifies a method of appointing an arbitrator, that designation or method shall be followed. The notice of appointment, with the name and address of the arbitrator, shall be filed with the AAA by the appointing party. Upon the request of any appointing party, the AAA shall submit a list of members of the National Roster from which the party may, if it so desires, make the appointment.

(b) Where the parties have agreed that each party is to name one arbitrator, the arbitrators so named must meet the standards of Section R–17 with respect to impartiality and independence unless the parties have specifically agreed pursuant to Section R–17(a) that the party-appointed arbitrators are to be non-neutral and need not meet those standards.

(c) If the agreement specifies a period of time within which an arbitrator shall be appointed and any party fails to make the appointment within that period, the AAA shall make the appointment.

(d) If no period of time is specified in the agreement, the AAA shall notify the party to make the appointment. If within 15 days after such notice has been sent, an arbitrator has not been appointed by a party, the AAA shall make the appointment.

R–13.   Appointment of Chairperson by Party–Appointed Arbitrators or Parties

(a) If, pursuant to Section R–12, either the parties have directly appointed arbitrators, or the arbitrators have been appointed by the AAA, and the parties have authorized them to appoint a chairperson within a specified time and no appointment is made within that time or any agreed extension, the AAA may appoint the chairperson.

(b) If no period of time is specified for appointment of the chairperson and the party-appointed arbitrators or the parties do not make the appointment within 15 days from the date of the appointment of the last party-appointed arbitrator, the AAA may appoint the chairperson.

(c) If the parties have agreed that their party-appointed arbitrators shall appoint the chairperson from the National Roster, the AAA shall furnish to the party-appointed arbitrators, in the manner provided in Section R–11, a list selected from the National Roster, and the appointment of the chairperson shall be made as provided in that Section.

R–14. Nationality of Arbitrator

Where the parties are nationals of different countries, the AAA, at the request of any party or on its own initiative, may appoint as arbitrator a national of a country other than that of any of the parties. The request must be made before the time set for the appointment of the arbitrator as agreed by the parties or set by these rules.

R–15. Number of Arbitrators

If the arbitration agreement does not specify the number of arbitrators, the dispute shall be heard and determined by one arbitrator, unless the AAA, in its discretion, directs that three arbitrators be appointed. A party may request three arbitrators in the demand or answer, which request the AAA will consider in exercising its discretion regarding the number of arbitrators appointed to the dispute.

R–16. Disclosure

(a) Any person appointed or to be appointed as an arbitrator shall disclose to the AAA any circumstance likely to give rise to justifiable doubt as to the arbitrator's impartiality or independence, including any bias or any financial or personal interest in the result of the arbitration or any past or present relationship with the parties or their representatives. Such obligation shall remain in effect throughout the arbitration.

(b) Upon receipt of such information from the arbitrator or another source, the AAA shall communicate the information to the parties and, if it deems it appropriate to do so, to the arbitrator and others.

(c) In order to encourage disclosure by arbitrators, disclosure of information pursuant to this Section R–16 is not to be construed as an indication that the arbitrator considers that the disclosed circumstance is likely to affect impartiality or independence.

R–17. Disqualification of Arbitrator

(a) Any arbitrator shall be impartial and independent and shall perform his or her duties with diligence and in good faith, and shall be subject to disqualification for

(i) partiality or lack of independence,

(ii) inability or refusal to perform his or her duties with diligence and in good faith, and

(iii) any grounds for disqualification provided by applicable law. The parties may agree in writing, however, that arbitrators directly appointed by a party pursuant to Section R–12 shall be nonneutral, in which case such arbitrators need not be impartial or independent and shall not be subject to disqualification for partiality or lack of independence.

(b) Upon objection of a party to the continued service of an arbitrator, or on its own initiative, the AAA shall determine whether the arbitrator should be disqualified under the grounds set out above, and shall inform the parties of its decision, which decision shall be conclusive.

R–18. Communication with Arbitrator

(a) No party and no one acting on behalf of any party shall communicate ex parte with an arbitrator or a candidate for arbitrator concerning the arbitration, except that a party, or someone acting on behalf of a party, may communicate ex parte with a candidate for direct appointment pursuant to Section R–12 in order to advise the candidate of the general nature of the controversy and of the anticipated proceedings and to discuss the candidate's qualifications, availability, or independence in relation to the parties or to discuss the suitability of candidates for selection as a third arbitrator where the parties or party-designated arbitrators are to participate in that selection.

(b) Section R–18(a) does not apply to arbitrators directly appointed by the parties who, pursuant to Section R–17(a), the parties have agreed in writing are non-neutral. Where the parties have so agreed under Section R–17(a), the AAA shall as an administrative practice suggest to the parties that they agree further that Section R–18(a) should nonetheless apply prospectively.

R–19. Vacancies

(a) If for any reason an arbitrator is unable to perform the duties of the office, the AAA may, on proof satisfactory to it, declare the office vacant. Vacancies shall be filled in accordance with the applicable provisions of these rules.

(b) In the event of a vacancy in a panel of neutral arbitrators after the hearings have commenced, the remaining arbitrator or arbitrators may continue with the hearing and determination of the controversy, unless the parties agree otherwise.

(c) In the event of the appointment of a substitute arbitrator, the panel of arbitrators shall determine in its sole discretion whether it is necessary to repeat all or part of any prior hearings.

R–20. Preliminary Hearing

(a) At the request of any party or at the discretion of the arbitrator or the AAA, the arbitrator may schedule as soon as practicable a preliminary hearing with the parties and/or their representatives. The preliminary hearing may be conducted by telephone at the arbitrator's discretion.

(b) During the preliminary hearing, the parties and the arbitrator should discuss the future conduct of the case, including clarification of the issues and claims, a schedule for the hearings and any other preliminary matters.

R–21. Exchange of Information

(a) At the request of any party or at the discretion of the arbitrator, consistent with the expedited nature of arbitration, the arbitrator may direct

       i) the production of documents and other information, and

       ii) the identification of any witnesses to be called.

(b) At least five business days prior to the hearing, the parties shall exchange copies of all exhibits they intend to submit at the hearing.

(c) The arbitrator is authorized to resolve any disputes concerning the exchange of information.

R–22. Date, Time, and Place of Hearing

The arbitrator shall set the date, time, and place for each hearing. The parties shall respond to requests for hearing dates in a timely manner, be cooperative in scheduling the earliest practicable date, and adhere to the established hearing schedule. The AAA shall send a notice of hearing to the parties at least 10 days in advance of the hearing date, unless otherwise agreed by the parties.

R–23. Attendance at Hearings

The arbitrator and the AAA shall maintain the privacy of the hearings unless the law provides to the contrary. Any person having a direct interest in the arbitration is entitled to attend hearings. The arbitrator shall otherwise have the power to require the exclusion of any witness, other than a party or other essential person, during the testimony of any other witness. It shall be discretionary with the arbitrator to determine the propriety of the attendance of any other person other than a party and its representatives.

R–24. Representation

Any party may be represented by counsel or other authorized representative. A party intending to be so represented shall notify the other party and the AAA of the name and address of the representative at least three days prior to the date set for the hearing at which that person is first to appear. When such a representative initiates an arbitration or responds for a party, notice is deemed to have been given.

R–25. Oaths

Before proceeding with the first hearing, each arbitrator may take an oath of office and, if required by law, shall do so. The arbitrator may require witnesses to testify under oath administered by any duly qualified person and, if it is required by law or requested by any party, shall do so.

R–26. Stenographic Record

Any party desiring a stenographic record shall make arrangements directly with a stenographer and shall notify the other parties of these arrangements at least three days in advance of the hearing. The requesting party or parties shall pay the cost of the record. If the transcript is agreed by the parties, or determined by the arbitrator to be the official record of the proceeding, it must be provided to the arbitrator and made available to the other parties for inspection, at a date, time, and place determined by the arbitrator.

R–27. Interpreters

Any party wishing an interpreter shall make all arrangements directly with the interpreter and shall assume the costs of the service.

R–28. Postponements

The arbitrator may postpone any hearing upon agreement of the parties, upon request of a party for good cause shown, or upon the arbitrator's own initiative.

R–29. Arbitration in the Absence of a Party or Representative

Unless the law provides to the contrary, the arbitration may proceed in the absence of any party or representative who, after due notice, fails to be present or fails to obtain a postponement. An award shall not be made solely on the default of a party. The arbitrator shall require the party who is present to submit such evidence as the arbitrator may require for the making of an award.

R–30. Conduct of Proceedings

(a) The claimant shall present evidence to support its claim. The respondent shall then present evidence to support its defense. Witnesses for each party shall also submit to questions from the arbitrator and the adverse party. The arbitrator has the discretion to vary this procedure, provided that the parties are treated with equality and that each party has the right to be heard and is given a fair opportunity to present its case.

(b) The arbitrator, exercising his or her discretion, shall conduct the proceedings with a view to expediting the resolution of the dispute and may direct the order of proof, bifurcate proceedings and direct the parties to focus their presentations on issues the decision of which could dispose of all or part of the case.

(c) The parties may agree to waive oral hearings in any case.

R–31. Evidence

(a) The parties may offer such evidence as is relevant and material to the dispute and shall produce such evidence as the arbitrator may deem necessary to an understanding and determination of the dispute. Conformity to legal rules of evidence shall not be necessary. All evidence shall be taken in the presence of all of the arbitrators and all of the parties, except where any of the parties is absent, in default or has waived the right to be present.

(b) The arbitrator shall determine the admissibility, relevance, and materiality of the evidence offered and may exclude evidence deemed by the arbitrator to be cumulative or irrelevant.

(c) The arbitrator shall take into account applicable principles of legal privilege, such as those involving the confidentiality of communications between a lawyer and client.

(d) An arbitrator or other person authorized by law to subpoena witnesses or documents may do so upon the request of any party or independently.

R–32. Evidence by Affidavit and Post-hearing Filing of Documents or Other Evidence

(a) The arbitrator may receive and consider the evidence of witnesses by declaration or affidavit, but shall give it only such weight as the arbitrator deems it entitled to after consideration of any objection made to its admission.

(b) If the parties agree or the arbitrator directs that documents or other evidence be submitted to the arbitrator after the hearing, the documents or other evidence shall be filed with the AAA for transmission to the arbitrator. All parties shall be afforded an opportunity to examine and respond to such documents or other evidence.

R–33. Inspection or Investigation

An arbitrator finding it necessary to make an inspection or investigation in connection with the arbitration shall direct the AAA to so advise the parties. The arbitrator shall set the date and time and the AAA shall notify the parties. Any party who so desires may be present at such an inspection or investigation. In the event that one or all parties are not present at the inspection or investigation, the arbitrator shall make an oral or written report to the parties and afford them an opportunity to comment.

R–34. Interim Measures**

(a) The arbitrator may take whatever interim measures he or she deems necessary, including injunctive relief and measures for the protection or conservation of property and disposition of perishable goods.

(b) Such interim measures may take the form of an interim award, and the arbitrator may require security for the costs of such measures.

** The Optional Rules may be found below.

(c) A request for interim measures addressed by a party to a judicial authority shall not be deemed incompatible with the agreement to arbitrate or a waiver of the right to arbitrate.

R–35. Closing of Hearing

The arbitrator shall specifically inquire of all parties whether they have any further proofs to offer or witnesses to be heard. Upon receiving negative replies or if satisfied that the record is complete, the arbitrator shall declare the hearing closed. If briefs are to be filed, the hearing shall b e declared closed as of the final date set by the arbitrator for the receipt of briefs. If documents are to be filed as provided in Section R–32 and the date set for their receipt is later than that set for the receipt of briefs, the later date shall be the closing date of the hearing. The time limit within which the arbitrator is required to make the award shall commence, in the absence of other agreements by the parties, upon the closing of the hearing.

R–36. Reopening of Hearing

The hearing may be reopened on the arbitrator's initiative, or upon application of a party, at any time before the award is made. If reopening the hearing would prevent the making of the award within the specific time agreed on by the parties in the contract(s) out of which the controversy has arisen, the matter may not be reopened unless the parties agree on an extension of time. When no specific date is fixed in the contract, the arbitrator may reopen the hearing and shall have 30 days from the closing of the reopened hearing within which to make an award.

R–37. Waiver of Rules

Any party who proceeds with the arbitration after knowledge that any provision or requirement of these rules has not been complied with and who fails to state an objection in writing shall be deemed to have waived the right to object.

R–38. Extensions of Time

The parties may modify any period of time by mutual agreement. The AAA or the arbitrator may for good cause extend any period of time established by these rules, except the time for making the award. The AAA shall notify the parties of any extension.

R–39. Serving of Notice

(a) Any papers, notices, or process necessary or proper for the initiation or continuation of an arbitration under these rules, for any court action in connection therewith, or for the entry of judgment on any award made under these rules may be served on a party by mail addressed to the party, or its representative at the last known address or by personal service, in or outside the state where the arbitration is to be held, provided that reasonable opportunity to be heard with regard to the dispute is or has been granted to the party.

(b) The AAA, the arbitrator and the parties may also use overnight delivery or electronic facsimile transmission (fax), to give the notices required by these rules. Where all parties and the arbitrator agree, notices may be transmitted by electronic mail (E-mail), or other methods of communication.

(c) Unless otherwise instructed by the AAA or by the arbitrator, any documents submitted by any party to the AAA or to the arbitrator shall simultaneously be provided to the other party or parties to the arbitration.

R–40. Majority Decision

When the panel consists of more than one arbitrator, unless required by law or by the arbitration agreement, a majority of the arbitrators must make all decisions.

R–41. Time of Award

The award shall be made promptly by the arbitrator and, unless otherwise agreed by the parties or specified by law, no later than 30 days from the date of closing the hearing, or, if oral hearings have been waived, from the date of the AAA's transmittal of the final statements and proofs to the arbitrator.

R–42. Form of Award

(a) Any award shall be in writing and signed by a majority of the arbitrators. It shall be executed in the manner required by law.

(b) The arbitrator need not render a reasoned award unless the parties request such an award in writing prior to appointment of the arbitrator or unless the arbitrator determines that a reasoned award is appropriate.

R–43. Scope of Award

(a) The arbitrator may grant any remedy or relief that the arbitrator deems just and equitable and within the scope of the agreement of the parties, including, but not limited to, specific performance of a contract.

(b) In addition to a final award, the arbitrator may make other decisions, including interim, interlocutory, or partial rulings, orders, and awards. In any interim, interlocutory, or partial award, the arbitrator may assess and apportion the fees, expenses, and compensation related to such award as the arbitrator determines is appropriate.

(c) In the final award, the arbitrator shall assess the fees, expenses, and compensation provided in Sections R–49, R–50, and R–51. The arbitrator may apportion such fees, expenses, and compensation among the parties in such amounts as the arbitrator determines is appropriate.

(d) The award of the arbitrator(s) may include:

(i) interest at such rate and from such date as the arbitrator(s) may deem appropriate; and

(ii) an award of attorneys' fees if all parties have requested such an award or it is authorized by law or their arbitration agreement.

R–44. Award upon Settlement

If the parties settle their dispute during the course of the arbitration and if the parties so request, the arbitrator may set forth the terms of the settlement in a "consent award." A consent award must include an allocation of arbitration costs, including administrative fees and expenses as well as arbitrator fees and expenses.

R–45. Delivery of Award to Parties

Parties shall accept as notice and delivery of the award the placing of the award or a true copy thereof in the mail addressed to the parties or their representatives at the last known addresses, personal or electronic service of the award, or the filing of the award in any other manner that is permitted by law.

R–46. Modification of Award

Within 20 days after the transmittal of an award, any party, upon notice to the other parties, may request the arbitrator, through the AAA, to correct any clerical, typographical, or computational errors in the award. The arbitrator is not empowered to redetermine the merits of any claim already decided. The other parties shall be given 10 days to respond to the request. The arbitrator shall dispose of the request within 20 days after transmittal by the AAA to the arbitrator of the request and any response thereto.

R–47. Release of Documents for Judicial Proceedings

The AAA shall, upon the written request of a party, furnish to the party, at the party's expense, certified copies of any papers in the AAA's possession that may be required in judicial proceedings relating to the arbitration.

R–48. Applications to Court and Exclusion of Liability

(a) No judicial proceeding by a party relating to the subject matter of the arbitration shall be deemed a waiver of the party's right to arbitrate.

(b) Neither the AAA nor any arbitrator in a proceeding under these rules is a necessary or proper party in judicial proceedings relating to the arbitration.

(c) Parties to an arbitration under these rules shall be deemed to have consented that judgment upon the arbitration award may be entered in any federal or state court having jurisdiction thereof.

(d) Parties to an arbitration under these rules shall be deemed to have consented that neither the AAA nor any arbitrator shall be liable to any party in any action for damages or injunctive relief for any act or omission in connection with any arbitration under these rules.

R–49.   Administrative Fees

As a not-for-profit organization, the AAA shall prescribe an initial filing fee and a case service fee to compensate it for the cost of providing administrative services. The fees in effect when the fee or charge is incurred shall be applicable. The filing fee shall be advanced by the party or parties making a claim or counterclaim, subject to final apportionment by the arbitrator in the award. The AAA may, in the event of extreme hardship on the part of any party, defer or reduce the administrative fees.

R–50.   Expenses

The expenses of witnesses for either side shall be paid by the party producing such witnesses. All other expenses of the arbitration, including required travel and other expenses of the arbitrator, AAA representatives, and any witness and the cost of any proof produced at the direct request of the arbitrator, shall be borne equally by the parties, unless they agree otherwise or unless the arbitrator in the award assesses such expenses or any part thereof against any specified party or parties.

R–51.   Neutral Arbitrator's Compensation

(a) Arbitrators shall be compensated at a rate consistent with the arbitrator's stated rate of compensation.

(b) If there is disagreement concerning the terms of compensation, an appropriate rate shall be established with the arbitrator by the AAA and confirmed to the parties.

(c) Any arrangement for the compensation of a neutral arbitrator shall be made through the AAA and not directly between the parties and the arbitrator.

R–52.   Deposits

The AAA may require the parties to deposit in advance of any hearings such sums of money as it deems necessary to cover the expense of the arbitration, including the arbitrator's fee, if any, and shall render an accounting to the parties and return any unexpended balance at the conclusion of the case.

R–53.   Interpretation and Application of Rules

The arbitrator shall interpret and apply these rules insofar as they relate to the arbitrator's powers and duties. When there is more than one arbitrator and a difference arises among them concerning the meaning or application of these rules, it shall be decided by a majority vote. If that is not possible, either an arbitrator or a party may refer the question to the AAA for final decision. All other rules shall be interpreted and applied by the AAA.

R–54.   Suspension for Nonpayment

If arbitrator compensation or administrative charges have not been paid in full, the AAA may so inform the parties in order that one of them may advance the required payment. If such payments are not made, the arbitrator may order the suspension or termination of the proceedings. If no arbitrator has yet been appointed, the AAA may suspend the proceedings.

EXPEDITED PROCEDURES

E–1. Limitation on Extensions

Except in extraordinary circumstances, the AAA or the arbitrator may grant a party no more than one seven-day extension of time to respond to the demand for arbitration or counterclaim as provided in Section R–4.

E–2. Changes of Claim or Counterclaim

A claim or counterclaim may be increased in amount, or a new or different claim or counterclaim added, upon the agreement of the other party, or the consent of the arbitrator. After the arbitrator is appointed, however, no new or different claim or counterclaim may be submitted except with the arbitrator's consent. If an increased claim or counterclaim exceeds $75,000, the case will be administered under the regular procedures unless all parties and the arbitrator agree that the case may continue to be processed under the Expedited Procedures.

E–3. Serving of Notices

In addition to notice provided by Section R–39(b), the parties shall also accept notice by telephone. Telephonic notices by the AAA shall subsequently be confirmed in writing to the parties. Should there be a failure to confirm in writing any such oral notice, the proceeding shall nevertheless be valid if notice has, in fact, been given by telephone.

E–4. Appointment and Qualifications of Arbitrator

(a) The AAA shall simultaneously submit to each party an identical list of five proposed arbitrators drawn from its National Roster from which one arbitrator shall be appointed.

(b) The parties are encouraged to agree to an arbitrator from this list and to advise the AAA of their agreement. If the parties are unable to agree upon an arbitrator, each party may strike two names from the list and return it to the AAA within seven days from the date of the AAA's mailing to the parties. If for any reason the appointment of an arbitrator cannot be made from the list, the AAA may make the appointment from other members of the panel without the submission of additional lists.

(c) The parties will be given notice by the AAA of the appointment of the arbitrator, who shall be subject to disqualification for the reasons specified in Section R–17. The parties shall notify the AAA within seven days of any objection to the arbitrator appointed. Any such objection shall be for cause and shall be confirmed in writing to the AAA with a copy to the other party or parties.

E–5. Exchange of Exhibits

At least two business days prior to the hearing, the parties shall exchange copies of all exhibits they intend to submit at the hearing. The arbitrator shall resolve disputes concerning the exchange of exhibits.

E–6. Proceedings on Documents

Where no party's claim exceeds $10,000, exclusive of interest and arbitration costs, and other cases in which the parties agree, the dispute shall be resolved by submission of documents, unless any party requests an oral hearing, or the arbitrator determines that an oral hearing is necessary. The arbitrator shall establish a fair and equitable procedure for the submission of documents.

E–7. Date, Time, and Place of Hearing

In cases in which a hearing is to be held, the arbitrator shall set the date, time, and place of the hearing, to be scheduled to take place within 30 days of confirmation of the arbitrator's appointment. The AAA will notify the parties in advance of the hearing date.

E–8. The Hearing

(a) Generally, the hearing shall not exceed one day. Each party shall have equal opportunity to submit its proofs and complete its case. The arbitrator shall determine the order of the hearing, and may require further submission of documents within two days after the hearing. For good cause shown, the arbitrator may schedule additional hearings within seven business days after the initial day of hearings.

(b) Generally, there will be no stenographic record. Any party desiring a stenographic record may arrange for one pursuant to the provisions of Section R–26.

E–9. Time of Award

Unless otherwise agreed by the parties, the award shall be rendered not later than 14 days from the date of the closing of the hearing or, if oral hearings have been waived, from the date of the AAA's transmittal of the final statements and proofs to the arbitrator.

E–10. Arbitrator's Compensation

Arbitrators will receive compensation at a rate to be suggested by the AAA regional office.

PROCEDURES FOR LARGE, COMPLEX COMMERCIAL DISPUTES

L–1. Administrative Conference

Prior to the dissemination of a list of potential arbitrators, the AAA shall, unless the parties agree otherwise, conduct an administrative conference with the parties and/or their attorneys or other representatives by conference call. The conference will take place within 14 days after the commencement of the arbitration. In the event the parties are unable to agree on a mutually acceptable time for the conference, the

AAA may contact the parties individually to discuss the issues contemplated herein. Such administrative conference shall be conducted for the following purposes and for such additional purposes as the parties or the AAA may deem appropriate:

(a) to obtain additional information about the nature and magnitude of the dispute and the anticipated length of hearing and scheduling;

(b) to discuss the views of the parties about the technical and other qualifications of the arbitrators;

(c) to obtain conflicts statements from the parties; and

(d) to consider, with the parties, whether mediation or other non-adjudicative methods of dispute resolution might be appropriate.

L–2. Arbitrators

(a) Large, Complex Commercial Cases shall be heard and determined by either one or three arbitrators, as may be agreed upon by the parties. If the parties are unable to agree upon the number of arbitrators and a claim or counterclaim involves at least $1,000,000, then three arbitrator(s) shall hear and determine the case. If the parties are unable to agree on the number of arbitrators and each claim and counterclaim is less than $1,000,000, then one arbitrator shall hear and determine the case.

(b) The AAA shall appoint arbitrator(s) as agreed by the parties. If they are unable to agree on a method of appointment, the AAA shall appoint arbitrators from the Large, Complex Commercial Case Panel, in the manner provided in the Regular Commercial Arbitration Rules. Absent agreement of the parties, the arbitrator(s) shall not have served as the mediator in the mediation phase of the instant proceeding.

L–3. Preliminary Hearing

As promptly as practicable after the selection of the arbitrator(s), a preliminary hearing shall be held among the parties and/or their attorneys or other representatives and the arbitrator(s). Unless the parties agree otherwise, the preliminary hearing will be conducted by telephone conference call rather than in person. At the preliminary hearing the matters to be considered shall include, without limitation:

(a) service of a detailed statement of claims, damages and defenses, a statement of the issues asserted by each party and positions with respect thereto, and any legal authorities the parties may wish to bring to the attention of the arbitrator(s);

(b) stipulations to uncontested facts;

(c) the extent to which discovery shall be conducted;

(d) exchange and premarking of those documents which each party believes may be offered at the hearing;

(e) the identification and availability of witnesses, including experts, and such matters with respect to witnesses including their biographies and expected testimony as may be appropriate;

(f) whether, and the extent to which, any sworn statements and/or depositions may be introduced;

(g) the extent to which hearings will proceed on consecutive days;

(h) whether a stenographic or other official record of the proceedings shall be maintained;

(i) the possibility of utilizing mediation or other non-adjudicative methods of dispute resolution; and

(j) the procedure for the issuance of subpoenas.

By agreement of the parties and/or order of the arbitrator(s), the pre-hearing activities and the hearing procedures that will govern the arbitration will be memorialized in a Scheduling and Procedure Order.

L–4. Management of Proceedings

(a) Arbitrator(s) shall take such steps as they may deem necessary or desirable to avoid delay and to achieve a just, speedy and cost-effective resolution of Large, Complex Commercial Cases.

(b) Parties shall cooperate in the exchange of documents, exhibits and information within such party's control if the arbitrator(s) consider such production to be consistent with the goal of achieving a just, speedy and cost-effective resolution of a Large, Complex Commercial Case.

(c) The parties may conduct such discovery as may be agreed to by all the parties provided, however, that the arbitrator(s) may place such limitations on the conduct of such discovery as the arbitrator(s) shall deem appropriate. If the parties cannot agree on production of documents and other information, the arbitrator(s), consistent with the expedited nature of arbitration, may establish the extent of the discovery.

(d) At the discretion of the arbitrator(s), upon good cause shown and consistent with the expedited nature of arbitration, the arbitrator(s) may order depositions of, or the propounding of interrogatories to, such persons who may possess information determined by the arbitrator(s) to be necessary to determination of the matter.

(e) The parties shall exchange copies of all exhibits they intend to submit at the hearing 10 business days prior to the hearing unless the arbitrator(s) determine otherwise.

(f) The exchange of information pursuant to this rule, as agreed by the parties and/or directed by the arbitrator(s), shall be included within the Scheduling and Procedure Order.

(g) The arbitrator is authorized to resolve any disputes concerning the exchange of information.

(h) Generally hearings will be scheduled on consecutive days or in blocks of consecutive days in order to maximize efficiency and minimize costs.

OPTIONAL RULES FOR EMERGENCY MEASURES OF PROTECTION

O–1. Applicability

Where parties by special agreement or in their arbitration clause have adopted these rules for emergency measures of protection, a party in need of emergency relief prior to the constitution of the panel shall notify the AAA and all other parties in writing of the nature of the relief sought and the reasons why such relief is required on an emergency basis. The application shall also set forth the reasons why the party is entitled to such relief. Such notice may be given by facsimile transmission, or other reliable means, but must include a statement certifying that all other parties have been notified or an explanation of the steps taken in good faith to notify other parties.

O–2. Appointment of Emergency Arbitrator

Within one business day of receipt of notice as provided in Section O 1, the AAA shall appoint a single emergency arbitrator from a special AAA panel of emergency arbitrators designated to rule on emergency applications. The emergency arbitrator shall immediately disclose any circumstance likely, on the basis of the facts disclosed in the application, to affect such arbitrator's impartiality or independence. Any challenge to the appointment of the emergency arbitrator must be made within one business day of the communication by the AAA to the parties of the appointment of the emergency arbitrator and the circumstances disclosed.

O–3. Schedule

The emergency arbitrator shall as soon as possible, but in any event within two business days of appointment, establish a schedule for consideration of the application for emergency relief. Such schedule shall provide a reasonable opportunity to all parties to be heard, but may provide for proceeding by telephone conference or on written submissions as alternatives to a formal hearing.

O–4. Interim Award

If after consideration the emergency arbitrator is satisfied that the party seeking the emergency relief has shown that immediate and irreparable loss or damage will result in the absence of emergency relief, and that such party is entitled to such relief, the emergency arbitrator may enter an interim award granting the relief and stating the reasons therefore.

O–5. Constitution of the Panel

Any application to modify an interim award of emergency relief must be based on changed circumstances and may be made to the emergency arbitrator until the panel is constituted; thereafter such a request shall be addressed to the panel. The emergency arbitrator shall have no further power to act after the panel is constituted unless the parties agree that the emergency arbitrator is named as a member of the panel.

O–6. Security

Any interim award of emergency relief may be conditioned on provision by the party seeking such relief of appropriate security.

O–7. Special Master

A request for interim measures addressed by a party to a judicial authority shall not be deemed incompatible with the agreement to arbitrate or a waiver of the right to arbitrate. If the AAA is directed by a judicial authority to nominate a special master to consider and report on an application for emergency relief, the AAA shall proceed as provided in Section O–1 of this article and the references to the emergency arbitrator shall be read to mean the special master, except that the special master shall issue a report rather than an interim award.

O–8. Costs

The costs associated with applications for emergency relief shall initially be apportioned by the emergency arbitrator or special master, subject to the power of the panel to determine finally the apportionment of such costs.

ADMINISTRATIVE FEES

The administrative fees of the AAA are based on the amount of the claim or counterclaim. Arbitrator compensation is not included in this schedule. Unless the parties agree otherwise, arbitrator compensation and administrative fees are subject to allocation by the arbitrator in the award.

In an effort to make arbitration costs reasonable for consumers, the AAA has a separate fee schedule for consumer-related disputes. Please refer to Section C–8 of the Supplementary Procedures for Consumer–Related Disputes when filing a consumer-related claim.

The AAA applies the Supplementary Procedures for Consumer–Related Disputes to arbitration clauses in agreements between individual consumers and businesses where the business has a standardized, systematic application of arbitration clauses with customers and where the terms and conditions of the purchase of standardized, consumable goods or services are non-negotiable or primarily non-negotiable in most or all of its terms, conditions, features, or choices. The product or service must be for personal or household use. The AAA will have the discretion to apply or not to apply the Supplementary Procedures and the parties will be able to bring any disputes concerning the application or non-application to the attention of the arbitrator. Consumers are not prohibited from seeking relief in a small claims court for disputes or claims within the scope of its jurisdiction, even in consumer arbitration cases filed by the business.

Fees

An initial filing fee is payable in full by a filing party when a claim, counterclaim or additional claim is filed. A case service fee will be incurred for all cases that proceed to their first hearing. This fee will be payable in advance at the time that the first hearing is scheduled. This fee will be refunded at the conclusion of the case if no hearings have occurred. However, if the Association is not notified at least 24 hours before the time of the scheduled hearing, the case service fee will remain due and will not be refunded.

These fees will be billed in accordance with the following schedule:

Amount of Claim
Initial Filing Fee
Case Service Fee

Above $0 to $10,000
$500
$200

Above $10,000 to $75,000
$750
$300

Above $75,000 to $150,000
$1,500
$750

Above $150,000 to $300,000
$2,750
$1,250

Above $300,000 to $500,000
$4,250
$1,750

Above $500,000 to $1,000,000
$6,000
$2,500

Above $1,000,000 to $5,000,000
$8,000
$3,250

Above $5,000,000 to $10,000,000
$10,000
$4,000

Above $10,000,000
*
*

Nonmonetary Claims**
$3,250
$1,250

** This fee is applicable only when a claim or counterclaim is not for a monetary amount. Where a monetary claim amount is not known, parties will be required to state a range of claims or be subject to the highest possible filing fee.

Fee Schedule for Claims in Excess of $10 Million.

The following is the fee schedule for use in disputes involving claims in excess of $10 million. If you have any questions, please consult your local AAA office or case management center.

Claim Size
Fee Case Service Fee

$10 million and above
Base fee of $12,500 plus .01% of the amount of claim above $10 million. $6,000

Filing fees capped at $65,000

Fees are subject to increase if the amount of a claim or counterclaim is modified after the initial filing date. Fees are subject to decrease if the amount of a claim or counterclaim is modified before the first hearing.

The minimum fees for any case having three or more arbitrators are $2,750 for the filing fee, plus a $1,250 case service fee. Expedited Procedures are applied in any case where no disclosed claim or counterclaim exceeds $75,000, exclusive of interest and arbitration costs.

Parties on cases held in abeyance for one year by agreement, will be assessed an annual abeyance fee of $300. If a party refuses to pay the assessed fee, the other party or parties may pay the entire fee on behalf of all parties, otherwise the matter will be closed.

Refund Schedule

The AAA offers a refund schedule on filing fees. For cases with claims up to $75,000, a minimum filing fee of $300 will not be refunded. For all other cases, a minimum fee of $500 will not be refunded. Subject to the minimum fee requirements, refunds will be calculated as follows:

100% of the filing fee, above the minimum fee, will be refunded if the case is settled or withdrawn within five calendar days of filing.

50% of the filing fee, in any case with filing fees in excess of $500, will be refunded if the case is settled or withdrawn between six and 30 calendar days of filing. Where the filing fee is $500, the refund will be $200.

25% of the filing fee will be refunded if the case is settled or withdrawn between 31 and 60 calendar days of filing.

No refund will be made once an arbitrator has been appointed (this includes one arbitrator on a three-arbitrator panel). No refunds will be granted on awarded cases.

Note: the date of receipt of the demand for arbitration with the AAA will be used to calculate refunds of filing fees for both claims and counterclaims.

AMERICAN ARBITRATION ASSOCIATION INTERNATIONAL ARBITRATION RULES

2001

ARTICLE 1

1. Where parties have agreed in writing to arbitrate disputes under these International Arbitration Rules or have provided for arbitration of an international dispute by the International Centre for Dispute Resolution or the American Arbitration Association without designating particular rules, the arbitration shall take place in accordance with these rules, as in effect at the date of commencement of the arbitration, subject to whatever modifications the parties may adopt in writing.

2. These rules govern the arbitration, except that, where any such rule is in conflict with any provision of the law applicable to the arbitration from which the parties cannot derogate, that provision shall prevail.

3. These rules specify the duties and responsibilities of the administrator, the International Centre for Dispute Resolution, a division of the American Arbitration Association. The administrator may provide services through its Centre, located in New York, or through the facilities of arbitral institutions with which it has agreements of cooperation.

R–1. Commencing the Arbitration

Notice of Arbitration and Statement of Claim

ARTICLE 2

1. The party initiating arbitration ("claimant") shall give written notice of arbitration to the administrator and at the same time to the party against whom a claim is being made ("respondent").

2. Arbitral proceedings shall be deemed to commence on the date on which the administrator receives the notice of arbitration.

3. The notice of arbitration shall contain a statement of claim including the following:

(a) a demand that the dispute be referred to arbitration;

(b) the names, addresses and telephone numbers of the parties;

(c) a reference to the arbitration clause or agreement that is invoked;

(d) a reference to any contract out of or in relation to which the dispute arises;

(e) a description of the claim and an indication of the facts supporting it;

(f) the relief or remedy sought and the amount claimed; and

(g) may include proposals as to the means of designating and the number of arbitrators, the place of arbitration and the language(s) of the arbitration.

4. Upon receipt of the notice of arbitration, the administrator shall communicate with all parties with respect to the arbitration and shall acknowledge the commencement of the arbitration.

Statement of Defense and Counterclaim

ARTICLE 3

1. Within 30 days after the commencement of the arbitration, a respondent shall submit a written statement of defense, responding to the issues raised in the notice of arbitration, to the claimant and any other parties, and to the administrator.

2. At the time a respondent submits its statement of defense, a respondent may make counterclaims or assert setoffs as to any claim covered by the agreement to arbitrate, as to which the claimant shall within 30 days submit a written statement of defense to the respondent and any other parties and to the administrator.

3. A respondent shall respond to the administrator, the claimant and other parties within 30 days after the commencement of the arbitration as to any proposals the claimant may have made as to the number of arbitrators, the place of the arbitration or the language(s) of the arbitration, except to the extent that the parties have previously agreed as to these matters.

4. The arbitral tribunal, or the administrator if the arbitral tribunal has not yet been formed, may extend any of the time limits established in this article if it considers such an extension justified.

Amendments to Claims

ARTICLE 4

During the arbitral proceedings, any party may amend or supplement its claim, counterclaim or defense, unless the tribunal considers it inappropriate to allow such amendment or supplement because of the party's delay in making it, prejudice to the other parties or any other circumstances. A party may not amend or supplement a claim or counterclaim if the amendment or supplement would fall outside the scope of the agreement to arbitrate.

R–2. The Tribunal

Number of Arbitrators

ARTICLE 5

If the parties have not agreed on the number of arbitrators, one arbitrator shall be appointed unless the administrator determines in its discretion that three arbitrators are appropriate because of the large size, complexity or other circumstances of the case.

Appointment of Arbitrators

ARTICLE 6

1.   The parties may mutually agree upon any procedure for appointing arbitrators and shall inform the administrator as to such procedure.

2.   The parties may mutually designate arbitrators, with or without the assistance of the administrator. When such designations are made, the parties shall notify the administrator so that notice of the appointment can be communicated to the arbitrators, together with a copy of these rules.

3.   If within 45 days after the commencement of the arbitration, all of the parties have not mutually agreed on a procedure for appointing the arbitrator(s) or have not mutually agreed on the designation of the arbitrator(s), the administrator shall, at the written request of any party, appoint the arbitrator(s) and designate the presiding arbitrator. If all of the parties have mutually agreed upon a procedure for appointing the arbitrator(s), but all appointments have not been made within the time limits provided in that procedure, the administrator shall, at the written request of any party, perform all functions provided for in that procedure that remain to be performed.

4.   In making such appointments, the administrator, after inviting consultation with the parties, shall endeavor to select suitable arbitrators. At the request of any party or on its own initiative, the administrator may appoint nationals of a country other than that of any of the parties.

5.   Unless the parties have agreed otherwise no later than 45 days after the commencement of the arbitration, if the notice of arbitration names two or more claimants or two or more respondents, the administrator shall appoint all the arbitrators.

Impartiality and Independence of Arbitrators

ARTICLE 7

1.   Arbitrators acting under these rules shall be impartial and independent. Prior to accepting appointment, a prospective arbitrator shall disclose to the administrator any circumstance likely to give rise to justifiable doubts as to the arbitrator's impartiality or independence. If, at any stage during the arbitration, new circumstances arise that may give rise to such doubts, an arbitrator shall promptly disclose such circumstances to the parties and to the administrator. Upon receipt of such information from an arbitrator or a party, the administrator shall communicate it to the other parties and to the tribunal.

2.   No party or anyone acting on its behalf shall have any ex parte communication relating to the case with any arbitrator, or with any candidate for appointment as party-appointed arbitrator except to advise the candidate of the general nature of the controversy and of the anticipated proceedings and to discuss the candidate's qualifications, availability or independence in relation to the parties, or to discuss the

suitability of candidates for selection as a third arbitrator where the parties or party designated arbitrators are to participate in that selection. No party or anyone acting on its behalf shall have any ex parte communication relating to the case with any candidate for presiding arbitrator.

Challenge of Arbitrators

ARTICLE 8

1. A party may challenge any arbitrator whenever circumstances exist that give rise to justifiable doubts as to the arbitrator's impartiality or independence. A party wishing to challenge an arbitrator shall send notice of the challenge to the administrator within 15 days after being notified of the appointment of the arbitrator or within 15 days after the circumstances giving rise to the challenge become known to that party.

2. The challenge shall state in writing the reasons for the challenge.

3. Upon receipt of such a challenge, the administrator shall notify the other parties of the challenge. When an arbitrator has been challenged by one party, the other party or parties may agree to the acceptance of the challenge and, if there is agreement, the arbitrator shall withdraw. The challenged arbitrator may also withdraw from office in the absence of such agreement. In neither case does withdrawal imply acceptance of the validity of the grounds for the challenge.

ARTICLE 9

If the other party or parties do not agree to the challenge or the challenged arbitrator does not withdraw, the administrator in its sole discretion shall make the decision on the challenge.

Replacement of an Arbitrator

ARTICLE 10

If an arbitrator withdraws after a challenge, or the administrator sustains the challenge, or the administrator determines that there are sufficient reasons to accept the resignation of an arbitrator, or an arbitrator dies, a substitute arbitrator shall be appointed pursuant to the provisions of Article 6, unless the parties otherwise agree.

ARTICLE 11

1. If an arbitrator on a three-person tribunal fails to participate in the arbitration for reasons other than those identified in Article 10, the two other arbitrators shall have the power in their sole discretion to continue the arbitration and to make any decision, ruling or award, notwithstanding the failure of the third arbitrator to participate. In determining whether to continue the arbitration or to render any decision, ruling or award without the participation of an arbitrator, the two other arbitrators shall take into account the stage of the arbitration, the reason, if any, expressed by the third arbitrator for such nonparticipa-

tion, and such other matters as they consider appropriate in the circumstances of the case. In the event that the two other arbitrators determine not to continue the arbitration without the participation of the third arbitrator, the administrator on proof satisfactory to it shall declare the office vacant, and a substitute arbitrator shall be appointed pursuant to the provisions of Article 6, unless the parties otherwise agree.

2. If a substitute arbitrator is appointed under either Article 10 or Article 11, the tribunal shall determine at its sole discretion whether all or part of any prior hearings shall be repeated.

R–3. General Conditions

Representation

ARTICLE 12

Any party may be represented in the arbitration. The names, addresses and telephone numbers of representatives shall be communicated in writing to the other parties and to the administrator. Once the tribunal has been established, the parties or their representatives may communicate in writing directly with the tribunal.

Place of Arbitration

ARTICLE 13

1. If the parties disagree as to the place of arbitration, the administrator may initially determine the place of arbitration, subject to the power of the tribunal to determine finally the place of arbitration within 60 days after its constitution. All such determinations shall be made having regard for the contentions of the parties and the circumstances of the arbitration.

2. The tribunal may hold conferences or hear witnesses or inspect property or documents at any place it deems appropriate. The parties shall be given sufficient written notice to enable them to be present at any such proceedings.

Language

ARTICLE 14

If the parties have not agreed otherwise, the language(s) of the arbitration shall be that of the documents containing the arbitration agreement, subject to the power of the tribunal to determine otherwise based upon the contentions of the parties and the circumstances of the arbitration. The tribunal may order that any documents delivered in another language shall be accompanied by a translation into the language(s) of the arbitration.

Pleas as to Jurisdiction

ARTICLE 15

1. The tribunal shall have the power to rule on its own jurisdiction, including any objections with respect to the existence, scope or validity of the arbitration agreement.

2. The tribunal shall have the power to determine the existence or validity of a contract of which an arbitration clause forms a part. Such an arbitration clause shall be treated as an agreement independent of the other terms of the contract. A decision by the tribunal that the contract is null and void shall not for that reason alone render invalid the arbitration clause.

3. A party must object to the jurisdiction of the tribunal or to the arbitrability of a claim or counterclaim no later than the filing of the statement of defense, as provided in Article 3, to the claim or counterclaim that gives rise to the objection. The tribunal may rule on such objections as a preliminary matter or as part of the final award.

Conduct of the Arbitration

ARTICLE 16

1. Subject to these rules, the tribunal may conduct the arbitration in whatever manner it considers appropriate, provided that the parties are treated with equality and that each party has the right to be heard and is given a fair opportunity to present its case.

2. The tribunal, exercising its discretion, shall conduct the proceedings with a view to expediting the resolution of the dispute. It may conduct a preparatory conference with the parties for the purpose of organizing, scheduling and agreeing to procedures to expedite the subsequent proceedings.

3. The tribunal may in its discretion direct the order of proof, bifurcate proceedings, exclude cumulative or irrelevant testimony or other evidence, and direct the parties to focus their presentations on issues the decision of which could dispose of all or part of the case.

4. Documents or information supplied to the tribunal by one party shall at the same time be communicated by that party to the other party or parties.

Further Written Statements

ARTICLE 17

1. The tribunal may decide whether the parties shall present any written statements in addition to statements of claims and counterclaims and statements of defense, and it shall fix the periods of time for submitting any such statements.

2. The periods of time fixed by the tribunal for the communication of such written statements should not exceed 45 days. However, the tribunal may extend such time limits if it considers such an extension justified.

Notices

ARTICLE 18

1. Unless otherwise agreed by the parties or ordered by the tribunal, all notices, statements and written communications may be served

on a party by air mail, air courier, facsimile transmission, telex, telegram or other written forms of electronic communication addressed to the party or its representative at its last known address or by personal service.

2. For the purpose of calculating a period of time under these rules, such period shall begin to run on the day following the day when a notice, statement or written communication is received. If the last day of such period is an official holiday at the place received, the period is extended until the first business day which follows. Official holidays occurring during the running of the period of time are included in calculating the period.

Evidence

ARTICLE 19

1. Each party shall have the burden of proving the facts relied on to support its claim or defense.

2. The tribunal may order a party to deliver to the tribunal and to the other parties a summary of the documents and other evidence which that party intends to present in support of its claim, counterclaim or defense.

3. At any time during the proceedings, the tribunal may order parties to produce other documents, exhibits or other evidence it deems necessary or appropriate.

Hearings

ARTICLE 20

1. The tribunal shall give the parties at least 30 days advance notice of the date, time and place of the initial oral hearing. The tribunal shall give reasonable notice of subsequent hearings.

2. At least 15 days before the hearings, each party shall give the tribunal and the other parties the names and addresses of any witnesses it intends to present, the subject of their testimony and the languages in which such witnesses will give their testimony.

3. At the request of the tribunal or pursuant to mutual agreement of the parties, the administrator shall make arrangements for the interpretation of oral testimony or for a record of the hearing.

4. Hearings are private unless the parties agree otherwise or the law provides to the contrary. The tribunal may require any witness or witnesses to retire during the testimony of other witnesses. The tribunal may determine the manner in which witnesses are examined.

5. Evidence of witnesses may also be presented in the form of written statements signed by them.

6. The tribunal shall determine the admissibility, relevance, materiality and weight of the evidence offered by any party. The tribunal shall take into account applicable principles of legal privilege, such as

those involving the confidentiality of communications between a lawyer and client.

Interim Measures of Protection

ARTICLE 21

1.   At the request of any party, the tribunal may take whatever interim measures it deems necessary, including injunctive relief and measures for the protection or conservation of property.

2.   Such interim measures may take the form of an interim award, and the tribunal may require security for the costs of such measures.

3.   A request for interim measures addressed by a party to a judicial authority shall not be deemed incompatible with the agreement to arbitrate or a waiver of the right to arbitrate.

4.   The tribunal may in its discretion apportion costs associated with applications for interim relief in any interim award or in the final award.

Experts

ARTICLE 22

1.   The tribunal may appoint one or more independent experts to report to it, in writing, on specific issues designated by the tribunal and communicated to the parties.

2.   The parties shall provide such an expert with any relevant information or produce for inspection any relevant documents or goods that the expert may require. Any dispute between a party and the expert as to the relevance of the requested information or goods shall be referred to the tribunal for decision.

3.   Upon receipt of an expert's report, the tribunal shall send a copy of the report to all parties and shall give the parties an opportunity to express, in writing, their opinion on the report. A party may examine any document on which the expert has relied in such a report.

4.   At the request of any party, the tribunal shall give the parties an opportunity to question the expert at a hearing. At this hearing, parties may present expert witnesses to testify on the points at issue.

Default

ARTICLE 23

1.   If a party fails to file a statement of defense within the time established by the tribunal without showing sufficient cause for such failure, as determined by the tribunal, the tribunal may proceed with the arbitration.

2.   If a party, duly notified under these rules, fails to appear at a hearing without showing sufficient cause for such failure, as determined by the tribunal, the tribunal may proceed with the arbitration.

3.   If a party, duly invited to produce evidence or take any other steps in the proceedings, fails to do so within the time established by the tribunal without showing sufficient cause for such failure, as determined by the tribunal, the tribunal may make the award on the evidence before it.

Closure of Hearing

ARTICLE 24

1.   After asking the parties if they have any further testimony or evidentiary submissions and upon receiving negative replies or if satisfied that the record is complete, the tribunal may declare the hearings closed.

2.   The tribunal in its discretion, on its own motion or upon application of a party, may reopen the hearings at any time before the award is made.

Waiver of Rules

ARTICLE 25

A party who knows that any provision of the rules or requirement under the rules has not been complied with, but proceeds with the arbitration without promptly stating an objection in writing thereto, shall be deemed to have waived the right to object.

Awards, Decisions and Rulings

ARTICLE 26

1.   When there is more than one arbitrator, any award, decision or ruling of the arbitral tribunal shall be made by a majority of the arbitrators. If any arbitrator fails to sign the award, it shall be accompanied by a statement of the reason for the absence of such signature.

2.   When the parties or the tribunal so authorize, the presiding arbitrator may make decisions or rulings on questions of procedure, subject to revision by the tribunal.

Form and Effect of the Award

ARTICLE 27

1.   Awards shall be made in writing, promptly by the tribunal, and shall be final and binding on the parties. The parties undertake to carry out any such award without delay.

2.   The tribunal shall state the reasons upon which the award is based, unless the parties have agreed that no reasons need be given.

3.   The award shall contain the date and the place where the award was made, which shall be the place designated pursuant to Article 13.

4.   An award may be made public only with the consent of all parties or as required by law.

5. Copies of the award shall be communicated to the parties by the administrator.

6. If the arbitration law of the country where the award is made requires the award to be filed or registered, the tribunal shall comply with such requirement.

7. In addition to making a final award, the tribunal may make interim, interlocutory or partial orders and awards.

8. Unless otherwise agreed by the parties, the administrator may publish or otherwise make publicly available selected awards, decisions and rulings that have been edited to conceal the names of the parties and other identifying details or that have been made publicly available in the course of enforcement or otherwise.

Applicable Laws and Remedies

ARTICLE 28

1. The tribunal shall apply the substantive law(s) or rules of law designated by the parties as applicable to the dispute. Failing such a designation by the parties, the tribunal shall apply such law(s) or rules of law as it determines to be appropriate.

2. In arbitrations involving the application of contracts, the tribunal shall decide in accordance with the terms of the contract and shall take into account usages of the trade applicable to the contract.

3. The tribunal shall not decide as amiable compositeur or ex aequo et bono unless the parties have expressly authorized it to do so.

4. A monetary award shall be in the currency or currencies of the contract unless the tribunal considers another currency more appropriate, and the tribunal may award such pre-award and post-award interest, simple or compound, as it considers appropriate, taking into consideration the contract and applicable law.

5. Unless the parties agree otherwise, the parties expressly waive and forego any right to punitive, exemplary or similar damages unless a statute requires that compensatory damages be increased in a specified manner. This provision shall not apply to any award of arbitration costs to a party to compensate for dilatory or bad faith conduct in the arbitration.

Settlement or Other Reasons for Termination

ARTICLE 29

1. If the parties settle the dispute before an award is made, the tribunal shall terminate the arbitration and, if requested by all parties, may record the settlement in the form of an award on agreed terms. The tribunal is not obliged to give reasons for such an award.

2. If the continuation of the proceedings becomes unnecessary or impossible for any other reason, the tribunal shall inform the parties of its intention to terminate the proceedings. The tribunal shall thereafter

issue an order terminating the arbitration, unless a party raises justifiable grounds for objection.

Interpretation or Correction of the Award

ARTICLE 30

1. Within 30 days after the receipt of an award, any party, with notice to the other parties, may request the tribunal to interpret the award or correct any clerical, typographical or computation errors or make an additional award as to claims presented but omitted from the award.

2. If the tribunal considers such a request justified, after considering the contentions of the parties, it shall comply with such a request within 30 days after the request.

Costs

ARTICLE 31

The tribunal shall fix the costs of arbitration in its award. The tribunal may apportion such costs among the parties if it determines that such apportionment is reasonable, taking into account the circumstances of the case.

Such costs may include:

(a) the fees and expenses of the arbitrators;

(b) the costs of assistance required by the tribunal, including its experts;

(c) the fees and expenses of the administrator;

(d) the reasonable costs for legal representation of a successful party; and

(e) any such costs incurred in connection with an application for interim or emergency relief pursuant to Article 21.

Compensation of Arbitrators

ARTICLE 32

Arbitrators shall be compensated based upon their amount of service, taking into account their stated rate of compensation and the size and complexity of the case. The administrator shall arrange an appropriate daily or hourly rate, based on such considerations, with the parties and with each of the arbitrators as soon as practicable after the commencement of the arbitration. If the parties fail to agree on the terms of compensation, the administrator shall establish an appropriate rate and communicate it in writing to the parties.

Deposit of Costs

ARTICLE 33

1. When a party files claims, the administrator may request the filing party to deposit appropriate amounts as an advance for the costs referred to in Article 31, paragraphs (a), (b) and (c).

2. During the course of the arbitral proceedings, the tribunal may request supplementary deposits from the parties.

3. If the deposits requested are not paid in full within 30 days after the receipt of the request, the administrator shall so inform the parties, in order that one or the other of them may make the required payment. If such payments are not made, the tribunal may order the suspension or termination of the proceedings.

4. After the award has been made, the administrator shall render an accounting to the parties of the deposits received and return any unexpended balance to the parties.

Confidentiality

ARTICLE 34

Confidential information disclosed during the proceedings by the parties or by witnesses shall not be divulged by an arbitrator or by the administrator. Except as provided in Article 27, unless otherwise agreed by the parties, or required by applicable law, the members of the tribunal and the administrator shall keep confidential all matters relating to the arbitration or the award.

Exclusion of Liability

ARTICLE 35

The members of the tribunal and the administrator shall not be liable to any party for any act or omission in connection with any arbitration conducted under these rules, except that they may be liable for the consequences of conscious and deliberate wrongdoing.

Interpretation of Rules

ARTICLE 36

The tribunal shall interpret and apply these rules insofar as they relate to its powers and duties. The administrator shall interpret and apply all other rules.

ADMINISTRATIVE FEES

The administrative fees of the ICDR are based on the amount of the claim or counterclaim. Arbitrator compensation is not included in this schedule. Unless the parties agree otherwise, arbitrator compensation and administrative fees are subject to allocation by the arbitrator in the award.

In an effort to make arbitration costs reasonable for consumers, the AAA has a separate fee schedule for consumer related disputes. Please refer to Section C–8 of the *Supplementary Procedures for Consumer–Related Disputes* when filing a consumer related claim.

Fees

An initial filing fee is payable in full by a filing party when a claim, counterclaim or additional claim is filed. A case service fee will be incurred for all cases that proceed to their first hearing. This fee will be payable in advance at the time that the first hearing is scheduled. This fee will be refunded at the conclusion of the case if no hearings have occurred.

However, if the administrator is not notified at least 24 hours before the time of the scheduled hearing, the case service fee will remain due and will not be refunded.

These fees will be billed in accordance with the following schedule:

Amount of Claim	Initial Filing Fee	Case Service Fee
Above $0 to $10,000	$500	200
Above $10,000 to $75,000	$750	300
Above $75,000 to $150,000	$1,500	$750
Above $150,000 to $300,000	$2,750	$1,250
Above $300,000 to $500,000	$4,250	$1,750
Above $500,000 to $1,000,000	$6,000	$2,500
Above $1,000,000 to $5,000,000	$8,000	$3,500
Above $5,000,000 to $10,000,000	$10,000	$4,000
Above $10,000,000*		
Nonmonetary Claims**	$3,250	$1,250

* Contact the ICDR's New York office for fees for claims in excess of $10 million.

** This fee is applicable only when a claim or a counterclaim is not for a monetary amount. Where a monetary claim amount is not known, parties will be required to state a range of claims or be subject to the highest possible filing fee.

The minimum fees for any case having three or more arbitrators are $2,750 for the filing fee, plus a $1,250 case service fee.

Parties on cases held in abeyance for one year by agreement, will be assessed an annual abeyance fee of $300. If a party refuses to pay the assessed fee, the other party or parties may pay the entire fee on behalf of all parties, otherwise the matter will be closed.

Refund Schedule

The ICDR offers a refund schedule on filing fees. For cases with claims up to $75,000, a minimum filing fee of $300 will not be refunded. For all other cases, a minimum fee of $500 will not be refunded. Subject to the minimum fee requirements, refunds will be calculated as follows:

100% of the filing fee, above the minimum fee, will be refunded if the case is settled or withdrawn within five calendar days of filing.

50% of the filing fee, in any case with filing fees in excess of $500, will be refunded if the case is settled or withdrawn between six and 30 calendar days of filing. Where the filing fee is $500, the refund will be $200.

25% of the filing fee will be refunded if the case is settled or withdrawn between 31 and 60 calendar days of filing. No refund will be made once an arbitrator has been appointed (this includes one arbitrator on a three-arbitrator panel). No refunds will be granted on awarded cases.

Note: the date of receipt of the demand for arbitration with the ICDR will be used to calculate refunds of filing fees for both claims and counterclaims.

Suspension for Nonpayment

If arbitrator compensation or administrative charges have not been paid in full, the administrator may so inform the parties in order that one of them may advance the required payment. If such payments are not made, the tribunal may order the suspension or termination of the proceedings. If no arbitrator has yet been appointed, the ICDR may suspend the proceedings.

INTERNATIONAL CHAMBER OF COMMERCE
RULES OF ARBITRATION
(effective 1 January 1998)

INTRODUCTORY PROVISIONS

Article 1

International Court of Arbitration

1.   The International Court of Arbitration (the "Court") of the International Chamber of Commerce (the "ICC") is the arbitration body attached to the ICC. The statutes of the Court are set forth in Appendix I. Members of the Court are appointed by the Council of the ICC. The function of the Court is to provide for the settlement by arbitration of business disputes of an international character in accordance with the Rules of Arbitration of the International Chamber of Commerce (the "Rules"). If so empowered by an arbitration agreement, the Court shall also provide for the settlement by arbitration in accordance with these Rules of business disputes not of an international character.

2.   The Court does not itself settle disputes. It has the function of ensuring the application of these Rules. It draws up its own Internal Rules (Appendix II).

3.   The Chairman of the Court, or, in the Chairman's absence or otherwise at his request, one of its Vice–Chairmen shall have the power to take urgent decisions on behalf of the Court, provided that any such decision is reported to the Court at its next session.

4.   As provided for in its Internal Rules, the Court may delegate to one or more committees composed of its members the power to take certain decisions, provided that any such decision is reported to the Court at its next session.

5.   The Secretariat of the Court (the "Secretariat") under the direction of its Secretary General (the "Secretary General") shall have its seat at the headquarters of the ICC.

Article 2

Definitions

In these Rules:

(i)   "Arbitral Tribunal" includes one or more arbitrators.

(ii)   "Claimant" includes one or more claimants and "Respondent" includes one or more respondents.

(iii)   "Award" includes, inter alia, an interim, partial or final Award.

Article 3

Written Notifications or Communications; Time Limits

1.   All pleadings and other written communications submitted by any party, as well as all documents annexed thereto, shall be supplied in

a number of copies sufficient to provide one copy for each party, plus one for each arbitrator, and one for the Secretariat. A copy of any communication from the Arbitral Tribunal to the parties shall be sent to the Secretariat.

2. All notifications or communications from the Secretariat and the Arbitral Tribunal shall be made to the last address of the party or its representative for whom the same are intended, as notified either by the party in question or by the other party. Such notification or communication may be made by delivery against receipt, registered post, courier, facsimile transmission, telex, telegram or any other means of telecommunication that provides a record of the sending thereof.

3. A notification or communication shall be deemed to have been made on the day it was received by the party itself or by its representative, or would have been received if made in accordance with the preceding paragraph.

4. Periods of time specified in, or fixed under the present Rules, shall start to run on the day following the date a notification or communication is deemed to have been made in accordance with the preceding paragraph. When the day next following such date is an official holiday, or a non-business day in the country where the notification or communication is deemed to have been made, the period of time shall commence on the first following business day. Official holidays and non-business days are included in the calculation of the period of time. If the last day of the relevant period of time granted is an official holiday or a non-business day in the country where the notification or communication is deemed to have been made, the period of time shall expire at the end of the first following business day.

COMMENCING THE ARBITRATION

Article 4

Request for Arbitration

1. A party wishing to have recourse to arbitration under these Rules shall submit its Request for Arbitration (the "Request") to the Secretariat, which shall notify the Claimant and Respondent of the receipt of the Request and the date of such receipt.

2. The date on which the Request is received by the Secretariat shall, for all purposes, be deemed to be the date of the commencement of the arbitral proceedings.

3. The Request shall, inter alia, contain the following information:

(a) the name in full, description and address of each of the parties;

(b) a description of the nature and circumstances of the dispute giving rise to the claims;

(c) a statement of the relief sought, including, to the extent possible, an indication of any amount(s) claimed;

(d) the relevant agreements and, in particular, the arbitration agreement;

(e) all relevant particulars concerning the number of arbitrators and their choice in accordance with the provisions of Articles 8, 9 and 10, and any nomination of an arbitrator required thereby; and

(f) any comments as to the place of arbitration, the applicable rules of law and the language of the arbitration.

4. Together with the Request, the Claimant shall submit the number of copies thereof required by Article 3(1) and shall make the advance payment on administrative expenses required by Appendix III ("Arbitration Costs and Fees") in force on the date the Request is submitted. In the event that the Claimant fails to comply with either of these requirements, the Secretariat may fix a time limit within which the Claimant must comply, failing which the file shall be closed without prejudice to the right of the Claimant to submit the same claims at a later date in another Request.

5. The Secretariat shall send a copy of the Request and the documents annexed thereto to the Respondent for its Answer to the Request once the Secretariat has sufficient copies of the Request and the required advance payment.

6. When a party submits a Request in connection with a legal relationship in respect of which arbitration proceedings between the same parties are already pending under these Rules, the Court may, at the request of a party, decide to include the claims contained in the Request in the pending proceedings provided that the Terms of Reference have not been signed or approved by the Court. Once the Terms of Reference have been signed or approved by the Court, claims may only be included in the pending proceedings subject to the provisions of Article 19.

Article 5

Answer to the Request; Counterclaims

1. Within 30 days from the receipt of the Request from the Secretariat, the Respondent shall file an Answer (the "Answer") which shall, inter alia, contain the following information:

(a) its name in full, description and address;

(b) its comments as to the nature and circumstances of the dispute giving rise to the claim(s);

(c) its response to the relief sought;

(d) any comments concerning the number of arbitrators and their choice in light of the Claimant's proposals and in accordance with the provisions of Articles 8, 9 and 10, and any nomination of an arbitrator required thereby; and

(e) any comments as to the place of arbitration, the applicable rules of law and the language of the arbitration.

2. The Secretariat may grant the Respondent an extension of the time for filing the Answer, provided the application for such an extension contains the Respondent's comments concerning the number of arbitrators and their choice, and, where required by Articles 8, 9 and 10, the nomination of an arbitrator. If the Respondent fails to do so, the Court shall proceed in accordance with these Rules.

3. The Answer shall be supplied to the Secretariat in the number of copies specified by Article 3(1).

4. A copy of the Answer and the documents annexed thereto shall be communicated by the Secretariat to the Claimant.

5. Any counterclaim(s) made by the Respondent shall be filed with its Answer and shall provide:

(a) a description of the nature and circumstances of the dispute giving rise to the counterclaim(s); and

(b) a statement of the relief sought, including, to the extent possible, an indication of any amount(s) counter-claimed.

6. The Claimant shall file a Reply to any counterclaim within 30 days from the date of receipt of the counterclaim(s) communicated by the Secretariat. The Secretariat may grant the Claimant an extension of time for filing the Reply.

Article 6

Effect of the Arbitration Agreement

1. Where the parties have agreed to submit to arbitration under the Rules, they shall be deemed to have submitted ipso facto to the Rules in effect on the date of commencement of the arbitration proceedings unless they have agreed to submit to the Rules in effect on the date of their arbitration agreement.

2. If the Respondent does not file an Answer, as provided by Article 5, or if any party raises one or more pleas concerning the existence, validity or scope of the arbitration agreement, the Court may decide, without prejudice to the admissibility or merits of the plea or pleas, that the arbitration shall proceed if it is prima facie satisfied that an arbitration agreement under the Rules may exist. In such a case, any decision as to the jurisdiction of the Arbitral Tribunal shall be taken by the Arbitral Tribunal itself. If the Court is not so satisfied, the parties shall be notified that the arbitration cannot proceed. In such a case, any party retains the right to ask any court having jurisdiction whether or not there is a binding arbitration agreement.

3. If any of the parties refuses or fails to take part in the arbitration or any stage thereof, the arbitration shall proceed notwithstanding such refusal or failure.

4. Unless otherwise agreed, the Arbitral Tribunal shall not cease to have jurisdiction by reason of any claim that the contract is null and void or allegation that it is non-existent provided that the Arbitral Tribunal

upholds the validity of the arbitration agreement. The Arbitral Tribunal shall continue to have jurisdiction to determine the respective rights of the parties and to adjudicate their claims and pleas even though the contract itself may be non-existent or null and void.

THE ARBITRAL TRIBUNAL

arbitration clause is severable from contract

Article 7

General Provisions

1. Every arbitrator must be and remain independent of the parties involved in the arbitration.

2. Before appointment or confirmation, a prospective arbitrator shall sign a statement of independence and disclose in writing to the Secretariat any facts or circumstances which might be of such a nature as to call into question the arbitrator's independence in the eyes of the parties. The Secretariat shall provide such information to the parties in writing and fix a time limit for any comments from them.

3. An arbitrator shall immediately disclose in writing to the Secretariat and to the parties any facts or circumstances of a similar nature which may arise during the arbitration.

4. The decisions of the Court as to the appointment, confirmation, challenge or replacement of an arbitrator shall be final and the reasons for such decisions shall not be communicated.

5. By accepting to serve, every arbitrator undertakes to carry out his responsibilities in accordance with these Rules.

6. Insofar as the parties have not provided otherwise, the Arbitral Tribunal shall be constituted in accordance with the provisions of Articles 8, 9 and 10.

Article 8

Number of Arbitrators

1. The disputes shall be decided by a sole arbitrator or by three arbitrators.

2. Where the parties have not agreed upon the number of arbitrators, the Court shall appoint a sole arbitrator, save where it appears to the Court that the dispute is such as to warrant the appointment of three arbitrators. In such case, the Claimant shall nominate an arbitrator within a period of 15 days from the receipt of the notification of the decision of the Court, and the Respondent shall nominate an arbitrator within a period of 15 days from the receipt of the notification of the nomination made by the Claimant.

3. Where the parties have agreed that the dispute shall be settled by a sole arbitrator, they may, by agreement, nominate the sole arbitrator for confirmation. If the parties fail to nominate a sole arbitrator within 30 days from the date when the Claimant's Request for Arbitration has been received by the other party, or within such additional time

as may be allowed by the Secretariat, the sole arbitrator shall be appointed by the Court.

4. Where the dispute is to be referred to three arbitrators, each party shall nominate in the Request and the Answer, respectively, one arbitrator for confirmation by the Court. If a party fails to nominate an arbitrator, the appointment shall be made by the Court. The third arbitrator, who will act as chairman of the Arbitral Tribunal, shall be appointed by the Court, unless the parties have agreed upon another procedure for such appointment, in which case the nomination will be subject to confirmation pursuant to Article 9. Should such procedure not result in a nomination within the time limit fixed by the parties or the Court, the third arbitrator shall be appointed by the Court. Article 9.

Article 9

Appointment and Confirmation of the Arbitrators

1. In confirming or appointing arbitrators, the Court shall consider the prospective arbitrator's nationality, residence and other relationships with the countries of which the parties or the other arbitrators are nationals and the prospective arbitrator's availability and ability to conduct the arbitration in accordance with these Rules. The same shall apply where the Secretary General confirms arbitrators pursuant to Article 9(2).

2. The Secretary General may confirm as co-arbitrators, sole arbitrators and chairmen of Arbitral Tribunals persons nominated by the parties or pursuant to their particular agreements, provided they have filed a statement of independence without qualification or a qualified statement of independence has not given rise to objections. Such confirmation shall be reported to the Court at its next session. If the Secretary General considers that a co-arbitrator, sole arbitrator or chairman of an Arbitral Tribunal should not be confirmed, the matter shall be submitted to the Court.

3. Where the Court is to appoint a sole arbitrator or the chairman of an Arbitral Tribunal, it shall make the appointment upon a proposal of a National Committee of the ICC that it considers to be appropriate. If the Court does not accept the proposal made, or if the National Committee fails to make the proposal requested within the time limit fixed by the Court, the Court may repeat its request or may request a proposal from another National Committee that it considers to be appropriate.

4. Where the Court considers that the circumstances so demand, it may choose the sole arbitrator or the chairman of the Arbitral Tribunal from a country where there is no National Committee, provided that neither of the parties objects within the time limit fixed by the Court.

5. The sole arbitrator or the chairman of the Arbitral Tribunal shall be of a nationality other than those of the parties. However, in suitable circumstances and provided that neither of the parties objects within the time limit fixed by the Court, the sole arbitrator or the

chairman of the Arbitral Tribunal may be chosen from a country of which any of the parties is a national.

6.   Where the Court is to appoint an arbitrator on behalf of a party which has failed to nominate one, it shall make the appointment upon a proposal of the National Committee of the country of which that party is a national. If the Court does not accept the proposal made, or if the National Committee fails to make the proposal requested within the time limit fixed by the Court, or if the country of which the said party is a national has no National Committee, the Court shall be at liberty to choose any person whom it regards as suitable. The Secretariat shall inform the National Committee, if one exists, of the country of which such person is a national.

Article 10

Multiple Parties

1.   Where there are multiple parties, whether as Claimant or as Respondent, and where the dispute is to be referred to three arbitrators, the multiple Claimants, jointly, and the multiple Respondents, jointly, shall nominate an arbitrator for confirmation pursuant to Article 9.

2.   In the absence of such a joint nomination and where all parties are unable to agree to a method for the constitution of the Arbitral Tribunal, the Court may appoint each member of the Arbitral Tribunal and shall designate one of them to act as chairman. In such case, the Court shall be at liberty to choose any person it regards as suitable to act as arbitrator, applying Article 9 when it considers this appropriate.

Article 11

Challenge of Arbitrators

1.   A challenge of an arbitrator, whether for an alleged lack of independence or otherwise, shall be made by the submission to the Secretariat of a written statement specifying the facts and circumstances on which the challenge is based.

2.   For a challenge to be admissible, it must be sent by a party either within 30 days from receipt by that party of the notification of the appointment or confirmation of the arbitrator, or within 30 days from the date when the party making the challenge was informed of the facts and circumstances on which the challenge is based if such date is subsequent to the receipt of such notification.

3.   The Court shall decide on the admissibility, and, at the same time, if necessary, on the merits of a challenge after the Secretariat has afforded an opportunity for the arbitrator concerned, the other party or parties and any other members of the Arbitral Tribunal, to comment in writing within a suitable period of time. Such comments shall be communicated to the parties and to the arbitrators.

Article 12

Replacement of Arbitrators

1.   An arbitrator shall be replaced upon his death, upon the acceptance by the Court of the arbitrator's resignation, upon acceptance by the Court of a challenge or upon the request of all the parties.

2.   An arbitrator shall also be replaced on the Court's own initiative when it decides that he is prevented de jure or de facto from fulfilling his functions, or that he is not fulfilling his functions in accordance with the Rules or within the prescribed time limits.

3.   When, on the basis of information that has come to its attention, the Court considers applying Article 12(2), it shall decide on the matter after the arbitrator concerned, the parties and any other members of the Arbitral Tribunal have had an opportunity to comment in writing within a suitable period of time. Such comments shall be communicated to the parties and to the arbitrators.

4.   When an arbitrator is to be replaced, the Court has discretion to decide whether or not to follow the original nominating process. Once reconstituted, and after having invited the parties to comment, the Arbitral Tribunal shall determine if and to what extent prior proceedings shall be repeated before the reconstituted Arbitral Tribunal.

5.   Subsequent to the closing of the proceedings, instead of replacing an arbitrator who has died or been removed by the Court pursuant to Articles 12(1) and 12(2), the Court may decide, when it considers it appropriate, that the remaining arbitrators shall continue the arbitration. In making such determination, the Court shall take into account the views of the remaining arbitrators and of the parties and such other matters that it considers appropriate in the circumstances.

THE ARBITRAL PROCEEDINGS

Article 13

Transmission of the File to the Arbitral Tribunal

The Secretariat shall transmit the file to the Arbitral Tribunal as soon as it has been constituted, provided the advance on costs requested by the Secretariat at this stage has been paid.

Article 14

Place of the Arbitration

1.   The place of the arbitration shall be fixed by the Court unless agreed upon by the parties.

2.   The Arbitral Tribunal may, after consultation with the parties, conduct hearings and meetings at any location it considers appropriate unless otherwise agreed by the parties.

3.   The Arbitral Tribunal may deliberate at any location it considers appropriate.

Article 15

Rules Governing the Proceedings

1. The proceedings before the Arbitral Tribunal shall be governed by these Rules, and, where these Rules are silent, by any rules which the parties or, failing them, the Arbitral Tribunal may settle on, whether or not reference is thereby made to the rules of procedure of a national law to be applied to the arbitration.

2. In all cases, the Arbitral Tribunal shall act fairly and impartially and ensure that each party has a reasonable opportunity to present its case.

Article 16

Language of the Arbitration

In the absence of an agreement by the parties, the Arbitral Tribunal shall determine the language or languages of the arbitration, due regard being given to all relevant circumstances, including the language of the contract.

Article 17

Applicable Rules of Law

1. The parties shall be free to agree upon the rules of law to be applied by the Arbitral Tribunal to the merits of the dispute. In the absence of any such agreement, the Arbitral Tribunal shall apply the rules of law which it determines to be appropriate.

2. In all cases the Arbitral Tribunal shall take account of the provisions of the contract and the relevant trade usages.

3. The Arbitral Tribunal shall assume the powers of an *amiable compositeur* or decide *ex aequo et bono* only if the parties have agreed to give it such powers.

Article 18

Terms of Reference; Procedural Timetable

1. As soon as it has received the file from the Secretariat, the Arbitral Tribunal shall draw up, on the basis of documents or in the presence of the parties and in the light of their most recent submissions, a document defining its Terms of Reference. This document shall include the following particulars:

(a) the full names and descriptions of the parties;

(b) the addresses of the parties to which notifications and communications arising in the course of the arbitration may be made;

(c) a summary of the parties' respective claims and of the relief sought by each party, with an indication to the extent possible of the amounts claimed or counterclaimed;

(d) unless the Arbitral Tribunal considers it inappropriate, a list of issues to be determined;

(e) the full names, descriptions and addresses of the arbitrators;

(f) the place of the arbitration; and

(g) particulars of the applicable procedural rules and, if such is the case, reference to the power conferred upon the Arbitral Tribunal to act as *amiable compositeur* or to decide *ex aequo et bono*.)

2. The Terms of Reference shall be signed by the parties and the Arbitral Tribunal. Within two months of the date on which the file has been transmitted to it, the Arbitral Tribunal shall transmit to the Court the Terms of Reference signed by it and by the parties. The Court may extend this time limit pursuant to a reasoned request from the Arbitral Tribunal or on its own initiative if it decides it is necessary to do so.

3. If any of the parties refuses to take part in the drawing up of the Terms of Reference or to sign the same, they shall be submitted to the Court for approval. When the Terms of Reference are signed in accordance with Article 18(2) or approved by the Court, the arbitration shall proceed.

4. When drawing up the Terms of Reference, or as soon as possible thereafter, the Arbitral Tribunal, after having consulted the parties, shall establish in a separate document a provisional timetable that it intends to follow for the conduct of the arbitration and shall communicate it to the Court and the parties. Any subsequent modifications of the provisional timetable shall be communicated to the Court and the parties.

Article 19

New Claims

After the Terms of Reference have been signed or approved by the Court, no party shall make new claims or counterclaims which fall outside the limits of the Terms of Reference unless it has been authorized to do so by the Arbitral Tribunal, which shall consider the nature of such new claims or counterclaims, the stage of the arbitration and other relevant circumstances.

Article 20

Establishing the Facts of the Case

1. The Arbitral Tribunal shall proceed within as short a time as possible to establish the facts of the case by all appropriate means.

2. After studying the written submissions of the parties and all documents relied upon, the Arbitral Tribunal shall hear the parties together in person if any of them so requests or, failing such a request, it may of its own motion decide to hear them.

3.   The Arbitral Tribunal may decide to hear witnesses, experts appointed by the parties or any other person, in the presence of the parties, or in their absence provided they have been duly summoned.

4.   The Arbitral Tribunal, after having consulted the parties, may appoint one or more experts, define their terms of reference and receive their reports. At the request of a party, the parties shall be given the opportunity to question at a hearing any such expert appointed by the Tribunal.

5.   At any time during the proceedings, the Arbitral Tribunal may summon any party to provide additional evidence.

6.   The Arbitral Tribunal may decide the case solely on the documents submitted by the parties unless any of the parties requests a hearing.

7.   The Arbitral Tribunal may take measures for protecting trade secrets and confidential information.

Article 21

Hearings

1.   When a hearing is to be held, the Arbitral Tribunal, giving reasonable notice, shall summon the parties to appear before it on the day and at the place fixed by it.

2.   If any of the parties, although duly summoned, fails to appear without valid excuse, the Arbitral Tribunal shall have the power to proceed with the hearing.

3.   The Arbitral Tribunal shall be in full charge of the hearings, at which all the parties shall be entitled to be present. Save with the approval of the Arbitral Tribunal and the parties, persons not involved in the proceedings shall not be admitted.

4.   The parties may appear in person or through duly authorized representatives. In addition, they may be assisted by advisers.

Article 22

Closing of the Proceedings

1.   When it is satisfied that the parties have had a reasonable opportunity to present their cases, the Arbitral Tribunal shall declare the proceedings closed. Thereafter, no further submission or argument may be made, or evidence produced, unless requested or authorized by the Arbitral Tribunal.

2.   When the Arbitral Tribunal has declared the proceedings closed, it shall indicate to the Secretariat an approximate date by which the draft Award will be submitted to the Court for approval pursuant to Article 27. Any postponement of that date shall be communicated to the Secretariat by the Arbitral Tribunal.

Article 23

Conservatory and Interim Measures

1. Unless the parties have otherwise agreed, as soon as the file has been transmitted to it, the Arbitral Tribunal may, at the request of a party, order any interim or conservatory measure it deems appropriate. The Arbitral Tribunal may make the granting of any such measure subject to appropriate security being furnished by the requesting party. Any such measure shall take the form of an order, giving reasons, or of an Award, as the Arbitral Tribunal considers appropriate.

2. Before the file is transmitted to the Arbitral Tribunal, and in appropriate circumstances even thereafter, the parties may apply to any competent judicial authority for interim or conservatory measures. The application of a party to a judicial authority for such measures or for the implementation of any such measures ordered by an Arbitral Tribunal shall not be deemed to be an infringement or a waiver of the arbitration agreement and shall not affect the relevant powers reserved to the Arbitral Tribunal. Any such application and any measures taken by the judicial authority must be notified without delay to the Secretariat. The Secretariat shall inform the Arbitral Tribunal thereof.

AWARDS

Article 24

Time Limit for the Award

1. The time limit within which the Arbitral Tribunal must render its final Award is six months. Such time limit shall start to run from the date of the last signature by the Arbitral Tribunal or of the parties of the Terms of Reference, or, in the case of application of Article 18(3), the date of the notification to the Arbitral Tribunal by the Secretariat of the approval of the Terms of Reference by the Court.

2. The Court may extend this time limit pursuant to a reasoned request from the Arbitral Tribunal or on its own initiative if it decides it is necessary to do so.

Article 25

Making of the Award

1. When the Arbitral Tribunal is composed of more than one arbitrator, an Award is given by a majority decision. If there be no majority, the Award shall be made by the chairman of the Arbitral Tribunal alone.

2. The Award shall state the reasons upon which it is based.

3. The Award shall be deemed to be made at the place of the arbitration and on the date stated therein.

Article 26

Award by Consent

If the parties reach a settlement after the file has been transmitted to the Arbitral Tribunal in accordance with Article 13, the settlement shall be recorded in the form of an Award made by consent of the parties if so requested by the parties and if the Arbitral Tribunal agrees to do so.

Article 27

Scrutiny of the Award by the Court

Before signing any Award, the Arbitral Tribunal shall submit it in draft form to the Court. The Court may lay down modifications as to the form of the Award and, without affecting the Arbitral Tribunal's liberty of decision, may also draw its attention to points of substance. No Award shall be rendered by the Arbitral Tribunal until it has been approved by the Court as to its form.

Article 28

Notification, Deposit and Enforceability of the Award

1. Once an Award has been made, the Secretariat shall notify to the parties the text signed by the Arbitral Tribunal, provided always that the costs of the arbitration have been fully paid to the ICC by the parties or by one of them.

2. Additional copies certified true by the Secretary General shall be made available on request and at any time to the parties, but to no one else.

3. By virtue of the notification made in accordance with Paragraph 1 of this Article, the parties waive any other form of notification or deposit on the part of the Arbitral Tribunal.

4. An original of each Award made in accordance with the present Rules shall be deposited with the Secretariat.

5. The Arbitral Tribunal and the Secretariat shall assist the parties in complying with whatever further formalities may be necessary.

6. Every Award shall be binding on the parties. By submitting the dispute to arbitration under these Rules, the parties undertake to carry out any Award without delay and shall be deemed to have waived their right to any form of recourse insofar as such waiver can validly be made.

Article 29

Correction and Interpretation of the Award

1. On its own initiative, the Arbitral Tribunal may correct a clerical, computational or typographical error, or any errors of similar nature contained in an Award, provided such correction is submitted for approval to the Court within 30 days of the date of such Award.

2. Any application of a party for the correction of an error of the kind referred to in Article 29(1), or for the interpretation of an Award, must be made to the Secretariat within 30 days of the receipt of the Award by such party, in a number of copies as stated in Article 3(1). After transmittal of the application to the Arbitral Tribunal, it shall grant the other party a short time limit, normally not exceeding 30 days,

from the receipt of the application by that party to submit any comments thereon. If the Arbitral Tribunal decides to correct or interpret the Award, it shall submit its decision in draft form to the Court not later than 30 days following the expiration of the time limit for the receipt of any comments from the other party or within such other period as the Court may decide.

3.   The decision to correct or to interpret the Award shall take the form of an addendum and shall constitute part of the Award. The provisions of Articles 25, 27 and 28 shall apply mutatis mutandis.

COSTS

Article 30

Advance to Cover the Costs of the Arbitration

1.   After receipt of the Request, the Secretary General may request the Claimant to pay a provisional advance in an amount intended to cover the costs of arbitration until the Terms of Reference have been drawn up.

2.   As soon as practicable, the Court shall fix the advance on costs in an amount likely to cover the fees and expenses of the arbitrators and the ICC administrative costs for the claims and counterclaims which have been referred to it by the parties. This amount may be subject to readjustment at any time during the arbitration. Where, apart from the claims, counterclaims are submitted, the Court may fix separate advances on costs for the claims and the counterclaims.

3.   The advance on costs fixed by the Court shall be payable in equal shares by the Claimant and the Respondent. Any provisional advance paid on the basis of Article 30(1) will be considered as a partial payment thereof. However, any party shall be free to pay the whole of the advance on costs in respect of the principal claim or the counterclaim should the other party fail to pay its share. When the Court has set separate advances on costs in accordance with Article 30(2), each of the parties shall pay the advance on costs corresponding to its claims.

4.   When a request for an advance on costs has not been complied with, and after consultation with the Arbitral Tribunal, the Secretary General may direct the Arbitral Tribunal to suspend its work and set a time limit, which must be not less than 15 days, on the expiry of which the relevant claims, or counterclaims, shall be considered as withdrawn. Should the party in question wish to object to this measure it must make a request within the aforementioned period for the matter to be decided by the Court. Such party shall not be prevented on the ground of such withdrawal from reintroducing the same claims or counterclaims at a later date in another proceeding.

5.   If one of the parties claims a right to a set-off with regard to either claims or counterclaims, such set-off shall be taken into account in determining the advance to cover the costs of arbitration in the same

way as a separate claim insofar as it may require the Arbitral Tribunal to consider additional matters.

Article 31
Decision as to the Costs of the Arbitration

1. The costs of the arbitration shall include the fees and expenses of the arbitrators and the ICC administrative costs fixed by the Court, in accordance with the scale in force at the time of the commencement of the arbitral proceedings, as well as the fees and expenses of any experts appointed by the Arbitral Tribunal and the reasonable legal and other costs incurred by the parties for the arbitration.

2. The Court may fix the fees of the arbitrators at a figure higher or lower than that which would result from the application of the relevant scale should this be deemed necessary due to the exceptional circumstances of the case. Decisions on costs other than those fixed by the Court may be taken by the Arbitral Tribunal at any time during the proceedings.

3. The final Award shall fix the costs of the arbitration and decide which of the parties shall bear them or in what proportion they shall be borne by the parties.

MISCELLANEOUS
Article 32
Modified Time Limits

1. The parties may agree to shorten the various time limits set out in these Rules. Any such agreement entered into subsequent to the constitution of an Arbitral Tribunal shall become effective only upon the approval of the Arbitral Tribunal.

2. The Court, on its own initiative, may extend any time limit which has been modified pursuant to Article 32(1) if it decides that it is necessary to do so in order that the Arbitral Tribunal or the Court may fulfil their responsibilities in accordance with these Rules.

Article 33
Waiver

A party which proceeds with the arbitration without raising its objection to a failure to comply with any provision of these Rules, or of any other rules applicable to the proceedings, any direction given by the Arbitral Tribunal, or any requirement under the arbitration agreement relating to the constitution of the Arbitral Tribunal, or to the conduct of the proceedings, shall be deemed to have waived its right to object.

Article 34
Exclusion of Liability

Neither the arbitrators, nor the Court and its members, nor the ICC and its employees, nor the ICC National Committees shall be liable to any person for any act or omission in connection with the arbitration.

Article 35

General Rule

In all matters not expressly provided for in these Rules, the Court and the Arbitral Tribunal shall act in the spirit of these Rules and shall make every effort to make sure that the Award is enforceable at law.

APPENDIX I

STATUTES OF THE INTERNATIONAL COURT OF ARBITRATION OF THE ICC

Article 1

Function

1. The function of the International Court of Arbitration of the International Chamber of Commerce (the Court) is to ensure the application of the Rules of Arbitration and the Rules of Conciliation of the International Chamber of Commerce, and it has all the necessary powers for that purpose.

2. As an autonomous body, it carries out these functions in complete independence from the ICC and its organs.

3. Its members are independent from the ICC National Committees.

Article 2

Composition of the Court

The Court shall consist of a Chairman, Vice–Chairmen, and members and alternate members (collectively designated as members). In its work it is assisted by its Secretariat (Secretariat of the Court).

Article 3

Appointment

1. The Chairman is elected by the ICC Council upon recommendation of the Executive Board of the ICC.

2. The ICC Council appoints the Vice–Chairmen of the Court from among the members of the Court or otherwise.

3. Its members are appointed by the ICC Council on the proposal of National Committees, one member for each Committee.

4. On the proposal of the Chairman of the Court, the Council may appoint alternate members.

5. The term of office of all members is three years. If a member is no longer in a position to exercise his functions, his successor is appointed by the Council for the remainder of the term.

Article 4

Plenary Session of the Court

The Plenary Sessions of the Court are presided over by the Chairman, or, in his absence, by one of the Vice–Chairmen designated by him.

The deliberations shall be valid when at least six members are present. Decisions are taken by a majority vote, the Chairman having a casting vote in the event of a tie.

Article 5

Committees

The Court may set up one or more Committees and establish the functions and organization of such Committees.

Article 6

Confidentiality

The work of the Court is of a confidential nature and must be respected by everyone who participates in that work in whatever capacity. The Court lays down the rules regarding the persons who can attend the meetings of the Court and its Committees and who are entitled to have access to the materials submitted to the Court and its Secretariat.

Article 7

Modification of the Rules of Arbitration

Any proposal of the Court for a modification of the Rules is laid before the Commission on International Arbitration before submission to the Executive Board and the Council of the ICC for approval.

APPENDIX II

INTERNAL RULES OF THE INTERNATIONAL COURT OF ARBITRATION OF THE ICC

Article 1

Confidential Character of the Work of the International Court of Arbitration

1. The sessions of the Court, whether plenary or those of a Committee of the Court, are open only to its members and to the Secretariat.

2. However, in exceptional circumstances, the Chairman of the Court may invite other persons to attend. Such persons must respect the confidential nature of the work of the Court.

3. The documents submitted to the Court, or drawn up by it in the course of its proceedings, are communicated only to the members of the Court and to the Secretariat and to persons authorized by the Chairman to attend Court sessions.

4. The Chairman or the Secretary General of the Court may authorize researchers undertaking work of a scientific nature on international trade law to acquaint themselves with awards and other documents of general interest, with the exception of memoranda, notes, statements and documents remitted by the parties within the framework of arbitration proceedings.

5.   Such authorization shall not be given unless the beneficiary has undertaken to respect the confidential character of the documents made available and to refrain from any publication in their respect without having previously submitted the text for approval to the Secretary General of the Court.

6.   The Secretariat will in each case submitted to arbitration under the Rules retain in the archives of the Court all awards, terms of reference, and decisions of the Court as well as copies of the pertinent correspondence of the Secretariat.

7.   Any documents, communications or correspondence submitted by the parties or the arbitrators may be destroyed unless a party or an arbitrator requests in writing within a period fixed by the Secretariat the return of such documents. All related costs and expenses for the return of those documents shall be paid by such party or arbitrator.

Article 2

Participation of Members of the International Court of Arbitration in ICC Arbitration

1.   The Chairman and the members of the Secretariat of the Court may not act as arbitrators or as counsel in cases submitted to ICC arbitration.

2.   The Court shall not appoint Vice–Chairmen or members of the Court as arbitrators. They may, however, be proposed for such duties by one or more of the parties, or, pursuant to any other procedure agreed upon by the parties, subject to confirmation by the Court.

3.   When the Chairman, a Vice–Chairman or a member of the Court or of the Secretariat is involved in any capacity whatsoever in proceedings pending before the Court, such person must inform the Secretary General of the Court upon becoming aware of such involvement.

4.   Such person must refrain from participating in the discussions or in the decisions of the Court concerning the proceedings and must be absent from the courtroom whenever the matter is considered.

5.   Such person will not receive any material documentation or information pertaining to such proceedings.

Article 3

Relations between the Members of the Court and the ICC National Committees

1.   By virtue of their capacity, the members of the Court are independent of the ICC National Committees which proposed them for appointment by the ICC Council.

2.   Furthermore, they must regard as confidential, vis-à-vis the said National Committees, any information concerning individual cases with which they have become acquainted in their capacity as members of the Court, except when they have been requested by the Chairman of the

Court or by its Secretary General to communicate specific information to their respective National Committee.

Article 4

Committee of the Court

1. In accordance with the provisions of Article 1 (4) of the Rules and Article 5 of its Statutes (Appendix I), the Court hereby establishes a Committee of the Court.

2. The members of the Committee consist of a Chairman and at least two other members. The Chairman of the Court acts as the Chairman of the Committee. If absent, the Chairman may designate a Vice–Chairman of the Court or, in exceptional circumstances, another member of the Court as Chairman of the Committee.

3. The other two members of the Committee are appointed by the Court from among the Vice–Chairmen or the other members of the Court. At each Plenary Session the Court appoints the members who are to attend the meetings of the Committee to be held before the next Plenary Session.

4. The Committee meets when convened by its Chairman. Two members constitute a quorum.

5.

(a) The Court shall determine the decisions that may be taken by the Committee.

(b) The decisions of the Committee are taken unanimously.

(c) When the Committee cannot reach a decision or deems it preferable to abstain, it transfers the case to the next Plenary Session, making any suggestions it deems appropriate.

(d) The Committee's decisions are brought to the notice of the Court at its next Plenary Session.

Article 5

Court Secretariat

1. In case of absence, the Secretary General may delegate to the General Counsel and Deputy Secretary General the authority to confirm arbitrators, to certify true copies of awards and to request the payment of a provisional advance, respectively provided for in Articles 9(2), 28(2) and 30(1) of the Rules.

2. The Secretariat may, with the approval of the Court, issue notes and other documents for the information of the parties and the arbitrators, or as necessary for the proper conduct of the arbitral proceedings.

Article 6

Scrutiny of Arbitral Awards

When the Court scrutinizes draft awards in accordance with Article 27 of the Rules, it considers, to the extent practicable, the requirements of mandatory law at the place of arbitration.

APPENDIX III

ARBITRATION COSTS AND FEES

Article 1

Advance on Costs

1. Each request to commence an arbitration pursuant to the Rules must be accompanied by an advance payment of US$2500 on the administrative expenses. Such payment is nonrefundable, and shall be credited to the Claimant's portion of the advance on costs.

2. The provisional advance fixed by the Secretary General according to Article 30(1) of the Rules shall normally not exceed the amount obtained by adding together the administrative expenses, the minimum of the fees (as set out in the scale hereinafter) based upon the amount of the claim and the expected reimbursable expenses of the Arbitral Tribunal incurred with respect to the drafting of the Terms of Reference. If such amount is not quantified, the provisional advance shall be fixed at the discretion of the Secretary General. Payment by the Claimant shall be credited to its share of the advance on costs fixed by the Court.

3. In general, after the Terms of Reference have been signed or approved by the Court and the provisional timetable has been established, the Arbitral Tribunal shall, in accordance with Article 30(4) of the Rules, proceed only with respect to those claims or counterclaims in regard to which the whole of the advance on costs has been paid.

4. The advance on costs fixed by the Court according to Article 30(2) of the Rules comprises the fees of the arbitrator or arbitrators (hereinafter referred to as "arbitrator"), any arbitration-related expenses of the arbitrator and the administrative expenses.

5. Each party shall pay in cash its share of the total advance on costs. However, if its share exceeds an amount fixed from time to time by the Court, a party may post a bank guarantee for this additional amount.

6. A party that has already paid in full its share of the advance on costs fixed by the Court may, in accordance with Article 30(3) of the Rules, pay the unpaid portion of the advance owed by the defaulting party by posting a bank guarantee.

7. When the Court has fixed separate advances on costs pursuant to Article 30(2) of the Rules, the Secretariat shall invite each party to pay the amount of the advance corresponding to its respective claim(s).

8. When, as a result of the fixing of separate advances on costs, the separate advance fixed for the claim of either party exceeds one half of such global advance as was previously fixed (in respect of the same claims and counterclaims that are the subject of separate advances), a bank guarantee may be posted to cover any such excess amount. In the event that the amount of the separate advance is subsequently increased, at least one half of the increase shall be paid in cash.

9. The Secretariat shall establish the terms governing all bank guarantees which the parties may post pursuant to the above provisions.

10. As provided in Article 30(2) of the Rules, the advance on costs may be subject to readjustment at any time during the arbitration, in particular to take into account fluctuations in the amount in dispute, changes in the amount of the estimated expenses of the arbitrator, or the evolving difficulty or complexity of arbitration proceedings.

11. Before any expertise ordered by the Arbitral Tribunal can be commenced, the parties, or one of them, shall pay an advance on costs fixed by the Arbitral Tribunal sufficient to cover the expected fees and expenses of the expert as determined by the Arbitral Tribunal. The Arbitral Tribunal shall be responsible for ensuring the payment by the parties of such fees and expenses.

Article 2

Costs and Fees

1. Subject to Article 31(2) of the Rules, the Court shall fix the fees of the arbitrator in accordance with the scale hereinafter set out or, where the sum in dispute is not stated, at its discretion.

2. In setting the arbitrator's fees, the Court shall take into consideration the diligence of the arbitrator, the time spent, the rapidity of the proceedings, and the complexity of the dispute so as to arrive at a figure within the limits specified or, in exceptional circumstances (Article 31(2) of the Rules), at a figure higher or lower than those limits.

3. When a case is submitted to more than one arbitrator, the Court, at its discretion, shall have the right to increase the total fees up to a maximum which shall normally not exceed three times the fees of one arbitrator.

4. The arbitrator's fees and expenses shall be fixed exclusively by the Court as required by the Rules. Separate fee arrangements between the parties and the arbitrator are contrary to the Rules.

5. The Court shall fix the administrative expenses of each arbitration in accordance with the scale hereinafter set out or, where the sum in dispute is not stated, at its discretion. In exceptional circumstances, the Court may fix the administrative expenses at a lower or higher figure than that which would result from the application of such scale, provided that such expenses shall normally not exceed the maximum amount of the scale. Further, the Court may require the payment of administrative expenses in addition to those provided in the scale of administrative expenses as a condition to holding an arbitration in abeyance at the request of the parties or of one of them with the acquiescence of the other.

6. If an arbitration terminates before the rendering of a final Award, the Court shall fix the costs of the arbitration at its discretion, taking into account the stage attained by the arbitral proceedings and any other relevant circumstances.

7. In the case of an application under Article 29(2) of the Rules, the Court may fix an advance to cover additional fees and expenses of the Arbitral Tribunal and may make the transmission of such application to the Arbitral Tribunal subject to the prior cash payment in full to the ICC of such advance. The Court shall fix at its discretion any possible fees of the arbitrator when approving the decision of the Arbitral Tribunal.

8. When an arbitration is preceded by an attempt at amicable resolution pursuant to the ICC ADR Rules, one half of the administrative expenses paid for such ADR proceedings shall be credited to the administrative expenses of the arbitration.

9. Amounts paid to the arbitrator do not include any possible value added taxes (VAT) or other taxes or charges and imposts applicable to the arbitrator's fees. Parties have a duty to pay any such taxes or charges; however, the recovery of any such charges or taxes is a matter solely between the arbitrator and the parties.

Article 3

ICC as Appointing Authority

Any request received for an authority of the ICC to act as appointing authority will be treated in accordance with the Rules of ICC as Appointing Authority in UNCITRAL or Other Ad Hoc Arbitration Proceedings and shall be accompanied by a non-refundable sum of US$2,500. No request shall be processed unless accompanied by the said sum. For additional services, ICC may at its discretion fix administrative expenses, which shall be commensurate with the services provided and shall not exceed the maximum sum of US$10,000.

Article 4

Scales of Administrative Expenses and Arbitrator's Fees

1. The Scales of Administrative Expenses and Arbitrator's Fees set forth below shall be effective as of 1 July 2003 in respect of all arbitrations commenced on or after such date, irrespective of the version of the Rules applying to such arbitrations.

2. To calculate the administrative expenses and the arbitrator's fees, the amounts calculated for each successive slice of the sum in dispute must be added together, except that where the sum in dispute is over US$80 million, a flat amount of US$88,800 shall constitute the entirety of the administrative expenses.

A. Administrative Expenses

	Sum in dispute (in US dollars)	Administrative expenses(*)
up to	50 000	$2 500
from	50 001 to 100 000	3.50%
from	100 001 to 500 000	1.70%
from	500 001 to 1 000 000	1.15%

	Sum in dispute (in US dollars)	Administrative expenses(*)
from	1 000 001 to 2 000 000	0.70%
from	2 000 001 to 5 000 000	0.30%
from	5 000 001 to 10 000 000	0.20%
from	10,000,001 to 50,000,000	0.07%
from	50,000,001 to 80,000,000	0.06%
over	80 000 000	$88 800

(*) For illustrative purposes only. The table on the following page indicates the resulting administrative expenses in US $ when the proper calculations have been made.

B. Arbitrator's Fees

	Sum in dispute (in US dollars)	Fees(**)	
		Minimum	Maximum
up to	50 000	$2500	17.00%
from	50 001 to 100 000	2.00%	11.00%
from	100 001 to 500 000	1.00%	5.50%
from	500 001 to 1 000 000	0.75%	3.50%
from	1 000 001 to 2 000 000	0.50%	2.75%
from	2 000 001 to 5 000 000	0.25%	1.12%
from	5 000 001 to 10 000 000	0.10%	0.616%
from	10 000 001 to 50 000 000	0.05%	0.193%
from	50 000 001 to 80 000 000	0.03%	0.136%
from	80 000 001 to 100 000 000	0.02%	0.112%
over	100 000 000	0.01%	0.056%

** For illustrative purposes only. The table on the following page indicates the resulting range of fees when the proper calculations have been made.

SUM IN DISPUTE (in US Dollars)	A. ADMINISTRATIVE EXPENSES (in US Dollars)	B. ARBITRATOR'S FEES (in US Dollars)	
		Minimum	Maximum
up to 50 000	2500	2500	17.00% of amount in dispute
from 50 001 to 100 000	2500 + 3.50% of amt. over 50 000	2500 + 2.00% of amt. over 50 000	8500 + 11.00% of amt. over 50 000
from 100 001 to 500 000	4250 + 1.70% of amt. over 100 000	3500 + 1.00% of amt. over 100 000	14 000 + 5.50% of amt. over 100 000
from 500 001 to 1 000 000	11 050 + 1.15% of amt. over 500 000	7500+ 0.75% of amt. over 500 000	36 000 + 3.50% of amt. over 500 000
from 1 000 001 to 2 000 000	16 800 + 0.70% of amt. over 1 000 000	11 250 + 0.50% of amt. over 1 000 000	53 500 + 2.75% of amt. over 1 000 000
from 2 000 001 to 5 000 000	23 800 + 0.30% of amt. over 2 000 000	16 250 + 0.25% of amt. over 2 000 000	81 000 + 1.12% of amt. over 2 000 000
from 5 000 001 to 10 000 000	32 800 + 0.20% of amt. over 5 000 000	23 750 + 0.10% of amt. over 5 000 000	114 600 + 0.616% of amt. over 5 000 000
from 10 000 001 to 50 000 000	42 800 + 0.07% of amt. over 10 000 000	28 750 + 0.05% of amt. over 10 000 000	145 400 + 0.193% of amt. over 10 000 000
from 50 000 001 to 80 000 000	70 800 + 0.06% of amt. over 50 000 000	48 750 + 0.03% of amt. over 50 000 000	222 600 + 0.136% of amt. over 50 000 000
from 80 000 001 to 100 000 000	88 800	57 750 + 0.02% of amt. over 80 000 000	263 400+ 0.112% of amt. over 80 000 000
over 100 000 000	88 800		

LONDON COURT OF INTERNATIONAL ARBITRATION
RULES

(effective 1 January 1998)

Where any agreement, submission or reference provides in writing and in whatsoever manner for arbitration under the rules of the LCIA or by the Court of the LCIA ("the LCIA Court"), the parties shall be taken to have agreed in writing that the arbitration shall be conducted in accordance with the following rules ("the Rules") or such amended rules as the LCIA may have adopted hereafter to take effect before the commencement of the arbitration. The Rules include the Schedule of Costs in effect at the commencement of the arbitration, as separately amended from time to time by the LCIA Court.

Article 1. The Request for Arbitration

Any party wishing to commence an arbitration under these Rules ("the Claimant") shall send to the Registrar of the LCIA Court ("the Registrar") a written request for arbitration ("the Request"), containing or accompanied by:

(a) the names, addresses, telephone, facsimile, telex and e-mail numbers (if known) of the parties to the arbitration and of their legal representatives;

(b) a copy of the written arbitration clause or separate written arbitration agreement invoked by the Claimant ("the Arbitration Agreement"), together with a copy of the contractual documentation in which the arbitration clause is contained or in respect of which the arbitration arises;

(c) a brief statement describing the nature and circumstances of the dispute, and specifying the claims advanced by the Claimant against another party to the arbitration ("the Respondent");

(d) a statement of any matters (such as the seat or language(s) of the arbitration, or the number of arbitrators, or their qualifications or identities) on which the parties have already agreed in writing for the arbitration or in respect of which the Claimant wishes to make a proposal;

(e) if the Arbitration Agreement calls for party nomination of arbitrators, the name, address, telephone, facsimile, telex and e-mail numbers (if known) of the Claimant's nominee;

(f) the fee prescribed in the Schedule of Costs (without which the Request shall be treated as not having been received by the Registrar and the arbitration as not having been commenced);

(g) confirmation to the Registrar that copies of the Request (including all accompanying documents) have been or are being served simultaneously on all other parties to the arbitration by one or more means of service to be identified in such confirmation.

The date of receipt by the Registrar of the Request shall be treated as the date on which the arbitration has commenced for all purposes. The Request (including all accompanying documents) should be submitted to the Registrar in two copies where a sole arbitrator should be appointed, or, if the parties have agreed or the Claimant considers that three arbitrators should be appointed, in four copies.

Article 2.   The Response

Within 30 days of service of the Request on the Respondent, (or such lesser period fixed by the LCIA Court), the Respondent shall send to the Registrar a written response to the Request ("the Response"), containing or accompanied by:

(a) confirmation or denial of all or part of the claims advanced by the Claimant in the Request;

(b) a brief statement describing the nature and circumstances of any counterclaims advanced by the Respondent against the Claimant;

(c) comment in response to any statements contained in the Request, as called for under Article 1.1(d), on matters relating to the conduct of the arbitration;

(d) if the Arbitration Agreement calls for party nomination of arbitrators, the name, address, telephone, facsimile, telex and e-mail numbers (if known) of the Respondent's nominee; and

(e) confirmation to the Registrar that copies of the Response (including all accompanying documents) have been or are being served simultaneously on all other parties to the arbitration by one or more means of service to be identified in such confirmation.

The Response (including all accompanying documents) should be submitted to the Registrar in two copies, or if the parties have agreed or the Respondent considers that three arbitrators should be appointed, in four copies.

Failure to send a Response shall not preclude the Respondent from denying any claim or from advancing a counterclaim in the arbitration. However, if the Arbitration Agreement calls for party nomination of arbitrators, failure to send a Response or to nominate an arbitrator within time or at all shall constitute an irrevocable waiver of that party's opportunity to nominate an arbitrator.

Article 3.   The LCIA Court and Registrar

The functions of the LCIA Court under these Rules shall be performed in its name by the President or a Vice–President of the LCIA Court or by a division of three or five members of the LCIA Court appointed by the President or a Vice–President of the LCIA Court, as determined by the President.

The functions of the Registrar under these Rules shall be performed by the Registrar or any deputy Registrar of the LCIA Court under the supervision of the LCIA Court.

All communications from any party or arbitrator to the LCIA Court shall be addressed to the Registrar.

Article 4.   Notices and Periods of Time

Any notice or other communication that may be or is required to be given by a party under these Rules shall be in writing and shall be delivered by registered postal or courier service or transmitted by facsimile, telex, e-mail or any other means of telecommunication that provide a record of its transmission.

A party's last-known residence or place of business during the arbitration shall be a valid address for the purpose of any notice or other communication in the absence of any notification of a change to such address by that party to the other parties, the Arbitral Tribunal and the Registrar.

For the purpose of determining the date of commencement of a time limit, a notice or other communication shall be treated as having been received on the day it is delivered or, in the case of telecommunications, transmitted in accordance with Articles 4.1 and 4.2.

For the purpose of determining compliance with a time limit, a notice or other communication shall be treated as having been sent, made or transmitted if it is dispatched in accordance with Articles 4.1 and 4.2 prior to or on the date of the expiration of the time-limit.

Notwithstanding the above, any notice or communication by one party may be addressed to another party in the manner agreed in writing between them or, failing such agreement, according to the practice followed in the course of their previous dealings or in whatever manner ordered by the Arbitral Tribunal.

For the purpose of calculating a period of time under these Rules, such period shall begin to run on the day following the day when a notice or other communication is received. If the last day of such period is an official holiday or a non-business day at the residence or place of business of the addressee, the period is extended until the first business day which follows. Official holidays or non-business days occurring during the running of the period of time are included in calculating that period.

The Arbitral Tribunal may at any time extend (even where the period of time has expired) or abridge any period of time prescribed under these Rules or under the Arbitration Agreement for the conduct of the arbitration, including any notice or communication to be served by one party on any other party.

Article 5.   Formation of the Arbitral Tribunal

The expression "the Arbitral Tribunal" in these Rules includes a sole arbitrator or all the arbitrators where more than one. All references to an arbitrator shall include the masculine and feminine. (References to the President, Vice–President and members of the LCIA Court, the Registrar or deputy Registrar, expert, witness, party and legal representative shall be similarly understood).

All arbitrators conducting an arbitration under these Rules shall be and remain at all times impartial and independent of the parties; and none shall act in the arbitration as advocates for any party. No arbitrator, whether before or after appointment, shall advise any party on the merits or outcome of the dispute.

Before appointment by the LCIA Court, each arbitrator shall furnish to the Registrar a written résumé of his past and present professional positions; he shall agree in writing upon fee rates conforming to the Schedule of Costs; and he shall sign a declaration to the effect that there are no circumstances known to him likely to give rise to any justified doubts as to his impartiality or independence, other than any circumstances disclosed by him in the declaration. Each arbitrator shall thereby also assume a continuing duty forthwith to disclose any such circumstances to the LCIA Court, to any other members of the Arbitral Tribunal and to all the parties if such circumstances should arise after the date of such declaration and before the arbitration is concluded.

The LCIA Court shall appoint the Arbitral Tribunal as soon as practicable after receipt by the Registrar of the Response or after the expiry of 30 days following service of the Request upon the Respondent if no Response is received by the Registrar (or such lesser period fixed by the LCIA Court). The LCIA Court may proceed with the formation of the Arbitral Tribunal notwithstanding that the Request is incomplete or the Response is missing, late or incomplete. A sole arbitrator shall be appointed unless the parties have agreed in writing otherwise, or unless the LCIA Court determines that in view of all the circumstances of the case a three-member tribunal is appropriate.

The LCIA Court alone is empowered to appoint arbitrators. The LCIA Court will appoint arbitrators with due regard for any particular method or criteria of selection agreed in writing by the parties. In selecting arbitrators consideration will be given to the nature of the transaction, the nature and circumstances of the dispute, the nationality, location and languages of the parties and (if more than two) the number of parties.

In the case of a three-member Arbitral Tribunal, the chairman (who will not be a party-nominated arbitrator) shall be appointed by the LCIA Court.

Article 6.   Nationality of Arbitrators

Where the parties are of different nationalities, a sole arbitrator or chairman of the Arbitral Tribunal shall not have the same nationality as any party unless the parties who are not of the same nationality as the proposed appointee all agree in writing otherwise.

The nationality of parties shall be understood to include that of controlling shareholders or interests.

For the purpose of this Article, a person who is a citizen of two or more states shall be treated as a national of each state; and citizens of the European Union shall be treated as nationals of its different Member States and shall not be treated as having the same nationality.

Article 7.   Party and Other Nominations

If the parties have agreed that any arbitrator is to be appointed by one or more of them or by any third person, that agreement shall be treated as an agreement to nominate an arbitrator for all purposes. Such nominee may only be appointed by the LCIA Court as arbitrator subject to his prior compliance with Article 5.3. The LCIA Court may refuse to appoint any such nominee if it determines that he is not suitable or independent or impartial.

Where the parties have howsoever agreed that the Respondent or any third person is to nominate an arbitrator and such nomination is not made within time or at all, the LCIA Court may appoint an arbitrator notwithstanding the absence of the nomination and without regard to any late nomination. Likewise, if the Request for Arbitration does not contain a nomination by the Claimant where the parties have howsoever agreed that the Claimant or a third person is to nominate an arbitrator, the LCIA Court may appoint an arbitrator notwithstanding the absence of the nomination and without regard to any late nomination.

Article 8.   Three or More Parties

Where the Arbitration Agreement entitles each party howsoever to nominate an arbitrator, the parties to the dispute number more than two and such parties have not all agreed in writing that the disputant parties represent two separate sides for the formation of the Arbitral Tribunal as Claimant and Respondent respectively, the LCIA Court shall appoint the Arbitral Tribunal without regard to any party's nomination.

In such circumstances, the Arbitration Agreement shall be treated for all purposes as a written agreement by the parties for the appointment of the Arbitral Tribunal by the LCIA Court.

Article 9.   Expedited Formation

In exceptional urgency, on or after the commencement of the arbitration, any party may apply to the LCIA Court for the expedited formation of the Arbitral Tribunal, including the appointment of any replacement arbitrator under Articles 10 and 11 of these Rules.

Such an application shall be made in writing to the LCIA Court, copied to all other parties to the arbitration; and it shall set out the specific grounds for exceptional urgency in the formation of the Arbitral Tribunal.

The LCIA Court may, in its complete discretion, abridge or curtail any time-limit under these Rules for the formation of the Arbitral

Tribunal, including service of the Response and of any matters or documents adjudged to be missing from the Request. The LCIA Court shall not be entitled to abridge or curtail any other time-limit.

Article 10. Revocation of Arbitrator's Appointment

If either (a) any arbitrator gives written notice of his desire to resign as arbitrator to the LCIA Court, to be copied to the parties and the other arbitrators (if any) or (b) any arbitrator dies, falls seriously ill, refuses, or becomes unable or unfit to act, either upon challenge by a party or at the request of the remaining arbitrators, the LCIA Court may revoke that arbitrator's appointment and appoint another arbitrator. The LCIA Court shall decide upon the amount of fees and expenses to be paid for the former arbitrator's services (if any) as it may consider appropriate in all the circumstances.

If any arbitrator acts in deliberate violation of the Arbitration Agreement (including these Rules) or does not act fairly and impartially as between the parties or does not conduct or participate in the arbitration proceedings with reasonable diligence, avoiding unnecessary delay or expense, that arbitrator may be considered unfit in the opinion of the LCIA Court.

An arbitrator may also be challenged by any party if circumstances exist that give rise to justifiable doubts as to his impartiality or independence. A party may challenge an arbitrator it has nominated, or in whose appointment it has participated, only for reasons of which it becomes aware after the appointment has been made.

A party who intends to challenge an arbitrator shall, within 15 days of the formation of the Arbitral Tribunal or (if later) after becoming aware of any circumstances referred to in Article 10.1, 10.2 or 10.3, send a written statement of the reasons for its challenge to the LCIA Court, the Arbitral Tribunal and all other parties. Unless the challenged arbitrator withdraws or all other parties agree to the challenge within 15 days of receipt of the written statement, the LCIA Court shall decide on the challenge.

Article 11. Nomination and Replacement of Arbitrators

In the event that the LCIA Court determines that any nominee is not suitable or independent or impartial or if an appointed arbitrator is to be replaced for any reason, the LCIA Court shall have a complete discretion to decide whether or not to follow the original nominating process.

If the LCIA Court should so decide, any opportunity given to a party to make a re-nomination shall be waived if not exercised within 15 days (or such lesser time as the LCIA Court may fix), after which the LCIA Court shall appoint the replacement arbitrator.

Article 12. Majority Power to Continue Proceedings

If any arbitrator on a three-member Arbitral Tribunal refuses or persistently fails to participate in its deliberations, the two other arbitrators shall have the power, upon their written notice of such refusal or failure to the LCIA Court, the parties and the third arbitrator, to continue the arbitration (including the making of any decision, ruling or award), notwithstanding the absence of the third arbitrator.

In determining whether to continue the arbitration, the two other arbitrators shall take into account the stage of the arbitration, any explanation made by the third arbitrator for his non-participation and such other matters as they consider appropriate in the circumstances of the case. The reasons for such determination shall be stated in any award, order or other decision made by the two arbitrators without the participation of the third arbitrator.

In the event that the two other arbitrators determine at any time not to continue the arbitration without the participation of the third arbitrator missing from their deliberations, the two arbitrators shall notify in writing the parties and the LCIA Court of such determination; and in that event, the two arbitrators or any party may refer the matter to the LCIA Court for the revocation of that third arbitrator's appointment and his replacement under Article 10.

Article 13. Communications between Parties and the Arbitral Tribunal

Until the Arbitral Tribunal is formed, all communications between parties and arbitrators shall be made through the Registrar.

Thereafter, unless and until the Arbitral Tribunal directs that communications shall take place directly between the Arbitral Tribunal and the parties (with simultaneous copies to the Registrar), all written communications between the parties and the Arbitral Tribunal shall continue to be made through the Registrar.

Where the Registrar sends any written communication to one party on behalf of the Arbitral Tribunal, he shall send a copy to each of the other parties. Where any party sends to the Registrar any communication (including Written Statements and Documents under Article 15), it shall include a copy for each arbitrator; and it shall also send copies direct to all other parties and confirm to the Registrar in writing that it has done or is doing so.

Article 14. Conduct of the Proceedings

The parties may agree on the conduct of their arbitral proceedings and they are encouraged to do so, consistent with the Arbitral Tribunal's general duties at all times:

    (i) to act fairly and impartially as between all parties, giving each a reasonable opportunity of putting its case and dealing with that of its opponent; and

    (ii) to adopt procedures suitable to the circumstances of the arbitration, avoiding unnecessary delay or expense, so as to provide a fair and efficient means for the final resolution of the parties' dispute.

Such agreements shall be made by the parties in writing or recorded in writing by the Arbitral Tribunal at the request of and with the authority of the parties.

Unless otherwise agreed by the parties under Article 14.1, the Arbitral Tribunal shall have the widest discretion to discharge its duties allowed under such law(s) or rules of law as the Arbitral Tribunal may determine to be applicable; and at all times the parties shall do everything necessary for the fair, efficient and expeditious conduct of the arbitration.

In the case of a three-member Arbitral Tribunal the chairman may, with the prior consent of the other two arbitrators, make procedural rulings alone.

Article 15.   Submission of Written Statements and Documents

Unless the parties have agreed otherwise under Article 14.1 or the Arbitral Tribunal should determine differently, the written stage of the proceedings shall be as set out below.

Within 30 days of receipt of written notification from the Registrar of the formation of the Arbitral Tribunal, the Claimant shall send to the Registrar a Statement of Case setting out in sufficient detail the facts and any contentions of law on which it relies, together with the relief claimed against all other parties, save and insofar as such matters have not been set out in its Request.

Within 30 days of receipt of the Statement of Case or written notice from the Claimant that it elects to treat the Request as its Statement of Case, the Respondent shall send to the Registrar a Statement of Defence setting out in sufficient detail which of the facts and contentions of law in the Statement of Case or Request (as the case may be) it admits or denies, on what grounds and on what other facts and contentions of law it relies. Any counterclaims shall be submitted with the Statement of Defence in the same manner as claims are to be set out in the Statement of Case.

Within 30 days of receipt of the Statement of Defence, the Claimant shall send to the Registrar a Statement of Reply which, where there are any counterclaims, shall include a Defence to Counterclaim in the same manner as a defence is to be set out in the Statement of Defence.

If the Statement of Reply contains a Defence to Counterclaim, within 30 days of its receipt the Respondent shall send to the Registrar a Statement of Reply to Counterclaim.

All Statements referred to in this Article shall be accompanied by copies (or, if they are especially voluminous, lists) of all essential documents on which the party concerned relies and which have not previously been submitted by any party, and (where appropriate) by any relevant samples and exhibits.

As soon as practicable following receipt of the Statements specified in this Article, the Arbitral Tribunal shall proceed in such manner as has been agreed in writing by the parties or pursuant to its authority under these Rules.

If the Respondent fails to submit a Statement of Defence or the Claimant a Statement of Defence to Counterclaim, or if at any point any party fails to avail itself of the opportunity to present its case in the manner determined by Article 15.2 to 15.6 or directed by the Arbitral Tribunal, the Arbitral Tribunal may nevertheless proceed with the arbitration and make an award.

Article 16.   Seat of Arbitration and Place of Hearings

The parties may agree in writing the seat (or legal place) of their arbitration. Failing such a choice, the seat of arbitration shall be London, unless and until the LCIA Court determines in view of all the circumstances, and after having given the parties an opportunity to make written comment, that another seat is more appropriate.

The Arbitral Tribunal may hold hearings, meetings and deliberations at any convenient geographical place in its discretion; and if elsewhere than the seat of the arbitration, the arbitration shall be treated as an arbitration conducted at the seat of the arbitration and any award as an award made at the seat of the arbitration for all purposes.

The law applicable to the arbitration (if any) shall be the arbitration law of the seat of arbitration, unless and to the extent that the parties have expressly agreed in writing on the application of another arbitration law and such agreement is not prohibited by the law of the arbitral seat.

Article 17.   Language of Arbitration

The initial language of the arbitration shall be the language of the Arbitration Agreement, unless the parties have agreed in writing otherwise and providing always that a non-participating or defaulting party shall have no cause for complaint if communications to and from the Registrar and the arbitration proceedings are conducted in English.

In the event that the Arbitration Agreement is written in more than one language, the LCIA Court may, unless the Arbitration Agreement provides that the arbitration proceedings shall be conducted in more than one language, decide which of those languages shall be the initial language of the arbitration.

Upon the formation of the Arbitral Tribunal and unless the parties have agreed upon the language or languages of the arbitration, the Arbitration Tribunal shall decide upon the language(s) of the arbitration, after giving the parties an opportunity to make written comment and taking into account the initial language of the arbitration and any other matter it may consider appropriate in all the circumstances of the case.

If any document is expressed in a language other than the language(s) of the arbitration and no translation of such document is submitted by the party relying upon the document, the Arbitral Tribunal or (if the Arbitral Tribunal has not been formed) the LCIA Court may order that party to submit a translation in a form to be determined by the Arbitral Tribunal or the LCIA Court, as the case may be.

Article 18.   Party Representation

Any party may be represented by legal practitioners or any other representatives.

At any time the Arbitral Tribunal may require from any party proof of authority granted to its representative(s) in such form as the Arbitral Tribunal may determine.

Article 19.   Hearings

Any party which expresses a desire to that effect has the right to be heard orally before the Arbitral Tribunal on the merits of the dispute, unless the parties have agreed in writing on documents-only arbitration.

The Arbitral Tribunal shall fix the date, time and physical place of any meetings and hearings in the arbitration, and shall give the parties reasonable notice thereof.

The Arbitral Tribunal may in advance of any hearing submit to the parties a list of questions which it wishes them to answer with special attention.

All meetings and hearings shall be in private unless the parties agree otherwise in writing or the Arbitral Tribunal directs otherwise.

The Arbitral Tribunal shall have the fullest authority to establish time-limits for meetings and hearings, or for any parts thereof.

Article 20.   Witnesses

Before any hearing, the Arbitral Tribunal may require any party to give notice of the identity of each witness that party wishes to call (including rebuttal witnesses), as well as the subject matter of that witness's testimony, its content and its relevance to the issues in the arbitration.

The Arbitral Tribunal may also determine the time, manner and form in which such materials should be exchanged between the parties and presented to the Arbitral Tribunal; and it has a discretion to allow, refuse, or limit the appearance of witnesses (whether witness of fact or expert witness).

Subject to any order otherwise by the Arbitral Tribunal, the testimony of a witness may be presented by a party in written form, either as a signed statement or as a sworn affidavit.

Subject to Article 14.1 and 14.2, any party may request that a witness, on whose testimony another party seeks to rely, should attend for oral questioning at a hearing before the Arbitral Tribunal. If the Arbitral Tribunal orders that other party to produce the witness and the witness fails to attend the oral hearing without good cause, the Arbitral Tribunal may place such weight on the written testimony (or exclude the same altogether) as it considers appropriate in the circumstances of the case.

Any witness who gives oral evidence at a hearing before the Arbitral Tribunal may be questioned by each of the parties under the control of the Arbitral Tribunal. The Arbitral Tribunal may put questions at any stage of his evidence.

Subject to the mandatory provisions of any applicable law, it shall not be improper for any party or its legal representatives to interview any witness or potential witness for the purpose of presenting his testimony in written form or producing him as an oral witness.

Any individual intending to testify to the Arbitral Tribunal on any issue of fact or expertise shall be treated as a witness under these Rules notwithstanding that the individual is a party to the arbitration or was or is an officer, employee or shareholder of any party.

Article 21.   Experts to the Arbitral Tribunal

Unless otherwise agreed by the parties in writing, the Arbitral Tribunal:

(a) may appoint one or more experts to report to the Arbitral Tribunal on specific issues, who shall be and remain impartial and independent of the parties throughout the arbitration proceedings; and

(b) may require a party to give any such expert any relevant information or to provide access to any relevant documents, goods, samples, property or site for inspection by the expert.

Unless otherwise agreed by the parties in writing, if a party so requests or if the Arbitral Tribunal considers it necessary, the expert shall, after delivery of his written or oral report to the Arbitral Tribunal and the parties, participate in one or more hearings at which the parties shall have the opportunity to question the expert on his report and to present expert witnesses in order to testify on the points at issue.

The fees and expenses of any expert appointed by the Arbitral Tribunal under this Article shall be paid out of the deposits payable by the parties under Article 24 and shall form part of the costs of the arbitration.

Article 22.   Additional Powers of the Arbitral Tribunal

Unless the parties at any time agree otherwise in writing, the Arbitral Tribunal shall have the power, on the application of any party or of its own motion, but in either case only after giving the parties a reasonable opportunity to state their views:

(a) to allow any party, upon such terms (as to costs and otherwise) as it shall determine, to amend any claim, counterclaim, defence and reply

(b) to extend or abbreviate any time-limit provided by the Arbitration Agreement or these Rules for the conduct of the arbitration or by the Arbitral Tribunal's own orders;

(c) to conduct such enquiries as may appear to the Arbitral Tribunal to be necessary or expedient, including whether and to what extent the Arbitral Tribunal should itself take the initiative in identifying the issues and ascertaining the relevant facts and the law(s) or rules of law applicable to the arbitration, the merits of the parties' dispute and the Arbitration Agreement;

(d) to order any party to make any property, site or thing under its control and relating to the subject matter of the arbitration available for inspection by the Arbitral Tribunal, any other party, its expert or any expert to the Arbitral Tribunal;

(e) to order any party to produce to the Arbitral Tribunal, and to the other parties for inspection, and to supply copies of, any documents or classes of documents in their possession, custody or power which the Arbitral Tribunal determines to be relevant;

(f) to decide whether or not to apply any strict rules of evidence (or any other rules) as to the admissibility, relevance or weight of any material tendered by a party on any matter of fact or expert opinion; and to determine the time, manner and form in which such material should be exchanged between the parties and presented to the Arbitral Tribunal;

(g) to order the correction of any contract between the parties or the Arbitration Agreement, but only to the extent required to rectify any mistake which the Arbitral Tribunal determines to be common to the parties and then only if and to the extent to which the law(s) or rules of law applicable to the contract or Arbitration Agreement permit such correction; and

(h) to allow, only upon the application of a party, one or more third persons to be joined in the arbitration as a party provided any such third person and the applicant party have consented thereto in writing, and thereafter to make a single final award, or separate awards, in respect of all parties so implicated in the arbitration;

By agreeing to arbitration under these Rules, the parties shall be treated as having agreed not to apply to any state court or other judicial authority for any order available from the Arbitral Tribunal under Article 22.1, except with the agreement in writing of all parties.

The Arbitral Tribunal shall decide the parties' dispute in accordance with the law(s) or rules of law chosen by the parties as applicable to the merits of their dispute. If and to the extent that the Arbitral Tribunal determines that the parties have made no such choice, the Arbitral Tribunal shall apply the law(s) or rules of law which it considers appropriate.

The Arbitral Tribunal shall only apply to the merits of the dispute principles deriving from "ex aequo et bono", "amiable composition" or "honourable engagement" where the parties have so agreed expressly in writing.

Article 23.   Jurisdiction of the Arbitral Tribunal

The Arbitral Tribunal shall have the power to rule on its own jurisdiction, including any objection to the initial or continuing existence, validity or effectiveness of the Arbitration Agreement. For that purpose, an arbitration clause which forms or was intended to form part of another agreement shall be treated as an arbitration agreement independent of that other agreement. A decision by the Arbitral Tribunal that such other agreement is non-existent, invalid or ineffective shall not entail ipso jure the non-existence, invalidity or ineffectiveness of the arbitration clause.

A plea by a Respondent that the Arbitral Tribunal does not have jurisdiction shall be treated as having been irrevocably waived unless it is raised not later than the Statement of Defence; and a like plea by a Respondent to Counterclaim shall be similarly treated unless it is raised no later than the Statement of Defence to Counterclaim. A plea that the Arbitral Tribunal is exceeding the scope of its authority shall be raised promptly after the Arbitral Tribunal has indicated its intention to decide on the matter alleged by any party to be beyond the scope of its authority, failing which such plea shall also be treated as having been waived irrevocably. In any case, the Arbitral Tribunal may nevertheless admit an untimely plea if it considers the delay justified in the particular circumstances.

The Arbitral Tribunal may determine the plea to its jurisdiction or authority in an award as to jurisdiction or later in an award on the merits, as it considers appropriate in the circumstances.

By agreeing to arbitration under these Rules, the parties shall be treated as having agreed not to apply to any state court or other judicial authority for any relief regarding the Arbitral Tribunal's jurisdiction or authority, except with the agreement in writing of all parties to the arbitration or the prior authorisation of the Arbitral Tribunal or following the latter's award ruling on the objection to its jurisdiction or authority.

Article 24.   Deposits

The LCIA Court may direct the parties, in such proportions as it thinks appropriate, to make one or several interim or final payments on account of the costs of the arbitration. Such deposits shall be made to and held by the LCIA and from time to time may be released by the LCIA Court to the arbitrator(s), any expert appointed by the Arbitral Tribunal and the LCIA itself as the arbitration progresses.

The Arbitral Tribunal shall not proceed with the arbitration without ascertaining at all times from the Registrar or any deputy Registrar that the LCIA is in requisite funds.

In the event that a party fails or refuses to provide any deposit as directed by the LCIA Court, the LCIA Court may direct the other party or parties to effect a substitute payment to allow the arbitration to proceed (subject to any award on costs). In such circumstances, the party paying the substitute payment shall be entitled to recover that amount as a debt immediately due from the defaulting party.

Failure by a claimant or counterclaiming party to provide promptly and in full the required deposit may be treated by the LCIA Court and the Arbitral Tribunal as a withdrawal of the claim or counterclaim respectively.

Article 25. Interim and Conservatory Measures

The Arbitral Tribunal shall have the power, unless otherwise agreed by the parties in writing, on the application of any party:

(a) to order any respondent party to a claim or counterclaim to provide security for all or part of the amount in dispute, by way of deposit or bank guarantee or in any other manner and upon such terms as the Arbitral Tribunal considers appropriate. Such terms may include the provision by the claiming or counterclaiming party of a cross-indemnity, itself secured in such manner as the Arbitral Tribunal considers appropriate, for any costs or losses incurred by such respondent in providing security. The amount of any costs and losses payable under such cross-indemnity may be determined by the Arbitral Tribunal in one or more awards;

(b) to order the preservation, storage, sale or other disposal of any property or thing under the control of any party and relating to the subject matter of the arbitration; and

(c) to order on a provisional basis, subject to final determination in an award, any relief which the Arbitral Tribunal would have power to grant in an award, including a provisional order for the payment of money or the disposition of property as between any parties.

The Arbitral Tribunal shall have the power, upon the application of a party, to order any claiming or counterclaiming party to provide security for the legal or other costs of any other party by way of deposit or bank guarantee or in any other manner and upon such terms as the Arbitral Tribunal considers appropriate. Such terms may include the provision by that other party of a cross-indemnity, itself secured in such manner as the Arbitral Tribunal considers appropriate, for any costs and losses incurred by such claimant or counterclaimant in providing security. The amount of any costs and losses payable under such cross-indemnity may be determined by the Arbitral Tribunal in one or more awards. In the event that a claiming or counterclaiming party does not comply with any order to provide security, the Arbitral Tribunal may stay that party's claims or counterclaims or dismiss them in an award.

The power of the Arbitral Tribunal under Article 25.1 shall not prejudice howsoever any party's right to apply to any state court or other judicial authority for interim or conservatory measures before the formation of the Arbitral Tribunal and, in exceptional cases, thereafter. Any application and any order for such measures after the formation of the Arbitral Tribunal shall be promptly communicated by the applicant to the Arbitral Tribunal and all other parties. However, by agreeing to arbitration under these Rules, the parties shall be taken to have agreed not to apply to any state court or other judicial authority for any order for security for its legal or other costs available from the Arbitral Tribunal under Article 25.2.

Article 26.   The Award

The Arbitral Tribunal shall make its award in writing and, unless all parties agree in writing otherwise, shall state the reasons upon which its award is based. The award shall also state the date when the award is made and the seat of the arbitration; and it shall be signed by the Arbitral Tribunal or those of its members assenting to it.

If any arbitrator fails to comply with the mandatory provisions of any applicable law relating to the making of the award, having been given a reasonable opportunity to do so, the remaining arbitrators may proceed in his absence and state in their award the circumstances of the other arbitrator's failure to participate in the making of the award.

Where there are three arbitrators and the Arbitral Tribunal fails to agree on any issue, the arbitrators shall decide that issue by a majority. Failing a majority decision on any issue, the chairman of the Arbitral Tribunal shall decide that issue.

If any arbitrator refuses or fails to sign the award, the signatures of the majority or (failing a majority) of the chairman shall be sufficient, provided that the reason for the omitted signature is stated in the award by the majority or chairman.

The sole arbitrator or chairman shall be responsible for delivering the award to the LCIA Court, which shall transmit certified copies to the parties provided that the costs of arbitration have been paid to the LCIA in accordance with Article 28.

An award may be expressed in any currency. The Arbitral Tribunal may order that simple or compound interest shall be paid by any party on any sum awarded at such rates as the Arbitral Tribunal determines to be appropriate, without being bound by legal rates of interest imposed by any state court, in respect of any period which the Arbitral Tribunal determines to be appropriate ending not later than the date upon which the award is complied with.

The Arbitral Tribunal may make separate awards on different issues at different times. Such awards shall have the same status and effect as any other award made by the Arbitral Tribunal.

In the event of a settlement of the parties' dispute, the Arbitral Tribunal may render an award recording the settlement if the parties so request in writing (a "Consent Award"), provided always that such award contains an express statement that it is an award made by the parties' consent. A Consent Award need not contain reasons. If the parties do not require a consent award, then on written confirmation by the parties to the LCIA Court that a settlement has been reached, the Arbitral Tribunal shall be discharged and the arbitration proceedings concluded, subject to payment by the parties of any outstanding costs of the arbitration under Article 28.

All awards shall be final and binding on the parties. By agreeing to arbitration under these Rules, the parties undertake to carry out any award immediately and without any delay (subject only to Article 27); and the parties also waive irrevocably their right to any form of appeal, review or recourse to any state court or other judicial authority, insofar as such waiver may be validly made.

Article 27.   Correction of Awards and Additional Awards

Within 30 days of receipt of any award, or such lesser period as may be agreed in writing by the parties, a party may by written notice to the Registrar (copied to all other parties) request the Arbitral Tribunal to correct in the award any errors in computation, clerical or typographical errors or any errors of a similar nature. If the Arbitral Tribunal considers the request to be justified, it shall make the corrections within 30 days of receipt of the request. Any correction shall take the form of separate memorandum dated and signed by the Arbitral Tribunal or (if three arbitrators) those of its members assenting to it; and such memorandum shall become part of the award for all purposes.

The Arbitral Tribunal may likewise correct any error of the nature described in Article 27.1 on its own initiative within 30 days of the date of the award, to the same effect.

Within 30 days of receipt of the final award, a party may by written notice to the Registrar (copied to all other parties), request the Arbitral Tribunal to make an additional award as to claims or counterclaims presented in the arbitration but not determined in any award. If the Arbitral Tribunal considers the request to be justified, it shall make the additional award within 60 days of receipt of the request. The provisions of Article 26 shall apply to any additional award.

Article 28.   Arbitration and Legal Costs

The costs of the arbitration (other than the legal or other costs incurred by the parties themselves) shall be determined by the LCIA Court in accordance with the Schedule of Costs. The parties shall be jointly and severally liable to the Arbitral Tribunal and the LCIA for such arbitration costs.

The Arbitral Tribunal shall specify in the award the total amount of the costs of the arbitration as determined by the LCIA Court. Unless the parties agree otherwise in writing, the Arbitral Tribunal shall determine the proportions in which the parties shall bear all or part of such arbitration costs. If the Arbitral Tribunal has determined that all or any part of the arbitration costs shall be borne by a party other than a party which has already paid them to the LCIA, the latter party shall have the right to recover the appropriate amount from the former party.

The Arbitral Tribunal shall also have the power to order in its award that all or part of the legal or other costs incurred by a party be paid by another party, unless the parties agree otherwise in writing. The Arbitral Tribunal shall determine and fix the amount of each item comprising such costs on such reasonable basis as it thinks fit.

Unless the parties otherwise agree in writing, the Arbitral Tribunal shall make its orders on both arbitration and legal costs on the general principle that costs should reflect the parties' relative success and failure in the award or arbitration, except where it appears to the Arbitral Tribunal that in the particular circumstances this general approach is inappropriate. Any order for costs shall be made with reasons in the award containing such order.

If the arbitration is abandoned, suspended or concluded, by agreement or otherwise, before the final award is made, the parties shall remain jointly and severally liable to pay to the LCIA and the Arbitral Tribunal the costs of the arbitration as determined by the LCIA Court in accordance with the Schedule of Costs. In the event that such arbitration costs are less than the deposits made by the parties, there shall be a refund by the LCIA in such proportion as the parties may agree in writing, or failing such agreement, in the same proportions as the deposits were made by the parties to the LCIA.

Article 29.   Decisions by the LCIA Court

The decisions of the LCIA Court with respect to all matters relating to the arbitration shall be conclusive and binding upon the parties and the Arbitral Tribunal. Such decisions are to be treated as administrative in nature and the LCIA Court shall not be required to give any reasons.

To the extent permitted by the law of the seat of the arbitration, the parties shall be taken to have waived any right of appeal or review in respect of any such decisions of the LCIA Court to any state court or other judicial authority. If such appeals or review remain possible due to mandatory provisions of any applicable law, the LCIA Court shall, subject to the provisions of that applicable law, decide whether the arbitral proceedings are to continue, notwithstanding an appeal or review.

Article 30.   Confidentiality

Unless the parties expressly agree in writing to the contrary, the parties undertake as a general principle to keep confidential all awards in their arbitration, together with all materials in the proceedings created for the purpose of the arbitration and all other documents produced by another party in the proceedings not otherwise in the public domain—save and to the extent that disclosure may be required of a party by legal duty, to protect or pursue a legal right or to enforce or challenge an award in bona fide legal proceedings before a state court or other judicial authority.

The deliberations of the Arbitral Tribunal are likewise confidential to its members, save and to the extent that disclosure of an arbitrator's refusal to participate in the arbitration is required of the other members of the Arbitral Tribunal under Articles 10, 12 and 26.

The LCIA Court does not publish any award or any part of an award without the prior written consent of all parties and the Arbitral Tribunal.

Article 31.   Exclusion of Liability

None of the LCIA, the LCIA Court (including its President, Vice–Presidents and individual members), the Registrar, any deputy Registrar, any arbitrator and any expert to the Arbitral Tribunal shall be liable to any party howsoever for any act or omission in connection with any arbitration conducted by reference to these Rules, save where the act or omission is shown by that party to constitute conscious and deliberate wrongdoing committed by the body or person alleged to be liable to that party.

After the award has been made and the possibilities of correction and additional awards referred to in Article 27 have lapsed or been exhausted, neither the LCIA, the LCIA Court (including its President, Vice–Presidents and individual members), the Registrar, any deputy Registrar, any arbitrator or expert to the Arbitral Tribunal shall be under any legal obligation to make any statement to any person about any matter concerning the arbitration, nor shall any party seek to make any of these persons a witness in any legal or other proceedings arising out of the arbitration.

Article 32.   General Rules

A party who knows that any provision of the Arbitration Agreement (including these Rules) has not been complied with and yet proceeds with the arbitration without promptly stating its objection to such non-compliance, shall be treated as having irrevocably waived its right to object.

In all matters not expressly provided for in these Rules, the LCIA Court, the Arbitral Tribunal and the parties shall act in the spirit of these Rules and shall make every reasonable effort to ensure that an award is legally enforceable.

SCHEDULE OF ARBITRATION
FEES AND COSTS
(effective 1 June 2003)

For arbitrations under the LCIA Rules; under UNCITRAL Rules when administered by the LCIA; when the LCIA acts as Appointing Authority only; and when the LCIA is appointed to decide challenges.

1. Administrative charges under LCIA and UNCITRAL Rules*

a. Registration Fee (payable in advance with Request for Arbitration non-refundable). £1,500

b. Time spent** by the Registrar and his/her deputy, and by the Secretariat of the LCIA in the administration of the arbitration.***

   Registrar and his/her deputy £200 per hour

   Secretariat £100 per hour

c. A sum equivalent to 5% of the fees of the Tribunal (excluding expenses) in respect of the LCIA's general overhead. * * *

d. Expenses incurred by the Secretariat in connection with the arbitration (such as postage, telephone, facsimile, travel etc.), and additional arbitration support services, whether provided by the Secretariat from its own resources or otherwise. * * * at applicable hourly rates or at cost

e. The LCIA's fees and expenses will be invoiced in sterling, but may be paid in other convertible currencies, at rates prevailing at the time of payment, provided that any transfer and/or currency exchange charges shall be borne by the payer.

2. Request to Act as Appointing Authority only*

a. Appointment Fee (payable in advance with request—non-refundable). £1,000

b. As for 1(b) and 1(d), above.

3. Request to act in deciding challenges to arbitrators in non-LCIA arbitrations

a. As for 2(a) and 2(b), above; plus

b. Time spent by members of the LCIA Court in carrying out their functions in deciding the challenges. at hourly rates advised by members of the LCIA Court

4. Fees and Expenses of the Tribunal

a. The Tribunal's fees will be calculated by reference to work done by its members in connection with the arbitration and will be charged at rates appropriate to the particular circumstances of the case, including its complexity and the special qualifications of the arbitrators. The Tribunal shall agree in writing upon fee rates conforming to this Schedule of Fees and Costs prior to its appointment by the LCIA Court. The rates will be advised by the Registrar to the parties at the time of the appointment of

---

* Charges may be subject to Value Added Tax at the prevailing rate.

** Minimum unit of time in all cases: 15 minutes.

*** Items 1(b), 1(c), and 1(d) above, are payable on interim invoice; with the award, or as directed by the LCIA Court under Article 24.1 of the Rules.

the Tribunal, but may be reviewed annually if the duration of the arbitration requires.

The fee rates shall be within the following range: £150 to £350 per hour.

However, in exceptional cases, the rate may be higher or lower, provided that, in such cases, (a) the fees of the Tribunal shall be fixed by the LCIA Court on the recommendation of the Registrar, following consultations with the arbitrator(s), and (b) the fees shall be agreed expressly by all parties.

b. The Tribunal's fees may include a charge for time spent travelling.

c. The Tribunal's fees may also include a charge for time reserved but not used as a result of late postponement or cancellation, provided that the basis for such charge shall be advised in writing to, and approved by, the LCIA Court.

d. The Tribunal may also recover such expenses as are reasonably incurred in connection with the arbitration, and as are in a reasonable amount, provided that claims for expenses should be supported by invoices or receipts.

e. Tribunal's fees may be invoiced either in the currency of account between the Tribunal and the parties, or in sterling. The Tribunal's expenses may be invoiced in the currency in which they were incurred, or in sterling.

f. In the event of the revocation of the appointment of any arbitrator, pursuant to the provisions of Article 10 of the LCIA Rules, the LCIA Court shall decide upon the amount of fees and expenses to be paid for the former arbitrator's services (if any) as it may consider appropriate in all the circumstances.

5. Deposits

a. The LCIA Court may direct the parties, in such proportions as it thinks appropriate, to make one or several interim or final payments on account of the costs of the arbitration. The LCIA Court may limit such payments to a sum sufficient to cover fees, expenses and costs for the next stage of the arbitration.

b. The Tribunal shall not proceed with the arbitration without ascertaining at all times from the Registrar or any deputy Registrar that the LCIA is in requisite funds.

c. In the event that a party fails or refuses to provide any deposit as directed by the LCIA Court, the LCIA Court may direct the other party or parties to effect a substitute payment to allow the arbitration to proceed (subject to any award on costs). In such circumstances, the party paying the substitute payment shall be entitled to recover that amount as a debt immediately due from the defaulting party.

d. Failure by a claimant or counterclaiming party to provide promptly and in full the required deposit may be treated by the LCIA Court and the Arbitral Tribunal as a withdrawal of the claim or counterclaim, respectively.

e. Funds lodged by the parties on account of the fees and expenses of the Tribunal and of the LCIA are held on trust in client bank accounts which are controlled by reference to each individual case and are disbursed by the LCIA, in accordance with the LCIA Rules and with this Schedule of Arbitration Fees and Costs. In the event that funds lodged by the parties exceed the costs of the arbitration at the conclusion of the arbitration, surplus monies will be returned to the parties as the ultimate default beneficiaries under the trust.

6. Interest on Deposits

Interest on sums deposited shall be credited to the account of each party depositing them, at the rate applicable to an amount equal to the amount so credited.

7. Interim Payments

a. When interim payments are required to cover the LCIA's administrative costs or the Tribunal's fees or expenses, including the fees or expenses of any expert appointed by the Tribunal, such payments may be made out of deposits held, upon the approval of the LCIA Court.

b. The LCIA may, in any event, submit interim invoices in respect of all current arbitrations, in March, June, September and December of each year, for payment direct by the parties or from funds held on deposit.

8. Registrar's Authority

a. For the purposes of sections 5(a) and 5(c) above, and of Articles 24.1 and 24.3 of the LCIA Rules, the Registrar has the authority of the LCIA Court to make the directions referred to, under the supervision of the Court.

b. For the purposes of section 7(a) above, and of Article 24.1 of the LCIA Rules, the Registrar has the authority of the LCIA Court to approve the payments referred to.

c. Any request by an arbitrator for payment on account of his fees shall be supported by a fee note, which shall include, or be accompanied by, details of the time spent at the rates that have been advised to the parties by the LCIA.

d. Any dispute regarding administration costs or the fees and expenses of the Tribunal shall be determined by the LCIA Court.

9. Notes

a. The parties shall be jointly and severally liable to the Arbitral Tribunal and the LCIA for the arbitration costs (other than the legal or other costs incurred by the parties themselves).

b. The Tribunal's Award(s) shall be transmitted to the parties by the LCIA Court provided that the costs of the arbitration have been paid in accordance with Article 28 of the LCIA Rules.

RESOLUTION 31/98 ADOPTED BY THE GENERAL ASSEMBLY ON 15 DECEMBER 1976

31/98. Arbitration Rules of the United Nations Commission on International Trade Law

The General Assembly,

Recognizing the value of arbitration as a method of settling disputes arising in the context of international commercial relations,

Being convinced that the establishment of rules for ad hoc arbitration that are acceptable in countries with different legal, social and economic systems would significantly contribute to the development of harmonious international economic relations,

Bearing in mind that the Arbitration Rules of the United Nations Commission on International Trade Law have been prepared after extensive consultation with arbitral institutions and centres of international commercial arbitration,

Noting that the Arbitration Rules were adopted by the United Nations Commission on International Trade Law at its ninth session[1] after due deliberation,

1. Recommends the use of the Arbitration Rules of the United Nations Commission on International Trade Law in the settlement of disputes arising in the context of international commercial relations, particularly by reference to the Arbitration Rules in commercial contracts;

2. Requests the Secretary-General to arrange for the widest possible distribution of the Arbitration Rules.

UNCITRAL ARBITRATION RULES

Section I. Introductory rules

SCOPE OF APPLICATION

Article 1

1. Where the parties to a contract have agreed in writing that disputes in relation to that contract shall be referred to arbitration under the UNCITRAL Arbitration Rules, then such disputes shall be settled in accordance with these Rules subject to such modification as the parties may agree in writing.

2. These Rules shall govern the arbitration except that where any of these Rules is in conflict with a provision of the law applicable to the arbitration from which the parties cannot derogate, that provision shall prevail.

---

[1]. Official Records of the General Assembly, Thirty-first Session, Supplement No. 17 (A/31/17), chap. V, sect. C.

NOTICE, CALCULATION OF PERIODS OF TIME

Article 2

1. For the purposes of these Rules, any notice, including a notification, communication or proposal, is deemed to have been received if it is physically delivered to the addressee or if it is delivered at his habitual residence, place of business or mailing address, or, if none of these can be found after making reasonable inquiry, then at the addressee's last-known residence or place of business. Notice shall be deemed to have been received on the day it is so delivered.

2. For the purposes of calculating a period of time under these Rules, such period shall begin to run on the day following the day when a notice, notification, communication or proposal is received. If the last day of such period is an official holiday or a non-business day at the residence or place of business of the addressee, the period is extended until the first business day which follows. Official holidays or non-business days occurring during the running of the period of time are included in calculating the period.

NOTICE OF ARBITRATION

Article 3

1. The party initiating recourse to arbitration (hereinafter called the "claimant") shall give to the other party (hereinafter called the "respondent") a notice of arbitration.

2. Arbitral proceedings shall be deemed to commence on the date on which the notice of arbitration is received by the respondent.

3. The notice of arbitration shall include the following:

   (a) A demand that the dispute be referred to arbitration;

   (b) The names and addresses of the parties;

   (c) A reference to the arbitration clause or the separate arbitration agreement that is invoked;

   (d) A reference to the contract out of or in relation to which the dispute arises;

   (e) The general nature of the claim and an indication of the amount involved, if any;

   (f) The relief or remedy sought;

   (g) A proposal as to the number of arbitrators (i.e. one or three), if the parties have not previously agreed thereon.

4. The notice of arbitration may also include:

   (a) The proposals for the appointments of a sole arbitrator and an appointing authority referred to in article 6, paragraph 1;

   (b) The notification of the appointment of an arbitrator referred to in article 7;

   (c) The statement of claim referred to in article 18.

REPRESENTATION AND ASSISTANCE

Article 4

The parties may be represented or assisted by persons of their choice. The names and addresses of such persons must be communicated in writing to the other party; such communication must specify whether the appointment is being made for purposes of representation or assistance.

Section II. Composition of the arbitral tribunal
NUMBER OF ARBITRATORS

Article 5

If the parties have not previously agreed on the number of arbitrators (i.e. one or three), and if within fifteen days after the receipt by the respondent of the notice of arbitration the parties have not agreed that there shall be only one arbitrator, three arbitrators shall be appointed.

APPOINTMENT OF ARBITRATORS (ARTICLES 6 TO 8)

Article 6

1.   If a sole arbitrator is to be appointed, either party may propose to the other:

(a) The names of one or more persons, one of whom would serve as the sole arbitrator; and

(b) If no appointing authority has been agreed upon by the parties, the name or names of one or more institutions or persons, one of whom would serve as appointing authority.

2.   If within thirty days after receipt by a party of a proposal made in accordance with paragraph 1 the parties have not reached agreement on the choice of a sole arbitrator, the sole arbitrator shall be appointed by the appointing authority agreed upon by the parties. If no appointing authority has been agreed upon by the parties, or if the appointing authority agreed upon refuses to act or fails to appoint the arbitrator within sixty days of the receipt of a party's request therefor, either party may request the Secretary-General of the Permanent Court of Arbitration at The Hague to designate an appointing authority.

3.   The appointing authority shall, at the request of one of the parties, appoint the sole arbitrator as promptly as possible. In making the appointment the appointing authority shall use the following list-procedure, unless both parties agree that the list-procedure should not be used or unless the appointing authority determines in its discretion that the use of the list-procedure is not appropriate for the case:

(a) At the request of one of the parties the appointing authority shall communicate to both parties an identical list containing at least three names;

(b) Within fifteen days after the receipt of this list, each party may return the list to the appointing authority after having deleted the name or names to which he objects and numbered the remaining names on the list in the order of his preference;

(c) After the expiration of the above period of time the appointing authority shall appoint the sole arbitrator from among the names approved on the lists returned to it and in accordance with the order of preference indicated by the parties;

(d) If for any reason the appointment cannot be made according to this procedure, the appointing authority may exercise its discretion in appointing the sole arbitrator.

4.   In making the appointment, the appointing authority shall have regard to such considerations as are likely to secure the appointment of an independent and impartial arbitrator and shall take into account as well the advisability of appointing an arbitrator of a nationality other than the nationalities of the parties.

Article 7

1.   If three arbitrators are to be appointed, each party shall appoint one arbitrator. The two arbitrators thus appointed shall choose the third arbitrator who will act as the presiding arbitrator of the tribunal.

2.   If within thirty days after the receipt of a party's notification of the appointment of an arbitrator the other party has not notified the first party of the arbitrator he has appointed:

(a) The first party may request the appointing authority previously designated by the parties to appoint the second arbitrator; or

(b) If no such authority has been previously designated by the parties, or if the appointing authority previously designated refuses to act or fails to appoint the arbitrator within thirty days after receipt of a party's request therefor, the first party may request the Secretary–General of the Permanent Court of Arbitration at The Hague to designate the appointing authority. The first party may then request the appointing authority so designated to appoint the second arbitrator. In either case, the appointing authority may exercise its discretion in appointing the arbitrator.*

3.   If within thirty days after the appointment of the second arbitrator the two arbitrators have not agreed on the choice of the presiding arbitrator, the presiding arbitrator shall be appointed by an appointing authority in the same way as a sole arbitrator would be appointed under article 6.

Article 8

1.   When an appointing authority is requested to appoint an arbitrator pursuant to article 6 or article 7, the party which makes the request shall send to the appointing authority a copy of the notice of

* This   sub-paragraph   is   inapplicable when parties have named AAA as appointing authority.

arbitration, a copy of the contract out of or in relation to which the dispute has arisen and a copy of the arbitration agreement if it is not contained in the contract. The appointing authority may require from either party such information as it deems necessary to fulfill its function.

2. Where the names of one or more persons are proposed for appointment as arbitrators, their full names, addresses and nationalities shall be indicated, together with a description of their qualifications.

CHALLENGE OF ARBITRATORS (ARTICLES 9 TO 12)

Article 9

A prospective arbitrator shall disclose to those who approach him in connexion with his possible appointment any circumstances likely to give rise to justifiable doubts as to his impartiality or independence. An arbitrator, once appointed or chosen, shall disclose such circumstances to the parties unless they have already been informed by him of these circumstances.

Article 10

1. Any arbitrator may be challenged if circumstances exist that give rise to justifiable doubts as to the arbitrator's impartiality or independence.

2. A party may challenge the arbitrator appointed by him only for reasons of which he becomes aware after the appointment has been made.

Article 11

1. A party who intends to challenge an arbitrator shall send notice of his challenge within fifteen days after the appointment of the challenged arbitrator has been notified to the challenging party or within fifteen days after the circumstances mentioned in articles 9 and 10 became known to that party.

2. The challenge shall be notified to the other party, to the arbitrator who is challenged and to the other members of the arbitral tribunal. The notification shall be in writing and shall state the reasons for the challenge.

3. When an arbitrator has been challenged by one party, the other party may agree to the challenge. The arbitrator may also, after the challenge, withdraw from his office. In neither case does this imply acceptance of the validity of the grounds for the challenge. In both cases the procedure provided in article 6 or 7 shall be used in full for the appointment of the substitute arbitrator, even if during the process of appointing the challenged arbitrator a party had failed to exercise his right to appoint or to participate in the appointment.

Article 12

1. If the other party does not agree to the challenge and the challenged arbitrator does not withdraw, the decision on the challenge will be made:

(a) When the initial appointment was made by an appointing authority, by that authority;

(b) When the initial appointment was not made by an appointing authority, but an appointing authority has been previously designated, by that authority;

(c) In all other cases, by the appointing authority to be designated in accordance with the procedure for designating an appointing authority as provided for in article 6.

2. If the appointing authority sustains the challenge, a substitute arbitrator shall be appointed or chosen pursuant to the procedure applicable to the appointment or choice of an arbitrator as provided in articles 6 to 9 except that, when this procedure would call for the designation of an appointing authority, the appointment of the arbitrator shall be made by the appointing authority which decided on the challenge.

REPLACEMENT OF AN ARBITRATOR

Article 13

1. In the event of the death or resignation of an arbitrator during the course of the arbitral proceedings, a substitute arbitrator shall be appointed or chosen pursuant to the procedure provided for in articles 6 to 9 that was applicable to the appointment or choice of the arbitrator being replaced.

2. In the event that an arbitrator fails to act or in the event of the *de jure* or *de facto* impossibility of his performing his functions, the procedure in respect of the challenge and replacement of an arbitrator as provided in the preceding articles shall apply.

REPETITION OF HEARINGS IN THE EVENT OF THE REPLACEMENT OF AN ARBITRATOR

Article 14

If under articles 11 to 13 the sole or presiding arbitrator is replaced, any Hearings held previously shall be repeated: if any other arbitrator is replaced, such prior hearings may be repeated at the discretion of the arbitral tribunal.

Section III. Arbitral proceedings
GENERAL PROVISIONS

Article 15

1. Subject to these Rules, the arbitral tribunal may conduct the arbitration in such manner as it considers appropriate, provided that the parties are treated with equality and that at any stage of the proceedings each party is given a full opportunity of presenting his case.

2. If either party so requests at any stage of the proceedings, the arbitral tribunal shall hold hearings for the presentation of evidence by witnesses, including expert witnesses, or for oral argument. In the

absence of such a request, the arbitral tribunal shall decide whether to hold such hearings or whether the proceedings shall be conducted on the basis of documents and other materials.

3.   All documents or information supplied to the arbitral tribunal by one party shall at the same time be communicated by that party to the other party.

PLACE OF ARBITRATION

Article 16

1.   Unless the parties have agreed upon the place where the arbitration is to be held, such place shall be determined by the arbitral tribunal, having regard to the circumstances of the arbitration.

2.   The arbitral tribunal may determine the locale of the arbitration within the country agreed upon by the parties. It may hear witnesses and hold meetings for consultation among its members at any place it deems appropriate, having regard to the circumstances of the arbitration.

3.   The arbitral tribunal may meet at any place it deems appropriate for the inspection of goods, other property or documents. The parties shall be given sufficient notice to enable them to be present at such inspection.

4.   The award shall be made at the place of arbitration.

LANGUAGE

Article 17

1.   Subject to an agreement by the parties, the arbitral tribunal shall, promptly after its appointment, determine the language or languages to be used in the proceedings. This determination shall apply to the statement of claim, the statement of defence, and any further written statements and, if oral hearings take place, to the language or languages to be used in such hearings.

2.   The arbitral tribunal may order that any documents annexed to the statement of claim or statement of defence, and any supplementary documents or exhibits submitted in the course of the proceedings, delivered in their original language, shall be accompanied by a translation into the language or languages agreed upon by the parties or determined by the arbitral tribunal.

STATEMENT OF CLAIM

Article 18

1.   Unless the statement of claim was contained in the notice of arbitration, within a period of time to be determined by the arbitral tribunal, the claimant shall communicate his statement of claim in writing to the respondent and to each of the arbitrators. A copy of the contract, and of the arbitration agreement if not contained in the contract, shall be annexed thereto.

2. The statement of claim shall include the following particulars:

   (a) The names and addresses of the parties;

   (b) A statement of the facts supporting the claim;

   (c) The points at issue;

   (d) The relief or remedy sought.

The claimant may annex to his statement of claim all documents he deems relevant or may add a reference to the documents or other evidence he will submit.

STATEMENT OF DEFENCE

Article 19

1. Within a period of time to be determined by the arbitral tribunal, the respondent shall communicate his statement of defence in writing to the claimant and to each of the arbitrators.

2. The statement of defence shall reply to the particulars (b), (c) and (d) of the statement of claim (article 18, para. 2). The respondent may annex to his statement the documents on which he relies for his defence or may add a reference to the documents or other evidence he will submit.

3. In his statement of defence, or at a later stage in the arbitral proceedings if the arbitral tribunal decides that the delay was justified under the circumstances, the respondent may make a counter-claim arising out of the same contract or rely on a claim arising out of the same contract for the purpose of a set-off.

4. The provisions of article 18, paragraph 2, shall apply to a counter-claim and a claim relied on for the purpose of a set-off.

AMENDMENTS TO THE CLAIM OR DEFENCE

Article 20

During the course of the arbitral proceedings either party may amend or supplement his claim or defence unless the arbitral tribunal considers it inappropriate to allow such amendment having regard to the delay in making it or prejudice to the other party or any other circumstances. However, a claim may not be amended in such a manner that the amended claim falls outside the scope of the arbitration clause or separate arbitration agreement.

PLEAS AS TO THE JURISDICTION OF THE ARBITRAL TRIBUNAL

Article 21

1. The arbitral tribunal shall have the power to rule on objections that it has no jurisdiction, including any objections with respect to the existence or validity of the arbitration clause or of the separate arbitration agreement.

2. The arbitral tribunal shall have the power to determine the existence or the validity of the contract of which an arbitration clause forms a part. For the purposes of article 21, an arbitration clause which forms part of a contract and which provides for arbitration under these Rules shall be treated as an agreement independent of the other terms of the contract. A decision by the arbitral tribunal that the contract is null and void shall not entail *ipso jure* the invalidity of the arbitration clause.

3. A plea that the arbitral tribunal does not have jurisdiction shall be raised not later than in the statement of defence or, with respect to a counter-claim, in the reply to the counter-claim.

4. In general, the arbitral tribunal should rule on a plea concerning its jurisdiction as a preliminary question. However, the arbitral tribunal may proceed with the arbitration and rule on such a plea in their final award.

FURTHER WRITTEN STATEMENTS

Article 22

The arbitral tribunal shall decide which further written statements, in addition to the statement of claim and the statement of defence, shall be required from the parties or may be presented by them and shall fix the periods of time for communicating such statements.

PERIODS OF TIME

Article 23

The periods of time fixed by the arbitral tribunal for the communication of written statements (including the statement of claim and statement of defence) should not exceed forty-five days. However, the arbitral tribunal may extend the time-limits if it concludes that an extension is justified.

EVIDENCE AND HEARINGS (ARTICLES 24 AND 25)

Article 24

1. Each party shall have the burden of proving the facts relied on to support his claim or defence.

2. The arbitral tribunal may, if it considers it appropriate, require a party to deliver to the tribunal and to the other party, within such a period of time as the arbitral tribunal shall decide, a summary of the documents and other evidence which that party intends to present in support of the facts in issue set out in his statement of claim or statement of defence.

3. At any time during the arbitral proceedings the arbitral tribunal may require the parties to produce documents, exhibits or other evidence within such a period of time as the tribunal shall determine.

Article 25

1. In the event of an oral hearing, the arbitral tribunal shall give the parties adequate advance notice of the date, time and place thereof.

2. If witnesses are to be heard, at least fifteen days before the hearing each party shall communicate to the arbitral tribunal and to the other party the names and addresses of the witnesses he intends to present, the subject upon and the languages in which such witnesses will give their testimony.

3. The arbitral tribunal shall make arrangements for the translation of oral statements made at a hearing and for a record of the hearing if either is deemed necessary by the tribunal under the circumstances of the case, or if the parties have agreed thereto and have communicated such agreement to the tribunal at least fifteen days before the hearing.

4. Hearings shall be held *in camera* unless the parties agree otherwise. The arbitral tribunal may require the retirement of any witness or witnesses during the testimony of other witnesses. The arbitral tribunal is free to determine the manner in which witnesses are examined.

5. Evidence of witnesses may also be presented in the form of written statements signed by them.

6. The arbitral tribunal shall determine the admissibility, relevance, materiality and weight of the evidence offered.

INTERIM MEASURES OF PROTECTION

Article 26

1. At the request of either party, the arbitral tribunal may take any interim measures it deems necessary in respect of the subject-matter of the dispute, including measures for the conservation of the goods forming the subject-matter in dispute, such as ordering their deposit with a third person or the sale of perishable goods.

2. Such interim measures may be established in the form of an interim award. The arbitral tribunal shall be entitled to require security for the costs of such measures.

3. A request for interim measures addressed by any party to a judicial authority shall not be deemed incompatible with the agreement to arbitrate, or as a waiver of that agreement.

EXPERTS

Article 27

1. The arbitral tribunal may appoint one or more experts to report to it, in writing, on specific issues to be determined by the tribunal. A copy of the expert's terms of reference, established by the arbitral tribunal, shall be communicated to the parties.

2. The parties shall give the expert any relevant information or produce for his inspection any relevant documents or goods that he may require of them. Any dispute between a party and such expert as to the relevance of the required information or production shall be referred to the arbitral tribunal for decision.

3.   Upon receipt of the expert's report, the arbitral tribunal shall communicate a copy of the report to the parties who shall be given the opportunity to express, in writing, their opinion on the report. A party shall be entitled to examine any document on which the expert has relied in his report.

4.   At the request of either party the expert, after delivery of the report, may be heard at a hearing where the parties shall have the opportunity to be present and to interrogate the expert. At this hearing either party may present expert witnesses in order to testify on the points at issue. The provisions of article 25 shall be applicable to such proceedings.

DEFAULT

Article 28

1.   If, within the period of time fixed by the arbitral tribunal, the claimant has failed to communicate his claim without showing sufficient cause for such failure, the arbitral tribunal shall issue an order for the termination of the arbitral proceedings. If, within the period of time fixed by the arbitral tribunal, the respondent has failed to communicate his statement of defence without showing sufficient cause for such failure, the arbitral tribunal shall order that the proceedings continue.

2.   If one of the parties, duly notified under these Rules, fails to appear at a hearing, without showing sufficient cause for such failure, the arbitral tribunal may proceed with the arbitration.

3.   If one of the parties, duly invited to produce documentary evidence, fails to do so within the established period of time, without showing sufficient cause for such failure, the arbitral tribunal may make the award on the evidence before it.

CLOSURE OF HEARINGS

Article 29

1.   The arbitral tribunal may inquire of the parties if they have any further proof to offer or witnesses to be heard or submissions to make and, if there are none, it may declare the hearings closed.

2.   The arbitral tribunal may, if it considers it necessary owing to exceptional circumstances, decide, on its own motion or upon application of a party, to reopen the hearings at any time before the award is made.

WAIVER OF RULES

Article 30

A party who knows that any provision of, or requirement under, these Rules has not been complied with and yet proceeds with the arbitration without promptly stating his objection to such non-compliance, shall be deemed to have waived his right to object.

Section IV. The award

DECISIONS

Article 31

1. When there are three arbitrators, any award or other decision of the arbitral tribunal shall be made by a majority of the arbitrators.

2. In the case of questions of procedure, when there is no majority or when the arbitral tribunal so authorizes, the presiding arbitrator may decide on his own, subject to revision, if any, by the arbitral tribunal.

FORM AND EFFECT OF THE AWARD

Article 32

1. In addition to making a final award, the arbitral tribunal shall be entitled to make interim, interlocutory, or partial awards.

2. The award shall be made in writing and shall be final and binding on the parties. The parties undertake to carry out the award without delay.

3. The arbitral tribunal shall state the reasons upon which the award is based, unless the parties have agreed that no reasons are to be given.

4. An award shall be signed by the arbitrators and it shall contain the date on which and the place where the award was made. Where there are three arbitrators and one of them fails to sign, the award shall state the reason for the absence of the signature.

5. The award may be made public only with the consent of both parties.

6. Copies of the award signed by the arbitrators shall be communicated to the parties by the arbitral tribunal.

7. If the arbitration law of the country where the award is made requires that the award be filed or registered by the arbitral tribunal, the tribunal shall comply with this requirement within the period of time required by law.

APPLICABLE LAW, AMIABLE COMPOSITEUR

Article 33

1. The arbitral tribunal shall apply the law designated by the parties as applicable to the substance of the dispute. Failing such designation by the parties, the arbitral tribunal shall apply the law determined by the conflict of laws rules which it considers applicable.

2. The arbitral tribunal shall decide as *amiable compositeur* or *ex aequo et bono* only if the parties have expressly authorized the arbitral tribunal to do so and if the law applicable to the arbitral procedure permits such arbitration.

3.   In all cases, the arbitral tribunal shall decide in accordance with the terms of the contract and shall take into account the usages of the trade applicable to the transaction.

SETTLEMENT OR OTHER GROUNDS FOR TERMINATION

Article 34

1.   If, before the award is made, the parties agree on a settlement of the dispute, the arbitral tribunal shall either issue an order for the termination of the arbitral proceedings or, if requested by both parties and accepted by the tribunal, record the settlement in the form of an arbitral award on agreed terms. The arbitral tribunal is not obliged to give reasons for such an award.

2.   If, before the award is made, the continuation of the arbitral proceedings becomes unnecessary or impossible for any reason not mentioned in paragraph 1, the arbitral tribunal shall inform the parties of its intention to issue an order for the termination of the proceedings. The arbitral tribunal shall have the power to issue such an order unless a party raises justifiable grounds for objection.

3.   Copies of the order for termination of the arbitral proceedings or of the arbitral award on agreed terms, signed by the arbitrators, shall be communicated by the arbitral tribunal to the parties. Where an arbitral award on agreed terms is made, the provisions of article 32, paragraphs 2 and 4 to 7, shall apply.

INTERPRETATION OF THE AWARD

Article 35

1.   Within thirty days after the receipt of the award, either party, with notice to the other party, may request that the arbitral tribunal give an interpretation of the award.

2.   The interpretation shall be given in writing within forty-five days after the receipt of the request. The interpretation shall form part of the award and the provisions of article 32, paragraphs 2 to 7, shall apply.

CORRECTION OF THE AWARD

Article 36

1.   Within thirty days after the receipt of the award, either party, with notice to the other party, may request the arbitral tribunal to correct in the award any errors in computation, any clerical or typographical errors, or any errors of similar nature. The arbitral tribunal may within thirty days after the communication of the award make such corrections on its own initiative.

2.   Such corrections shall be in writing, and the provisions of article 32, paragraphs 2 to 7, shall apply.

ADDITIONAL AWARD

Article 37

1. Within thirty days after the receipt of the award, either party, with notice to the other party, may request the arbitral tribunal to make an additional award as to claims presented in the arbitral proceedings but omitted from the award.

2. If the arbitral tribunal considers the request for an additional award to be justified and considers that the omission can be rectified without any further hearings or evidence, it shall complete its award within sixty days after the receipt of the request.

3. When an additional award is made, the provisions of article 32, paragraphs 2 to 7, shall apply.

COSTS (ARTICLES 38 TO 40)

Article 38

The arbitral tribunal shall fix the costs of arbitration in its award. The term "costs" includes only:

(a) The fees of the arbitral tribunal to be stated separately as to each arbitrator and to be fixed by the tribunal itself in accordance with article 39;

(b) The travel and other expenses incurred by the arbitrators;

(c) The costs of expert advice and of other assistance required by the arbitral tribunal;

(d) The travel and other expenses of witnesses to the extent such expenses are approved by the arbitral tribunal;

(e) The costs for legal representation and assistance of the successful party if such costs were claimed during the arbitral proceedings, and only to the extent that the arbitral tribunal determines that the amount of such costs is reasonable;

(f) Any fees and expenses of the appointing authority as well as the expenses of the Secretary–General of the Permanent Court of Arbitration at The Hague.

Article 39

1. The fees of the arbitral tribunal shall be reasonable in amount, taking into account the amount in dispute, the complexity of the subject-matter, the time spent by the arbitrators and any other relevant circumstances of the case.

2. If an appointing authority has been agreed upon by the parties or designated by the Secretary–General of the Permanent Court of Arbitration at The Hague, and if that authority has issued a schedule of fees for arbitrators in international cases which it administers, the arbitral tribunal in fixing its fees shall take that schedule of fees into account to the extent that it considers appropriate in the circumstances of the case.

3. If such appointing authority has not issued a schedule of fees for arbitrators in international cases, any party may at any time request the appointing authority to furnish a statement setting forth the basis for establishing fees which is customarily followed in international cases in which the authority appoints arbitrators. If the appointing authority consents to provide such a statement, the arbitral tribunal in fixing its fees shall take such information into account to the extent that it considers appropriate in the circumstances of the case.

4. In cases referred to in paragraphs 2 and 3, when a party so requests and the appointing authority consents to perform the function, the arbitral tribunal shall fix its fees only after consultation with the appointing authority which may make any comment it deems appropriate to the arbitral tribunal concerning the fees.

Article 40

1. Except as provided in paragraph 2, the costs of arbitration shall in principle be borne by the unsuccessful party. However, the arbitral tribunal may apportion each of such costs between the parties if it determines that apportionment is reasonable, taking into account the circumstances of the case.

2. With respect to the costs of legal representation and assistance referred to in article 38, paragraph (e), the arbitral tribunal, taking into account the circumstances of the case, shall be free to determine which party shall bear such costs or may apportion such costs between the parties if it determines that apportionment is reasonable.

3. When the arbitral tribunal issues an order for the termination of the arbitral proceedings or makes an award on agreed terms, it shall fix the costs of arbitration referred to in article 38 and article 39, paragraph 1, in the text of that order or award.

4. No additional fees may be charged by an arbitral tribunal for interpretation or correction or completion of its award under articles 35 to 37.

DEPOSIT OF COSTS

Article 41

1. The arbitral tribunal, on its establishment, may request each party to deposit an equal amount as an advance for the costs referred to in article 38, paragraphs (a), (b) and (c).

2. During the course of the arbitral proceedings the arbitral tribunal may request supplementary deposits from the parties.

3. If an appointing authority has been agreed upon by the parties or designated by the Secretary–General of the Permanent Court of Arbitration at The Hague, and when a party so requests and the appointing authority consents to perform the function, the arbitral tribunal shall fix the amounts of any deposits or supplementary deposits only after consultation with the appointing authority which may make

any comments to the arbitral tribunal which it deems appropriate concerning the amount of such deposits and supplementary deposits.

4. If the required deposits are not paid in full within thirty days after the receipt of the request, the arbitral tribunal shall so inform the parties in order that one or another of them may make the required payment. If such payment is not made, the arbitral tribunal may order the suspension or termination of the arbitral proceedings.

5. After the award has been made, the arbitral tribunal shall render an accounting to the parties of the deposits received and return any unexpended balance to the parties.

THE UNITED STATES ARBITRATION ACT (FAA)

Title 9, U.S. Code §§ 1–14, was first enacted February 12, 1925 (43 Stat. 883), codified July 30, 1947 (61 Stat. 669), and amended September 3, 1954 (68 Stat. 1233). Chapter 2 was added July 31, 1970 (84 Stat. 692), sections 15 and 16 were passed by Congress in October of 1988, and Chapter 3 was added on May 31, 1990.

Chapter 1. GENERAL PROVISIONS

§ 1. "Maritime transactions" and "commerce" defined; exceptions to operation of title
§ 2. Validity, irrevocability, and enforcement of agreements to arbitrate
§ 3. Stay of proceedings where issue therein referable to arbitration
§ 4. Failure to arbitrate under agreement; petition to united states court having jurisdiction for order to compel arbitration; notice and service thereof; hearing and determination
§ 5. Appointment of arbitrators or umpire
§ 6. Application heard as motion
§ 7. Witnesses before arbitrators; fees; compelling attendance
§ 8. Proceedings begun by libel in admiralty and seizure of vessel or property
§ 9. Award of arbitrators; confirmation; jurisdiction; procedure
§ 10. Same; vacation; grounds; rehearing
§ 11. Same; modification or correction; grounds; order
§ 12. Notice of motions to vacate or modify; service; stay of proceedings
§ 13. Papers filed with order on motions; judgment; docketing; force and effect; enforcement
§ 14. Contracts not affected
§ 15. Inapplicability of the act of state doctrine
§ 16. Appeals

Chapter 2. CONVENTION ON THE RECOGNITION AND ENFORCEMENT OF FOREIGN ARBITRAL AWARDS

§ 201. Enforcement of Convention
§ 202. Agreement or award falling under the Convention
§ 203. Jurisdiction; amount in controversy
§ 204. Venue
§ 205. Removal of cases from State courts
§ 206. Order to compel arbitration; appointment of arbitrators
§ 207. Award of arbitrators; confirmation; jurisdiction; proceeding
§ 208. Chapter 1; residual application

Chapter 3. INTER-AMERICAN CONVENTION ON INTERNATIONAL COMMERCIAL ARBITRATION

Chapter 1. GENERAL PROVISIONS

§ 1. "Maritime transactions" and "commerce" defined; exceptions to operation of title

"Maritime transaction", as herein defined, means charter parties, bills of lading of water carriers, agreements relating to wharfage, supplies furnished vessels or repairs to vessels, collisions, or any other matters in foreign commerce which, if the subject of controversy, would be embraced within admiralty jurisdiction; "commerce", as herein defined, means commerce among the several States or with foreign nations, or in any Territory of the United States or in the District of Columbia, or between any such Territory and another, or between any such Territory and any State or foreign nation, or between the District of Columbia and any State or Territory or foreign nation, but nothing herein contained shall apply to contracts of employment of seamen, railroad employees, or any other class of workers engaged in foreign or interstate commerce.

§ 2. Validity, irrevocability, and enforcement of agreements to arbitrate

A written provision in any maritime transaction or a contract evidencing a transaction involving commerce to settle by arbitration a controversy thereafter arising out of such contract or transaction, or the refusal to perform the whole or any part thereof, or an agreement in writing to submit to arbitration an existing controversy arising out of such a contract, transaction, or refusal, shall be valid, irrevocable, and enforceable, save upon such grounds as exist at law or in equity for the revocation of any contract.

§ 3. Stay of proceedings where issue therein referable to arbitration

If any suit or proceeding be brought in any of the courts of the United States upon any issue referable to arbitration under an agreement in writing for such arbitration, the court in which such suit is pending, upon being satisfied that the issue involved in such suit or proceeding is referable to arbitration under such an agreement, shall on application of one of the parties stay the trial of the action until such arbitration has been had in accordance with the terms of the agreement, providing the applicant for the stay is not in default in proceeding with such arbitration.

§ 4. Failure to arbitrate under agreement; petition to United States court having jurisdiction for order to compel arbitration; notice and service thereof; hearing and determination

A party aggrieved by the alleged failure, neglect, or refusal of another to arbitrate under a written agreement for arbitration may petition any United States district court which, save for such agreement, would have jurisdiction under Title 28, in a civil action or in admiralty of the subject matter of a suit arising out of the controversy between the parties, for an order directing that such arbitration proceed in the manner provided for in such agreement. Five days' notice in writing of such application shall be served upon the party in default. Service thereof shall be made in the manner provided by the Federal Rules of Civil Procedure. The court shall hear the parties, and upon being satisfied that the making of the agreement for arbitration or the failure to comply therewith is not in issue, the court shall make an order directing the parties to proceed to arbitration in accordance with the terms of the agreement. The hearing and proceedings, under such agreement, shall be within the district in which the petition for an order directing such arbitration is filed. If the making of the arbitration agreement or the failure, neglect, or refusal to perform the same be in issue, the court shall proceed summarily to the trial thereof. If no jury trial be demanded by the party alleged to be in default, or if the matter in dispute is within admiralty jurisdiction, the court shall hear and determine such issue. Where such an issue is raised, the party alleged to be in default may, except in cases of admiralty, on or before the return day of the notice of application, demand a jury trial of such issue, and upon such demand the court shall make an order referring the issue or issues to a jury in the manner provided by the Federal Rules of Civil Procedure, or may specially call a jury for that purpose. If the jury find that no agreement in writing for arbitration was made or that there is no default in proceeding thereunder, the proceeding shall be dismissed. If the jury find that an agreement for arbitration was made in writing and that there is a default in proceeding thereunder, the court shall make an order summarily directing the parties to proceed with the arbitration in accordance with the terms thereof.

§ 5. Appointment of arbitrators or umpire

If in the agreement provision be made for a method of naming or appointing an arbitrator or arbitrators or an umpire, such method shall be followed; but if no method be provided therein, or if a method be provided and any party thereto shall fail to avail himself of such method, or if for any other reason there shall be a lapse in the naming of an arbitrator or arbitrators or umpire, or in filling a vacancy, then upon the application of either party to the controversy the court shall designate and appoint an arbitrator or arbitrators or umpire, as the case may require, who shall act under the said agreement with the same force and effect as if he or they had been specifically named therein; and unless otherwise provided in the agreement the arbitration shall be by a single arbitrator.

§ 6. Application heard as motion

Any application to the court hereunder shall be made and heard in the manner provided by law for the making and hearing of motions, except as otherwise herein expressly provided.

§ 7. Witnesses before arbitrators; fees; compelling attendance

The arbitrators selected either as prescribed in this title or otherwise, or a majority of them, may summon in writing any person to attend before them or any of them as a witness and in a proper case to bring with him or them any book, record, document, or paper which may be deemed material as evidence in the case. The fees for such attendance shall be the same as the fees of witnesses before masters of the United States courts. Said summons shall issue in the name of the arbitrator or arbitrators, or a majority of them, and shall be signed by the arbitrators, or a majority of them, and shall be directed to the said person and shall be served in the same manner as subpoenas to appear and testify before the court; if any person or persons so summoned to testify shall refuse or neglect to obey said summons, upon petition the United States district court for the district in which such arbitrators, or a majority of them, are sitting may compel the attendance of such person or persons before said arbitrator or arbitrators, or punish said person or persons for contempt in the same manner provided by law for securing the attendance of witnesses or their punishment for neglect or refusal to attend in the courts of the United States.

§ 8. Proceedings begun by libel in admiralty and seizure of vessel or property

If the basis of jurisdiction be a cause of action otherwise justiciable in admiralty, then, notwithstanding anything herein to the contrary, the party claiming to be aggrieved may begin his proceeding hereunder by libel and seizure of the vessel or other property of the other party according to the usual course of admiralty proceedings, and the court shall then have jurisdiction to direct the parties to proceed with the arbitration and shall retain jurisdiction to enter its decree upon the award.

§ 9. Award of arbitrators; confirmation; jurisdiction; procedure

If the parties in their agreement have agreed that a judgment of the court shall be entered upon the award made pursuant to the arbitration, and shall specify the court, then at any time within one year after the award is made any party to the arbitration may apply to the court so specified for an order confirming the award, and thereupon the court must grant such an order unless the award is vacated, modified, or corrected as prescribed in sections 10 and 11 of this title. If no court is specified in the agreement of the parties, then such application may be made to the United States court in and for the district within which such award was made. Notice of the application shall be served upon the adverse party, and thereupon the court shall have jurisdiction of such party as though he had appeared generally in the proceeding. If the adverse party is a resident of the district within which the award was made, such service shall be made upon the adverse party or his attorney as prescribed by law for service of notice of motion in an action in the same court. If the adverse party shall be a nonresident, then the notice of the application shall be served by the marshal of any district within which the adverse party may be found in like manner as other process of the court.

§ 10. Same; vacation; grounds; rehearing

In either of the following cases the United States court in and for the district wherein the award was made may make an order vacating the award upon the application of any party to the arbitration—

(a) Where the award was procured by corruption, fraud, or undue means.

(b) Where there was evident partiality or corruption in the arbitrators, or either of them.

(c) Where the arbitrators were guilty of misconduct in refusing to postpone the hearing, upon sufficient cause shown, or in refusing to hear evidence pertinent and material to the controversy; or of any other misbehavior by which the rights of any party have been prejudiced.

(d) Where the arbitrators exceeded their powers, or so imperfectly executed them that a mutual, final, and definite award upon the subject matter submitted was not made.

(e) Where an award is vacated and the time within which the agreement required the award to be made has not expired the court may, in its discretion, direct a rehearing by the arbitrators.

§ 11. Same; modification or correction; grounds; order

In either of the following cases the United States court in and for the district wherein the award was made may make an order modifying or correcting the award upon the application of any party to the arbitration—

(a) Where there was an evident material miscalculation of figures or an evident material mistake in the description of any person, thing, or property referred to in the award.

(b) Where the arbitrators have awarded upon a matter not submitted to them, unless it is a matter not affecting the merits of the decision upon the matter submitted.

(c) Where the award is imperfect in matter of form not affecting the merits of the controversy.

The order may modify and correct the award, so as to effect the intent thereof and promote justice between the parties.

§ 12. Notice of motions to vacate or modify; service; stay of proceedings

Notice of a motion to vacate, modify, or correct an award must be served upon the adverse party or his attorney within three months after the award is filed or delivered. If the adverse party is a resident of the district within which the award was made, such service shall be made upon the adverse party or his attorney as prescribed by law for service of notice of motion in an action in the same court. If the adverse party shall be a nonresident then the notice of the application shall be served by the marshal of any district within which the adverse party may be found in like manner as other process of the court. For the purposes of the motion any judge who might make an order to stay the proceedings in an action brought in the same court may make an order, to be served with the notice of motion, staying the proceedings of the adverse party to enforce the award.

§ 13. Papers filed with order on motions; judgment; docketing; force and effect; enforcement

The party moving for an order confirming, modifying, or correcting an award shall, at the time such order is filed with the clerk for the entry of judgment thereon, also file the following papers with the clerk:

(a) The agreement; the selection or appointment, if any, of an additional arbitrator or umpire; and each written extension of the time, if any, within which to make the award.

(b) The award.

(c) Each notice, affidavit, or other paper used upon an application to confirm, modify, or correct the award, and a copy of each order of the court upon such an application.

The judgment shall be docketed as if it was rendered in an action.

The judgment so entered shall have the same force and effect, in all respects, as, and be subject to all the provisions of law relating to, a judgment in an action; and it may be enforced as if it had been rendered in an action in the court in which it is entered.

§ 14. Contracts not affected

This title shall not apply to contracts made prior to January 1, 1926.

§ 15. Inapplicability of the Act of State doctrine

Enforcement of arbitral agreements, confirmation of arbitral awards, and execution upon judgments based on orders confirming such awards shall not be refused on the basis of the Act of State doctrine.

§ 16. Appeals

(a) An appeal may be taken from—

(1) an order—

(A) refusing a stay of any action under section 3 of this title,

(B) denying a petition under section 4 of this title to order arbitration to proceed,

(C) denying an application under section 206 of this title to compel arbitration,

(D) confirming or denying confirmation of an award or partial award, or

(E) modifying, correcting, or vacating an award;

(2) an interlocutory order granting, continuing, or modifying an injunction against an arbitration that is subject to this title; or

(3) a final decision with respect to an arbitration that is subject to this title.

(b) Except as otherwise provided in section 1292(b) of title 28, an appeal may not be taken from an interlocutory order—

(1) granting a stay of any action under section 3 of this title;

(2) directing arbitration to proceed under section 4 of this title;

(3) compelling arbitration under section 206 of this title; or

(4) refusing to enjoin an arbitration that is subject to this title.

Chapter 2. CONVENTION ON THE RECOGNITION AND ENFORCEMENT OF FOREIGN ARBITRAL AWARDS

§ 201. Enforcement of Convention

The Convention on the Recognition and Enforcement of Foreign Arbitral Awards of June 10, 1958, shall be enforced in United States courts in accordance with this chapter.

§ 202. Agreement or award falling under the Convention

An arbitration agreement or arbitral award arising out of a legal relationship, whether contractual or not, which is considered as commercial, including a transaction, contract, or agreement described in section 2 of this title, falls under the Convention. An agreement or award arising out of such a relationship which is entirely between citizens of the United States shall be deemed not to fall under the Convention unless that relationship involves property located abroad, envisages performance or enforcement abroad, or has some other reasonable relation with one or more foreign states. For the purpose of this section a corporation is a citizen of the United States if it is incorporated or has its principal place of business in the United States.

§ 203. Jurisdiction; amount in controversy

An action or proceeding falling under the Convention shall be deemed to arise under the laws and treaties of the United States. The district courts of the United States (including the courts enumerated in section 460 of title 28) shall have original jurisdiction over such an action or proceeding, regardless of the amount in controversy.

§ 204. Venue

An action or proceeding over which the district courts have jurisdiction pursuant to section 203 of this title may be brought in any such court in which save for the arbitration agreement an action or proceeding with respect to the controversy between the parties could be brought, or in such court for the district and division which embraces the place designated in the agreement as the place of arbitration if such place is within the United States.

§ 205. Removal of cases from State courts

Where the subject matter of an action or proceeding pending in a State court relates to an arbitration agreement or award falling under the Convention, the defendant or the defendants may, at any time before the trial thereof, remove such action or proceeding to the district court of the United States for the district and division embracing the place where the action or proceeding is pending. The procedure for removal of causes otherwise provided by law shall apply, except that the ground for removal provided in this section need not appear on the face of the complaint but may be shown in the petition for removal. For the purposes of Chapter 1 of this title any action or proceeding removed under this section shall be deemed to have been brought in the district court to which it is removed.

§ 206. Order to compel arbitration; appointment of arbitrators

A court having jurisdiction under this chapter may direct that arbitration be held in accordance with the agreement at any place therein provided for, whether that place is within or without the United States. Such court may also appoint arbitrators in accordance with the provisions of the agreement.

§ 207. Award of arbitrators; confirmation; jurisdiction; proceeding

Within three years after an arbitral award falling under the Convention is made, any party to the arbitration may apply to any court having jurisdiction under this chapter for an order confirming the award as against any other party to the arbitration. The court shall confirm the award unless it finds one of the grounds for refusal or deferral of recognition or enforcement of the award specified in the said Convention.

§ 208. Chapter 1; residual application

Chapter 1 applies to actions and proceedings brought under this chapter to the extent that chapter is not in conflict with this chapter or the Convention as ratified by the United States.

Chapter 3. INTER-AMERICAN CONVENTION ON INTERNATIONAL COMMERCIAL ARBITRATION

§ 301. Enforcement of Convention

The Inter–American Convention on International Commercial Arbitration of January 30, 1975, shall be enforced in United States courts in accordance with this chapter.

§ 302. Incorporation by reference

Sections 202, 203, 204, 205, and 207 of this title shall apply to this chapter as if specifically set forth herein, except that for the purposes of this chapter "the Convention" shall mean the Inter American Convention.

§ 303. Order to compel arbitration; appointment of arbitrators; locale

(a) A court having jurisdiction under this chapter may direct that arbitration be held in accordance with the agreement at any place therein provided for, whether that place is within or without the United States. The court may also appoint arbitrators in accordance with the provisions of the agreement.

(b) In the event the agreement does not make provision for the place of arbitration or the appointment of arbitrators, the court shall direct that the arbitration shall be held and the arbitrators be appointed in accordance with Article 3 of the Inter–American Convention.

§ 304. Recognition and enforcement of foreign arbitral decisions and awards; reciprocity

Arbitral decisions or awards made in the territory of a foreign State shall, on the basis of reciprocity, be recognized and enforced under this chapter only if that State has ratified or acceded to the Inter–American Convention.

§ 305. Relationship between the Inter–American Convention and the Convention on the Recognition and Enforcement of Foreign Arbitral Awards of June 10, 1958

When the requirements for application of both the Inter–American Convention and the Convention on the Recognition and Enforcement of Foreign Arbitral Awards of June 10, 1958, are met, determination as to which Convention applies shall, unless otherwise expressly agreed, be made as follows:

(1) If a majority of the parties to the arbitration agreement are citizens of a State or States that have ratified or acceded to the Inter–American Convention and are member States of the Organization of American States, the Inter–American Convention shall apply.

(2) In all other cases the Convention on the Recognition and Enforcement of Foreign Arbitral Awards of June 10, 1958, shall apply.

§ 306. Applicable rules of Inter–American Commercial Arbitration Commission

(a) For the purposes of this chapter the rules of procedure of the Inter–American Commercial Arbitration Commission referred to in Article 3 of the Inter–American Convention shall, subject to subsection (b) of this section, be those rules as promulgated by the Commission on July 1, 1988.

(b) In the event the rules of procedure of the Inter–American Commercial Arbitration Commission are modified or amended in accordance with the procedures for amendment of the rules of that Commission, the Secretary of State, by regulation in accordance with section 553 of title 5, consistent with the aims and purposes of this Convention, may prescribe that such modifications or amendments shall be effective for purposes of this chapter.

§ 307. Chapter 1; residual application

Chapter 1 applies to actions and proceedings brought under this chapter to the extent chapter 1 is not in conflict with this chapter or the Inter–American Convention as ratified by the United States.

UNITED KINGDOM: ARBITRATION ACT 1996*

An Act to restate and improve the law relating to arbitration pursuant to an arbitration agreement; to make other provision relating to arbitration and arbitration awards; and for connected purposes.

[17th June 1996]

BE IT ENACTED by the Queen's most Excellent Majesty, by and with the advice and consent of the Lords Spiritual and Temporal, and Commons, in this present Parliament assembled, and by the authority of the same, as follows:—

PART I

ARBITRATION PURSUANT TO AN ARBITRATION AGREEMENT

Introductory

General principles.

1.—The provisions of this Part are founded on the following principles, and shall be construed accordingly—

(a) the object of arbitration is to obtain the fair resolution of disputes by an impartial tribunal without unnecessary delay or expense;

(b) the parties should be free to agree how their disputes are resolved, subject only to such safeguards as are necessary in the public interest;

(c) in matters governed by this Part the court should not intervene except as provided by this Part.

Scope of application of provisions.

2.—(1) The provisions of this Part apply where the seat of the arbitration is in England and Wales or Northern Ireland.

(2) The following sections apply even if the seat of the arbitration is outside England and Wales or Northern Ireland or no seat has been designated or determined—

(a) sections 9 to 11 (stay of legal proceedings, & c.), and

(b) section 66 (enforcement of arbitral awards).

(3) The powers conferred by the following sections apply even if the seat of the arbitration is outside England and Wales or Northern Ireland or no seat has been designated or determined—

(a) section 43 (securing the attendance of witnesses), and

(b) section 44 (court powers exercisable in support of arbitral proceedings);

* 1996 Laws, c. 23.

but the court may refuse to exercise any such power if, in the opinion of the court, the fact that the seat of the arbitration is outside England and Wales or Northern Ireland, or that when designated or determined the seat is likely to be outside England and Wales or Northern Ireland, makes it inappropriate to do so.

(4) The court may exercise a power conferred by any provision of this Part not mentioned in subsection (2) or (3) for the purpose of supporting the arbitral process where—

> (a) no seat of the arbitration has been designated or determined, and

> (b) by reason of a connection with England and Wales or Northern Ireland the court is satisfied that it is appropriate to do so.

(5) Section 7 (separability of arbitration agreement) and section 8 (death of a party) apply where the law applicable to the arbitration agreement is the law of England and Wales or Northern Ireland even if the seat of the arbitration is outside England and Wales or Northern Ireland or has not been designated or determined.

The seat of the arbitration.

3.—In this Part "the seat of the arbitration" means the juridical seat of the arbitration designated—

> (a) by the parties to the arbitration agreement, or

> (b) by any arbitral or other institution or person vested by the parties with powers in that regard, or

> (c) by the arbitral tribunal if so authorised by the parties,

or determined, in the absence of any such designation, having regard to the parties' agreement and all the relevant circumstances.

Mandatory and non-mandatory provisions.

4.—(1) The mandatory provisions of this Part are listed in Schedule 1 and have effect notwithstanding any agreement to the contrary.

(2) The other provisions of this Part (the "non-mandatory provisions") allow the parties to make their own arrangements by agreement but provide rules which apply in the absence of such agreement.

(3) The parties may make such arrangements by agreeing to the application of institutional rules or providing any other means by which a matter may be decided.

(4) It is immaterial whether or not the law applicable to the parties' agreement is the law of England and Wales or, as the case may be, Northern Ireland.

(5) The choice of a law other than the law of England and Wales or Northern Ireland as the applicable law in respect of a matter provided for by a non-mandatory provision of this Part is equivalent to an agreement making provision about that matter.

For this purpose an applicable law determined in accordance with the parties' agreement, or which is objectively determined in the absence of any express or implied choice, shall be treated as chosen by the parties.

Agreements to be in writing.

5.—(1) The provisions of this Part apply only where the arbitration agreement is in writing, and any other agreement between the parties as to any matter is effective for the purposes of this Part only if in writing.

The expressions "agreement", "agree" and "agreed" shall be construed accordingly.

(2) There is an agreement in writing—

(a) if the agreement is made in writing (whether or not it is signed by the parties),

(b) if the agreement is made by exchange of communications in writing, or

(c) if the agreement is evidenced in writing.

(3) Where parties agree otherwise than in writing by reference to terms which are in writing, they make an agreement in writing.

(4) An agreement is evidenced in writing if an agreement made otherwise than in writing is recorded by one of the parties, or by a third party, with the authority of the parties to the agreement.

(5) An exchange of written submissions in arbitral or legal proceedings in which the existence of an agreement otherwise than in writing is alleged by one party against another party and not denied by the other party in his response constitutes as between those parties an agreement in writing to the effect alleged.

(6) References in this Part to anything being written or in writing include its being recorded by any means.

The Arbitration Agreement

Definition of arbitration agreement.

6.—(1) In this Part an "arbitration agreement" means an agreement to submit to arbitration present or future disputes (whether they are contractual or not).

(2) The reference in an agreement to a written form of arbitration clause or to a document containing an arbitration clause constitutes an arbitration agreement if the reference is such as to make that clause part of the agreement.

Separability of arbitration agreement.

7. Unless otherwise agreed by the parties, an arbitration agreement which forms or was intended to form part of another agreement (whether or not in writing) shall not be regarded as invalid, non-existent or ineffective because that other agreement is invalid, or did not come into existence or has become ineffective, and it shall for that purpose be treated as a distinct agreement.

Whether agreement discharged by death of a party.

8.—(1) Unless otherwise agreed by the parties, an arbitration agreement is not discharged by the death of a party and may be enforced by or against the personal representatives of that party.

(2) Subsection (1) does not affect the operation of any enactment or rule of law by virtue of which a substantive right or obligation is extinguished by death.

Stay of Legal Proceedings

Stay of legal proceedings.

9.—(1) A party to an arbitration agreement against whom legal proceedings are brought (whether by way of claim or counterclaim) in respect of a matter which under the agreement is to be referred to arbitration may (upon notice to the other parties to the proceedings) apply to the court in which the proceedings have been brought to stay the proceedings so far as they concern that matter.

(2) An application may be made notwithstanding that the matter is to be referred to arbitration only after the exhaustion of other dispute resolution procedures.

(3) An application may not be made by a person before taking the appropriate procedural step (if any) to acknowledge the legal proceedings against him or after he has taken any step in those proceedings to answer the substantive claim.

(4) On an application under this section the court shall grant a stay unless satisfied that the arbitration agreement is null and void, inoperative, or incapable of being performed.

(5) If the court refuses to stay the legal proceedings, any provision that an award is a condition precedent to the bringing of legal proceedings in respect of any matter is of no effect in relation to those proceedings.

Reference of interpleader issue to arbitration.

10.—(1) Where in legal proceedings relief by way of interpleader is granted and any issue between the claimants is one in respect of which there is an arbitration agreement between them, the court granting the relief shall direct that the issue be determined in accordance with the agreement unless the circumstances are such that proceedings brought by a claimant in respect of the matter would not be stayed.

(2) Where subsection (1) applies but the court does not direct that the issue be determined in accordance with the arbitration agreement, any provision that an award is a condition precedent to the bringing of legal proceedings in respect of any matter shall not affect the determination of that issue by the court.

Retention of security where Admiralty proceedings stayed.

11.—(1) Where Admiralty proceedings are stayed on the ground that the dispute in question should be submitted to arbitration, the court granting the stay may, if in those proceedings property has been arrested or bail or other security has been given to prevent or obtain release from arrest—

(a) order that the property arrested be retained as security for the satisfaction of any award given in the arbitration in respect of that dispute, or

(b) order that the stay of those proceedings be conditional on the provision of equivalent security for the satisfaction of any such award.

(2) Subject to any provision made by rules of court and to any necessary modifications, the same law and practice shall apply in relation to property retained in pursuance of an order as would apply if it were held for the purposes of proceedings in the court making the order.

Commencement of Arbitral Proceedings

Power of court to extend time for beginning arbitral proceedings, etc.

12.—(1) Where an arbitration agreement to refer future disputes to arbitration provides that a claim shall be barred, or the claimant's right extinguished, unless the claimant takes within a time fixed by the agreement some step—

(a) to begin arbitral proceedings, or

(b) to begin other dispute resolution procedures which must be exhausted before arbitral proceedings can be begun,

the court may by order extend the time for taking that step.

(2) Any party to the arbitration agreement may apply for such an order (upon notice to the other parties), but only after a claim has arisen and after exhausting any available arbitral process for obtaining an extension of time.

(3) The court shall make an order only if satisfied—

(a) that the circumstances are such as were outside the reasonable contemplation of the parties when they agreed the provision in question, and that it would be just to extend the time, or

(b) that the conduct of one party makes it unjust to hold the other party to the strict terms of the provision in question.

(4) The court may extend the time for such period and on such terms as it thinks fit, and may do so whether or not the time previously fixed (by agreement or by a previous order) has expired.

(5) An order under this section does not affect the operation of the Limitation Acts (see section 13).

(6) The leave of the court is required for any appeal from a decision of the court under this section.

Application of Limitation Acts.

13.—(1) The Limitation Acts apply to arbitral proceedings as they apply to legal proceedings.

(2) The court may order that in computing the time prescribed by the Limitation Acts for the commencement of proceedings (including arbitral proceedings) in respect of a dispute which was the subject matter—

    (a) of an award which the court orders to be set aside or declares to be of no effect, or

    (b) of the affected part of an award which the court orders to be set aside in part, or declares to be in part of no effect,

the period between the commencement of the arbitration and the date of the order referred to in paragraph (a) or (b) shall be excluded.

(3) In determining for the purposes of the Limitation Acts when a cause of action accrued, any provision that an award is a condition precedent to the bringing of legal proceedings in respect of a matter to which an arbitration agreement applies shall be disregarded.

(4) In this Part "the Limitation Acts" means—

    (a) in England and Wales, the Limitation Act 1980, the Foreign Limitation Periods Act 1984 and any other enactment (whenever passed) relating to the limitation of actions;

    (b) in Northern Ireland, the Limitation (Northern Ireland) Order 1989, the Foreign Limitation Periods (Northern Ireland) Order 1985 and any other enactment (whenever passed) relating to the limitation of actions.

Commencement of arbitral proceedings.

14.—(1) The parties are free to agree when arbitral proceedings are to be regarded as commenced for the purposes of this Part and for the purposes of the Limitation Acts.

(2) If there is no such agreement the following provisions apply.

(3) Where the arbitrator is named or designated in the arbitration agreement, arbitral proceedings are commenced in respect of a matter when one party serves on the other party or parties a notice in writing requiring him or them to submit that matter to the person so named or designated.

(4) Where the arbitrator or arbitrators are to be appointed by the parties, arbitral proceedings are commenced in respect of a matter when one party serves on the other party or parties notice in writing requiring him or them to appoint an arbitrator or to agree to the appointment of an arbitrator in respect of that matter.

(5) Where the arbitrator or arbitrators are to be appointed by a person other than a party to the proceedings, arbitral proceedings are commenced in respect of a matter when one party gives notice in writing to that person requesting him to make the appointment in respect of that matter.

The Arbitral Tribunal

The arbitral tribunal.

15.—(1) The parties are free to agree on the number of arbitrators to form the tribunal and whether there is to be a chairman or umpire.

(2) Unless otherwise agreed by the parties, an agreement that the number of arbitrators shall be two or any other even number shall be understood as requiring the appointment of an additional arbitrator as chairman of the tribunal.

(3) If there is no agreement as to the number of arbitrators, the tribunal shall consist of a sole arbitrator.

Procedure for appointment of arbitrators.

16.—(1) The parties are free to agree on the procedure for appointing the arbitrator or arbitrators, including the procedure for appointing any chairman or umpire.

(2) If or to the extent that there is no such agreement, the following provisions apply.

(3) If the tribunal is to consist of a sole arbitrator, the parties shall jointly appoint the arbitrator not later than 28 days after service of a request in writing by either party to do so.

(4) If the tribunal is to consist of two arbitrators, each party shall appoint one arbitrator not later than 14 days after service of a request in writing by either party to do so.

(5) If the tribunal is to consist of three arbitrators—

(a) each party shall appoint one arbitrator not later than 14 days after service of a request in writing by either party to do so, and

(b) the two so appointed shall forthwith appoint a third arbitrator as the chairman of the tribunal.

(6) If the tribunal is to consist of two arbitrators and an umpire—

(a) each party shall appoint one arbitrator not later than 14 days after service of a request in writing by either party to do so, and

(b) the two so appointed may appoint an umpire at any time after they themselves are appointed and shall do so before any substantive hearing or forthwith if they cannot agree on a matter relating to the arbitration.

(7) In any other case (in particular, if there are more than two parties) section 18 applies as in the case of a failure of the agreed appointment procedure.

Power in case of default to appoint sole arbitrator.

17.—(1) Unless the parties otherwise agree, where each of two parties to an arbitration agreement is to appoint an arbitrator and one party ("the party in default") refuses to do so, or fails to do so within the time specified, the other party, having duly appointed his arbitrator, may give notice in writing to the party in default that he proposes to appoint his arbitrator to act as sole arbitrator.

(2) If the party in default does not within 7 clear days of that notice being given—

    (a) make the required appointment, and

    (b) notify the other party that he has done so,

the other party may appoint his arbitrator as sole arbitrator whose award shall be binding on both parties as if he had been so appointed by agreement.

(3) Where a sole arbitrator has been appointed under subsection (2), the party in default may (upon notice to the appointing party) apply to the court which may set aside the appointment.

(4) The leave of the court is required for any appeal from a decision of the court under this section.

Failure of appointment procedure.

18.—(1) The parties are free to agree what is to happen in the event of a failure of the procedure for the appointment of the arbitral tribunal.

There is no failure if an appointment is duly made under section 17 (power in case of default to appoint sole arbitrator), unless that appointment is set aside.

(2) If or to the extent that there is no such agreement any party to the arbitration agreement may (upon notice to the other parties) apply to the court to exercise its powers under this section.

(3) Those powers are—

    (a) to give directions as to the making of any necessary appointments;

    (b) to direct that the tribunal shall be constituted by such appointments (or any one or more of them) as have been made;

    (c) to revoke any appointments already made;

    (d) to make any necessary appointments itself.

(4) An appointment made by the court under this section has effect as if made with the agreement of the parties.

(5) The leave of the court is required for any appeal from a decision of the court under this section.

Court to have regard to agreed qualifications.

19. In deciding whether to exercise, and in considering how to exercise, any of its powers under section 16 (procedure for appointment of arbitrators) or section 18 (failure of appointment procedure), the court shall have due regard to any agreement of the parties as to the qualifications required of the arbitrators.

Chairman.

20.—(1) Where the parties have agreed that there is to be a chairman, they are free to agree what the functions of the chairman are to be in relation to the making of decisions, orders and awards.

(2) If or to the extent that there is no such agreement, the following provisions apply.

(3) Decisions, orders and awards shall be made by all or a majority of the arbitrators (including the chairman).

(4) The view of the chairman shall prevail in relation to a decision, order or award in respect of which there is neither unanimity nor a majority under subsection (3).

Umpire

21.—(1) Where the parties have agreed that there is to be an umpire, they are free to agree what the functions of the umpire are to be, and in particular—

    (a) whether he is to attend the proceedings, and

    (b) when he is to replace the other arbitrators as the tribunal with power to make decisions, orders and awards.

(2) If or to the extent that there is no such agreement, the following provisions apply.

(3) The umpire shall attend the proceedings and be supplied with the same documents and other materials as are supplied to the other arbitrators.

(4) Decisions, orders and awards shall be made by the other arbitrators unless and until they cannot agree on a matter relating to the arbitration.

In that event they shall forthwith give notice in writing to the parties and the umpire, whereupon the umpire shall replace them as the tribunal with power to make decisions, orders and awards as if he were sole arbitrator.

(5) If the arbitrators cannot agree but fail to give notice of that fact, or if any of them fails to join in the giving of notice, any party to the arbitral proceedings may (upon notice to the other parties and to the tribunal) apply to the court which may order that the umpire shall replace the other arbitrators as the tribunal with power to make decisions, orders and awards as if he were sole arbitrator.

(6) The leave of the court is required for any appeal from a decision of the court under this section.

Decision-making where no chairman or umpire.

22.—(1) Where the parties agree that there shall be two or more arbitrators with no chairman or umpire, the parties are free to agree how the tribunal is to make decisions, orders and awards.

(2) If there is no such agreement, decisions, orders and awards shall be made by all or a majority of the arbitrators.

Revocation of arbitrator's authority.

23.—(1) The parties are free to agree in what circumstances the authority of an arbitrator may be revoked.

(2) If or to the extent that there is no such agreement the following provisions apply.

(3) The authority of an arbitrator may not be revoked except—

    (a) by the parties acting jointly, or

    (b) by an arbitral or other institution or person vested by the parties with powers in that regard.

(4) Revocation of the authority of an arbitrator by the parties acting jointly must be agreed in writing unless the parties also agree (whether or not in writing) to terminate the arbitration agreement.

(5) Nothing in this section affects the power of the court—

    (a) to revoke an appointment under section 18 (powers exercisable in case of failure of appointment procedure), or

    (b) to remove an arbitrator on the grounds specified in section 24.

Power of court to remove arbitrator.

24.—(1) A party to arbitral proceedings may (upon notice to the other parties, to the arbitrator concerned and to any other arbitrator) apply to the court to remove an arbitrator on any of the following grounds—

    (a) that circumstances exist that give rise to justifiable doubts as to his impartiality;

    (b) that he does not possess the qualifications required by the arbitration agreement;

    (c) that he is physically or mentally incapable of conducting the proceedings or there are justifiable doubts as to his capacity to do so;

    (d) that he has refused or failed—

        (i) properly to conduct the proceedings, or

        (ii) to use all reasonable despatch in conducting the proceedings or making an award, and that substantial injustice has been or will be caused to the applicant.

(2) If there is an arbitral or other institution or person vested by the parties with power to remove an arbitrator, the court shall not exercise its power of removal unless satisfied that the applicant has first exhausted any available recourse to that institution or person.

(3) The arbitral tribunal may continue the arbitral proceedings and make an award while an application to the court under this section is pending.

(4) Where the court removes an arbitrator, it may make such order as it thinks fit with respect to his entitlement (if any) to fees or expenses, or the repayment of any fees or expenses already paid.

(5) The arbitrator concerned is entitled to appear and be heard by the court before it makes any order under this section.

(6) The leave of the court is required for any appeal from a decision of the court under this section.

Resignation of arbitrator.

25.—(1) The parties are free to agree with an arbitrator as to the consequences of his resignation as regards—

    (a) his entitlement (if any) to fees or expenses, and

    (b) any liability thereby incurred by him.

(2) If or to the extent that there is no such agreement the following provisions apply.

(3) An arbitrator who resigns his appointment may (upon notice to the parties) apply to the court—

    (a) to grant him relief from any liability thereby incurred by him, and

    (b) to make such order as it thinks fit with respect to his entitlement (if any) to fees or expenses or the repayment of any fees or expenses already paid.

(4) If the court is satisfied that in all the circumstances it was reasonable for the arbitrator to resign, it may grant such relief as is mentioned in subsection (3)(a) on such terms as it thinks fit.

(5) The leave of the court is required for any appeal from a decision of the court under this section.

Death of arbitrator or person appointing him.

26.—(1) The authority of an arbitrator is personal and ceases on his death.

(2) Unless otherwise agreed by the parties, the death of the person by whom an arbitrator was appointed does not revoke the arbitrator's authority.

Filling of vacancy, & c.

27.—(1) Where an arbitrator ceases to hold office, the parties are free to agree—

    (a) whether and if so how the vacancy is to be filled,

    (b) whether and if so to what extent the previous proceedings should stand, and

    (c) what effect (if any) his ceasing to hold office has on any appointment made by him (alone or jointly).

(2) If or to the extent that there is no such agreement, the following provisions apply.

(3) The provisions of sections 16 (procedure for appointment of arbitrators) and 18 (failure of appointment procedure) apply in relation to the filling of the vacancy as in relation to an original appointment.

(4) The tribunal (when reconstituted) shall determine whether and if so to what extent the previous proceedings should stand.

This does not affect any right of a party to challenge those proceedings on any ground which had arisen before the arbitrator ceased to hold office.

(5) His ceasing to hold office does not affect any appointment by him (alone or jointly) of another arbitrator, in particular any appointment of a chairman or umpire.

Joint and several liability of parties to arbitrators for fees and expenses.

28.—(1) The parties are jointly and severally liable to pay to the arbitrators such reasonable fees and expenses (if any) as are appropriate in the circumstances.

(2) Any party may apply to the court (upon notice to the other parties and to the arbitrators) which may order that the amount of the arbitrators' fees and expenses shall be considered and adjusted by such means and upon such terms as it may direct.

(3) If the application is made after any amount has been paid to the arbitrators by way of fees or expenses, the court may order the repayment of such amount (if any) as is shown to be excessive, but shall not do so unless it is shown that it is reasonable in the circumstances to order repayment.

(4) The above provisions have effect subject to any order of the court under section 24(4) or 25(3)(b) (order as to entitlement to fees or expenses in case of removal or resignation of arbitrator).

(5) Nothing in this section affects any liability of a party to any other party to pay all or any of the costs of the arbitration (see sections 59 to 65) or any contractual right of an arbitrator to payment of his fees and expenses.

(6) In this section references to arbitrators include an arbitrator who has ceased to act and an umpire who has not replaced the other arbitrators.

Immunity of arbitrator.

29.—(1) An arbitrator is not liable for anything done or omitted in the discharge or purported discharge of his functions as arbitrator unless the act or omission is shown to have been in bad faith.

(2) Subsection (1) applies to an employee or agent of an arbitrator as it applies to the arbitrator himself.

(3) This section does not affect any liability incurred by an arbitrator by reason of his resigning (but see section 25).

Jurisdiction of the Arbitral Tribunal

Competence of tribunal to rule on its own jurisdiction.

30.—(1) Unless otherwise agreed by the parties, the arbitral tribunal may rule on its own substantive jurisdiction, that is, as to—

    (a) whether there is a valid arbitration agreement,

    (b) whether the tribunal is properly constituted, and

    (c) what matters have been submitted to arbitration in accordance with the arbitration agreement.

(2) Any such ruling may be challenged by any available arbitral process of appeal or review or in accordance with the provisions of this Part.

Objection to substantive jurisdiction of tribunal.

31.—(1) An objection that the arbitral tribunal lacks substantive jurisdiction at the outset of the proceedings must be raised by a party not later than the time he takes the first step in the proceedings to contest the merits of any matter in relation to which he challenges the tribunal's jurisdiction.

A party is not precluded from raising such an objection by the fact that he has appointed or participated in the appointment of an arbitrator.

(2) Any objection during the course of the arbitral proceedings that the arbitral tribunal is exceeding its substantive jurisdiction must be made as soon as possible after the matter alleged to be beyond its jurisdiction is raised.

(3) The arbitral tribunal may admit an objection later than the time specified in subsection (1) or (2) if it considers the delay justified.

(4) Where an objection is duly taken to the tribunal's substantive jurisdiction and the tribunal has power to rule on its own jurisdiction, it may—

    (a) rule on the matter in an award as to jurisdiction, or

    (b) deal with the objection in its award on the merits.

If the parties agree which of these courses the tribunal should take, the tribunal shall proceed accordingly.

(5) The tribunal may in any case, and shall if the parties so agree, stay proceedings whilst an application is made to the court under section 32 (determination of preliminary point of jurisdiction).

Determination of preliminary point of jurisdiction.

32.—(1) The court may, on the application of a party to arbitral proceedings (upon notice to the other parties), determine any question as to the substantive jurisdiction of the tribunal.

A party may lose the right to object (see section 73).

(2) An application under this section shall not be considered unless—

(a) it is made with the agreement in writing of all the other parties to the proceedings, or

(b) it is made with the permission of the tribunal and the court is satisfied—

(i) that the determination of the question is likely to produce substantial savings in costs,

(ii) that the application was made without delay, and

(iii) that there is good reason why the matter should be decided by the court.

(3) An application under this section, unless made with the agreement of all the other parties to the proceedings, shall state the grounds on which it is said that the matter should be decided by the court.

(4) Unless otherwise agreed by the parties, the arbitral tribunal may continue the arbitral proceedings and make an award while an application to the court under this section is pending.

(5) Unless the court gives leave, no appeal lies from a decision of the court whether the conditions specified in subsection (2) are met.

(6) The decision of the court on the question of jurisdiction shall be treated as a judgment of the court for the purposes of an appeal.

But no appeal lies without the leave of the court which shall not be given unless the court considers that the question involves a point of law which is one of general importance or is one which for some other special reason should be considered by the Court of Appeal.

The Arbitral Proceedings

General duty of the tribunal.

33.—(1) The tribunal shall—

(a) act fairly and impartially as between the parties, giving each party a reasonable opportunity of putting his case and dealing with that of his opponent, and

(b) adopt procedures suitable to the circumstances of the particular case, avoiding unnecessary delay or expense, so as to provide a fair means for the resolution of the matters falling to be determined.

(2) The tribunal shall comply with that general duty in conducting the arbitral proceedings, in its decisions on matters of procedure and evidence and in the exercise of all other powers conferred on it.

Procedural and evidential matters.

34.—(1) It shall be for the tribunal to decide all procedural and evidential matters, subject to the right of the parties to agree any matter.

(2) Procedural and evidential matters include—

(a) when and where any part of the proceedings is to be held;

(b) the language or languages to be used in the proceedings and whether translations of any relevant documents are to be supplied;

(c) whether any and if so what form of written statements of claim and defence are to be used, when these should be supplied and the extent to which such statements can be later amended;

(d) whether any and if so which documents or classes of documents should be disclosed between and produced by the parties and at what stage;

(e) whether any and if so what questions should be put to and answered by the respective parties and when and in what form this should be done;

(f) whether to apply strict rules of evidence (or any other rules) as to the admissibility, relevance or weight of any material (oral, written or other) sought to be tendered on any matters of fact or opinion, and the time, manner and form in which such material should be exchanged and presented;

(g) whether and to what extent the tribunal should itself take the initiative in ascertaining the facts and the law;

(h) whether and to what extent there should be oral or written evidence or submissions.

(3) The tribunal may fix the time within which any directions given by it are to be complied with, and may if it thinks fit extend the time so fixed (whether or not it has expired).

Consolidation of proceedings and concurrent hearings.

35.—(1) The parties are free to agree—

(a) that the arbitral proceedings shall be consolidated with other arbitral proceedings, or

(b) that concurrent hearings shall be held,

on such terms as may be agreed.

(2) Unless the parties agree to confer such power on the tribunal, the tribunal has no power to order consolidation of proceedings or concurrent hearings.

Legal or other representation.

36. Unless otherwise agreed by the parties, a party to arbitral proceedings may be represented in the proceedings by a lawyer or other person chosen by him.

Power to appoint experts, legal advisers or assessors.

37.—(1) Unless otherwise agreed by the parties—

    (a) the tribunal may—

        (i) appoint experts or legal advisers to report to it and the parties, or

        (ii) appoint assessors to assist it on technical matters,

and may allow any such expert, legal adviser or assessor to attend the proceedings; and.

    (b) the parties shall be given a reasonable opportunity to comment on any information, opinion or advice offered by any such person.

(2) The fees and expenses of an expert, legal adviser or assessor appointed by the tribunal for which the arbitrators are liable are expenses of the arbitrators for the purposes of this Part.

General powers exercisable by the tribunal.

38.—(1) The parties are free to agree on the powers exercisable by the arbitral tribunal for the purposes of and in relation to the proceedings.

(2) Unless otherwise agreed by the parties the tribunal has the following powers.

(3) The tribunal may order a claimant to provide security for the costs of the arbitration.

This power shall not be exercised on the ground that the claimant is—

    (a) an individual ordinarily resident outside the United Kingdom, or

    (b) a corporation or association incorporated or formed under the law of a country outside the United Kingdom, or whose central management and control is exercised outside the United Kingdom.

(4) The tribunal may give directions in relation to any property which is the subject of the proceedings or as to which any question arises

in the proceedings, and which is owned by or is in the possession of a party to the proceedings—

(a) for the inspection, photographing, preservation, custody or detention of the property by the tribunal, an expert or a party, or

(b) ordering that samples be taken from, or any observation be made of or experiment conducted upon, the property.

(5) The tribunal may direct that a party or witness shall be examined on oath or affirmation, and may for that purpose administer any necessary oath or take any necessary affirmation.

(6) The tribunal may give directions to a party for the preservation for the purposes of the proceedings of any evidence in his custody or control.

Power to make provisional awards.

39.—(1) The parties are free to agree that the tribunal shall have power to order on a provisional basis any relief which it would have power to grant in a final award.

(2) This includes, for instance, making—

(a) a provisional order for the payment of money or the disposition of property as between the parties, or

(b) an order to make an interim payment on account of the costs of the arbitration.

(3) Any such order shall be subject to the tribunal's final adjudication; and the tribunal's final award, on the merits or as to costs, shall take account of any such order.

(4) Unless the parties agree to confer such power on the tribunal, the tribunal has no such power.

This does not affect its powers under section 47 (awards on different issues, etc.).

General duty of parties.

40.—(1) The parties shall do all things necessary for the proper and expeditious conduct of the arbitral proceedings.

(2) This includes—

(a) complying without delay with any determination of the tribunal as to procedural or evidential matters, or with any order or directions of the tribunal, and

(b) where appropriate, taking without delay any necessary steps to obtain a decision of the court on a preliminary question of jurisdiction or law (see sections 32 and 45).

Powers of tribunal in case of party's default.

41.—(1) The parties are free to agree on the powers of the tribunal in case of a party's failure to do something necessary for the proper and expeditious conduct of the arbitration.

(2) Unless otherwise agreed by the parties, the following provisions apply.

(3) If the tribunal is satisfied that there has been inordinate and inexcusable delay on the part of the claimant in pursuing his claim and that the delay—

    (a) gives rise, or is likely to give rise, to a substantial risk that it is not possible to have a fair resolution of the issues in that claim, or

    (b) has caused, or is likely to cause, serious prejudice to the respondent,

the tribunal may make an award dismissing the claim.

(4) If without showing sufficient cause a party—

    (a) fails to attend or be represented at an oral hearing of which due notice was given, or

    (b) where matters are to be dealt with in writing, fails after due notice to submit written evidence or make written submissions;

the tribunal may continue the proceedings in the absence of that party or, as the case may be, without any written evidence or submissions on his behalf, and may make an award on the basis of the evidence before it.

(5) If without showing sufficient cause a party fails to comply with any order or directions of the tribunal, the tribunal may make a peremptory order to the same effect, prescribing such time for compliance with it as the tribunal considers appropriate.

(6) If a claimant fails to comply with a peremptory order of the tribunal to provide security for costs, the tribunal may make an award dismissing his claim.

(7) If a party fails to comply with any other kind of peremptory order, then, without prejudice to section 42 (enforcement by court of tribunal's peremptory orders), the tribunal may do any of the following—

    (a) direct that the party in default shall not be entitled to rely upon any allegation or material which was the subject matter of the order;

    (b) draw such adverse inferences from the act of non-compliance as the circumstances justify;

    (c) proceed to an award on the basis of such materials as have been properly provided to it;

    (d) make such order as it thinks fit as to the payment of costs of the arbitration incurred in consequence of the non-compliance.

Powers of Court in Relation to Arbitral Proceedings

Enforcement of peremptory orders of tribunal.

42.—(1) Unless otherwise agreed by the parties, the court may make an order requiring a party to comply with a peremptory order made by the tribunal.

(2) An application for an order under this section may be made—

(a) by the tribunal (upon notice to the parties),

(b) by a party to the arbitral proceedings with the permission of the tribunal (and upon notice to the other parties), or

(c) where the parties have agreed that the powers of the court under this section shall be available.

(3) The court shall not act unless it is satisfied that the applicant has exhausted any available arbitral process in respect of failure to comply with the tribunal's order.

(4) No order shall be made under this section unless the court is satisfied that the person to whom the tribunal's order was directed has failed to comply with it within the time prescribed in the order or, if no time was prescribed, within a reasonable time.

(5) The leave of the court is required for any appeal from a decision of the court under this section.

Securing the attendance of witnesses.

43. (1) A party to arbitral proceedings may use the same court procedures as are available in relation to legal proceedings to secure the attendance before the tribunal of a witness in order to give oral testimony or to produce documents or other material evidence.

(2) This may only be done with the permission of the tribunal or the agreement of the other parties.

(3) The court procedures may only be used if—

(a) the witness is in the United Kingdom, and

(b) the arbitral proceedings are being conducted in England and Wales or, as the case may be, Northern Ireland.

(4) A person shall not be compelled by virtue of this section to produce any document or other material evidence which he could not be compelled to produce in legal proceedings.

Court powers exercisable in support of arbitral proceedings.

44.—(1) Unless otherwise agreed by the parties, the court has for the purposes of and in relation to arbitral proceedings the same power of making orders about the matters listed below as it has for the purposes of and in relation to legal proceedings.

(2) Those matters are—

(a) the taking of the evidence of witnesses;

(b) the preservation of evidence;

(c) making orders relating to property which is the subject of the proceedings or as to which any question arises in the proceedings—

(i) for the inspection, photographing, preservation, custody or detention of the property, or

(ii) ordering that samples be taken from, or any observation be made of or experiment conducted upon, the property;

and for that purpose authorising any person to enter any premises in the possession or control of a party to the arbitration;

(d) the sale of any goods the subject of the proceedings;

(e) the granting of an interim injunction or the appointment of a receiver.

(3) If the case is one of urgency, the court may, on the application of a party or proposed party to the arbitral proceedings, make such orders as it thinks necessary for the purpose of preserving evidence or assets.

(4) If the case is not one of urgency, the court shall act only on the application of a party to the arbitral proceedings (upon notice to the other parties and to the tribunal) made with the permission of the tribunal or the agreement in writing of the other parties.

(5) In any case the court shall act only if or to the extent that the arbitral tribunal, and any arbitral or other institution or person vested by the parties with power in that regard, has no power or is unable for the time being to act effectively.

(6) If the court so orders, an order made by it under this section shall cease to have effect in whole or in part on the order of the tribunal or of any such arbitral or other institution or person having power to act in relation to the subject-matter of the order.

(7) The leave of the court is required for any appeal from a decision of the court under this section.

Determination of preliminary point of law.

45.—(1) Unless otherwise agreed by the parties, the court may on the application of a party to arbitral proceedings (upon notice to the other parties) determine any question of law arising in the course of the proceedings which the court is satisfied substantially affects the rights of one or more of the parties.

An agreement to dispense with reasons for the tribunal's award shall be considered an agreement to exclude the court's jurisdiction under this section.

(2) An application under this section shall not be considered unless—

(a) it is made with the agreement of all the other parties to the proceedings, or

(b) it is made with the permission of the tribunal and the court is satisfied—

(i) that the determination of the question is likely to produce substantial savings in costs, and

(ii) that the application was made without delay.

(3) The application shall identify the question of law to be determined and, unless made with the agreement of all the other parties to the proceedings, shall state the grounds on which it is said that the question should be decided by the court.

(4) Unless otherwise agreed by the parties, the arbitral tribunal may continue the arbitral proceedings and make an award while an application to the court under this section is pending.

(5) Unless the court gives leave, no appeal lies from a decision of the court whether the conditions specified in subsection (2) are met.

(6) The decision of the court on the question of law shall be treated as a judgment of the court for the purposes of an appeal.

But no appeal lies without the leave of the court which shall not be given unless the court considers that the question is one of general importance, or is one which for some other special reason should be considered by the Court of Appeal.

The Award

Rules applicable to substance of dispute.

46.—(1) The arbitral tribunal shall decide the dispute—

(a) in accordance with the law chosen by the parties as applicable to the substance of the dispute, or

(b) if the parties so agree, in accordance with such other considerations as are agreed by them or determined by the tribunal.

(2) For this purpose the choice of the laws of a country shall be understood to refer to the substantive laws of that country and not its conflict of laws rules.

(3) If or to the extent that there is no such choice or agreement, the tribunal shall apply the law determined by the conflict of laws rules which it considers applicable.

Awards on different issues, & c.

47.—(1) Unless otherwise agreed by the parties, the tribunal may make more than one award at different times on different aspects of the matters to be determined.

(2) The tribunal may, in particular, make an award relating—

(a) to an issue affecting the whole claim, or

(b) to a part only of the claims or cross-claims submitted to it for decision.

(3) If the tribunal does so, it shall specify in its award the issue, or the claim or part of a claim, which is the subject matter of the award.

Remedies.

48.—(1) The parties are free to agree on the powers exercisable by the arbitral tribunal as regards remedies.

(2) Unless otherwise agreed by the parties, the tribunal has the following powers.

(3) The tribunal may make a declaration as to any matter to be determined in the proceedings.

(4) The tribunal may order the payment of a sum of money, in any currency.

(5) The tribunal has the same powers as the court—

(a) to order a party to do or refrain from doing anything;

(b) to order specific performance of a contract (other than a contract relating to land);

(c) to order the rectification, setting aside or cancellation of a deed or other document.

Interest.

49.—(1) The parties are free to agree on the powers of the tribunal as regards the award of interest.

(2) Unless otherwise agreed by the parties the following provisions apply.

(3) The tribunal may award simple or compound interest from such dates, at such rates and with such rests as it considers meets the justice of the case—

(a) on the whole or part of any amount awarded by the tribunal, in respect of any period up to the date of the award;

(b) on the whole or part of any amount claimed in the arbitration and outstanding at the commencement of the arbitral proceedings but paid before the award was made, in respect of any period up to the date of payment.

(4) The tribunal may award simple or compound interest from the date of the award (or any later date) until payment, at such rates and with such rests as it considers meets the justice of the case, on the outstanding amount of any award (including any award of interest under subsection (3) and any award as to costs).

(5) References in this section to an amount awarded by the tribunal include an amount payable in consequence of a declaratory award by the tribunal.

(6) The above provisions do not affect any other power of the tribunal to award interest.

Extension of time for making award.

50.—(1) Where the time for making an award is limited by or in pursuance of the arbitration agreement, then, unless otherwise agreed by the parties, the court may in accordance with the following provisions by order extend that time.

(2) An application for an order under this section may be made—

(a) by the tribunal (upon notice to the parties), or

(b) by any party to the proceedings (upon notice to the tribunal and the other parties);

but only after exhausting any available arbitral process for obtaining an extension of time.

(3) The court shall only make an order if satisfied that a substantial injustice would otherwise be done.

(4) The court may extend the time for such period and on such terms as it thinks fit, and may do so whether or not the time previously fixed (by or under the agreement or by a previous order) has expired.

(5) The leave of the court is required for any appeal from a decision of the court under this section.

Settlement.

51.—(1) If during arbitral proceedings the parties settle the dispute, the following provisions apply unless otherwise agreed by the parties.

(2) The tribunal shall terminate the substantive proceedings and, if so requested by the parties and not objected to by the tribunal, shall record the settlement in the form of an agreed award.

(3) An agreed award shall state that it is an award of the tribunal and shall have the same status and effect as any other award on the merits of the case.

(4) The following provisions of this Part relating to awards (sections 52 to 58) apply to an agreed award.

(5) Unless the parties have also settled the matter of the payment of the costs of the arbitration, the provisions of this Part relating to costs (sections 59 to 65) continue to apply.

Form of award.

52.—(1) The parties are free to agree on the form of an award.

(2) If or to the extent that there is no such agreement, the following provisions apply.

(3) The award shall be in writing signed by all the arbitrators or all those assenting to the award.

(4) The award shall contain the reasons for the award unless it is an agreed award or the parties have agreed to dispense with reasons.

(5) The award shall state the seat of the arbitration and the date when the award is made.

Place where award treated as made.

53.   Unless otherwise agreed by the parties, where the seat of the arbitration is in England and Wales or Northern Ireland, any award in the proceedings shall be treated as made there, regardless of where it was signed, despatched or delivered to any of the parties.

Date of award.

54.—(1) Unless otherwise agreed by the parties, the tribunal may decide what is to be taken to be the date on which the award was made.

(2) In the absence of any such decision, the date of the award shall be taken to be the date on which it is signed by the arbitrator or, where more than one arbitrator signs the award, by the last of them.

Notification of award.

55.—(1) The parties are free to agree on the requirements as to notification of the award to the parties.

(2) If there is no such agreement, the award shall be notified to the parties by service on them of copies of the award, which shall be done without delay after the award is made.

(3) Nothing in this section affects section 56 (power to withhold award in case of non-payment).

Power to withhold award in case of non-payment.

56.—(1) The tribunal may refuse to deliver an award to the parties except upon full payment of the fees and expenses of the arbitrators.

(2) If the tribunal refuses on that ground to deliver an award, a party to the arbitral proceedings may (upon notice to the other parties and the tribunal) apply to the court, which may order that—

(a) the tribunal shall deliver the award on the payment into court by the applicant of the fees and expenses demanded, or such lesser amount as the court may specify;

(b) the amount of the fees and expenses properly payable shall be determined by such means and upon such terms as the court may direct, and

(c) out of the money paid into court there shall be paid out such fees and expenses as may be found to be properly payable and the balance of the money (if any) shall be paid out to the applicant.

(3) For this purpose the amount of fees and expenses properly payable is the amount the applicant is liable to pay under section 28 or any agreement relating to the payment of the arbitrators.

(4) No application to the court may be made where there is any available arbitral process for appeal or review of the amount of the fees or expenses demanded.

(5) References in this section to arbitrators include an arbitrator who has ceased to act and an umpire who has not replaced the other arbitrators.

(6) The above provisions of this section also apply in relation to any arbitral or other institution or person vested by the parties with powers in relation to the delivery of the tribunal's award.

As they so apply, the references to the fees and expenses of the arbitrators shall be construed as including the fees and expenses of that institution or person.

(7) The leave of the court is required for any appeal from a decision of the court under this section.

(8) Nothing in this section shall be construed as excluding an application under section 28 where payment has been made to the arbitrators in order to obtain the award.

Correction of award or additional award.

57.—(1) The parties are free to agree on the powers of the tribunal to correct an award or make an additional award.

(2) If or to the extent there is no such agreement, the following provisions apply.

(3) The tribunal may on its own initiative or on the application of a party—

(a) correct an award so as to remove any clerical mistake or error arising from an accidental slip or omission or clarify or remove any ambiguity in the award, or

(b) make an additional award in respect of any claim (including a claim for interest or costs) which was presented to the tribunal but was not dealt with in the award.

These powers shall not be exercised without first affording the other parties a reasonable opportunity to make representations to the tribunal.

(4) Any application for the exercise of those powers must be made within 28 days of the date of the award or such longer period as the parties may agree.

(5) Any correction of an award shall be made within 28 days of the date the application was received by the tribunal or, where the correction is made by the tribunal on its own initiative, within 28 days of the date of the award or, in either case, such longer period as the parties may agree.

(6) Any additional award shall be made within 56 days of the date of the original award or such longer period as the parties may agree.

(7) Any correction of an award shall form part of the award.

Effect of award.

58. Unless otherwise agreed by the parties, an award made by the tribunal pursuant to an arbitration agreement is final and binding both on the parties and on any persons claiming through or under them.

(2) This does not affect the right of a person to challenge the award by any available arbitral process of appeal or review or in accordance with the provisions of this Part.

Costs of the Arbitration

Costs of the arbitration.

59.—(1) References in this Part to the costs of the arbitration are to—

(a) the arbitrators' fees and expenses;

(b) the fees and expenses of any arbitral institution concerned, and

(c) the legal or other costs of the parties.

(2) Any such reference includes the costs of or incidental to any proceedings to determine the amount of the recoverable costs of the arbitration (see section 63).

Agreement to pay costs in any event.

60. An agreement which has the effect that a party is to pay the whole or part of the costs of the arbitration in any event is only valid if made after the dispute in question has arisen.

Award of costs.

61.—(1) The tribunal may make an award allocating the costs of the arbitration as between the parties, subject to any agreement of the parties.

(2) Unless the parties otherwise agree, the tribunal shall award costs on the general principle that costs should follow the event except where it appears to the tribunal that in the circumstances this is not appropriate in relation to the whole or part of the costs.

Effect of agreement or award about costs.

62. Unless the parties otherwise agree, any obligation under an agreement between them as to how the costs of the arbitration are to be borne, or under an award allocating the costs of the arbitration, extends only to such costs as are recoverable.

The recoverable costs of the arbitration.

63.—(1) The parties are free to agree what costs of the arbitration are recoverable.

(2) If or to the extent there is no such agreement, the following provisions apply.

(3) The tribunal may determine by award the recoverable costs of the arbitration on such basis as it thinks fit.

If it does so, it shall specify—

(a) the basis on which it has acted, and

(b) the items of recoverable costs and the amount referable to each.

(4) If the tribunal does not determine the recoverable costs of the arbitration, any party to the arbitral proceedings may apply to the court (upon notice to the other parties) which may—

(a) determine the recoverable costs of the arbitration on such basis as it thinks fit, or

(b) order that they shall be determined by such means and upon such terms as it may specify.

(5) Unless the tribunal or the court determines otherwise—

(a) the recoverable costs of the arbitration shall be determined on the basis that there shall be allowed a reasonable amount in respect of all costs reasonably incurred, and

(b) any doubt as to whether costs were reasonably incurred or were reasonable in amount shall be resolved in favour of the paying party.

(6) The above provisions have effect subject to section 64 (recoverable fees and expenses of arbitrators).

(7) Nothing in this section affects any right of the arbitrators, any expert, legal adviser or assessor appointed by the tribunal, or any arbitral institution, to payment of their fees and expenses.

Recoverable fees and expenses of arbitrators.

64.—(1) Unless otherwise agreed by the parties, the recoverable costs of the arbitration shall include in respect of the fees and expenses of the arbitrators only such reasonable fees and expenses as are appropriate in the circumstances.

(2) If there is any question as to what reasonable fees and expenses are appropriate in the circumstances, and the matter is not already before the court on an application under section 63(4), the court may on the application of any party (upon notice to the other parties)—

(a) determine the matter, or

(b) order that it be determined by such means and upon such terms as the court may specify.

(3) Subsection (1) has effect subject to any order of the court under section 24(4) or 25(3)(b) (order as to entitlement to fees or expenses in case of removal or resignation of arbitrator).

(4) Nothing in this section affects any right of the arbitrator to payment of his fees and expenses.

Power to limit recoverable costs.

65.—(1) Unless otherwise agreed by the parties, the tribunal may direct that the recoverable costs of the arbitration, or of any part of the arbitral proceedings, shall be limited to a specified amount.

(2) Any direction may be made or varied at any stage, but this must be done sufficiently in advance of the incurring of costs to which it relates, or the taking of any steps in the proceedings which may be affected by it, for the limit to be taken into account.

Powers of the Court in Relation to Award

Enforcement of the award.

66.—(1) An award made by the tribunal pursuant to an arbitration agreement may, by leave of the court, be enforced in the same manner as a judgment or order of the court to the same effect.

(2) Where leave is so given, judgment may be entered in terms of the award.

(3) Leave to enforce an award shall not be given where, or to the extent that, the person against whom it is sought to be enforced shows that the tribunal lacked substantive jurisdiction to make the award.

The right to raise such an objection may have been lost (see section 73).

(4) Nothing in this section affects the recognition or enforcement of an award under any other enactment or rule of law, in particular under Part II of the Arbitration Act 1950 (enforcement of awards under Geneva Convention) or the provisions of Part III of this Act relating to the recognition and enforcement of awards under the New York Convention or by an action on the award.

Challenging the award: substantive jurisdiction.

67.—(1) A party to arbitral proceedings may (upon notice to the other parties and to the tribunal) apply to the court—

    (a) challenging any award of the arbitral tribunal as to its substantive jurisdiction; or

    (b) for an order declaring an award made by the tribunal on the merits to be of no effect, in whole or in part, because the tribunal did not have substantive jurisdiction.

A party may lose the right to object (see section 73) and the right to apply is subject to the restrictions in section 70(2) and (3).

(2) The arbitral tribunal may continue the arbitral proceedings and make a further award while an application to the court under this section is pending in relation to an award as to jurisdiction.

(3) On an application under this section challenging an award of the arbitral tribunal as to its substantive jurisdiction, the court may by order—

(a) confirm the award;

(b) vary the award, or

(c) set aside the award in whole or in part.

(4) The leave of the court is required for any appeal from a decision of the court under this section.

Challenging the award: serious irregularity.

68.—(1) A party to arbitral proceedings may (upon notice to the other parties and to the tribunal) apply to the court challenging an award in the proceedings on the ground of serious irregularity affecting the tribunal, the proceedings or the award.

A party may lose the right to object (see section 73) and the right to apply is subject to the restrictions in section 70(2) and (3).

(2) Serious irregularity means an irregularity of one or more of the following kinds which the court considers has caused or will cause substantial injustice to the applicant—

(a) failure by the tribunal to comply with section 33 (general duty of tribunal);

(b) the tribunal exceeding its powers (otherwise than by exceeding its substantive jurisdiction: see section 67);

(c) failure by the tribunal to conduct the proceedings in accordance with the procedure agreed by the parties;

(d) failure by the tribunal to deal with all the issues that were put to it;

(e) any arbitral or other institution or person vested by the parties with powers in relation to the proceedings or the award exceeding its powers;

(f) uncertainty or ambiguity as to the effect of the award;

(g) the award being obtained by fraud or the award or the way in which it was procured being contrary to public policy;

(h) failure to comply with the requirements as to the form of the award; or

(i) any irregularity in the conduct of the proceedings or in the award which is admitted by the tribunal or by any arbitral or other institution or person vested by the parties with powers in relation to the proceedings or the award.

(3) If there is shown to be serious irregularity affecting the tribunal, the proceedings or the award, the court may—

(a) remit the award to the tribunal, in whole or in part, for reconsideration;

(b) set the award aside in whole or in part, or

(c) declare the award to be of no effect, in whole or in part.

The court shall not exercise its power to set aside or to declare an award to be of no effect, in whole or in part, unless it is satisfied that it would be inappropriate to remit the matters in question to the tribunal for reconsideration.

(4) The leave of the court is required for any appeal from a decision of the court under this section.

Appeal on point of law.

69.—(1) Unless otherwise agreed by the parties, a party to arbitral proceedings may (upon notice to the other parties and to the tribunal) appeal to the court on a question of law arising out of an award made in the proceedings.

An agreement to dispense with reasons for the tribunal's award shall be considered an agreement to exclude the court's jurisdiction under this section.

(2) An appeal shall not be brought under this section except—

(a) with the agreement of all the other parties to the proceedings, or

(b) with the leave of the court.

The right to appeal is also subject to the restrictions in section 70(2) and (3).

(3) Leave to appeal shall be given only if the court is satisfied—

(a) that the determination of the question will substantially affect the rights of one or more of the parties;

(b) that the question is one which the tribunal was asked to determine;

(c) that, on the basis of the findings of fact in the award—

(i) the decision of the tribunal on the question is obviously wrong, or

(ii) the question is one of general public importance and the decision of the tribunal is at least open to serious doubt, and.

(d) that, despite the agreement of the parties to resolve the matter by arbitration, it is just and proper in all the circumstances for the court to determine the question.

(4) An application for leave to appeal under this section shall identify the question of law to be determined and state the grounds on which it is alleged that leave to appeal should be granted.

(5) The court shall determine an application for leave to appeal under this section without a hearing unless it appears to the court that a hearing is required.

(6) The leave of the court is required for any appeal from a decision of the court under this section to grant or refuse leave to appeal.

(7) On an appeal under this section the court may by order—

(a) confirm the award,

(b) vary the award,

(c) remit the award to the tribunal, in whole or in part, for reconsideration in the light of the court's determination, or

(d) set aside the award in whole or in part.

The court shall not exercise its power to set aside an award, in whole or in part, unless it is satisfied that it would be inappropriate to remit the matters in question to the tribunal for reconsideration.

(8) The decision of the court on an appeal under this section shall be treated as a judgment of the court for the purposes of a further appeal.

But no such appeal lies without the leave of the court which shall not be given unless the court considers that the question is one of general importance or is one which for some other special reason should be considered by the Court of Appeal.

Challenge or appeal: supplementary provisions.

70.—(1) The following provisions apply to an application or appeal under section 67, 68 or 69

(2) An application or appeal may not be brought if the applicant or appellant has not first exhausted—

(a) any available arbitral process of appeal or review, and

(b) any available recourse under section 57 (correction of award or additional award).

(3) Any application or appeal must be brought within 28 days of the date of the award or, if there has been any arbitral process of appeal or review, of the date when the applicant or appellant was notified of the result of that process.

(4) If on an application or appeal it appears to the court that the award—

(a) does not contain the tribunal's reasons, or

(b) does not set out the tribunal's reasons in sufficient detail to enable the court properly to consider the application or appeal;

the court may order the tribunal to state the reasons for its award in sufficient detail for that purpose.

(5) Where the court makes an order under subsection (4), it may make such further order as it thinks fit with respect to any additional costs of the arbitration resulting from its order.

(6) The court may order the applicant or appellant to provide security for the costs of the application or appeal, and may direct that the application or appeal be dismissed if the order is not complied with.

The power to order security for costs shall not be exercised on the ground that the applicant or appellant is—

(a) an individual ordinarily resident outside the United Kingdom, or

(b) a corporation or association incorporated or formed under the law of a country outside the United Kingdom, or whose central management and control is exercised outside the United Kingdom.

(7) The court may order that any money payable under the award shall be brought into court or otherwise secured pending the determination of the application or appeal, and may direct that the application or appeal be dismissed if the order is not complied with.

(8) The court may grant leave to appeal subject to conditions to the same or similar effect as an order under subsection (6) or (7).

This does not affect the general discretion of the court to grant leave subject to conditions.

Challenge or appeal: effect of order of court.

71.—(1) The following provisions have effect where the court makes an order under section 67, 68 or 69 with respect to an award.

(2) Where the award is varied, the variation has effect as part of the tribunal's award.

(3) Where the award is remitted to the tribunal, in whole or in part, for reconsideration, the tribunal shall make a fresh award in respect of the matters remitted within three months of the date of the order for remission or such longer or shorter period as the court may direct.

(4) Where the award is set aside or declared to be of no effect, in whole or in part, the court may also order that any provision that an award is a condition precedent to the bringing of legal proceedings in respect of a matter to which the arbitration agreement applies, is of no effect as regards the subject matter of the award or, as the case may be, the relevant part of the award.

Miscellaneous

Saving for rights of person who takes no part in proceedings.

72.—(1) A person alleged to be a party to arbitral proceedings but who takes no part in the proceedings may question—

(a) whether there is a valid arbitration agreement,

(b) whether the tribunal is properly constituted, or

(c) what matters have been submitted to arbitration in accordance with the arbitration agreement,

by proceedings in the court for a declaration or injunction or other appropriate relief.

(2) He also has the same right as a party to the arbitral proceedings to challenge an award—

(a) by an application under section 67 on the ground of lack of substantive jurisdiction in relation to him, or

(b) by an application under section 68 on the ground of serious irregularity (within the meaning of that section) affecting him;

and section 70(2) (duty to exhaust arbitral procedures) does not apply in his case.

Loss of right to object.

73.—(1) If a party to arbitral proceedings takes part, or continues to take part, in the proceedings without making, either forthwith or within such time as is allowed by the arbitration agreement or the tribunal or by any provision of this Part, any objection—

(a) that the tribunal lacks substantive jurisdiction,

(b) that the proceedings have been improperly conducted,

(c) that there has been a failure to comply with the arbitration agreement or with any provision of this Part, or

(d) that there has been any other irregularity affecting the tribunal or the proceedings,

he may not raise that objection later, before the tribunal or the court, unless he shows that, at the time he took part or continued to take part in the proceedings, he did not know and could not with reasonable diligence have discovered the grounds for the objection.

(2) Where the arbitral tribunal rules that it has substantive jurisdiction and a party to arbitral proceedings who could have questioned that ruling—

(a) by any available arbitral process of appeal or review, or

(b) by challenging the award,

does not do so, or does not do so within the time allowed by the arbitration agreement or any provision of this Part, he may not object later to the tribunal's substantive jurisdiction on any ground which was the subject of that ruling.

Immunity of arbitral institutions, etc.

74.—(1) An arbitral or other institution or person designated or requested by the parties to appoint or nominate an arbitrator is not liable for anything done or omitted in the discharge or purported discharge of that function unless the act or omission is shown to have been in bad faith.

(2) An arbitral or other institution or person by whom an arbitrator is appointed or nominated is not liable, by reason of having appointed or nominated him, for anything done or omitted by the arbitrator (or his employees or agents) in the discharge or purported discharge of his functions as arbitrator.

(3) The above provisions apply to an employee or agent of an arbitral or other institution or person as they apply to the institution or person himself.

Charge to secure payment of solicitors' costs.

75. The powers of the court to make declarations and orders under section 73 of the Solicitors Act 1974 or Article 71H of the Solicitors (Northern Ireland) Order 1976 (power to charge property recovered in the proceedings with the payment of solicitors' costs) may be exercised in relation to arbitral proceedings as if those proceedings were proceedings in the court.

Supplementary

Service of notices, & c.

76.—(1) The parties are free to agree on the manner of service of any notice or other document required or authorised to be given or served in pursuance of the arbitration agreement or for the purposes of the arbitral proceedings.

(2) If or to the extent that there is no such agreement the following provisions apply.

(3) A notice or other document may be served on a person by any effective means.

(4) If a notice or other document is addressed, pre-paid and delivered by post—

(a) to the addressee's last known principal residence or, if he is or has been carrying on a trade, profession or business, his last known principal business address, or

(b) where the addressee is a body corporate, to the body's registered or principal office,

it shall be treated as effectively served.

(5) This section does not apply to the service of documents for the purposes of legal proceedings, for which provision is made by rules of court.

(6) References in this Part to a notice or other document include any form of communication in writing and references to giving or serving a notice or other document shall be construed accordingly.

Powers of court in relation to service of documents.

77.—(1) This section applies where service of a document on a person in the manner agreed by the parties, or in accordance with provisions of section 76 having effect in default of agreement, is not reasonably practicable.

(2) Unless otherwise agreed by the parties, the court may make such order as it thinks fit—

(a) for service in such manner as the court may direct, or

(b) dispensing with service of the document.

(3) Any party to the arbitration agreement may apply for an order, but only after exhausting any available arbitral process for resolving the matter.

(4) The leave of the court is required for any appeal from a decision of the court under this section.

Reckoning periods of time.

78.—(1) The parties are free to agree on the method of reckoning periods of time for the purposes of any provision agreed by them or any provision of this Part having effect in default of such agreement.

(2) If or to the extent there is no such agreement, periods of time shall be reckoned in accordance with the following provisions.

(3) Where the act is required to be done within a specified period after or from a specified date, the period begins immediately after that date.

(4) Where the act is required to be done a specified number of clear days after a specified date, at least that number of days must intervene between the day on which the act is done and that date.

(5) Where the period is a period of seven days or less which would include a Saturday, Sunday or a public holiday in the place where anything which has to be done within the period falls to be done, that day shall be excluded.

In relation to England and Wales or Northern Ireland, a "public holiday" means Christmas Day, Good Friday or a day which under the Banking and Financial Dealings Act 1971 is a bank holiday.

Power of court to extend time limits relating to arbitral proceedings.

79.—(1) Unless the parties otherwise agree, the court may by order extend any time limit agreed by them in relation to any matter relating to the arbitral proceedings or specified in any provision of this Part having effect in default of such agreement.

This section does not apply to a time limit to which section 12 applies (power of court to extend time for beginning arbitral proceedings, & c.).

(2) An application for an order may be made—

(a) by any party to the arbitral proceedings (upon notice to the other parties and to the tribunal), or

(b) by the arbitral tribunal (upon notice to the parties).

(3) The court shall not exercise its power to extend a time limit unless it is satisfied—

(a) that any available recourse to the tribunal, or to any arbitral or other institution or person vested by the parties with power in that regard, has first been exhausted, and

(b) that a substantial injustice would otherwise be done.

(4) The court's power under this section may be exercised whether or not the time has already expired.

(5) An order under this section may be made on such terms as the court thinks fit.

(6) The leave of the court is required for any appeal from a decision of the court under this section.

Notice and other requirements in connection with legal proceedings.

80.—(1) References in this Part to an application, appeal or other step in relation to legal proceedings being taken "upon notice" to the other parties to the arbitral proceedings, or to the tribunal, are to such notice of the originating process as is required by rules of court and do not impose any separate requirement.

(2) Rules of court shall be made—

(a) requiring such notice to be given as indicated by any provision of this Part, and

(b) as to the manner, form and content of any such notice.

(3) Subject to any provision made by rules of court, a requirement to give notice to the tribunal of legal proceedings shall be construed—

(a) if there is more than one arbitrator, as a requirement to give notice to each of them; and

(b) if the tribunal is not fully constituted, as a requirement to give notice to any arbitrator who has been appointed.

(4) References in this Part to making an application or appeal to the court within a specified period are to the issue within that period of the appropriate originating process in accordance with rules of court.

(5) Where any provision of this Part requires an application or appeal to be made to the court within a specified time, the rules of court relating to the reckoning of periods, the extending or abridging of periods, and the consequences of not taking a step within the period prescribed by the rules, apply in relation to that requirement.

(6) Provision may be made by rules of court amending the provisions of this Part—

(a) with respect to the time within which any application or appeal to the court must be made;

(b) so as to keep any provision made by this Part in relation to arbitral proceedings in step with the corresponding provision of rules of court applying in relation to proceedings in the court, or

(c) so as to keep any provision made by this Part in relation to legal proceedings in step with the corresponding provision of rules of court applying generally in relation to proceedings in the court.

(7) Nothing in this section affects the generality of the power to make rules of court.

Saving for certain matters governed by common law.

81.—(1) Nothing in this Part shall be construed as excluding the operation of any rule of law consistent with the provisions of this Part, in particular, any rule of law as to—

(a) matters which are not capable of settlement by arbitration;

(b) the effect of an oral arbitration agreement; or

(c) the refusal of recognition or enforcement of an arbitral award on grounds of public policy.

(2) Nothing in this Act shall be construed as reviving any jurisdiction of the court to set aside or remit an award on the ground of errors of fact or law on the face of the award.

Minor definitions.

82.—(1) In this Part—

"arbitrator", unless the context otherwise requires, includes an umpire;

"available arbitral process", in relation to any matter, includes any process of appeal to or review by an arbitral or other institution or person vested by the parties with powers in relation to that matter;

"claimant", unless the context otherwise requires, includes a counterclaimant, and related expressions shall be construed accordingly;

"dispute" includes any difference;

"enactment" includes an enactment contained in Northern Ireland legislation;

"legal proceedings" means civil proceedings in the High Court or a county court;

"peremptory order" means an order made under section 41(5) or made in exercise of any corresponding power conferred by the parties;

"premises" includes land, buildings, moveable structures, vehicles, vessels, aircraft and hovercraft;

"question of law" means—

(a) for a court in England and Wales, a question of the law of England and Wales, and

(b) for a court in Northern Ireland, a question of the law of Northern Ireland;

"substantive jurisdiction", in relation to an arbitral tribunal, refers to the matters specified in section 30(1)(a) to (c), and references to the tribunal exceeding its substantive jurisdiction shall be construed accordingly.

(2) References in this Part to a party to an arbitration agreement include any person claiming under or through a party to the agreement.

Index of defined expressions: Part I.

83. In this Part the expressions listed below are defined or otherwise explained by the provisions indicated—

agreement, agree and agreed
      section 5(1)

agreement in writing
      section 5(2) to (5)

arbitration agreement
      sections 6 and 5(1)

arbitrator
      section 82(1)

available arbitral process
      section 82(1)

claimant
      section 82(1)

commencement (in relation to arbitral proceedings)
      section 14

costs of the arbitration
      section 59

the court
      section 105

dispute
      section 82(1)

enactment
      section 82(1)

legal proceedings
      section 82(1)

Limitation Acts
      section 13(4)

notice (or other document)
      section 76(6)

party—

—in relation to an arbitration agreement
      section 82(2)

—where section 106(2) or (3) applies
      section 106(4)

peremptory order
      section 82(1) (and see section 41(5))

premises

section 82(1)

question of law

section 82(1)

recoverable costs

sections 63 and 64

seat of the arbitration

section 3

serve and service (of notice or other document)

section 76(6)

substantive jurisdiction (in relation to an arbitral tribunal)

section 82(1) (and see section 30(1)(a) to (c))

upon notice (to the parties or the tribunal)

section 80

written and in writing

section 5(6)

Transitional provisions.

84.—(1) The provisions of this Part do not apply to arbitral proceedings commenced before the date on which this Part comes into force.

(2) They apply to arbitral proceedings commenced on or after that date under an arbitration agreement whenever made.

(3) The above provisions have effect subject to any transitional provision made by an order under section 109(2) (power to include transitional provisions in commencement order).

PART II

OTHER PROVISIONS RELATING TO ARBITRATION

Domestic Arbitration Agreements

Modification of Part I in relation to domestic arbitration agreement.

85.[1]—(1) In the case of a domestic arbitration agreement the provisions of Part I are modified in accordance with the following sections.

(2) For this purpose a "domestic arbitration agreement" means an arbitration agreement to which none of the parties is—

    (a) an individual who is a national of, or habitually resident in, a state other than the United Kingdom, or

---

1. Sections 85–87 were not brought into effect when the Secretary of State promulgated the Act. *See* S.I. 1996 No. 3146, § 3 (Dec. 16, 1996). The effect is that both domestic and international arbitration agreements may now exclude the right to appeal to the courts.

(b) a body corporate which is incorporated in, or whose central control and management is exercised in, a state other than the United Kingdom,

and under which the seat of the arbitration (if the seat has been designated or determined) is in the United Kingdom.

(3) In subsection (2) "arbitration agreement" and "seat of the arbitration" have the same meaning as in Part I (see sections 3, 5(1) and 6).

Staying of legal proceedings.

86.—(1) In section 9 (stay of legal proceedings), subsection (4) (stay unless the arbitration agreement is null and void, inoperative, or incapable of being performed) does not apply to a domestic arbitration agreement.

(2) On an application under that section in relation to a domestic arbitration agreement the court shall grant a stay unless satisfied—

(a) that the arbitration agreement is null and void, inoperative, or incapable of being performed, or

(b) that there are other sufficient grounds for not requiring the parties to abide by the arbitration agreement.

(3) The court may treat as a sufficient ground under subsection (2)(b) the fact that the applicant is or was at any material time not ready and willing to do all things necessary for the proper conduct of the arbitration or of any other dispute resolution procedures required to be exhausted before resorting to arbitration.

(4) For the purposes of this section the question whether an arbitration agreement is a domestic arbitration agreement shall be determined by reference to the facts at the time the legal proceedings are commenced.

Effectiveness of agreement to exclude court's jurisdiction.

87.—(1) In the case of a domestic arbitration agreement any agreement to exclude the jurisdiction of the court under—

(a) section 45 (determination of preliminary point of law), or

(b) section 69 (challenging the award: appeal on point of law),

is not effective unless entered into after the commencement of the arbitral proceedings in which the question arises or the award is made.

(2) For this purpose the commencement of the arbitral proceedings has the same meaning as in Part I (see section 14).

(3) For the purposes of this section the question whether an arbitration agreement is a domestic arbitration agreement shall be determined by reference to the facts at the time the agreement is entered into.

Power to repeal or amend sections 85 to 87.

88.—(1) The Secretary of State may by order repeal or amend the provisions of sections 85 to 87.

(2) An order under this section may contain such supplementary, incidental and transitional provisions as appear to the Secretary of State to be appropriate.

(3) An order under this section shall be made by statutory instrument and no such order shall be made unless a draft of it has been laid before and approved by a resolution of each House of Parliament.

Consumer Arbitration Agreements

Application of unfair terms regulations to consumer arbitration agreements.

89.—(1) The following sections extend the application of the Unfair Terms in Consumer Contracts Regulations 1994 in relation to a term which constitutes an arbitration agreement.

For this purpose "arbitration agreement" means an agreement to submit to arbitration present or future disputes or differences (whether or not contractual).

(2) In those sections "the Regulations" means those regulations and includes any regulations amending or replacing those regulations.

(3) Those sections apply whatever the law applicable to the arbitration agreement.

Regulations apply where consumer is a legal person.

90. The Regulations apply where the consumer is a legal person as they apply where the consumer is a natural person.

Arbitration agreement unfair where modest amount sought.

91.—(1) A term which constitutes an arbitration agreement is unfair for the purposes of the Regulations so far as it relates to a claim for a pecuniary remedy which does not exceed the amount specified by order for the purposes of this section.

(2) Orders under this section may make different provision for different cases and for different purposes.

(3) The power to make orders under this section is exercisable—

(a) for England and Wales, by the Secretary of State with the concurrence of the Lord Chancellor,

(b) for Scotland, by the Secretary of State with the concurrence of the Lord Advocate, and

(c) for Northern Ireland, by the Department of Economic Development for Northern Ireland with the concurrence of the Lord Chancellor.

(4) Any such order for England and Wales or Scotland shall be made by statutory instrument which shall be subject to annulment in pursuance of a resolution of either House of Parliament.

(5) Any such order for Northern Ireland shall be a statutory rule for the purposes of the Statutory Rules (Northern Ireland) Order 1979 and shall be subject to negative resolution, within the meaning of section 41(6) of the Interpretation Act (Northern Ireland) 1954.

Small Claims Arbitration in the County Court

Exclusion of Part I in relation to small claims arbitration in the county court.

92. Nothing in Part I of this Act applies to arbitration under section 64 of the County Courts Act 1984.

Appointment of Judges as Arbitrators

Appointment of judges as arbitrators.

93.—(1) A judge of the Commercial Court or an official referee may, if in all the circumstances he thinks fit, accept appointment as a sole arbitrator or as umpire by or by virtue of an arbitration agreement.

(2) A judge of the Commercial Court shall not do so unless the Lord Chief Justice has informed him that, having regard to the state of business in the High Court and the Crown Court, he can be made available.

(3) An official referee shall not do so unless the Lord Chief Justice has informed him that, having regard to the state of official referees' business, he can be made available.

(4) The fees payable for the services of a judge of the Commercial Court or official referee as arbitrator or umpire shall be taken in the High Court.

(5) In this section—

"arbitration agreement" has the same meaning as in Part I; and

"official referee" means a person nominated under section 68(1)(a) of the Supreme Court Act 1981 to deal with official referees' business.

(6) The provisions of Part I of this Act apply to arbitration before a person appointed under this section with the modifications specified in Schedule 2.

Statutory Arbitrations

Application of Part I to statutory arbitrations.

94.—(1) The provisions of Part I apply to every arbitration under an enactment (a "statutory arbitration"), whether the enactment was passed or made before or after the commencement of this Act, subject to the adaptations and exclusions specified in sections 95 to 98.

(2) The provisions of Part I do not apply to a statutory arbitration if or to the extent that their application—

(a) is inconsistent with the provisions of the enactment concerned, with any rules or procedure authorised or recognised by it, or

(b) is excluded by any other enactment.

(3) In this section and the following provisions of this Part "enactment"—

(a) in England and Wales, includes an enactment contained in subordinate legislation within the meaning of the Interpretation Act 1978;

(b) in Northern Ireland, means a statutory provision within the meaning of section 1(f) of the Interpretation Act (Northern Ireland) 1954.

General adaptation of provisions in relation to statutory arbitrations.

95.—(1) The provisions of Part I apply to a statutory arbitration—

(a) as if the arbitration were pursuant to an arbitration agreement and as if the enactment were that agreement, and

(b) as if the persons by and against whom a claim subject to arbitration in pursuance of the enactment may be or has been made were parties to that agreement.

(2) Every statutory arbitration shall be taken to have its seat in England and Wales or, as the case may be, in Northern Ireland.

Specific adaptations of provisions in relation to statutory arbitrations.

96.—(1) The following provisions of Part I apply to a statutory arbitration with the following adaptations.

(2) In section 30(1) (competence of tribunal to rule on its own jurisdiction), the reference in paragraph (a) to whether there is a valid arbitration agreement shall be construed as a reference to whether the enactment applies to the dispute or difference in question.

(3) Section 35 (consolidation of proceedings and concurrent hearings) applies only so as to authorise the consolidation of proceedings, or concurrent hearings in proceedings, under the same enactment.

(4) Section 46 (rules applicable to substance of dispute) applies with the omission of subsection (1)(b) (determination in accordance with considerations agreed by parties).

Provisions excluded from applying to statutory arbitrations.

97. The following provisions of Part I do not apply in relation to a statutory arbitration—

(a) section 8 (whether agreement discharged by death of a party);

(b) section 12 (power of court to extend agreed time limits);

(c) sections 9(5), 10(2) and 71(4) (restrictions on effect of provision that award condition precedent to right to bring legal proceedings).

Power to make further provision by regulations.

98.—(1) The Secretary of State may make provision by regulations for adapting or excluding any provision of Part I in relation to statutory arbitrations in general or statutory arbitrations of any particular description.

(2) The power is exercisable whether the enactment concerned is passed or made before or after the commencement of this Act.

(3) Regulations under this section shall be made by statutory instrument which shall be subject to annulment in pursuance of a resolution of either House of Parliament.

PART III

RECOGNITION AND ENFORCEMENT OF CERTAIN FOREIGN AWARDS

Enforcement of Geneva Convention Awards

Continuation of Part II of the Arbitration Act 1950.

99. Part II of the Arbitration Act 1950 (enforcement of certain foreign awards) continues to apply in relation to foreign awards within the meaning of that Part which are not also New York Convention awards.

Recognition and Enforcement of New York Convention Awards

New York Convention awards.

100.—(1) In this Part a "New York Convention award" means an award made, in pursuance of an arbitration agreement, in the territory of a state (other than the United Kingdom) which is a party to the New York Convention.

(2) For the purposes of subsection (1) and of the provisions of this Part relating to such awards—

(a) "arbitration agreement" means an arbitration agreement in writing, and

(b) an award shall be treated as made at the seat of the arbitration, regardless of where it was signed, despatched or delivered to any of the parties.

In this subsection "agreement in writing" and "seat of the arbitration" have the same meaning as in Part I.

(3) If Her Majesty by Order in Council declares that a state specified in the Order is a party to the New York Convention, or is a party in

respect of any territory so specified, the Order shall, while in force, be conclusive evidence of that fact.

(4) In this section "the New York Convention" means the Convention on the Recognition and Enforcement of Foreign Arbitral Awards adopted by the United Nations Conference on International Commercial Arbitration on 10th June 1958.

Recognition and enforcement of awards.

101.—(1) A New York Convention award shall be recognised as binding on the persons as between whom it was made, and may accordingly be relied on by those persons by way of defence, set-off or otherwise in any legal proceedings in England and Wales or Northern Ireland.

(2) A New York Convention award may, by leave of the court, be enforced in the same manner as a judgment or order of the court to the same effect.

As to the meaning of "the court" see section 105.

(3) Where leave is so given, judgment may be entered in terms of the award.

Evidence to be produced by party seeking recognition or enforcement.

102.—(1) A party seeking the recognition or enforcement of a New York Convention award must produce—

(a) the duly authenticated original award or a duly certified copy of it, and

(b) the original arbitration agreement or a duly certified copy of it.

(2) If the award or agreement is in a foreign language, the party must also produce a translation of it certified by an official or sworn translator or by a diplomatic or consular agent.

Refusal of recognition or enforcement.

103.—(1) Recognition or enforcement of a New York Convention award shall not be refused except in the following cases.

(2) Recognition or enforcement of the award may be refused if the person against whom it is invoked proves—

(a) that a party to the arbitration agreement was (under the law applicable to him) under some incapacity;

(b) that the arbitration agreement was not valid under the law to which the parties subjected it or, failing any indication thereon, under the law of the country where the award was made;

(c) that he was not given proper notice of the appointment of the arbitrator or of the arbitration proceedings or was otherwise unable to present his case;

(d) that the award deals with a difference not contemplated by or not falling within the terms of the submission to arbitration or contains decisions on matters beyond the scope of the submission to arbitration (but see subsection (4));

(e) that the composition of the arbitral tribunal or the arbitral procedure was not in accordance with the agreement of the parties or, failing such agreement, with the law of the country in which the arbitration took place;

(f) that the award has not yet become binding on the parties, or has been set aside or suspended by a competent authority of the country in which, or under the law of which, it was made.

(3) Recognition or enforcement of the award may also be refused if the award is in respect of a matter which is not capable of settlement by arbitration, or if it would be contrary to public policy to recognise or enforce the award.

(4) An award which contains decisions on matters not submitted to arbitration may be recognised or enforced to the extent that it contains decisions on matters submitted to arbitration which can be separated from those on matters not so submitted.

(5) Where an application for the setting aside or suspension of the award has been made to such a competent authority as is mentioned in subsection (2)(f), the court before which the award is sought to be relied upon may, if it considers it proper, adjourn the decision on the recognition or enforcement of the award.

It may also on the application of the party claiming recognition or enforcement of the award order the other party to give suitable security.

Saving for other bases of recognition or enforcement.

104. Nothing in the preceding provisions of this Part affects any right to rely upon or enforce a New York Convention award at common law or under section 66.

PART IV

GENERAL PROVISIONS

Meaning of "the court": jurisdiction of High Court and county court.

105.—(1) In this Act "the court" means the High Court or a county court, subject to the following provisions.

(2) The Lord Chancellor may by order make provision—

(a) allocating proceedings under this Act to the High Court or to county courts; or

(b) specifying proceedings under this Act which may be commenced or taken only in the High Court or in a county court.

(3) The Lord Chancellor may by order make provision requiring proceedings of any specified description under this Act in relation to

which a county court has jurisdiction to be commenced or taken in one or more specified county courts.

Any jurisdiction so exercisable by a specified county court is exercisable throughout England and Wales or, as the case may be, Northern Ireland.

(4) An order under this section—

(a) may differentiate between categories of proceedings by reference to such criteria as the Lord Chancellor sees fit to specify, and

(b) may make such incidental or transitional provision as the Lord Chancellor considers necessary or expedient.

(5) An order under this section for England and Wales shall be made by statutory instrument which shall be subject to annulment in pursuance of a resolution of either House of Parliament.

(6) An order under this section for Northern Ireland shall be a statutory rule for the purposes of the Statutory Rules (Northern Ireland) Order 1979 which shall be subject to annulment in pursuance of a resolution of either House of Parliament in like manner as a statutory instrument and section 5 of the Statutory Instruments Act 1946 shall apply accordingly.

Crown application.

106.—(1) Part I of this Act applies to any arbitration agreement to which Her Majesty, either in right of the Crown or of the Duchy of Lancaster or otherwise, or the Duke of Cornwall, is a party.

(2) Where Her Majesty is party to an arbitration agreement otherwise than in right of the Crown, Her Majesty shall be represented for the purposes of any arbitral proceedings—

(a) where the agreement was entered into by Her Majesty in right of the Duchy of Lancaster, by the Chancellor of the Duchy or such person as he may appoint, and

(b) in any other case, by such person as Her Majesty may appoint in writing under the Royal Sign Manual.

(3) Where the Duke of Cornwall is party to an arbitration agreement, he shall be represented for the purposes of any arbitral proceedings by such person as he may appoint.

(4) References in Part I to a party or the parties to the arbitration agreement or to arbitral proceedings shall be construed, where subsection (2) or (3) applies, as references to the person representing Her Majesty or the Duke of Cornwall.

Consequential amendments and repeals.

107.—(1) The enactments specified in Schedule 3 are amended in accordance with that Schedule, the amendments being consequential on the provisions of this Act.

(2) The enactments specified in Schedule 4 are repealed to the extent specified.

Extent.

108.—(1) The provisions of this Act extend to England and Wales and, except as mentioned below, to Northern Ireland.

(2) The following provisions of Part II do not extend to Northern Ireland—

section 92 (exclusion of Part I in relation to small claims arbitration in the county court), and

section 93 and Schedule 2 (appointment of judges as arbitrators).

(3) Sections 89, 90 and 91 (consumer arbitration agreements) extend to Scotland and the provisions of Schedules 3 and 4 (consequential amendments and repeals) extend to Scotland so far as they relate to enactments which so extend, subject as follows.

(4) The repeal of the Arbitration Act 1975 extends only to England and Wales and Northern Ireland.

Commencement.

109.—(1) The provisions of this Act come into force on such day as the Secretary of State may appoint by order made by statutory instrument, and different days may be appointed for different purposes.

(2) An order under subsection (1) may contain such transitional provisions as appear to the Secretary of State to be appropriate.

Short title.

110.—This Act may be cited as the Arbitration Act 1996.

UNCITRAL MODEL LAW ON INTERNATIONAL COMMERCIAL ARBITRATION

*Adopted by the United Nations Commission on
International Trade Law 21 June 1985*

TABLE OF CONTENTS

Chapter VII. Recourse Against Award

Chapter VIII. Recognition and Enforcement of Award

CHAPTER I. GENERAL PROVISIONS

Article 1. Scope of application*

1. This Law applies to international commercial** arbitration, subject to any agreement in force between this State and any other State or States.

2. The provisions of this Law, except articles 8, 9, 35 and 36, apply only if the place of arbitration is in the territory of this State.

3. An arbitration is international if:

a. the parties to an arbitration agreement have, at the time of the conclusion of that agreement, their places of business in different States; or

b. one of the following places is situated outside the State in which the parties have their places of business;

(i) the place of arbitration if determined in, or pursuant to, the arbitration agreement;

(ii) any place where a substantial part of the obligations of the commercial relationship is to be performed or the place with which the subject-matter of the dispute is most closely connected; or

c. the parties have expressly agreed that the subject-matter of the arbitration agreement relates to more than one country.

---

* Article headings are for reference purposes only and are not to be used for purposes of interpretation.

** The term "commercial" should be given a wide interpretation so as to cover matters arising from all relationships of a commercial nature, whether contractual or not. Relationships of a commercial nature include, but are not limited to, the following transactions: any trade transaction for the supply or exchange of goods or services; distribution agreement; commercial representation or agency; factoring; leasing; construction of works; consulting; engineering; licensing; investment; financing; banking; insurance; exploitation agreement or concession; joint venture and other forms of industrial or business co-operation; carriage of goods or passengers by air, sea, rail or road.

4.   For the purposes of paragraph (3) of this article:

a.   if a party has more than one place of business, the place of business is that which has the closest relationship to the arbitration agreement;

b.   if a party does not have a place of business, reference is to be made to his habitual residence.

5.   This Law shall not affect any other law of this State by virtue of which certain disputes may not be submitted to arbitration or may be submitted to arbitration only according to provisions other than those of this Law.

Article 2.   Definitions and rules of interpretation

For the purposes of this Law:

a.   "arbitration" means any arbitration whether or not administered by a permanent arbitral institution;

b.   "arbitral tribunal" means a sole arbitrator or a panel of arbitrators;

c.   "court" means a body or organ of the judicial system of a State;

d.   where a provision of this Law, except article 28, leaves the parties free to determine a certain issue, such freedom includes the right of the parties to authorize a third party, including an institution, to make that determination;

e.   where a provision of this Law refers to the fact that the parties have agreed or that they may agree or in any other way refers to an agreement of the parties, such agreement includes any arbitration rules referred to in that agreement;

f.   where a provision of this Law, other than in articles 25(a) and 32(2)(a), refers to a claim, it also applies to a counter-claim, and where it refers to a defence, it also applies to a defence to such counter-claim.

Article 3.   Receipt of written communications

1.   Unless otherwise agreed by the parties:

a.   any written communication is deemed to have been received if it is delivered to the addressee personally or if it is delivered at his place of business, habitual residence or mailing address; if none of these can be found after making a reasonable inquiry, a written communication is deemed to have been received if it is sent to the addressee's last-known place of business, habitual residence or mailing address by registered letter or any other means which provides a record of the attempt to deliver it;

b.   the communication is deemed to have been received on the day it is so delivered.

2.   The provisions of this article do not apply to communications in court proceedings.

Article 4.   Waiver of right to object

A party who knows that any provision of this Law from which the parties may derogate or any requirement under the arbitration agreement has not been complied with and yet proceeds with the arbitration without stating his objection to such non-compliance without undue delay or, if a time-limit is provided therefor, within such period of time, shall be deemed to have waived his right to object.

Article 5.   Extent of court intervention

In matters governed by this Law, no court shall intervene except where so provided in this Law.

Article 6.   Court or other authority for certain functions of arbitration assistance and supervision

The functions referred to in articles 11(3), 11(4), 13(3), 14, 16(3) and 34(2) shall be performed by . . . [Each State enacting this model law specifies the court, courts or, where referred to therein, other authority competent to perform these functions.]

CHAPTER II.   ARBITRATION AGREEMENT

Article 7.   Definition and form of arbitration agreement

1.   "Arbitration agreement" is an agreement by the parties to submit to arbitration all or certain disputes which have arisen or which may arise between them in respect of a defined legal relationship, whether contractual or not. An arbitration agreement may be in the form of an arbitration clause in a contract or in the form of a separate agreement.

2.   The arbitration agreement shall be in writing. An agreement is in writing if it is contained in a document signed by the parties or in an exchange of letters, telex, telegrams or other means of telecommunication which provide a record of the agreement, or in an exchange of statements of claim and defence in which the existence of an agreement is alleged by one party and not denied by another. The reference in a contract to a document containing an arbitration clause constitutes an arbitration agreement provided that the contract is in writing and the reference is such as to make that clause part of the contract.

Article 8.   Arbitration agreement and substantive claim before court

1.   A court before which an action is brought in a matter which is the subject of an arbitration agreement shall, if a party so requests not later than when submitting his first statement on the substance of the dispute, refer the parties to arbitration unless it finds that the agreement is null and void, inoperative or incapable of being performed.

2.   Where an action referred to in paragraph (1) of this article has been brought, arbitral proceedings may nevertheless be commenced or

continued, and an award may be made, while the issue is pending before the court.

Article 9. Arbitration agreement and interim measures by court

It is not incompatible with an arbitration agreement for a party to request, before or during arbitral proceedings, from a court an interim measure of protection and for a court to grant such measure.

CHAPTER III. COMPOSITION OF ARBITRAL TRIBUNAL

Article 10. Number of arbitrators

1. The parties are free to determine the number of arbitrators.

2. Failing such determination, the number of arbitrators shall be three.

Article 11. Appointment of arbitrators

1. No person shall be precluded by reason of his nationality from acting as an arbitrator, unless otherwise agreed by the parties.

2. The parties are free to agree on a procedure of appointing the arbitrator or arbitrators, subject to the provisions of paragraphs (4) and (5) of this article.

3. Failing such agreement,

    a. in an arbitration with three arbitrators, each party shall appoint one arbitrator, and the two arbitrators thus appointed shall appoint the third arbitrator; if a party fails to appoint the arbitrator within thirty days of receipt of a request to do so from the other party, or if the two arbitrators fail to agree on the third arbitrator within thirty days of their appointment, the appointment shall be made, upon request of a party, by the court or other authority specified in article 6;

    b. in an arbitration with a sole arbitrator, if the parties are unable to agree on the arbitrator, he shall be appointed, upon request of a party, by the court or other authority specified in article 6.

4. Where, under an appointment procedure agreed upon by the parties,

    a. a party fails to act as required under such procedure, or

    b. the parties, or two arbitrators, are unable to reach an agreement expected of them under such procedure, or

    c. a third party, including an institution, fails to perform any function entrusted to it under such procedure,

any party may request the court or other authority specified in article 6 to take the necessary measure, unless the agreement on the appointment procedure provides other means for securing the appointment.

5.   A decision on a matter, entrusted by paragraph (3) or (4) of this article to the court or other authority specified in article 6 shall be subject to no appeal. The court or other authority, in appointing an arbitrator, shall have due regard to any qualifications required of the arbitrator by the agreement of the parties and to such considerations as are likely to secure the appointment of an independent and impartial arbitrator and, in the case of a sole or third arbitrator, shall take into account as well the advisability of appointing an arbitrator of a nationality other than those of the parties.

Article 12.   Grounds for challenge

1.   When a person is approached in connection with his possible appointment as an arbitrator, he shall disclose any circumstances likely to give rise to justifiable doubts as to his impartiality or independence. An arbitrator, from the time of his appointment and throughout the arbitral proceedings, shall without delay disclose any such circumstances to the parties unless they have already been informed of them by him.

2.   An arbitrator may be challenged only if circumstances exist that give rise to justifiable doubts as to his impartiality or independence, or if he does not possess qualifications agreed to by the parties. A party may challenge an arbitrator appointed by him, or in whose appointment he has participated, only for reasons of which he becomes aware after the appointment has been made.

Article 13.   Challenge procedure

1.   The parties are free to agree on a procedure for challenging an arbitrator, subject to the provisions of paragraph (3) of this article.

2.   Failing such agreement, a party who intends to challenge an arbitrator shall, within fifteen days after becoming aware of the constitution of the arbitral tribunal or after becoming aware of any circumstance referred to in article 12(2), send a written statement of the reasons for the challenge to the arbitral tribunal. Unless the challenged arbitrator withdraws from his office or the other party agrees to the challenge, the arbitral tribunal shall decide on the challenge.

3.   If a challenge under any procedure agreed upon by the parties or under the procedure of paragraph (2) of this article is not successful, the challenging party may request, within thirty days after having received notice of the decision rejecting the challenge, the court or other authority specified in article 6 to decide on the challenge, which decision shall be subject to no appeal; while such a request is pending, the arbitral tribunal, including the challenged arbitrator, may continue the arbitral proceedings and make an award.

Article 14.   Failure or impossibility to act

1.   If an arbitrator becomes *de jure* or *de facto* unable to perform his functions or for other reasons fails to act without undue delay, his mandate terminates if he withdraws from his office or if the parties agree on the termination. Otherwise, if a controversy remains concern-

ing any of these grounds, any party may request the court or other authority specified in article 6 to decide on the termination of the mandate, which decision shall be subject to no appeal.

2.   If, under this article or article 13(2), an arbitrator withdraws from his office or a party agrees to the termination of the mandate of an arbitrator, this does not imply acceptance of the validity of any ground referred to in this article or article 12(2).

Article 15.   Appointment of substitute arbitrator

Where the mandate of an arbitrator terminates under article 13 or 14 or because of his withdrawal from office for any other reason or because of the revocation of his mandate by agreement of the parties or in any other case of termination of his mandate, a substitute arbitrator shall be appointed according to the rules that were applicable to the appointment of the arbitrator being replaced.

CHAPTER IV.   JURISDICTION OF ARBITRAL TRIBUNAL

Article 16.   Competence of arbitral tribunal to rule on its jurisdiction

1.   The arbitral tribunal may rule on its own jurisdiction, including any objections with respect to the existence or validity of the arbitration agreement. For that purpose, an arbitration clause which forms part of a contract shall be treated as an agreement independent of the other terms of the contract. A decision by the arbitral tribunal that the contract is null and void shall not entail *ipso jure* the invalidity of the arbitration clause.

2.   A plea that the arbitral tribunal does not have jurisdiction shall be raised not later than the submission of the statement of defence. A party is not precluded from raising such a plea by the fact that he has appointed, or participated in the appointment of, an arbitrator. A plea that the arbitral tribunal is exceeding the scope of its authority shall be raised as soon as the matter alleged to be beyond the scope of its authority is raised during the arbitral proceedings. The arbitral tribunal may, in either case, admit a later plea if it considers the delay justified.

3.   The arbitral tribunal may rule on a plea referred to in paragraph (2) of this article either as a preliminary question or in an award on the merits. If the arbitral tribunal rules as a preliminary question that it has jurisdiction, any party may request, within thirty days after having received notice of that ruling, the court specified in article 6 to decide the matter, which decision shall be subject to no appeal; while such a request is pending, the arbitral tribunal may continue the arbitral proceedings and make an award.

Article 17.   Power of arbitral tribunal to order interim measures

Unless otherwise agreed by the parties, the arbitral tribunal may, at the request of a party, order any party to take such interim measure of protection as the arbitral tribunal may consider necessary in respect of the subject-matter of the dispute. The arbitral tribunal may require any party to provide appropriate security in connection with such measure.

CHAPTER V. CONDUCT OF ARBITRAL PROCEEDINGS

Article 18. Equal treatment of parties

The parties shall be treated with equality and each party shall be given a full opportunity of presenting his case.

Article 19. Determination of rules of procedure

1. Subject to the provisions of this Law, the parties are free to agree on the procedure to be followed by the arbitral tribunal in conducting the proceedings.

2. Failing such agreement, the arbitral tribunal may, subject to the provisions of this Law, conduct the arbitration in such manner as it considers appropriate. The power conferred upon the arbitral tribunal includes the power to determine the admissibility, relevance, materiality and weight of any evidence.

Article 20. Place of arbitration

1. The parties are free to agree on the place of arbitration. Failing such agreement, the place of arbitration shall be determined by the arbitral tribunal having regard to the circumstances of the case, including the convenience of the parties.

2. Notwithstanding the provisions of paragraph (1) of this article, the arbitral tribunal may, unless otherwise agreed by the parties, meet at any place it considers appropriate for consultation among its members, for hearing witnesses, experts or the parties, or for inspection of goods, other property or documents.

Article 21. Commencement of arbitral proceedings

Unless otherwise agreed by the parties, the arbitral proceedings in respect of a particular dispute commence on the date on which a request for that dispute to be referred to arbitration is received by the respondent.

Article 22. Language

1. The parties are free to agree on the language or languages to be used in the arbitral proceedings. Failing such agreement, the arbitral tribunal shall determine the language or languages to be used in the proceedings. This agreement or determination, unless otherwise specified therein, shall apply to any written statement by a party, any hearing and any award, decision or other communication by the arbitral tribunal.

2. The arbitral tribunal may order that any documentary evidence shall be accompanied by a translation into the language or languages agreed upon by the parties or determined by the arbitral tribunal.

Article 23. Statements of claim and defence

1. Within the period of time agreed by the parties or determined by the arbitral tribunal, the claimant shall state the facts supporting his claim, the points at issue and the relief or remedy sought, and the respondent shall state his defence in respect of these particulars, unless the parties have otherwise agreed as to the required elements of such statements. The parties may submit with their statements all documents they consider to be relevant or may add a reference to the documents or other evidence they will submit.

2. Unless otherwise agreed by the parties, either party may amend or supplement his claim or defence during the course of the arbitral proceedings, unless the arbitral tribunal considers it inappropriate to allow such amendment having regard to the delay in making it.

Article 24. Hearings and written proceedings

1. Subject to any contrary agreement by the parties, the arbitral tribunal shall decide whether to hold oral hearings for the presentation of evidence or for oral argument, or whether the proceedings shall be conducted on the basis of documents and other materials. However, unless the parties have agreed that no hearings shall be held, the arbitral tribunal shall hold such hearings at an appropriate stage of the proceedings, if so requested by a party.

2. The parties shall be given sufficient advance notice of any hearing and of any meeting of the arbitral tribunal for the purposes of inspection of goods, other property or documents.

3. All statements, documents or other information supplied to the arbitral tribunal by one party shall be communicated to the other party. Also any expert report or evidentiary document on which the arbitral tribunal may rely in making its decision shall be communicated to the parties.

Article 25. Default of a party

Unless otherwise agreed by the parties, if, without showing sufficient cause,

    a. the claimant fails to communicate his statement of claim in accordance with article 23(1), the arbitral tribunal shall terminate the proceedings;

    b. the respondent fails to communicate his statement of defence in accordance with article 23(1), the arbitral tribunal shall continue the proceedings without treating such failure in itself as an admission of the claimant's allegations;

    c. any party fails to appear at a hearing or to produce documentary evidence, the arbitral tribunal may continue the proceedings and make the award on the evidence before it.

Article 26.   Expert appointed by arbitral tribunal

1.   Unless otherwise agreed by the parties, the arbitral tribunal

a.   may appoint one or more experts to report to it on specific issues to be determined by the arbitral tribunal;

b.   may require a party to give the expert any relevant information or to produce, or to provide access to, any relevant documents, goods or other property for his inspection.

2.   Unless otherwise agreed by the parties, if a party so requests or if the arbitral tribunal considers it necessary, the expert shall, after delivery of his written or oral report, participate in a hearing where the parties have the opportunity to put questions to him and to present expert witnesses in order to testify on the points at issue.

Article 27.   Court assistance in taking evidence

The arbitral tribunal or a party with the approval of the arbitral tribunal may request from a competent court of this State assistance in taking evidence. The court may execute the request within its competence and according to its rules on taking evidence.

CHAPTER VI.   MAKING OF AWARD AND TERMINATION OF PROCEEDINGS

Article 28.   Rules applicable to substance of dispute

1.   The arbitral tribunal shall decide the dispute in accordance with such rules of law as are chosen by the parties as applicable to the substance of the dispute. Any designation of the law or legal system of a given State shall be construed, unless otherwise expressed, as directly referring to the substantive law of that State and not to its conflict of laws rules.

2.   Failing any designation by the parties, the arbitral tribunal shall apply the law determined by the conflict of laws rules which it considers applicable.

3.   The arbitral tribunal shall decide *ex aequo et bono* or as *amiable compositeur* only if the parties have expressly authorized it to do so.

4.   In all cases, the arbitral tribunal shall decide in accordance with the terms of the contract and shall take into account the usages of the trade applicable to the transaction.

Article 29.   Decision making by panel of arbitrators

In arbitral proceedings with more than one arbitrator, any decision of the arbitral tribunal shall be made, unless otherwise agreed by the parties, by a majority of all its members. However, questions of procedure may be decided by a presiding arbitrator, if so authorized by the parties or all members of the arbitral tribunal.

Article 30. Settlement

1. If, during arbitral proceedings, the parties settle the dispute, the arbitral tribunal shall terminate the proceedings and, if requested by the parties and not objected to by the arbitral tribunal, record the settlement in the form of an arbitral award on agreed terms.

2. An award on agreed terms shall be made in accordance with the provisions of article 31 and shall state that it is an award. Such an award has the same status and effect as any other award on the merits of the case.

Article 31. Form and contents of award

1. The award shall be made in writing and shall be signed by the arbitrator or arbitrators. In arbitral proceedings with more than one arbitrator, the signatures of the majority of all members of the arbitral tribunal shall suffice, provided that the reason for any omitted signature is stated.

2. The award shall state the reasons upon which it is based, unless the parties have agreed that no reasons are to be given or the award is an award on agreed terms under article 30.

3. The award shall state its date and the place of arbitration as determined in accordance with article 20(1). The award shall be deemed to have been made at that place.

4. After the award is made, a copy signed by the arbitrators in accordance with paragraph (1) of this article shall be delivered to each party.

Article 32. Termination of proceedings

1. The arbitral proceedings are terminated by the final award or by an order of the arbitral tribunal in accordance with paragraph (2) of this article.

2. The arbitral tribunal shall issue an order for the termination of the arbitral proceedings when:

    a. the claimant withdraws his claim, unless the respondent objects thereto and the arbitral tribunal recognizes a legitimate interest on his part in obtaining a final settlement of the dispute;

    b. the parties agree on the termination of the proceedings;

    c. the arbitral tribunal finds that the continuation of the proceedings has for any other reason become unnecessary or impossible.

3. The mandate of the arbitral tribunal terminates with the termination of the arbitral proceedings, subject to the provisions of articles 33 and 34(4).

Article 33. Correction and interpretation of award; additional award

1. Within thirty days of receipt of the award, unless another period of time has been agreed upon by the parties:

a. a party, with notice to the other party, may request the arbitral tribunal to correct in the award any errors in computation, any clerical or typographical errors or any errors of similar nature;

b. if so agreed by the parties, a party, with notice to the other party, may request the arbitral tribunal to give an interpretation of a specific point or part of the award.

If the arbitral tribunal considers the request to be justified, it shall make the correction or give the interpretation within thirty days of receipt of the request. The interpretation shall form part of the award.

2. The arbitral tribunal may correct any error of the type referred to in paragraph (1)(a) of this article on its own initiative within thirty days of the date of the award.

3. Unless otherwise agreed by the parties, a party, with notice to the other party, may request, within thirty days of receipt of the award, the arbitral tribunal to make an additional award as to claims presented in the arbitral proceedings but omitted from the award. If the arbitral tribunal considers the request to be justified, it shall make the additional award within sixty days.

4. The arbitral tribunal may extend, if necessary, the period of time within which it shall make a correction, interpretation or an additional award under paragraph (1) or (3) of this article.

5. The provisions of article 31 shall apply to a correction or interpretation of the award or to an additional award.

CHAPTER VII. RECOURSE AGAINST AWARD

Article 34. Application for setting aside as exclusive recourse against arbitral award

1. Recourse to a court against an arbitral award may be made only by an application for setting aside in accordance with paragraphs (2) and (3) of this article.

2. An arbitral award may be set aside by the court specified in article 6 only if:

a. the party making the application furnishes proof that:

(i) a party to the arbitration agreement referred to in article 7 was under some incapacity; or the said agreement is not valid under the law to which the parties have subjected it or, failing any indication thereon, under the law of this State; or

(ii) the party making the application was not given proper notice of the appointment of an arbitrator or of the arbitral proceedings or was otherwise unable to present his case; or

(iii) the award deals with a dispute not contemplated by or not falling within the terms of the submission to arbitration, or contains decisions on matters beyond the scope of the submission to arbitration, provided that, if the decisions on matters submitted to arbitration can be separated from those not so submitted, only that part of the award which contains decisions on matters not submitted to arbitration may be set aside; or

(iv) the composition of the arbitral tribunal or the arbitral procedure was not in accordance with the agreement of the parties, unless such agreement was in conflict with a provision of this Law from which the parties cannot derogate, or, failing such agreement, was not in accordance with this Law; or

b. the court finds that:

(i) the subject-matter of the dispute is not capable of settlement by arbitration under the law of this State; or

(ii) the award is in conflict with the public policy of this State.

3. An application for setting aside may not be made after three months have elapsed from the date on which the party making that application had received the award or, if a request had been made under article 33, from the date on which that request had been disposed of by the arbitral tribunal.

4. The court, when asked to set aside an award, may, where appropriate and so requested by a party, suspend the setting aside proceedings for a period of time determined by it in order to give the arbitral tribunal an opportunity to resume the arbitral proceedings or to take such other action as in the arbitral tribunal's opinion will eliminate the grounds for setting aside.

CHAPTER VIII. RECOGNITION AND ENFORCEMENT OF AWARDS

Article 35. Recognition and enforcement

1. An arbitral award, irrespective of the country in which it was made, shall be recognized as binding and, upon application in writing to the competent court, shall be enforced subject to the provisions of this article and of article 36.

2. The party relying on an award or applying for its enforcement shall supply the duly authenticated original award or a duly certified copy thereof, and the original arbitration agreement referred to in article 7 or a duly certified copy thereof. If the award or agreement is not made in an official language of this State, the party shall supply a duly certified translation thereof into such language.***

Article 36. Grounds for refusing recognition or enforcement

1. Recognition or enforcement of an arbitral award, irrespective of the country in which it was made, may be refused only:

*** The conditions set forth in this paragraph are intended to set maximum standards. It would, thus, not be contrary to the harmonization to be achieved by the model law if a State retained even less onerous conditions.

a. at the request of the party against whom it is invoked, if that party furnishes to the competent court where recognition or enforcement is sought proof that:

(i) a party to the arbitration agreement referred to in article 7 was under some incapacity; or the said agreement is not valid under the law to which the parties have subjected it or, failing any indication thereon, under the law of the country where the award was made; or

(ii) the party against whom the award is invoked was not given proper notice of the appointment of an arbitrator or of the arbitral proceedings or was otherwise unable to present his case; or

(iii) the award deals with a dispute not contemplated by or not falling within the terms of the submission to arbitration, or it contains decisions on matters beyond the scope of the submission to arbitration, provided that, if the decisions on matters submitted to arbitration can be separated from those not so submitted, that part of the award which contains decisions on matters submitted to arbitration may be recognized and enforced; or

(iv) the composition of the arbitral tribunal or the arbitral procedure was not in accordance with the agreement of the parties or, failing such agreement, was not in accordance with the law of the country where the arbitration took place; or

(v) the award has not yet become binding on the parties or has been set aside or suspended by a court of the country in which, or under the law of which, that award was made; or

b. if the court finds that:

(i) the subject-matter of the dispute is not capable of settlement by arbitration under the law of this State; or

(ii) the recognition or enforcement of the award would be contrary to the public policy of this State.

2. If an application for setting aside or suspension of an award has been made to a court referred to in paragraph (1)(a)(v) of this article, the court where recognition or enforcement is sought may, if it considers it proper, adjourn its decision and may also, on the application of the party claiming recognition or enforcement of the award, order the other party to provide appropriate security.

UNITED NATIONS CONVENTION ON THE RECOGNITION AND ENFORCEMENT OF FOREIGN ARBITRAL AWARDS

("New York Convention")

June 10, 1958

Article I

1.   This Convention shall apply to the recognition and enforcement of arbitral awards made in the territory of a State other than the State where the recognition and enforcement of such awards are sought, and arising out of differences between persons, whether physical or legal. It shall also apply to arbitral awards not considered as domestic awards in the State where their recognition and enforcement are sought.

2.   The term "arbitral awards" shall include not only awards made by arbitrators appointed for each case but also those made by permanent arbitral bodies to which the parties have submitted.

3.   When signing, ratifying or acceding to this Convention, or notifying extension under article X hereof, any State may on the basis of reciprocity declare that it will apply the Convention to the recognition and enforcement of awards made only in the territory of another Contracting State. It may also declare that it will apply the Convention only to differences arising out of legal relationships whether contractual or not, which are considered as commercial under the national law of the State making such declaration.

Article II

1.   Each Contracting State shall recognize an agreement in writing under which the parties undertake to submit to arbitration all or any differences which have arisen or which may arise between them in respect of a defined legal relationship, whether contractual or not, concerning a subject matter capable of settlement by arbitration.

2.   The term "agreement in writing" shall include an arbitral clause in a contract or an arbitration agreement, signed by the parties or contained in an exchange of letters or telegrams.

3.   The court of a Contracting State, when seized of an action in a matter in respect of which the parties have made an agreement within the meaning of this article, shall at the request of one of the parties, refer the parties to arbitration, unless it finds that the said agreement is null and void, inoperative or incapable of being performed.

Article III

Each Contracting State shall recognize arbitral awards as binding and enforce them in accordance with the rules of procedure of the territory where the award is relied upon, under the conditions laid down in the following articles. There shall not be imposed substantially more onerous conditions or higher fees or charges on the recognition or enforcement of arbitral awards to which this Convention applies than are imposed on the recognition or enforcement of domestic arbitral awards.

Article IV

1. To obtain the recognition and enforcement mentioned in the preceding article, the party applying for recognition and enforcement shall, at the time of the application, supply:

(a) the duly authenticated original award or a duly certified copy thereof;

(b) the original agreement referred to in article II or a duly certified copy thereof.

2. If the said award or agreement is not made in an official language of the country in which the award is relied upon, the party applying for recognition and enforcement of the award shall produce a translation of these documents into such language. The translation shall be certified by an official or sworn translator or by a diplomatic or consular agent.

Article V

1. Recognition and enforcement of the award may be refused, at the request of the party against whom it is invoked, only if that party furnishes to the competent authority where the recognition and enforcement is sought, proof that:

(a) the parties to the agreement referred to in article II were, under the law applicable to them, under some incapacity, or the said agreement is not valid under the law to which the parties have subjected it or, failing any indication thereon, under the law of the country where the award was made; or

(b) the party against whom the award is invoked was not given proper notice of the appointment of the arbitrator or of the arbitration proceedings or was otherwise unable to present his case; or

(c) the award deals with a difference not contemplated by or not falling within the terms of the submission to arbitration, or it contains decisions on matters beyond the scope of the submission to arbitration, provided that, if the decision on matters submitted to arbitration can be separated from those not so submitted, that part of the award which contains decisions on matters submitted to arbitration may be recognized and enforced; or

(d) the composition of the arbitral authority or the arbitral procedure was not in accordance with the agreement of the parties, or failing such agreement, was not in accordance with the law of the country where the arbitration took place; or

(e) the award has not yet become binding on the parties, or has been set aside or suspended by a competent authority of the country in which, or under the law of which, that award was made.

2.   Recognition and enforcement of an arbitral award may also be refused if the competent authority in the country where recognition and enforcement is sought finds that:

(a) the subject matter of the difference is not capable of settlement by arbitration under the law of that country; or

(b) the recognition or enforcement of the award would be contrary to the public policy of that country.

Article VI

If an application for the setting aside or suspension of the award has been made to a competent authority referred to in article V paragraph (1)(e), the authority before which the award is sought to be relied upon may, if it considers it proper, adjourn the decision on the enforcement of the award and may also, on the application of the party claiming enforcement of the award, order the other party to give suitable security.

Article VII

1.   The provisions of the present Convention shall not affect the validity of multilateral or bilateral agreements concerning the recognition and enforcement of arbitral awards entered into by the Contracting States nor deprive any interested party of any right he may have to avail himself by the law or the treaties of the country where such award is sought to be relied upon.

2.   The Geneva Protocol on Arbitration Clauses of 1923 and the Geneva Convention on the Execution of Foreign Arbitral Awards of 1927 shall cease to have effect between Contracting States on their becoming bound and to the extent that they become bound, by this Convention.

Article VIII

1.   This Convention shall be open until 31 December 1958 for signature on behalf of any Member of the United Nations and also on behalf of any other State which is or hereafter becomes a member of any specialized agency of the United Nations, or which is or hereafter becomes a party to the Statute of the International Court of Justice, or any other State to which an invitation has been addressed by the General Assembly of the United Nations.

2.   This Convention shall be ratified and the instrument of ratification shall be deposited with the Secretary–General of the United Nations.

Article IX

1.   This Convention shall be open for accession to all States referred to in article VIII.

2.   Accession shall be effected by the deposit of an instrument of accession with the Secretary–General of the United Nations.

Article X

1.   Any State may, at the time of signature, ratification or accession, declare that this Convention shall extend to all or any of the territories for the international relations of which it is responsible. Such a declaration shall take effect when the Convention enters into force for the State concerned.

2.   At any time thereafter any such extension shall be made by notification addressed to the Secretary–General of the United Nations and shall take effect as from the ninetieth day after the day of receipt by the Secretary–General of the United Nations of this notification, or as from the date of entry into force of the Convention for the State concerned, whichever is the later.

3.   With respect to those territories to which this Convention is not extended at the time of signature, ratification or accession, each State concerned shall consider the possibility of taking the necessary steps in order to extend the application of this Convention to such territories, subject, where necessary for constitutional reasons, to the consent of the Governments of such territories.

Article XI

1.   In the case of a federal or non-unitary State, the following provisions shall apply:

(a) With respect to those articles of this Convention that come within the legislative jurisdiction of the federal authority, the obligations of the federal Government shall to this extent be the same as those of Contracting States which are not federal States;

(b) With respect to those articles of this Convention that come within the legislative jurisdiction of constituent states or provinces which are not, under the constitutional system of the federation, bound to take legislative action, the federal Government shall bring such articles with a favourable recommendation to the notice of the appropriate authorities of constituent states or provinces at the earliest possible moment;

(c) A federal State party to this Convention shall, at the request of any other Contracting State transmitted through the Secretary–General of the United Nations, supply a statement of the law and practice of the federation and its constituent units in regard to any particular provisions of this Convention, showing the extent to which effect has been given to that provision by legislative or other action.

Article XII

1.   This Convention shall come into force on the ninetieth day following the date of deposit of the third instrument of ratification or accession.

2.   For each State ratifying or acceding to this Convention after the deposit of the third instrument of ratification or accession, this Conven-

tion shall enter into force on the ninetieth day after deposit by such State of its instrument of ratification or accession.

Article XIII

1. Any Contracting State may denounce this Convention by a written notification to the Secretary–General of the United Nations. Denunciation shall take effect one year after the date of receipt of the notification by the Secretary–General.

2. Any State which has made a declaration or notification under article X may, at any time thereafter, by notification to the Secretary–General of the United Nations, declare that this Convention shall cease to extend to the territory concerned one year after the date of the receipt of the notification by the Secretary–General.

3. This Convention shall continue to be applicable to arbitral awards in respect of which recognition or enforcement proceedings have been instituted before the denunciation takes effect.

Article XIV

A Contracting State shall not be entitled to avail itself of the present Convention against other Contracting States except to the extent that it is itself bound to apply the Convention.

Article XV

The Secretary–General of the United Nations shall notify the States contemplated in article VIII of the following:

(a) Signature and ratifications in accordance with article VIII;

(b) Accessions in accordance with article IX;

(c) Declarations and notifications under articles I, X and XI;

(d) The date upon which this Convention enters into force in accordance with article XII;

(e) Denunciations and notifications in accordance with article XIII.

Article XVI

1. This Convention, of which the Chinese, English, French, Russian and Spanish texts shall be equally authentic, shall be deposited in the archives of the United Nations.

2. The Secretary–General of the United Nations shall transmit a certified copy of this Convention to the States contemplated in article VIII.

PARTIES TO THE UNITED NATIONS CONVENTION ON THE RECOGNITION AND ENFORCEMENT OF ARBITRAL AWARDS

(as of December, 2004)

Albania
Algeria
Antigua and Barbuda
Argentina
Armenia
Australia
Austria
Azerbaijan
Bahrain
Bangladesh
Barbados
Belarus
Belgium
Benin
Bolivia
Bosnia and Herzegovina
Botswana
Brazil
Brunei Darussalam
Bulgaria
Burkina Faso
Cambodia
Cameroon
Canada
Central African Republic
Chile
People's Republic of China
Colombia
Costa Rica
Côte d'Ivoire
Croatia
Cuba
Cyprus
Czech Republic
Denmark
Djibouti
Dominica
Dominican Republican
Ecuador
Egypt
El Salvador
Estonia
Finland
France
Georgia
Germany
Ghana

Greece
Guatemala
Guinea
Haiti
Holy See (Vatican City)
Honduras
Hungary
Iceland
India
Indonesia
Iran
Ireland
Israel
Italy
Jamaica
Japan
Jordan
Kazakhstan
Kenya
Korea (South)
Kuwait
Kyrgyzstan
Lao People's Democratic Republic
Latvia
Lebanon
Lesotho
Lithuania
Luxembourg
Macedonia, Former Yugoslav
    Republic of
Madagascar
Malaysia
Mali
Malta
Mauritania
Mauritius
Mexico
Moldova
Monaco
Morocco
Mongolia
Mozambique
Nepal
Netherlands
New Zealand
Nicaragua

Niger
Nigeria
Norway
Oman
Pakistan*
Panama
Paraguay
Peru
Philippines
Poland
Portugal
Qatar
Romania
Russian Federation
St. Vincent & the Grenadines
San Marino
Saudi Arabia
Senegal
Serbia & Montenegro
Singapore
Slovakia

Slovenia
South Africa
Spain
Sri Lanka
Sweden
Switzerland
Syrian Arab Republic
Tanzania
Thailand
Trinidad and Tobago
Tunisia
Turkey
Uganda
Ukraine
United Kingdom
United States of America
Uruguay
Uzbekistan
Venezuela
Vietnam
Zimbabwe

* Signed but not ratified.

INTER–AMERICAN CONVENTION ON INTERNATIONAL COMMERCIAL ARBITRATION

(Signed in Panama January 30, 1975)

The Governments of the Member States of the Organization of American States, desirous of concluding a convention on international commercial arbitration, have agreed as follows:

Article 1. An agreement in which the parties undertake to submit to arbitral decision any differences that may arise or have arisen between them with respect to a commercial transaction is valid. The agreement shall be set forth in an instrument signed by the parties, or in the form of an exchange of letters, telegrams, or telex communications.

Article 2. Arbitrators shall be appointed in the manner agreed upon by the parties. Their appointment may be delegated to a third party, whether a natural or juridical person.

Arbitrators may be nationals or foreigners.

Article 3. In the absence of an express agreement between the parties, the arbitration shall be conducted in accordance with the rules of procedure of the Inter–American Commercial Arbitration Commission.

Article 4. An arbitral decision or award that is not appealable under the applicable law or procedural rules shall have the force of a final judicial judgment. Its execution or recognition may be ordered in the same manner as that of decisions handed down by national or foreign ordinary courts, in accordance with the procedural laws of the country where it is to be executed and the provisions of international treaties.

Article 5.1. The recognition and execution of the decision may be refused, at the request of the party against which it is made, only if such party is able to prove to the competent authority of the State in which recognition and execution are requested:

    a. That the parties to the agreement were subject to some incapacity under the applicable law or that the agreement is not valid under the law to which the parties have submitted it, or, if such law is not specified, under the law of the State in which the decision was made; or

    b. That the party against which the arbitral decision has been made was not duly notified of the appointment of the arbitrator or of the arbitration procedure to be followed, or was unable, for any other reason to present his defense; or

    c. That the decision concerns a dispute not envisaged in the agreement between the parties to submit to arbitration; nevertheless, if the provisions of the decision that refer to issues submitted to arbitration can be separated from those not submitted to arbitration, the former may be recognized and executed; or *d.* That the constitution of the arbitral tribunal or the arbitration procedure has not been carried out in accordance with the terms of the agreement signed by the parties or, in the absence of such agreement, that the constitution of the arbitral tribunal or the arbitration procedure has not been carried out in accordance with the law of the State where the arbitration took place; or

e. That the decision is not yet binding on the parties or has been annulled or suspended by a competent authority of the State in which, or according to the law of which, the decision has been made.

2. The recognition and execution of an arbitral decision may also be refused if the competent authority of the State in which the recognition and execution is requested finds:

a. That the subject of the dispute cannot be settled by arbitration under the law of that State; or

b. That the recognition or execution of the decision would be contrary to the public policy ("ordre public") of that State.

Article 6. If the competent authority mentioned in Article 5.1.e has been requested to annul or suspend the arbitral decision, the authority before which such decision is invoked may, if it deems it appropriate, postpone a decision on the execution of the arbitral decision and, at the request of the party requesting execution, may also instruct the other party to provide appropriate guaranties.

Article 7. This Convention shall be open for signature by the Member States of the Organization of American States.

Article 8. This Convention is subject to ratification. The instruments of ratification shall be deposited with the General Secretariat of the Organization of American States.

Article 9. This Convention shall remain open for accession by any other State. The instruments of accession shall be deposited with the General Secretariat of the Organization of American States.

Article 10. This Convention shall enter into force on the thirtieth day following the date of deposit of the second instrument of ratification.

For each State ratifying or acceding to the Convention after the deposit of the second instrument of ratification, the Convention shall enter into force on the thirtieth day after deposit by such State of its instrument of ratification or accession.

Article 11. If a State Party has two or more territorial units in which different systems of law apply in relation to the matters dealt with in this Convention, it may, at the time of signature, ratification or accession, declare that this Convention shall extend to all its territorial units or only to one or more of them.

Such declaration may be modified by subsequent declarations, which shall expressly indicate the territorial unit or units to which the Convention applies. Such subsequent declarations shall be transmitted to the

General Secretariat of the Organization of American States, and shall become effective thirty days after the date of their receipt.

Article 12. This Convention shall remain in force indefinitely, but any of the States Parties may denounce it. The instrument of denunciation shall be deposited with the General Secretariat of the Organization of American States. After one year from the date of deposit of the instrument of denunciation, the Convention shall no longer be in effect for the denouncing State, but shall remain in effect for the other States Parties.

Article 13. The original instrument of this Convention, the English, French, Portuguese and Spanish texts of which are equally authentic, shall be deposited with the General Secretariat of the Organization of American States. The Secretariat shall notify the Member States of the Organization of American States and the States that have acceded to the Convention of the signatures, deposits of instruments of ratification, accession, and denunciation as well as of reservations, if any. It shall also transmit the declarations referred to in Article 11 of this Convention.

IN WITNESS WHEREOF the undersigned Plenipotentiaries, being duly authorized thereto by their respective Governments, have signed this Convention.

DONE AT PANAMA CITY, Republic of Panama, this thirtieth day of January one thousand nine hundred and seventy-five.

PARTIES TO THE INTER–AMERICAN CONVENTION ON INTERNATIONAL COMMERCIAL ARBITRATION

(as of 2004)

Argentina
Bolivia
Brazil
Chile
Colombia
Costa Rica
Dominican Republic*
Ecuador
El Salvador
Guatemala

Honduras
Mexico
Nicaragua*
Panama
Paraguay
Peru
United States of America
Uruguay
Venezuela

* Signed but not ratified.

CONVENTION ON THE SETTLEMENT OF INVESTMENT DISPUTES BETWEEN STATES AND NATIONALS OF OTHER STATES

("ICSID Convention")

PREAMBLE

The Contracting States

Considering the need for international cooperation for economic development, and the role of private international investment therein;

Bearing in mind the possibility that from time to time disputes may arise in connection with such investment between Contracting States and nationals of other Contracting States;

Recognizing that while such disputes would usually be subject to national legal processes, international methods of settlement may be appropriate in certain cases;

Attaching particular importance to the availability of facilities for international conciliation or arbitration to which Contracting States and nationals of other Contracting States may submit such disputes if they so desire;

Desiring to establish such facilities under the auspices of the International Bank for Reconstruction and Development;

Recognizing that mutual consent by the parties to submit such disputes to conciliation or to arbitration through such facilities constitutes a binding agreement which requires in particular that due consideration be given to any recommendation of conciliators, and that any arbitral award be complied with; and

Declaring that no Contracting State shall by the mere fact of its ratification, acceptance or approval of this Convention and without its consent be deemed to be under any obligation to submit any particular dispute to conciliation or arbitration,

Have agreed as follows:

CHAPTER I

International Centre for Settlement of Investment Disputes

Section 1

Establishment and Organization

Article 1

(1) There is hereby established the International Centre for Settlement of Investment Disputes (hereinafter called the Centre).

(2) The purpose of the Centre shall be to provide facilities for conciliation and arbitration of investment disputes between Contracting States and nationals of other Contracting States in accordance with the provisions of this Convention.

Article 2

The seat of the Centre shall be at the principal office of the International Bank for Reconstruction and Development (hereinafter called the Bank). The seat may be moved to another place by decision of the Administrative Council adopted by a majority of two-thirds of its members.

Article 3

The Centre shall have an Administrative Council and a Secretariat and shall maintain a Panel of Conciliators and a Panel of Arbitrators.

Section 2

The Administrative Council

Article 4

(1) The Administrative Council shall be composed of one representative of each Contracting State. An alternate may act as representative in case of his principal's absence from a meeting or inability to act.

(2) In the absence of a contrary designation, each governor and alternate governor of the Bank appointed by a Contracting State shall be *ex officio* its representative and its alternate respectively.

Article 5

The President of the Bank shall be *ex officio* Chairman of the Administrative Council (hereinafter called the Chairman) but shall have no vote. During his absence or inability to act and during any vacancy in the office of President of the Bank, the person for the time being acting as President shall act as Chairman of the Administrative Council.

Article 6

(1) Without prejudice to the powers and functions vested in it by other provisions of this Convention, the Administrative Council shall:

(a) adopt the administrative and financial regulations of the Centre;

(b) adopt the rules of procedure for the institution of conciliation and arbitration proceedings;

(c) adopt the rules of procedure for conciliation and arbitration proceedings (hereinafter called the Conciliation Rules and the Arbitration Rules);

(d) approve arrangements with the Bank for the use of the Bank's administrative facilities and services;

(e) determine the conditions of service of the Secretary–General and of any Deputy Secretary–General;

(f) adopt the annual budget of revenues and expenditures of the Centre;

(g) approve the annual report on the operation of the Centre.

The decisions referred to in sub-paragraphs (a), (b), (c) and (f) above shall be adopted by a majority of two-thirds of the members of the Administrative Council.

(2) The Administrative Council may appoint such committees as it considers necessary.

(3) The Administrative Council shall also exercise such other powers and perform such other functions as it shall determine to be necessary for the implementation of the provisions of this Convention.

Article 7

(1) The Administrative Council shall hold an annual meeting and such other meetings as may be determined by the Council, or convened by the Chairman, or convened by the Secretary–General at the request of not less than five members of the Council.

(2) Each member of the Administrative Council shall have one vote and, except as otherwise herein provided, all matters before the Council shall be decided by a majority of the votes cast.

(3) A quorum for any meeting of the Administrative Council shall be a majority of its members.

(4) The Administrative Council may establish, by a majority of two-thirds of its members, a procedure whereby the Chairman may seek a vote of the Council without convening a meeting of the Council. The vote shall be considered valid only if the majority of the members of the Council cast their votes within the time limit fixed by the said procedure.

Article 8

Members of the Administrative Council and the Chairman shall serve without remuneration from the Centre.

Section 3

The Secretariat

Article 9

The Secretariat shall consist of a Secretary–General, one or more Deputy Secretaries–General and staff.

Article 10

(1) The Secretary–General and any Deputy Secretary–General shall be elected by the Administrative Council by a majority of two-thirds of its members upon the nomination of the Chairman for a term of service not exceeding six years and shall be eligible for re-election. After consulting the members of the Administrative Council, the Chairman shall propose one or more candidates for each such office.

(2) The offices of Secretary–General and Deputy Secretary–General shall be incompatible with the exercise of any political function. Neither the Secretary–General nor any Deputy Secretary–General may hold any

other employment or engage in any other occupation except with the approval of the Administrative Council.

(3) During the Secretary–General's absence or inability to act, and during any vacancy of the office of Secretary–General, the Deputy Secretary–General shall act as Secretary–General. If there shall be more than one Deputy Secretary–General, the Administrative Council shall determine in advance the order in which they shall act as Secretary–General.

Article 11

The Secretary–General shall be the legal representative and the principal officer of the Centre and shall be responsible for its administration, including the appointment of staff, in accordance with the provisions of this Convention and the rules adopted by the Administrative Council. He shall perform the function of registrar and shall have the power to authenticate arbitral awards rendered pursuant to this Convention, and to certify copies thereof.

Section 4
The Panels

Article 12

The Panel of Conciliators and the Panel of Arbitrators shall each consist of qualified persons, designated as hereinafter provided, who are willing to serve thereon.

Article 13

(1) Each Contracting State may designate to each Panel four persons who may but need not be its nationals.

(2) The Chairman may designate ten persons to each Panel. The persons so designated to a Panel shall each have a different nationality.

Article 14

(1) Persons designated to serve on the Panels shall be persons of high moral character and recognized competence in the fields of law, commerce, industry or finance, who may be relied upon to exercise independent judgment. Competence in the field of law shall be of particular importance in the case of persons on the Panel of Arbitrators.

(2) The Chairman, in designating persons to serve on the Panels, shall in addition pay due regard to the importance of assuring representation on the Panels of the principal legal systems of the world and of the main forms of economic activity.

Article 15

(1) Panel members shall serve for renewable periods of six years.

(2) In case of death or resignation of a member of a Panel, the authority which designated the member shall have the right to designate another person to serve for the remainder of that member's term.

(3) Panel members shall continue in office until their successors have been designated.

Article 16

(1) A person may serve on both Panels.

(2) If a person shall have been designated to serve on the same Panel by more than one Contracting State, or by one or more Contracting States and the Chairman, he shall be deemed to have been designated by the authority which first designated him or, if one such authority is the State of which he is a national, by that State.

(3) All designations shall be notified to the Secretary–General and shall take effect from the date on which the notification is received.

Section 5
Financing the Centre

Article 17

If the expenditure of the Centre cannot be met out of charges for the use of its facilities, or out of other receipts, the excess shall be borne by Contracting States which are members of the Bank in proportion to their respective subscriptions to the capital stock of the Bank, and by Contracting States which are not members of the Bank in accordance with rules adopted by the Administrative Council.

Section 6
Status, Immunities and Privileges

Article 18

The Centre shall have full international legal personality. The legal capacity of the Centre shall include the capacity:

    (a) to contract;

    (b) to acquire and dispose of movable and immovable property;

    (c) to institute legal proceedings.

Article 19

To enable the Centre to fulfil its functions, it shall enjoy in the territories of each Contracting State the immunities and privileges set forth in this Section.

Article 20

The Centre, its property and assets shall enjoy immunity from all legal process, except when the Centre waives this immunity.

Article 21

The Chairman, the members of the Administrative Council, persons acting as conciliators or arbitrators or members of a Committee appointed pursuant to paragraph (3) of Article 52, and the officers and employees of the Secretariat:

(a) shall enjoy immunity from legal process with respect to acts performed by them in the exercise of their functions, except when the Centre waives this immunity;

(b) not being local nationals, shall enjoy the same immunities from immigration restrictions, alien registration requirements and national service obligations, the same facilities as regards exchange restrictions and the same treatment in respect of travelling facilities as are accorded by Contracting States to the representatives, officials and employees of comparable rank of other Contracting States.

Article 22

The provisions of Article 21 shall apply to persons appearing in proceedings under this Convention as parties, agents, counsel, advocates, witnesses or experts; provided, however, that sub-paragraph (b) thereof shall apply only in connection with their travel to and from, and their stay at, the place where the proceedings are held.

Article 23

(1) The archives of the Centre shall be inviolable, wherever they may be.

(2) With regard to its official communications, the Centre shall be accorded by each Contracting State treatment not less favourable than that accorded to other international organizations.

Article 24

(1) The Centre, its assets, property and income, and its operations and transactions authorized by this Convention shall be exempt from all taxation and customs duties. The Centre shall also be exempt from liability for the collection or payment of any taxes or customs duties.

(2) Except in the case of local nationals, no tax shall be levied on or in respect of expense allowances paid by the Centre to the Chairman or members of the Administrative Council, or on or in respect of salaries, expense allowances or other emoluments paid by the Centre to officials or employees of the Secretariat.

(3) No tax shall be levied on or in respect of fees or expense allowances received by persons acting as conciliators, or arbitrators, or members of a Committee appointed pursuant to paragraph (3) of Article 52, in proceedings under this Convention, if the sole jurisdictional basis for such tax is the location of the Centre or the place where such proceedings are conducted or the place where such fees or allowances are paid.

CHAPTER II

Jurisdiction of the Centre

Article 25

(1) The jurisdiction of the Centre shall extend to any legal dispute arising directly out of an investment, between a Contracting State (or any constituent subdivision or agency of a Contracting State designated to the Centre by that State) and a national of another Contracting State, which the parties to the dispute consent in writing to submit to the Centre. When the parties have given their consent, no party may withdraw its consent unilaterally.

(2) "National of another Contracting State" means:

(a) any natural person who had the nationality of a Contracting State other than the State party to the dispute on the date on which the parties consented to submit such dispute to conciliation or arbitration as well as on the date on which the request was registered pursuant to paragraph (3) of Article 28 or paragraph (3) of Article 36, but does not include any person who on either date also had the nationality of the Contracting State party to the dispute; and

(b) any juridical person which had the nationality of a Contracting State other than the State party to the dispute on the date on which the parties consented to submit such dispute to conciliation or arbitration and any juridical person which had the nationality of the Contracting State party to the dispute on that date and which, because of foreign control, the parties have agreed should be treated as a national of another Contracting State for the purposes of this Convention.

(3) Consent by a constituent subdivision or agency of a Contracting State shall require the approval of that State unless that State notifies the Centre that no such approval is required.

(4) Any Contracting State may, at the time of ratification, acceptance or approval of this Convention or at any time thereafter, notify the Centre of the class or classes of disputes which it would or would not consider submitting to the jurisdiction of the Centre. The Secretary–General shall forthwith transmit such notification to all Contracting States. Such notification shall not constitute the consent required by paragraph (1).

Article 26

Consent of the parties to arbitration under this Convention shall, unless otherwise stated, be deemed consent to such arbitration to the exclusion of any other remedy. A Contracting State may require the exhaustion of local administrative or judicial remedies as a condition of its consent to arbitration under this Convention.

Article 27

(1) No Contracting State shall give diplomatic protection, or bring an international claim, in respect of a dispute which one of its nationals and another Contracting State shall have consented to submit or shall have submitted to arbitration under this Convention, unless such other Contracting State shall have failed to abide by and comply with the award rendered in such dispute.

(2) Diplomatic protection, for the purposes of paragraph (1), shall not include informal diplomatic exchanges for the sole purpose of facilitating a settlement of the dispute.

CHAPTER III

Conciliation

Section 1

Request for Conciliation

Article 28

(1) Any Contracting State or any national of a Contracting State wishing to institute conciliation proceedings shall address a request to that effect in writing to the Secretary–General who shall send a copy of the request to the other party.

(2) The request shall contain information concerning the issues in dispute, the identity of the parties and their consent to conciliation in accordance with the rules of procedure for the institution of conciliation and arbitration proceedings.

(3) The Secretary–General shall register the request unless he finds, on the basis of the information contained in the request, that the dispute is manifestly outside the jurisdiction of the Centre. He shall forthwith notify the parties of registration or refusal to register.

Section 2

Constitution of the Conciliation Commission

Article 29

(1) The Conciliation Commission (hereinafter called the Commission) shall be constituted as soon as possible after registration of a request pursuant to Article 28.

(2) (a) The Commission shall consist of a sole conciliator or any uneven number of conciliators appointed as the parties shall agree.

(b) Where the parties do not agree upon the number of conciliators and the method of their appointment, the Commission shall consist of three conciliators, one conciliator appointed by each party and the third, who shall be the president of the Commission, appointed by agreement of the parties.

Article 30

If the Commission shall not have been constituted within 90 days after notice of registration of the request has been dispatched by the Secretary–General in accordance with paragraph (3) of Article 28, or such other period as the parties may agree, the Chairman shall, at the request of either party and after consulting both parties as far as possible, appoint the conciliator or conciliators not yet appointed.

Article 31

(1) Conciliators may be appointed from outside the Panel of Conciliators, except in the case of appointments by the Chairman pursuant to Article 30.

(2) Conciliators appointed from outside the Panel of Conciliators shall possess the qualities stated in paragraph (1) of Article 14.

Section 3
Conciliation Proceedings

Article 32

(1) The Commission shall be the judge of its own competence.

(2) Any objection by a party to the dispute that that dispute is not within the jurisdiction of the Centre, or for other reasons is not within the competence of the Commission, shall be considered by the Commission which shall determine whether to deal with it as a preliminary question or to join it to the merits of the dispute.

Article 33

Any conciliation proceeding shall be conducted in accordance with the provisions of this Section and, except as the parties otherwise agree, in accordance with the Conciliation Rules in effect on the date on which the parties consented to conciliation. If any question of procedure arises which is not covered by this Section or the Conciliation Rules or any rules agreed by the parties, the Commission shall decide the question.

Article 34

(1) It shall be the duty of the Commission to clarify the issues in dispute between the parties and to endeavour to bring about agreement between them upon mutually acceptable terms. To that end, the Commission may at any stage of the proceedings and from time to time recommend terms of settlement to the parties. The parties shall cooperate in good faith with the Commission in order to enable the Commission to carry out its functions, and shall give their most serious consideration to its recommendations.

(2) If the parties reach agreement, the Commission shall draw up a report noting the issues in dispute and recording that the parties have reached agreement. If, at any stage of the proceedings, it appears to the Commission that there is no likelihood of agreement between the par-

ties, it shall close the proceedings and shall draw up a report noting the submission of the dispute and recording the failure of the parties to reach agreement. If one party fails to appear or participate in the proceedings, the Commission shall close the proceedings and shall draw up a report noting that party's failure to appear or participate.

Article 35

Except as the parties to the dispute shall otherwise agree, neither party to a conciliation proceeding shall be entitled in any other proceeding, whether before arbitrators or in a court of law or otherwise, to invoke or rely on any views expressed or statements or admissions or offers of settlement made by the other party in the conciliation proceedings, or the report or any recommendations made by the Commission.

CHAPTER IV

Arbitration

Section I

Request for Arbitration

Article 36

(1) Any Contracting State or any national of a Contracting State wishing to institute arbitration proceedings shall address a request to that effect in writing to the Secretary–General who shall send a copy of the request to the other party.

(2) The request shall contain information concerning the issues in dispute, the identity of the parties and their consent to arbitration in accordance with the rules of procedure for the institution of conciliation and arbitration proceedings.

(3) The Secretary–General shall register the request unless he finds, on the basis of the information contained in the request, that the dispute is manifestly outside the jurisdiction of the Centre. He shall forthwith notify the parties of registration or refusal to register.

Section 2

Constitution of the Tribunal

Article 37

(1) The Arbitral Tribunal (hereinafter called the Tribunal) shall be constituted as soon as possible after registration of a request pursuant to Article 36.

(2) (a) The Tribunal shall consist of a sole arbitrator or any uneven number of arbitrators appointed as the parties shall agree.

(b) Where the parties do not agree upon the number of arbitrators and the method of their appointment, the Tribunal shall consist of three arbitrators, one arbitrator appointed by each party and the third, who shall be the president of the Tribunal, appointed by agreement of the parties.

Article 38

If the Tribunal shall not have been constituted within 90 days after notice of registration of the request has been dispatched by the Secretary–General in accordance with paragraph (3) of Article 36, or such other period as the parties may agree, the Chairman shall, at the request of either party and after consulting both parties as far as possible, appoint the arbitrator or arbitrators not yet appointed. Arbitrators appointed by the Chairman pursuant to this Article shall not be nationals of the Contracting State party to the dispute or of the Contracting State whose national is a party to the dispute.

Article 39

The majority of the arbitrators shall be nationals of States other than the Contracting State party to the dispute and the Contracting State whose national is a party to the dispute; provided, however, that the foregoing provisions of this Article shall not apply if the sole arbitrator or each individual member of the Tribunal has been appointed by agreement of the parties.

Article 40

(1) Arbitrators may be appointed from outside the Panel of Arbitrators, except in the case of appointments by the Chairman pursuant to Article 38.

(2) Arbitrators appointed from outside the Panel of Arbitrators shall possess the qualities stated in paragraph (1) of Article 14.

Section 3
Powers and Functions of the Tribunal

Article 41

(1) The Tribunal shall be the judge of its own competence.

(2) Any objection by a party to the dispute that that dispute is not within the jurisdiction of the Centre, or for other reasons is not within the competence of the Tribunal, shall be considered by the Tribunal which shall determine whether to deal with it as a preliminary question or to join it to the merits of the dispute.

Article 42

(1) The Tribunal shall decide a dispute in accordance with such rules of law as may be agreed by the parties. In the absence of such agreement, the Tribunal shall apply the law of the Contracting State party to the dispute (including its rules on the conflict of laws) and such rules of international law as may be applicable.

(2) The Tribunal may not bring in a finding of *non liquet* on the ground of silence or obscurity of the law.

(3) The provisions of paragraphs (1) and (2) shall not prejudice the power of the Tribunal to decide a dispute *ex aequo et bono* if the parties so agree.

Article 43

Except as the parties otherwise agree, the Tribunal may, if it deems it necessary at any stage of the proceedings,

> (a) call upon the parties to produce documents or other evidence, and

> (b) visit the scene connected with the dispute, and conduct such inquiries there as it may deem appropriate.

Article 44

Any arbitration proceeding shall be conducted in accordance with the provisions of this Section and, except as the parties otherwise agree, in accordance with the Arbitration Rules in effect on the date on which the parties consented to arbitration. If any question of procedure arises which is not covered by this Section or the Arbitration Rules or any rules agreed by the parties, the Tribunal shall decide the question.

Article 45

(1) Failure of a party to appear or to present his case shall not be deemed an admission of the other party's assertions.

(2) If a party fails to appear or to present his case at any stage of the proceedings the other party may request the Tribunal to deal with the questions submitted to it and to render an award. Before rendering an award, the Tribunal shall notify, and grant a period of grace to, the party failing to appear or to present its case, unless it is satisfied that that party does not intend to do so.

Article 46

Except as the parties otherwise agree, the Tribunal shall, if requested by a party, determine any incidental or additional claims or counterclaims arising directly out of the subject-matter of the dispute provided that they are within the scope of the consent of the parties and are otherwise within the jurisdiction of the Centre.

Article 47

Except as the parties otherwise agree, the Tribunal may, if it considers that the circumstances so require, recommend any provisional measures which should be taken to preserve the respective rights of either party.

Section 4
The Award

Article 48

(1) The Tribunal shall decide questions by a majority of the votes of all its members.

(2) The award of the Tribunal shall be in writing and shall be signed by the members of the Tribunal who voted for it.

(3) The award shall deal with every question submitted to the Tribunal, and shall state the reasons upon which it is based.

(4) Any member of the Tribunal may attach his individual opinion to the award, whether he dissents from the majority or not, or a statement of his dissent.

(5) The Centre shall not publish the award without the consent of the parties.

Article 49

(1) The Secretary–General shall promptly dispatch certified copies of the award to the parties. The award shall be deemed to have been rendered on the date on which the certified copies were dispatched.

(2) The Tribunal upon the request of a party made within 45 days after the date on which the award was rendered may after notice to the other party decide any question which it had omitted to decide in the award, and shall rectify any clerical, arithmetical or similar error in the award. Its decision shall become part of the award and shall be notified to the parties in the same manner as the award. The periods of time provided for under paragraph (2) of Article 51 and paragraph (2) of Article 52 shall run from the date on which the decision was rendered.

Section 5
Interpretation, Revision and Annulment of the Award

Article 50

(1) If any dispute shall arise between the parties as to the meaning or scope of an award, either party may request interpretation of the award by an application in writing addressed to the Secretary–General.

(2) The request shall, if possible, be submitted to the Tribunal which rendered the award. If this shall not be possible, a new Tribunal shall be constituted in accordance with Section 2 of this Chapter. The Tribunal may, if it considers that the circumstances so require, stay enforcement of the award pending its decision.

Article 51

(1) Either party may request revision of the award by an application in writing addressed to the Secretary–General on the ground of discovery of some fact of such a nature as decisively to affect the award, provided that when the award was rendered that fact was unknown to the Tribunal and to the applicant and that the applicant's ignorance of that fact was not due to negligence.

(2) The application shall be made within 90 days after the discovery of such fact and in any event within three years after the date on which the award was rendered.

(3) The request shall, if possible, be submitted to the Tribunal which rendered the award. If this shall not be possible, a new Tribunal shall be constituted in accordance with Section 2 of this Chapter.

(4) The Tribunal may, if it considers that the circumstances so require, stay enforcement of the award pending its decision. If the applicant requests a stay of enforcement of the award in his application, enforcement shall be stayed provisionally until the Tribunal rules on such request.

Article 52

(1) Either party may request annulment of the award by an application in writing addressed to the Secretary–General on one or more of the following grounds:

(a) that the Tribunal was not properly constituted;

(b) that the Tribunal has manifestly exceeded its powers;

(c) that there was corruption on the part of a member of the Tribunal;

(d) that there has been a serious departure from a fundamental rule of procedure; or

(e) that the award has failed to state the reasons on which it is based.

(2) The application shall be made within 120 days after the date on which the award was rendered except that when annulment is requested on the ground of corruption such application shall be made within 120 days after discovery of the corruption and in any event within three years after the date on which the award was rendered.

(3) On receipt of the request the Chairman shall forthwith appoint from the Panel of Arbitrators an *ad hoc* Committee of three persons. None of the members of the Committee shall have been a member of the Tribunal which rendered the award, shall be of the same nationality as any such member, shall be a national of the State party to the dispute or of the State whose national is a party to the dispute, shall have been designated to the Panel of Arbitrators by either of those States, or shall have acted as a conciliator in the same dispute. The Committee shall have the authority to annul the award or any part thereof on any of the grounds set forth in paragraph (1).

(4) The provisions of Articles 41–45, 48, 49, 53 and 54, and of Chapters VI and VII shall apply *mutatis mutandis* to proceedings before the Committee.

(5) The Committee may, if it considers that the circumstances so require, stay enforcement of the award pending its decision. If the applicant requests a stay of enforcement of the award in his application, enforcement shall be stayed provisionally until the Committee rules on such request.

(6) If the award is annulled the dispute shall, at the request of either party, be submitted to a new Tribunal constituted in accordance with Section 2 of this Chapter.

Section 6
Recognition and Enforcement of the Award

Article 53

(1) The award shall be binding on the parties and shall not be subject to any appeal or to any other remedy except those provided for in this Convention. Each party shall abide by and comply with the terms of the award except to the extent that enforcement shall have been stayed pursuant to the relevant provisions of this Convention.

(2) For the purposes of this Section, "award" shall include any decision interpreting, revising or annulling such award pursuant to Articles 50, 51 or 52.

Article 54

(1) Each Contracting State shall recognize an award rendered pursuant to this Convention as binding and enforce the pecuniary obligations imposed by that award within its territories as if it were a final judgment of a court in that State. A Contracting State with a federal constitution may enforce such an award in or through its federal courts and may provide that such courts shall treat the award as if it were a final judgment of the courts of a constituent state.

(2) A party seeking recognition or enforcement in the territories of a Contracting State shall furnish to a competent court or other authority which such State shall have designated for this purpose a copy of the award certified by the Secretary–General. Each Contracting State shall notify the Secretary–General of the designation of the competent court or other authority for this purpose and of any subsequent change in such designation.

(3) Execution of the award shall be governed by the laws concerning the execution of judgments in force in the State in whose territories such execution is sought.

Article 55

Nothing in Article 54 shall be construed as derogating from the law in force in any Contracting State relating to immunity of that State or of any foreign State from execution.

CHAPTER V
Replacement and Disqualification of Conciliators and Arbitrators

Article 56

(1) After a Commission or a Tribunal has been constituted and proceedings have begun, its composition shall remain unchanged; provided,

however, that if a conciliator or an arbitrator should die, become incapacitated, or resign, the resulting vacancy shall be filled in accordance with the provisions of Section 2 of Chapter III or Section 2 of Chapter IV.

(2) A member of a Commission or Tribunal shall continue to serve in that capacity notwithstanding that he shall have ceased to be a member of the Panel.

(3) If a conciliator or arbitrator appointed by a party shall have resigned without the consent of the Commission or Tribunal of which he was a member, the Chairman shall appoint a person from the appropriate Panel to fill the resulting vacancy.

Article 57

A party may propose to a Commission or Tribunal the disqualification of any of its members on account of any fact indicating a manifest lack of the qualities required by paragraph (1) of Article 14. A party to arbitration proceedings may, in addition, propose the disqualification of an arbitrator on the ground that he was ineligible for appointment to the Tribunal under Section 2 of Chapter IV.

Article 58

The decision on any proposal to disqualify a conciliator or arbitrator shall be taken by the other members of the Commission or Tribunal as the case may be, provided that where those members are equally divided, or in the case of a proposal to disqualify a sole conciliator or arbitrator, or a majority of the conciliators or arbitrators, the Chairman shall take that decision. If it is decided that the proposal is well-founded the conciliator or arbitrator to whom the decision relates shall be replaced in accordance with the provisions of Section 2 of Chapter III or Section 2 of Chapter IV.

CHAPTER VI

Cost of Proceedings

Article 59

The charges payable by the parties for the use of the facilities of the Centre shall be determined by the Secretary–General in accordance with the regulations adopted by the Administrative Council.

Article 60

(1) Each Commission and each Tribunal shall determine the fees and expenses of its members within limits established from time to time by the Administrative Council and after consultation with the Secretary–General.

(2) Nothing in paragraph (1) of this Article shall preclude the parties from agreeing in advance with the Commission or Tribunal concerned upon the fees and expenses of its members.

Article 61

(1) In the case of conciliation proceedings the fees and expenses of members of the Commission as well as the charges for the use of the facilities of the Centre, shall be borne equally by the parties. Each party shall bear any other expenses it incurs in connection with the proceedings.

(2) In the case of arbitration proceedings the Tribunal shall, except as the parties otherwise agree, assess the expenses incurred by the parties in connection with the proceedings, and shall decide how and by whom those expenses, the fees and expenses of the members of the Tribunal and the charges for the use of the facilities of the Centre shall be paid. Such decision shall form part of the award.

CHAPTER VII
Place of Proceedings

Article 62

Conciliation and arbitration proceedings shall be held at the seat of the Centre except as hereinafter provided.

Article 63

Conciliation and arbitration proceedings may be held, if the parties so agree,

(a) at the seat of the Permanent Court of Arbitration or of any other appropriate institution, whether private or public, with which the Centre may make arrangements for that purpose; or

(b) at any other place approved by the Commission or Tribunal after consultation with the Secretary–General.

CHAPTER VIII
Disputes Between Contracting States

Article 64

Any dispute arising between Contracting States concerning the interpretation or application of this Convention which is not settled by negotiation shall be referred to the International Court of Justice by the application of any party to such dispute, unless the States concerned agree to another method of settlement.

CHAPTER IX
Amendment

Article 65

Any Contracting State may propose amendment of this Convention. The text of a proposed amendment shall be communicated to the Secretary–General not less than 90 days prior to the meeting of the Administrative Council at which such amendment is to be considered and shall forthwith be transmitted by him to all the members of the Administrative Council.

Article 66

(1) If the Administrative Council shall so decide by a majority of two-thirds of its members, the proposed amendment shall be circulated to all Contracting States for ratification, acceptance or approval. Each amendment shall enter into force 30 days after dispatch by the depositary of this Convention of a notification to Contracting States that all Contracting States have ratified, accepted or approved the amendment.

(2) No amendment shall affect the rights and obligations under this Convention of any Contracting State or of any of its constituent subdivisions or agencies, or of any national of such State arising out of consent to the jurisdiction of the Centre given before the date of entry into force of the amendment.

CHAPTER X
Final Provisions

Article 67

This Convention shall be open for signature on behalf of States members of the Bank. It shall also be open for signature on behalf of any other State which is a party to the Statute of the International Court of Justice and which the Administrative Council, by a vote of two-thirds of its members, shall have invited to sign the Convention.

Article 68

(1) This Convention shall be subject to ratification, acceptance or approval by the signatory States in accordance with their respective constitutional procedures.

(2) This Convention shall enter into force 30 days after the date of deposit of the twentieth instrument of ratification, acceptance or approval. It shall enter into force for each State which subsequently deposits its instrument of ratification, acceptance or approval 30 days after the date of such deposit.

Article 69

Each Contracting State shall take such legislative or other measures as may be necessary for making the provisions of this Convention effective in its territories.

Article 70

This Convention shall apply to all territories for whose international relations a Contracting State is responsible, except those which are excluded by such State by written notice to the depositary of this Convention either at the time of ratification, acceptance or approval or subsequently.

Article 71

Any Contracting State may denounce this Convention by written notice to the depositary of this Convention. The denunciation shall take effect six months after receipt of such notice.

Article 72

Notice by a Contracting State pursuant to Articles 70 or 71 shall not affect the rights or obligations under this Convention of that State or of any of its constituent subdivisions or agencies or of any national of that State arising out of consent to the jurisdiction of the Centre given by one of them before such notice was received by the depositary.

Article 73

Instruments of ratification, acceptance or approval of this Convention and of amendments thereto shall be deposited with the Bank which shall act as the depositary of this Convention. The depositary shall transmit certified copies of this Convention to States members of the Bank and to any other State invited to sign the Convention.

Article 74

The depositary shall register this Convention with the Secretariat of the United Nations in accordance with Article 102 of the Charter of the United Nations and the Regulations thereunder adopted by the General Assembly.

Article 75

The depositary shall notify all signatory States of the following:

(a) signatures in accordance with Article 67;

(b) deposits of instruments of ratification, acceptance and approval in accordance with Article 73;

(c) the date on which this Convention enters into force in accordance with Article 68;

(d) exclusions from territorial application pursuant to Article 70;

(e) the date on which any amendment of this Convention enters into force in accordance with Article 66; and

(f) denunciations in accordance with Article 71.

DONE at Washington, in the English, French and Spanish languages, all three texts being equally authentic, in a single copy which shall remain deposited in the archives of the International Bank for Reconstruction and Development, which has indicated by its signature below its agreement to fulfil the functions with which it is charged under this Convention.

List of Contracting States and other Signatories of the Convention (as of December 20, 2004)

Afghanistan
Albania
Algeria
Argentina
Armenia
Australia
Austria
Azerbaïjan
Bahamas
Bahrain
Bangladesh
Barbados
Belarus
Belgium
Belize*
Benin
Bolivia
Bosnia and Herzegovina
Botswana
Brunei Darussalam
Bulgaria
Burkina Faso
Burundi
Cambodia
Cameroon
Central African Republic
Chad
Chile
China
Colombia
Comoros
Congo
Congo, Democratic Rep. of
Costa Rica
Côte d'Ivoire
Croatia
Cyprus
Czech Republic
Dominican Republic*
Denmark
Ecuador
Egypt, Arab Rep. of
El Salvador
Estonia
Ethiopia*
Fiji
Finland
France
Gabon
Gambia, The
Georgia
Germany
Ghana

Greece
Grenada
Guatemala
Guinea
Guinea–Bissau*
Guyana
Haiti*
Honduras
Hungary
Iceland
Indonesia
Ireland
Israel
Italy
Jamaica
Japan
Jordan
Kazakhstan
Kenya
Kyrgyz, Rep. of*
Korea, Rep. of
Kuwait
Latvia
Lebanon
Lesotho
Liberia
Lithuania
Luxembourg
Macedonia, former Yugoslav
    Rep. of
Madagascar
Malawi
Malaysia
Mali
Malta
Mauritania
Mauritius
Micronesia
Moldova*
Mongolia
Morocco
Mozambique
Namibia*
Nepal
Netherlands
New Zealand
Nicaragua
Niger
Nigeria
Norway
Oman
Pakistan
Panama
Papua New Guinea

Paraguay
Peru
Philippines
Portugal
Romania
Russian Federation*
Rwanda
Saint Vincent and the Grenadines
Samoa
Sao Tome and Principe*
Saudi Arabia
Senegal
Serbia and Montenegro*
Seychelles
Sierra Leone
Singapore
Slovak Republic
Slovenia
Solomon Islands
Somalia
Spain
Sri Lanka
St. Kitts & Nevis
St. Lucia
Sudan

Swaziland
Sweden
Switzerland
Tanzania
Thailand*
Timor–Leste
Togo
Tonga
Trinidad and Tobago
Tunisia
Turkey
Turkmenistan
Uganda
Ukraine
United Arab Emirates
United Kingdom of Great Britain
   and Northern Ireland
United States of America
Uruguay
Uzbekistan
Venezuela
Yemen, Republic of
Zambia
Zimbabwe

*   Signed but not ratified.

BILATERAL INVESTMENT TREATY "BIT"

TREATY BETWEEN UNITED STATES OF AMERICA AND THE ARGENTINE REPUBLIC CONCERNING THE RECIPROCAL ENCOURAGEMENT AND PROTECTION OF INVESTMENT

1991

The United States of America and the Argentine Republic, hereinafter referred to as the Parties-

Desiring to promote greater economic cooperation between them, with respect to investment by nationals and companies of one Party in the territory of the other Party;

Recognizing that agreement upon the treatment to be accorded such investment will stimulate the flow of private capital and the economic development of the Parties;

Agreeing that fair and equitable treatment of investment is desirable in order to maintain a stable framework for investment and maximum effective use of economic resources;

Recognizing that the development of economic and business ties can contribute to the well-being of workers in both Parties and promote respect for internationally recognized worker rights and having resolved to conclude a Treaty concerning the encouragement and reciprocal protection of investment;

Have agreed as follows:

ARTICLE I

1. For the purposes of this Treaty,

    a) "investment" means every kind of investment in the territory of one Party owned or controlled directly or indirectly by nationals or companies of the other Party, such as equity, debt, and service and investment contracts; and includes without limitation:

    (i) tangible and intangible property, including rights, such as mortgages, liens and pledges;

    (ii) a company or shares of stock or other interests in a company or interests in the assets thereof;

    (iii) a claim to money or a claim to performance having economic value and directly related to an investment;

    (iv) intellectual property which includes, inter alia, rights relating to:

    literary and artistic works, including sound

    recordings,

inventions in all fields of human endeavor,

industrial designs,

semiconductor mask works,

trade secrets, know-how, and confidential

business information, and

trademarks, service marks, and trade names; and

(v) any right conferred by law or contract, and any licenses and permits pursuant to law;

b) "company" of a Party means any kind of corporation, company, association, state enterprise, or other organization, legally constituted under the laws and regulations of a Party or a political subdivision thereof whether or not organized for pecuniary gain, and whether privately or governmentally owned;

c) "national" of a Party means a natural person who is national of a Party under its applicable law;

d) "return" means an amount derived from or associated with an investment, including profit; dividend; interest; capital gain; royalty payment; management, technical assistance or other fee; or returns in kind;

e) "associated activities" include the organization, control, operation, maintenance and disposition of companies, branches, agencies, offices, factories or other facilities for the conduct of business; the making, performance and enforcement of contracts; the acquisition, use, protection and disposition of property of all kinds including intellectual and industrial property rights; and the borrowing of funds, the purchase, issuance, and sale of equity shares and other securities, and the purchase of foreign exchange for imports.

f) "territory" means the territory of the United States or the Argentine Republic, including the territorial sea established in accordance with international law as reflected in the 1982 United Nations Convention on the Law of the Sea. This Treaty also applies in the seas and seabed adjacent to the territorial sea in which the United States or the Argentine Republic has sovereign rights or jurisdiction in accordance with international law as reflected in the 1982 United Nations Convention on the Law of the Sea.

2. Each Party reserves the right to deny to any company of the other Party the advantages of this Treaty if (a) nationals of any third country, or nationals of such Party, control such company and the company has no substantial business activities in the territory of the other Party, or (b) the company is controlled by nationals of a third country with which the denying Party does not maintain normal economic relations.

3. Any alteration of the form in which assets are invested or reinvested shall not affect their character as investment.

ARTICLE II

1.   Each Party shall permit and treat investment, and activities associated therewith, on a basis no less favorable than that accorded in like situations to investment or associated activities of its own nationals or companies, or of nationals or companies of any third country, whichever is the more favorable, subject to the right of each Party to make or maintain exceptions falling within one of the sectors or matters listed in the Protocol to this Treaty. Each Party agrees to notify the other Party before or on the date of entry into force of this Treaty of all such laws and regulations of which it is aware concerning the sectors or matters listed in the Protocol. Moreover, each Party agrees to notify the other of any future exception with respect to the sectors or matters listed in the Protocol, and to limit such exceptions to a minimum. Any future exception by either Party shall not apply to investment existing in that sector or matter at the time the exception becomes effective. The treatment accorded pursuant to any exceptions shall, unless specified otherwise in the Protocol, be not less favorable than that accorded in like situations to investments and associated activities of nationals or companies of any third country.

2.   a) Investment shall at all times be accorded fair and equitable treatment, shall enjoy full protection and security and shall in no case be accorded treatment less than that required by international law.

   b) Neither Party shall in any way impair by arbitrary or discriminatory measures the management, operation, maintenance, use, enjoyment, acquisition, expansion, or disposal of investments. For the purposes of dispute resolution under Articles VII and VIII, a measure may be arbitrary or discriminatory notwithstanding the opportunity to review such measure in the courts or administrative tribunals of a Party.

   c) Each Party shall observe any obligation it may have entered into with regard to investments.

3.   Subject to the laws relating to the entry and sojourn of aliens, nationals of either Party shall be permitted to enter and to remain in the territory of the other Party for the purpose of establishing, developing, administering or advising on the operation of an investment to which they, or a company of the first Party that employs them, have committed or are in the process of committing a substantial amount of capital or other resources.

4.   Companies which are legally constituted under the applicable laws or regulations of one Party, and which are investments, shall be permitted to engage top managerial personnel of their choice, regardless of nationality.

5.   Neither Party shall impose performance requirements as a condition of establishment, expansion or maintenance of investments, which require or enforce commitments to export goods produced, or which specify

that goods or services must be purchased locally, or which impose any other similar requirements.

6.   Each Party shall provide effective means of asserting claims and enforcing rights with respect to investments, investment agreements, and investment authorizations.

7.   Each Party shall make public all laws, regulations, administrative practices and procedures, and adjudicatory decisions that pertain to or affect investments.

8.   The treatment accorded by the United States of America to investments and associated activities of nationals and companies of the Argentine Republic under the provisions of this Article shall in any State, Territory or possession of the United States of America be no less favorable than the treatment accorded therein to investments and associated activities of nationals of the United States of America resident in, and companies legally constituted under the laws and regulations of, other States, Territories or possessions of the United States of America.

9.   The most favored nation provisions of this Article shall not apply to advantages accorded by either Party to nationals or companies of any third country by virtue of that Party's binding obligations that derive from full membership in a regional customs union or free trade area, whether such an arrangement is designated as a customs union, free trade area, common market or otherwise.

ARTICLE III

This Treaty shall not preclude either Party from prescribing laws and regulations in connection with the admission of investments made in its territory by nationals or companies of the other Party or with the conduct of associated activities, provided, however, that such laws and regulations shall not impair the substance of any of the rights set forth in this Treaty.

ARTICLE IV

1.   Investments shall not be expropriated or nationalized either directly or indirectly through measures tantamount to expropriation or nationalization ("expropriation") except for a public purpose; in a non-discriminatory manner; upon payment of prompt, adequate and effective compensation; and in accordance with due process of law and the general principles of treatment provided for in Article II(2). Compensation shall be equivalent to the fair market value of the expropriated investment immediately before the expropriatory action was taken or became known, whichever is earlier; be paid without delay; include interest at a commercially reasonable rate from the date of expropriation; be fully realizable; and be freely transferable at the prevailing market rate of exchange on the date of expropriation.

2.   A national or company of either Party that asserts that all or part of its investment has been expropriated shall have a right to prompt review by the appropriate judicial or administrative authorities of the other

Party to determine whether any such expropriation has occurred and, if so, whether such expropriation, and any compensation therefore, conforms to the provisions of this Treaty and the principles of international law.

3.   Nationals or companies of either Party whose investments suffer losses in the territory of the other Party owing to war or other armed conflict, revolution, state of national emergency, insurrection, civil disturbance or other similar events shall be accorded treatment by such other Party no less favorable than that accorded to its own nationals or companies or to nationals or companies of any third country, whichever is the more favorable treatment, as regards any measures it adopts in relation to such losses.

ARTICLE V

1.   Each Party shall permit all transfers related to an investment to be made freely and without delay into and out of its territory. Such transfers include: (a) returns; (b) compensation pursuant to Article IV; (c) payments arising out of an investment dispute; (d) payments made under a contract, including amortization of principal and accrued interest payments made pursuant to a loan agreement directly related to an investment; (e) proceeds from the sale or liquidation of all or any part of an investment; and (f) additional contributions to capital for the maintenance or development of an investment.

2.   Except as provided in Article IV paragraph 1, transfers shall be made in a freely usable currency at the prevailing market rate of exchange on the date of transfer with respect to spot transactions in the currency to be transferred. The free transfer shall take place in accordance with the procedures established by each Party; such procedures shall not impair the rights set forth in this Treaty.

3.   Notwithstanding the provisions of paragraphs 1 and 2, either Party may maintain laws and regulations (a) requiring reports of currency transfer; and (b) imposing income taxes by such means as a withholding tax applicable to dividends or other transfers. Furthermore, either Party may protect the rights of creditors, or ensure the satisfaction of judgments in adjudicatory proceedings, through the equitable, nondiscriminatory and good faith application of its law.

ARTICLE VI

The Parties agree to consult promptly, on the request of either, to resolve any disputes in connection with the Treaty, or to discuss any matter relating to the interpretation or application of the Treaty.

ARTICLE VII

1.   For purposes of this Article, an investment dispute is a dispute between a Party and a national or company of the other Party arising out of or relating to (a) an investment agreement between that Party and such national or company; (b) an investment authorization granted by that Party's foreign investment authority (if any such authorization

exists) to such national or company; or (c) an alleged breach of any right conferred or created by this Treaty with respect to an investment.

2. In the event of an investment dispute, the parties to the dispute should initially seek a resolution through consultation and negotiation. If the dispute cannot be settled amicably, the national or company concerned may choose to submit the dispute for resolution:

(a) to the courts or administrative tribunals of the Party that is a party to the dispute; or

(b) in accordance with any applicable, previously agreed dispute-settlement procedures; or

(c) in accordance with the terms of paragraph 3.

3. (a) Provided that the national or company concerned has not submitted the dispute for resolution under paragraph 2 (a) or (b) and that six months have elapsed from the date on which the dispute arose, the national or company concerned may choose to consent in writing to the submission of the dispute for settlement by binding arbitration:

(i) to the International Centre for the Settlement of Investment Disputes ("Centre") established by the Convention on the Settlement of Investment Disputes between States and Nationals of other States, done at Washington, March 18, 1965 ("ICSID Convention"), provided that the Party is a party to such convention: or

(ii) to the Additional Facility of the Centre, if the Centre is not available; or

(iii) in accordance with the Arbitration Rules of the United Nations Commission on International Trade Law (UNICTRAL): or

(iv) to any other arbitration institution, or in accordance with any other arbitration rules, as may be mutually agreed between the parties to the dispute.

(b) Once the national or company concerned has so consented, either party to the dispute may initiate arbitration in accordance with the choice so specified in the consent.

4. Each Party hereby consents to the submission of any investment dispute for settlement by binding arbitration in accordance with the choice specified in the written consent of the national or company under paragraph 3. Such consent, together with the written consent of the national or company when given under paragraph 3 shall satisfy the requirement for:

(a) written consent of the parties to the dispute for purposes of Chapter II of the ICSID Convention (Jurisdiction of the Centre) and for purposes of the Additional Facility Rules; and

(b) an "agreement in writing" for purposes of Article II of the United Nations Convention on the Recognition and Enforcement of

Foreign Arbitral Awards," done at New York, June 10, 1958 ("New York Convention").

5. Any arbitration under paragraph 3(a)(ii), (iii) or (iv) of this Article shall be held in a state that is a party to the New York Convention.

6. Any arbitral award rendered pursuant to this Article shall be final and binding on the parties to the dispute. Each Party undertakes to carry out without delay the provisions of any such award and to provide in its territory for its enforcement.

7. In any proceeding involving an investment dispute, a Party shall not assert, as a defense, counterclaim, right of set-off or otherwise, that the national or company concerned has received or will receive, pursuant to an insurance or guarantee contract, indemnification or other compensation for all or Part of its alleged damages.

8. For purposes of an arbitration held under paragraph 3 of this Article, any company legally constituted under the applicable laws and regulations of a Party or a political subdivision thereof but that, immediately before the occurrence of the event or events giving rise to the dispute, was an investment of nationals or companies of the other Party, shall be treated as a national or company of such other Party in accordance with Article 25(2)(b) of the ICSID Convention.

ARTICLE VIII

1. Any dispute between the Parties concerning the interpretation or application of the Treaty which is not resolved through consultations or other diplomatic channels, shall be submitted, upon the request of either Party, to an arbitral tribunal for binding decision in accordance with the applicable rules of international law. In the absence of an agreement by the Parties to the contrary, the arbitration rules of the United Nations Commission on International Trade Law (UNCITRAL), except to the extent modified by the Parties or by the arbitrators, shall govern.

2. Within two months of receipt of a request, each Party shall appoint an arbitrator. The two arbitrators shall select a third arbitrator as Chairman, who is a national-of a third State. The UNCITRAL Rules for appointing members of three member panels shall apply mutatis mutandis to the appointment of the arbitral panel except that the appointing authority referenced in those rules shall be the Secretary General of the Permanent Court of Arbitration.

3. Unless otherwise agreed, all submissions shall be made and all hearings shall be completed within six months of the date of selection of the third arbitrator, and the Tribunal shall render its decisions within two months of the date of the final submissions or the date of the closing of the hearings, whichever is later.

4. Expenses incurred by the Chairman, the other arbitrators, and other costs of the proceedings shall be paid for equally by the Parties.

ARTICLE IX

The provisions of Article VII and VIII shall not apply to a dispute arising (a) under the export credit, guarantee or insurance programs of the Export–Import Bank of the United States or (b) under other official credit, guarantee or insurance arrangements pursuant to which the Parties have agreed to other means of settling disputes.

ARTICLE X

This Treaty shall not derogate from:

(a) laws and regulations, administrative practices or procedures, or administrative or adjudicatory decisions of either Party;

(b) international legal obligations; or

(c) obligations assumed by either Party, including those contained in an investment agreement or an investment authorization, that entitle investments or associated activities to treatment more favorable than that accorded by this Treaty in like situations

ARTICLE XI

This Treaty shall not preclude the application by either Party of measures necessary for the maintenance of public order, the fulfillment of its obligations with respect to the maintenance or restoration of international peace or security, or the Protection of its own essential security interests.

ARTICLE XII

1. With respect to its tax policies, each Party should strive to accord fairness and equity in the treatment of investment of nationals and companies of the other Party.

2. Nevertheless, the provisions of this Treaty, and in particular Article VII and VIII, shall apply to matters of taxation only with respect to the following:

(a) expropriation, pursuant to Article IV;

(b) transfers, pursuant to Article V; or

(c) the observance and enforcement of terms of an investment agreement or authorization as referred to in Article VII(1)(a) or (b),

to the extent they are not subject to the dispute settlement provisions of a Convention for the avoidance of double taxation between the two Parties, or have been raised under such settlement provisions and are not resolved within a reasonable period of time.

ARTICLE XIII

This Treaty shall apply to the political subdivisions of the Parties.

ARTICLE XIV

1. This Treaty shall enter into force thirty days after the date of exchange of instruments of ratification. It shall remain in force for a

period of ten years and shall continue in force unless terminated in accordance with paragraph 2 of this Article. It shall apply to investments existing at the time of entry into force as well as to investments made or acquired thereafter.

2.   Either Party may, by giving one year's written notice to the other Party, terminate this Treaty at the end of the initial ten year period or at any time thereafter.

3.   With respect to investments made or acquired prior to the date of termination of this Treaty and to which this Treaty otherwise applies, the provisions of all of the other Articles of this Treaty shall thereafter continue to be effective for a further period of ten years from such date of termination.

4.   The Protocol shall form an integral part of the Treaty.

IN WITNESS WHEREOF, the respective plenipotentiaries have signed this Treaty.

DONE in duplicate at Washington on the fourteenth day of November, 1991, in the English and Spanish languages, both texts being equally authentic.

FOR THE UNITED
STATES OF AMERICA:

FOR THE ARGENTINE
REPUBLIC:

_____   _____

PROTOCOL

During dispute settlement proceedings pursuant to Article VII, a party may be required to produce evidence of ownership or control consistent with Article I(1)(a).

2.   With reference to Article II, paragraph 1, the United States reserves the right to make or maintain limited exceptions to national treatment in the following sectors:

air transportation; ocean and coastal shipping; banking; insurance; energy and power production; custom house brokers; ownership and operation of broadcast or common carrier radio and television stations; ownership of real property; ownership of shares in the Communications Satellite Corporation; the provision of common carrier telephone and telegraph services; the provision of submarine cable services; use of land and natural resources

3.   With reference to Article II, paragraph 1, the United States reserves the right to make or maintain limited exceptions to national treatment with respect to certain programs involving government grants, loans, and insurance.

4.   With reference to Article II, paragraph 1, the United States reserves the right to make or maintain limited exceptions to national and most favored nation treatment in the following sectors, with respect to which treatment will be based on reciprocity:

mining on the public domain; maritime services and maritime-related services; primary dealership in United States government securities.

5. With reference to Article II, paragraph 1, the Argentine Republic reserves the right to make or maintain limited exceptions to national treatment in the following sectors:

real estate in the Border Areas; air transportation; shipbuilding; nuclear energy centers; uranium mining; insurance; mining; fishing.

6. The Parties understand that, with respect to rights reserved in Article XI of the Treaty, "obligations with respect to the maintenance or restoration of international peace or securities" means obligations under the Charter of the United Nations.

7. The Parties acknowledge and agree that, to the extent of any conflict or inconsistency between the terms of this Treaty, and the terms of the Treaty of Friendship, Commerce, and Navigation between the Parties, entered into force December 20, 1854 (the "FCN Treaty"), the terms of this Treaty shall supersede the terms of the FCN Treaty, and shall control the resolution of such conflict.

8. The Parties confirm their mutual understanding that the provisions of this Treaty do not bind either Party in relation to any act or fact which took place or any situation which ceased to exist before the date of the entry into force of this Treaty.

9. Notwithstanding Article II(5) and in accordance with the terms of this paragraph, the Government of the Argentine Republic may maintain, but not intensify, existing performance requirements in the automotive industry. The Government of the Argentine Republic shall exert best efforts to eliminate all such requirements within the shortest possible period, and shall ensure their elimination within eight years of the date of the entry into force of this Treaty. The Government of the Argentine Republic shall further ensure that such performance requirements are applied in a manner which does not place existing investments at a competitive disadvantage against new entrants in this industry. The Parties shall consult at the request of either on any matter concerning the implementation of these undertakings. For the purposes of this paragraph, "existing" means extant at the time of signature of this Treaty.

10. The Parties note that the Argentine Republic has had and may have in the future a debt-equity conversion program under which nationals or companies of the United States may choose to invest in the Argentine Republic through the purchase of debt at a discount.

The Parties agree that the rights provided in Article V, paragraph 1, with respect to the transfer of returns and of proceeds from the sale or liquidation of all or any part of an investment, remain or may be, as such rights would apply to that part of an investment financed through a debt-equity conversion, modified by the terms of any debt-equity conversion agreement between a national or company of the United States and the Government of the Argentine Republic, or any agency or instrumentality thereof.

The transfer of returns and of proceeds from the sale or liquidation of all or any part of an investment shall in no case be on terms less favorable than those accorded, in like circumstances, to nationals or companies of the Argentine Republic or any third country, whichever is more favorable.

11.   The Parties note with satisfaction that the Argentine Republic is engaged in a process of privatization of various industries, including public utilities. They agree that they will undertake their best efforts, including through consultations, to avoid any misinterpretation regarding the scope of Article II(5) that would adversely affect this privatization process.

LITIGATION INVOLVING FOREIGN GOVERNMENTS: STATUTES AND TREATIES

HICKENLOOPER AMENDMENTS TO FOREIGN ASSISTANCE ACT

(Through 1973)

SEC. 620. PROHIBITIONS AGAINST FURNISHING ASSISTANCE.*

(c)(1) The President shall suspend assistance to the government of any country to which assistance is provided under this or any other Act when the government of such country or any government agency or subdivision within such country on or after January 1, 1962—

(A) has nationalized or expropriated or seized ownership or control of property owned by any United States citizen or by any corporation, partnership, or association not less than 50 per centum beneficially owned by the United States citizen, or

(B) has taken steps to repudiate or nullify existing contracts or agreements with any United States citizen or any corporation, partnership, or association not less than 50 per centum beneficially owned by United States citizens, or

(C) has imposed or enforced discriminatory taxes or other exactions, or restrictive maintenance or operational conditions, or has taken other actions, which have the effect of nationalizing, expropriating, or otherwise seizing ownership or control of property so owned.

and such country, government agency, or government subdivision fails within a reasonable time (not more than six months after such action, or, in the event of a referral to the Foreign Claims Settlement Commission of the United States within such period as provided herein, not more than twenty days after the report of the Commission is received) to take appropriate steps, which may include arbitration, to discharge its obligations under international law toward such citizen or entity, including speedy compensation for such property in convertible foreign ex-

* 22 U.S.C. § 2370(e).

change, equivalent to the full value thereof, as required by international law, or fails to take steps designed to provide relief from such taxes, exactions, or conditions, as the case may be; and such suspension shall continue until the President is satisfied that appropriate steps are being taken, and no other provision of this Act shall be construed to authorize the President to waive the provisions of this subsection.

Upon request of the President (within seventy days after such action referred to in subparagraphs (A), (B), or (C) of paragraph (1) of this subsection), the Foreign Claims Settlement Commission of the United States (established pursuant to Reorganization Plan No. 1 of 1954, 68 Stat. 1279) is hereby authorized to evaluate expropriated property, determining the full value of any property nationalized, expropriated, or seized, or subject to discriminatory or other actions as aforesaid, for purposes of this subsection and to render an advisory report to the President within ninety days after such request. Unless authorized by the President, the Commission shall not publish its advisory report except to the citizen or entity owning such property. There is hereby authorized to be appropriated such amount, to remain available until expended, as may be necessary from time to time to enable the Commission to carry out expeditiously its functions under this subsection.

(2) Notwithstanding any other provision of law, no court in the United States shall decline on the ground of the federal act of state doctrine to make a determination on the merits giving effect to the principles of international law in a case in which a claim or title or other right to property is asserted by any party including a foreign state (or a party claiming through such state) based upon (or traced through) a confiscation or other taking after January 1, 1959, by an act of that state in violation of the principles of international law, including the principles of compensation and the other standards set out in this subsection: Provided, That this subparagraph shall not be applicable (1) in any case in which an act of a foreign state is not contrary to international law or with respect to a claim of title or other right to property acquired pursuant to an irrevocable letter of credit of not more than 180 days duration issued in good faith prior to the time of the confiscation or other taking, or (2) in any case with respect to which the President determines that application of the act of state doctrine is required in that particular case by the foreign policy interests of the United States and a suggestion to this effect is filed on his behalf in that case with the court.

1973 Amendment*

The first full paragraph of section 620(e)(1) of the Foreign Assistance Act of 1961 is amended by striking out "no other provision of this

* As enacted by section 15 of the Foreign Assistance Act of 1973, Pub.L. 93–189, 87 Stat. 722 (Dec. 17, 1973).

Act shall be construed to authorize the President to waive the provisions of this subsection," and inserting in lieu thereof "the provisions of this subsection shall not be waived with respect to any country unless the President determines and certifies that such a waiver is important to the national interests of the United States. Such certification shall be reported immediately to Congress."

UNITED STATES FOREIGN SOVEREIGN IMMUNITIES ACT OF 1976

(as amended)

Title 28, United States Code

§ 1330. Actions against foreign states

(a) The district courts shall have original jurisdiction without regard to amount in controversy of any nonjury civil action against a foreign state as defined in section 1603(a) of this title as to any claim for relief in personam with respect to which the foreign state is not entitled to immunity either under sections 1605–1607 of this title or under any applicable international agreement.

(b) Personal jurisdiction over a foreign state shall exist as to every claim for relief over which the district courts have jurisdiction under subsection (a) where service has been made under section 1608 of this title.

(c) For purposes of subsection (b), an appearance by a foreign state does not confer personal jurisdiction with respect to any claim for relief not arising out of any transaction or occurrence enumerated in sections 1605–1607 of this title.

§ 1332. Diversity of citizenship; amount in controversy; costs

(a) The district courts shall have original jurisdiction of all civil actions where the matter in controversy exceeds the sum or value of $75,000, exclusive of interest and costs, and is between—

(1) citizens of different States;

(2) citizens of a State and citizens or subjects of a foreign state;

(3) citizens of different States and in which citizens or subjects of a foreign state are additional parties; and

(4) a foreign state, defined in section 1603(a) of this title, as plaintiff and citizens of a State or of different States.

For the purposes of this section, section 1335, and section 1441, an alien admitted to the United States for permanent residence shall be deemed a citizen of the State in which such alien is domiciled.

(b) Except when express provision therefor is otherwise made in a statute of the United States, where the plaintiff who files the case originally in the Federal courts is finally adjudged to be entitled to recover less than the sum or value of $75,000, computed without regard to any setoff or counterclaim to which the defendant may be adjudged to be entitled, and exclusive of interest and costs, the district court may deny costs to the plaintiff and, in addition, may impose costs on the plaintiff.

(c) For the purposes of this section and section 1441 of this title—

(1) a corporation shall be deemed to be a citizen of any State by which it has been incorporated and of the State where it has its principal place of business, except that in any direct action against the insurer of a policy or contract of liability insurance, whether incorporated or unincorporated, to which action the insured is not joined as a party-defendant, such insurer shall be deemed a citizen of the State of which the insured is a citizen, as well as of any State by which the insurer has been incorporated and of the State where it has its principal place of business; and

(2) the legal representative of the estate of a decedent shall be deemed to be a citizen only of the same State as the decedent, and the legal representative of an infant or incompetent shall be deemed to be a citizen only of the same State as the infant or incompetent.

(d) The word "States", as used in this section, includes the Territories, the District of Columbia, and the Commonwealth of Puerto Rico.

§ 1391. Venue generally

. . .

(f) A civil action against a foreign state as defined in section 1603(a) of this title may be brought–

(1) in any judicial district in which a substantial part of the events or omissions giving rise to the claim occurred, or a substantial part of property that is the subject of the action is situated;

(2) in any judicial district in which the vessel or cargo of a foreign state is situated, if the claim is asserted under section 1605(b) of this title;

(3) in any judicial district in which the agency or instrumentality is licensed to do business or is doing business, if the action is brought against an agency or instrumentality of a foreign state as defined in section 1603(b) of this title; or

(4) in the United States District Court for the District of Columbia if the action is brought against a foreign state or political subdivision thereof.

§ 1441. Actions removable generally

. . .

(d) Any civil action brought in a State court against a foreign state as defined in section 1603(a) of this title may be removed by the foreign state to the district court of the United States for the district and division embracing the place where such action is pending. Upon removal the action shall be tried by the court without jury. Where removal is based upon this subsection, the time limitations of section 1446(b) of this chapter may be enlarged at any time for cause shown.

§ 1602. Findings and declaration of purpose

The Congress finds that the determination by United States courts of the claims of foreign states to immunity from the jurisdiction of such courts would serve the interests of justice and would protect the rights of both foreign states and litigants in United States courts. Under international law, states are not immune from the jurisdiction of foreign courts insofar as their commercial activities are concerned, and their commercial property may be levied upon for the satisfaction of judgments rendered against them in connection with their commercial activities. Claims of foreign states to immunity should henceforth be decided by courts of the United States and of the States in conformity with the principles set forth in this chapter.

§ 1603. Definitions

For purposes of this chapter—

(a) A "foreign state", except as used in section 1608 of this title, includes a political subdivision of a foreign state or an agency or instrumentality of a foreign state as defined in subsection (b).

(b) An "agency or instrumentality of a foreign state" means any entity—

(1) which is a separate legal person, corporate or otherwise, and

(2) which is an organ of a foreign state or political subdivision thereof, or a majority of whose shares or other ownership interest is owned by a foreign state or political subdivision thereof, and

(3) which is neither a citizen of a State of the United States as defined in section 1332 (c) and (d) of this title, nor created under the laws of any third country.

(c) The "United States" includes all territory and waters, continental or insular, subject to the jurisdiction of the United States.

(d) A "commercial activity" means either a regular course of commercial conduct or a particular commercial transaction or act. The commercial character of an activity shall be determined by reference to the nature of the course of conduct or particular transaction or act, rather than by reference to its purpose.

(e) A "commercial activity carried on in the United States by a foreign state" means commercial activity carried on by such state and having substantial contact with the United States.

§ 1604. Immunity of a foreign state from jurisdiction

Subject to existing international agreements to which the United States is a party at the time of enactment of this Act a foreign state shall be immune from the jurisdiction of the courts of the United States and of the States except as provided in sections 1605 to 1607 of this chapter.

§ 1605. General exceptions to the jurisdictional immunity of a foreign state

(a) A foreign state shall not be immune from the jurisdiction of courts of the United States or of the States in any case—

(1) in which the foreign state has waived its immunity either explicitly or by implication, notwithstanding any withdrawal of the waiver which the foreign state may purport to effect except in accordance with the terms of the waiver;

(2) in which the action is based upon a commercial activity carried on in the United States by the foreign state; or upon an act performed in the United States in connection with a commercial activity of the foreign state elsewhere; or upon an act outside the territory of the United States in connection with a commercial activity of the foreign state elsewhere and that act causes a direct effect in the United States;

(3) in which rights in property taken in violation of international law are in issue and that property or any property exchanged for such property is present in the United States in connection with a commercial activity carried on in the United States by the foreign state; or that property or any property exchanged for such property is owned or operated by an agency or instrumentality of the foreign state and that agency or instrumentality is engaged in a commercial activity in the United States;

(4) in which rights in property in the United States acquired by succession or gift or rights in immovable property situated in the United States are in issue;

(5) not otherwise encompassed in paragraph (2) above, in which money damages are sought against a foreign state for personal injury or death, or damage to or loss of property, occurring in the United States and caused by the tortious act or omission of that foreign state or of any official or employee of that foreign state while acting within the scope of his office or employment; except this paragraph shall not apply to—

(A) any claim based upon the exercise or performance or the failure to exercise or perform a discretionary function regardless of whether the discretion be abused, or

(B) any claim arising out of malicious prosecution, abuse of process, libel, slander, misrepresentation, deceit, or interference with contract rights;

(6)* in which the action is brought, either to enforce an agreement made by the foreign state with or for the benefit of a private party to submit to arbitration all or any differences which have arisen or which may arise between the parties with respect to a defined legal relationship, whether contractual or

* Added in 1988.

not, concerning a subject matter capable of settlement by arbitration under the laws of the United States, or to confirm an award made pursuant to such an agreement to arbitrate, if (A) the arbitration takes place or is intended to take place in the United States, (B) the agreement or award is or may be governed by a treaty or other international agreement in force for the United States calling for the recognition and enforcement of arbitral awards, (C) the underlying claim, save for the agreement to arbitrate, could have been brought in a United States court under this section or section 1607, or (D) paragraph (1) of this subsection is otherwise applicable; or

(7)** not otherwise covered by paragraph (2), in which money damages are sought against a foreign state for personal injury or death that was caused by an act of torture, extrajudicial killing, aircraft sabotage, hostage taking, or the provision of material support or resources (as defined in section 2339A of title 18) for such an act if such act or provision of material support is engaged in by an official, employee, or agent of such foreign state while acting within the scope of his or her office, employment, or agency, except that the court shall decline to hear a claim under this paragraph—

(A) if the foreign state was not designated as a state sponsor of terrorism under section 6(j) of the Export Administration Act of 1979 (50 U.S.C. App. 2405(j)) or section 620A of the Foreign Assistance Act of 1961 (22 U.S.C. 2371) at the time the act occurred, unless later so designated as a result of such act; and

(B) even if the foreign state is or was so designated, if—

(i) the act occurred in the foreign state against which the claim has been brought and the claimant has not afforded the foreign state a reasonable opportunity to arbitrate the claim in accordance with accepted international rules of arbitration; or

(ii) neither the claimant nor the victim was a national of the United States (as that term is defined in section 101(a)(22) of the Immigration and Nationality Act) when the act upon which the claim is based occurred.

(b) A foreign state shall not be immune from the jurisdiction of the courts of the United States in any case in which a suit in admiralty is brought to enforce a maritime lien against a vessel or cargo of the foreign state, which maritime lien is based upon a commercial activity of the foreign state: Provided, That—

(1) notice of the suit is given by delivery of a copy of the summons and of the complaint to the person, or his agent, having possession of the vessel or cargo against which the

** Added in 1996.

maritime lien is asserted; and if the vessel or cargo is arrested pursuant to process obtained on behalf of the party bringing the suit, the service of process of arrest shall be deemed to constitute valid delivery of such notice, but the party bringing the suit shall be liable for any damages sustained by the foreign state as a result of the arrest if the party bringing the suit had actual or constructive knowledge that the vessel or cargo of a foreign state was involved; and

(2) notice to the foreign state of the commencement of suit as provided in section 1608 of this title is initiated within ten days either of the delivery of notice as provided in paragraph (1) of this subsection or, in the case of a party who was unaware that the vessel or cargo of a foreign state was involved, of the date such party determined the existence of the foreign state's interest.

(c) Whenever notice is delivered under subsection (b)(1), the suit to enforce a maritime lien shall thereafter proceed and shall be heard and determined according to the principles of law and rules of practice of suits in rem whenever it appears that, had the vessel been privately owned and possessed, a suit in rem might have been maintained. A decree against the foreign state may include costs of the suit and, if the decree is for a money judgment, interest as ordered by the court, except that the court may not award judgment against the foreign state in an amount greater than the value of the vessel or cargo upon which the maritime lien arose. Such value shall be determined as of the time notice is served under subsection (b)(1). Decrees shall be subject to appeal and revision as provided in other cases of admiralty and maritime jurisdiction. Nothing shall preclude the plaintiff in any proper case from seeking relief in personam in the same action brought to enforce a maritime lien as provided in this section.

(d) A foreign state shall not be immune from the jurisdiction of the courts of the United States in any action brought to foreclose a preferred mortgage, as defined in the Ship Mortgage Act, 1920 (46 U.S.C. 911 and following). Such action shall be brought, heard, and determined in accordance with the provisions of that Act and in accordance with the principles of law and rules of practice of suits in rem, whenever it appears that had the vessel been privately owned and possessed a suit in rem might have been maintained.

(e)* For purposes of paragraph (7) of subsection (a)—

(1) the terms "torture" and "extrajudicial killing" have the meaning given those terms in section 3 of the Torture Victim Protection Act of 1991;

(2) the term "hostage taking" has the meaning given that term in Article 1 of the International Convention Against the Taking of Hostages; and

---

* Subsections (e) to (g) added in 1996.

(3) the term "aircraft sabotage" has the meaning given that term in Article 1 of the Convention for the Suppression of Unlawful Acts Against the Safety of Civil Aviation.

(f) No action shall be maintained under subsection (a)(7) unless the action is commenced not later than 10 years after the date on which the cause of action arose. All principles of equitable tolling, including the period during which the foreign state was immune from suit, shall apply in calculating this limitation period.

(g) Limitation on Discovery.—

(1) In general.—

(A) Subject to paragraph (2), if an action is filed that would otherwise be barred by section 1604, but for subsection (a)(7), the court, upon request of the Attorney General, shall stay any request, demand, or order for discovery on the United States that the Attorney General certifies would significantly interfere with a criminal investigation or prosecution, or a national security operation, related to the incident that gave rise to the cause of action, until such time as the Attorney General advises the court that such request, demand, or order will no longer so interfere.

(B) A stay under this paragraph shall be in effect during the 12-month period beginning on the date on which the court issues the order to stay discovery. The court shall renew the order to stay discovery for additional 12-month periods upon motion by the United States if the Attorney General certifies that discovery would significantly interfere with a criminal investigation or prosecution, or a national security operation, related to the incident that gave rise to the cause of action.

(2) Sunset.—

(A) Subject to subparagraph (B), no stay shall be granted or continued in effect under paragraph (1) after the date that is 10 years after the date on which the incident that gave rise to the cause of action occurred.

(B) After the period referred to in subparagraph (A), the court, upon request of the Attorney General, may stay any request, demand, or order for discovery on the United States that the court finds a substantial likelihood would—

(i) create a serious threat of death or serious bodily injury to any person;

(ii) adversely affect the ability of the United States to work in cooperation with foreign and international law enforcement agencies in investigating violations of United States law; or

(iii) obstruct the criminal case related to the incident that gave rise to the cause of action or undermine the potential for a conviction in such case.

(3) Evaluation of evidence.—The court's evaluation of any request for a stay under this subsection filed by the Attorney General shall be conducted ex parte and in camera.

(4) Bar on motions to dismiss.—A stay of discovery under this subsection shall constitute a bar to the granting of a motion to dismiss under rules 12(b)(6) and 56 of the Federal Rules of Civil Procedure.

(5) Construction.—Nothing in this subsection shall prevent the United States from seeking protective orders or asserting privileges ordinarily available to the United States.

§ 1606. Extent of liability

As to any claim for relief with respect to which a foreign state is not entitled to immunity under section 1605 or 1607 of this chapter, the foreign state shall be liable in the same manner and to the same extent as a private individual under like circumstances; but a foreign state except for an agency or instrumentality thereof shall not be liable for punitive damages, [except any action under section 1605(a)(7) or 1610(f)];* if, however, in any case wherein death was caused, the law of the place where the action or omission occurred provides, or has been construed to provide, for damages only punitive in nature, the foreign state shall be liable for actual or compensatory damages measured by the pecuniary injuries resulting from such death which were incurred by the persons for whose benefit the action was brought.

§ 1607. Counterclaims

In any action brought by a foreign state, or in which a foreign state intervenes, in a court of the United States or of a State, the foreign state shall not be accorded immunity with respect to any counterclaim—

(a) for which a foreign state would not be entitled to immunity under section 1605 of this chapter had such claim been brought in a separate action against the foreign state; or

(b) arising out of the transaction or occurrence that is the subject matter of the claim of the foreign state; or

(c) to the extent that the counterclaim does not seek relief exceeding in amount or differing in kind from that sought by the foreign state.

§ 1608. Service; time to answer; default

(a) Service in the courts of the United States and of the States shall be made upon a foreign state or political subdivision of a foreign state:

* Provision in brackets enacted in 1998   and repealed in 2000.

(1) by delivery of a copy of the summons and complaint in accordance with any special arrangement for service between the plaintiff and the foreign state or political subdivision; or

(2) if no special arrangement exists, by delivery of a copy of the summons and complaint in accordance with an applicable international convention on service of judicial documents; or

(3) if service cannot be made under paragraphs (1) or (2), by sending a copy of the summons and complaint and a notice of suit, together with a translation of each into the official language of the foreign state, by any form of mail requiring a signed receipt, to be addressed and dispatched by the clerk of the court to the head of the ministry of foreign affairs of the foreign state concerned, or

(4) if service cannot be made within 30 days under paragraph (3), by sending two copies of the summons and complaint and a notice of suit, together with a translation of each into the official language of the foreign state, by any form of mail requiring a signed receipt, to be addressed and dispatched by the clerk of the court to the Secretary of State in Washington, District of Columbia, to the attention of the Director of Special Consular Services—and the Secretary shall transmit one copy of the papers through diplomatic channels to the foreign state and shall send to the clerk of the court a certified copy of the diplomatic note indicating when the papers were transmitted. As used in this subsection, a "notice of suit" shall mean a notice addressed to a foreign state and in a form prescribed by the Secretary of State by regulation.

(b) Service in the courts of the United States and of the States shall be made upon an agency or instrumentality of a foreign state:

(1) by delivery of a copy of the summons and complaint in accordance with any special arrangement for service between the plaintiff and the agency or instrumentality; or

(2) if no special arrangement exists, by delivery of a copy of the summons and complaint either to an officer, a managing or general agent, or to any other agent authorized by appointment or by law to receive service of process in the United States; or in accordance with an applicable international convention on service of judicial documents; or

(3) if service cannot be made under paragraphs (1) or (2), and if reasonably calculated to give actual notice, by delivery of a copy of the summons and complaint, together with a translation of each into the official language of the foreign state—

(A) as directed by an authority of the foreign state or political subdivision in response to a letter rogatory or request or

(B) by any form of mail requiring a signed receipt, to be addressed and dispatched by the clerk of the court to the agency or instrumentality to be served, or

(C) as directed by order of the court consistent with the law of the place where service is to be made.

(c) Service shall be deemed to have been made—

(1) in the case of service under subsection (a)(4), as of the date of transmittal indicated in the certified copy of the diplomatic note; and (2) in any other case under this section, as of the date of receipt indicated in the certification, signed and returned postal receipt, or other proof of service applicable to the method of service employed.

(d) In any action brought in a court of the United States or of a State, a foreign state, a political subdivision thereof, or an agency or instrumentality of a foreign state shall serve an answer or other responsive pleading to the complaint within sixty days after service has been made under this section.

(e) No judgment by default shall be entered by a court of the United States or of a State against a foreign state, a political subdivision thereof, or an agency or instrumentality of a foreign state, unless the claimant establishes his claim or right to relief by evidence satisfactory to the court. A copy of any such default judgment shall be sent to the foreign state or political subdivision in the manner prescribed for service in this section.

§ 1609. Immunity from attachment and execution of property of a foreign state

Subject to existing international agreements to which the United States is a party at the time of enactment of this Act the property in the United States of a foreign state shall be immune from attachment arrest and execution except as provided in sections 1610 and 1611 of this chapter.

§ 1610. Exceptions to the immunity from attachment or execution

(a) The property in the United States of a foreign state, as defined in section 1603(a) of this chapter, used for a commercial activity in the United States, shall not be immune from attachment in aid of execution, or from execution, upon a judgment entered by a court of the United States or of a State after the effective date of this Act, if—

(1) the foreign state has waived its immunity from attachment in aid of execution or from execution either explicitly or by implication, notwithstanding any withdrawal of the waiver the foreign state may purport to effect except in accordance with the terms of the waiver, or

(2) the property is or was used for the commercial activity upon which the claim is based, or

(3) the execution relates to a judgment establishing rights in property which has been taken in violation of international law or which has been exchanged for property taken in violation of international law, or

(4) the execution relates to a judgment establishing rights in property—

> (A) which is acquired by succession or gift, or
>
> (B) which is immovable and situated in the United States: Provided, That such property is not used for purposes of maintaining a diplomatic or consular mission or the residence of the Chief of such mission, or

(5) the property consists of any contractual obligation or any proceeds from such a contractual obligation to indemnify or hold harmless the foreign state or its employees under a policy of automobile or other liability or casualty insurance covering the claim which merged into the judgment, or

(6)* the judgment is based on an order confirming an arbitral award rendered against the foreign state, provided that attachment in aid of execution, or execution, would not be inconsistent with any provision in the arbitral agreement, or

(7)** the judgment relates to a claim for which the foreign state is not immune under section 1605(a)(7), regardless of whether the property is or was involved with the act upon which the claim is based.

(b) In addition to subsection (a), any property in the United States of an agency or instrumentality of a foreign state engaged in commercial activity in the United States shall not be immune from attachment in aid of execution, or from execution, upon a judgment entered by a court of the United States or of a State after the effective date of this Act, if—

(1) the agency or instrumentality has waived its immunity from attachment in aid of execution or from execution either explicitly or implicitly, notwithstanding any withdrawal of the waiver the agency or instrumentality may purport to effect except in accordance with the terms of the waiver, or

(2) the judgment relates to a claim for which the agency or instrumentality is not immune by virtue of section 1605(a)(2), (3), (5), or (7), or 1605(b) of this chapter, regardless of whether the property is or was involved in the act upon which the claim is based.

---

* Added in 1988.   ** Added in 1996.

(c) No attachment or execution referred to in subsections (a) and (b) of this section shall be permitted until the court has ordered such attachment and execution after having determined that a reasonable period of time has elapsed following the entry of judgment and the giving of any notice required under section 1608(e) of this chapter.

(d) The property of a foreign state, as defined in section 1603(a) of this chapter, used for a commercial activity in the United States, shall not be immune from attachment prior to the entry of judgment in any action brought in a court of the United States or of a State, or prior to the elapse of the period of time provided in subsection (c) of this section, if—

> (1) the foreign state has explicitly waived its immunity from attachment prior to judgment, notwithstanding any withdrawal of the waiver the foreign state may purport to effect except in accordance with the terms of the waiver, and (2) the purpose of the attachment is to secure satisfaction of a judgment that has been or may ultimately be entered against the foreign state, and not to obtain jurisdiction.

(e) The vessels of a foreign state shall not be immune from arrest in rem, interlocutory sale, and execution in actions brought to foreclose a preferred mortgage as provided in section 1605(d).

(f)* (1)

> (A) Notwithstanding any other provision of law, including but not limited to section 208(f) of the Foreign Missions Act (22 U.S.C. 4308(f)), and except as provided in subparagraph (B), any property with respect to which financial transactions are prohibited or regulated pursuant to section 5(b) of the Trading with the Enemy Act (50 U.S.C. App. 5(b)), section 620(a) of the Foreign Assistance Act of 1961 (22 U.S.C. 2370(a)), sections 202 and 203 of the International Emergency Economic Powers Act (50 U.S.C. 1701 1702), or any other proclamation, order, regulation, or license issued pursuant thereto, shall be subject to execution or attachment in aid of execution of any judgment relating to a claim for which a foreign state (including any agency or instrumentality or such state) claiming such property is not immune under section 1605(a)(7).

> (B) Subparagraph (A) shall not apply if, at the time the property is expropriated or seized by the foreign state, the property has been held in title by a natural person or, if held in trust, has been held for the benefit of a natural person or persons.

---

* When this section was added in 1998, it authorized waiver by the President on national interest grounds, and the President granted such a waiver. *See* Alejandre v. Republic of Cuba, 42 F. Supp. 2d 1317 (S.D. Fla. 1999), *vacated by* Alejandre v. Telefonica Larga Distancia de Puerto Rico, Inc., 183 F.3d 1277 (11th Cir. 1999). In 1999, the waiver authority was repealed, and a judgment was entered ordering Cuban assets held under the Trading With the Enemy Act to be paid to the survivors of aircraft shot down by the Cuban Air Force in 1996.

(2)

(A) At the request of any party in whose favor a judgment has been issued with respect to a claim for which the foreign state is not immune under section 1605(a)(7), the Secretary of the Treasury and the Secretary of State shall fully, promptly, and effectively assist any judgment creditor or any court that has issued any such judgment in identifying, locating, and executing against the property of that foreign state or any agency or instrumentality of such state.

(B) In providing such assistance, the Secretaries—

(i) may provide such information to the court under seal; and

(ii) shall provide the information in a manner sufficient to allow the court to direct the United States Marshall's office to promptly and effectively execute against that property.

§ 1611. Certain types of property immune from execution

(a) Notwithstanding the provisions of section 1610 of this chapter, the property of those organizations designated by the President as being entitled to enjoy the privileges, exemptions, and immunities provided by the International Organizations Immunities Act shall not be subject to attachment or any other judicial process impeding the disbursement of funds to, or on the order of, a foreign state as the result of an action brought in the courts of the United States or of the States.

(b) Notwithstanding the provisions of section 1610 of this chapter, the property of a foreign state shall be immune from attachment and from execution, if—

(1) the property is that of a foreign central bank or monetary authority held for its own account, unless such bank or authority, or its parent foreign government, has explicitly waived its immunity from attachment in aid of execution, or from execution, notwithstanding any withdrawal of the waiver which the bank, authority or government may purport to effect except in accordance with the terms of the waiver; or

(2) the property is, or is intended to be, used in connection with a military activity and

(A) is of a military character, or

(B) is under the control of a military authority or defense agency.

(c) Notwithstanding the provisions of section 1610 of this chapter, the property of a foreign state shall be immune from attachment and from execution in an action brought under section 302 of the Cuban Liberty and Democratic Solidarity (LIBERTAD) Act of 1996 to the extent that the property is a facility or installation used by an accredited diplomatic mission for official purposes.

CIVIL LIABILITY FOR ACTS OF STATE SPONSORED TERRORISM*

(a) An official, employee, or agent of a foreign state designated as a state sponsor of terrorism designated under section 6(j) of the Export Administration Act of 1979 [section 2405(j) of the Appendix to Title 50, War and National Defense] while acting within the scope of his or her office, employment, or agency shall be liable to a United States national or national's legal representative for personal injury or death caused by acts of that official, employee, or agent for which the courts of the United States may maintain jurisdiction under section 1605(a)(7) of title 28, United States Code [subsec. (a)(7) of this section] for money damages which may include economic damages, solatium, pain and suffering, and punitive damages if the acts were among those described in section 1605(a)(7) of this section].

(b) Provisions related to statute of limitations and limitations on discovery that would apply to an action brought under 28 U.S.C. 1605(f) and (g) [subsecs. (f) and (g) of this section] shall also apply to actions brought under this section.

No action shall be maintained under this action [sic] if an official, employee, or agent of the United States, while acting within the scope of his or her office, employment, or agency would not be liable for such acts if carried out within the United States.

* Pub.L. 104–208, Div. A, Title I, § 101(c) [Title V, § 589], Sept. 30, 1996, 110 Stat. 3009–172, printed as Note following 28 U.S.C. § 1605.

UNITED KINGDOM
STATE IMMUNITY ACT 1978*

An Act to make new provision with respect to proceedings in the United Kingdom by or against other States; to provide for the effect of judgments given against the United Kingdom in the courts of States parties to the European Convention on State Immunity; to make new provision with respect to the immunities and privileges of heads of State; and for connected purposes.

Be it enacted by the Queen's most Excellent Majesty, by and with the advice and consent of the Lords Spiritual and Temporal, and Commons, in this present Parliament assembled, and by the authority of the same, as follows:

Part I

PROCEEDINGS IN UNITED KINGDOM BY OR AGAINST OTHER STATES

Immunity from jurisdiction

1.   (1) A State is immune from the jurisdiction of the courts of the United Kingdom except as provided in the following provisions of this Part of this Act.

(2) A court shall give effect to the immunity conferred by this section even though the State does not appear in the proceedings in question.

Exceptions from immunity

2.   (1) A State is not immune as respects proceedings in respect of which it has submitted to the jurisdiction of the courts of the United Kingdom.

(2) A State may submit after the dispute giving rise to the proceedings has arisen or by a prior written agreement; but a provision in any agreement that it is to be governed by the law of the United Kingdom is not to be regarded as a submission.

(3) A State is deemed to have submitted:

(a) if it has instituted the proceedings; or

(b) subject to subsections (4) and (5) below, if it has intervened or taken any step in the proceedings.

(4) Subsection (3)(b) above does not apply to intervention or any step taken for the purpose only of:

(a) claiming immunity; or

(b) asserting an interest in property in circumstances such that the State would have been entitled to immunity if the proceedings had been brought against it.

* 1978 Laws, c.33.

(5) Subsection (3)(b) above does not apply to any step taken by the State in ignorance of facts entitling it to immunity if those facts could not reasonably have been ascertained and immunity is claimed as soon as reasonably practicable.

(6) A submission in respect of any proceedings extends to any appeal but not to any counter–claim unless it arises out of the same legal relationship or facts as the claim.

(7) The head of a State's diplomatic mission in the United Kingdom, or the person for the time being performing his functions, shall be deemed to have authority to submit on behalf of the State in respect of any proceedings; and any person who has entered into a contract on behalf of and with the authority of a State shall be deemed to have authority to submit on its behalf in respect of proceedings arising out of the contract.

3. (1) A State is not immune as respects proceedings relating to:

(a) a commercial transaction entered into by the State; or

(b) an obligation of the State which by virtue of a contract (whether a commercial transaction or not) falls to be performed wholly or partly in the United Kingdom.

(2) This section does not apply if the parties to the dispute are States or have otherwise agreed in writing; and subsection (1)(b) above does not apply if the contract (not being a commercial transaction) was made in the territory of the State concerned and the obligation in question is governed by its administrative law.

(3) In this section "commercial transaction" means:

(a) any contract for the supply of goods or services;

(b) any loan or other transaction for the provision of finance and any guarantee or indemnity in respect of any such transaction or of any other financial obligation; and

(c) any other transaction or activity (whether of a commercial, industrial, financial, professional or other similar character) into which a State enters or in which it engages otherwise than in the exercise of sovereign authority;

but neither paragraph of subsection (1) above applies to a contract of employment between a State and an individual.

4. (1) A State is not immune as respects proceedings relating to a contract of employment between the State and an individual where the contract was made in the United Kingdom or the work is to be wholly or partly performed there.

(2) Subject to subsections (3) and (4) below, this section does not apply if:

(a) at the time when the proceedings are brought the individual is a national of the State concerned; or

(b) at the time when the contract was made the individual was neither a national of the United Kingdom nor habitually resident there; or

(c) the parties to the contract have otherwise agreed in writing.

(3) Where the work is for an office, agency or establishment maintained by the State in the United Kingdom for commercial purposes, subsection (2)(a) and (b) above do not exclude the application of this section unless the individual was, at the time when the contract was made, habitually resident in that State.

(4) Subsection (2)(c) above does not exclude the application of this section where the law of the United Kingdom requires the proceedings to be brought before a court of the United Kingdom.

(5) In subsection (2)(b) above "national of the United Kingdom" means a citizen of the United Kingdom and Colonies, a person who is a British subject by virtue of section 2, 13 or 16 of the British Nationality Act 1948 or by virtue of the British Nationality Act 1965, a British protected person within the meaning of the said Act of 1948 or a citizen of Southern Rhodesia.

(6) In this section "proceedings relating to a contract of employment" includes proceedings between the parties to such a contract in respect of any statutory rights or duties to which they are entitled or subject as employer or employee.

5.   A State is not immune as respects proceedings in respect of:

(a) death or personal injury; or

(b) damage to or loss of tangible property, caused by an act or omission in the United Kingdom.

6.   (1) A State is not immune as respects proceedings relating to:

(a) any interest of the State in, or its possession or use of, immovable property in the United Kingdom; or

(b) any obligation of the State arising out of its interest in, or its possession or use of, any such property.

(2) A State is not immune as respects proceedings relating to any interest of the State in movable or immovable property, being an interest arising by way of succession, gift or bona vacantia.

(3) The fact that a State has or claims an interest in any property shall not preclude any court from exercising in respect of it any jurisdiction relating to the estates of deceased persons or persons of unsound mind or to insolvency, the winding up of companies or the administration of trusts.

(4) A court may entertain proceedings against a person other than a State notwithstanding that the proceedings relate to property:

(a) which is in the possession or control of a State; or

(b) in which a State claims an interest,

if the State would not have been immune had the proceedings been brought against it or, in a case within paragraph (b) above, if the claim is neither admitted nor supported by prima facie evidence.

7.   A State is not immune as respects proceedings relating to:

(a) any patent, trade-mark, design or plant breeders' rights belonging to the State and registered or protected in the United Kingdom or for which the State has applied in the United Kingdom;

(b) an alleged infringement by the State in the United Kingdom of any patent, trade-mark, design, plant breeders' rights or copyright; or

(c) the right to use a trade or business name in the United Kingdom.

8.   (1) A State is not immune as respects proceedings relating to its membership of a body corporate, an unincorporated body or a partnership which:

(a) has members other than States; and

(b) is incorporated or constituted under the law of the United Kingdom or is controlled from or has its principal place of business in the United Kingdom,

being proceedings arising between the State and the body or its other members or, as the case may be, between the State and the other partners.

(2) This section does not apply if provision to the contrary has been made by an agreement in writing between the parties to the dispute or by the constitution or other instrument establishing or regulating the body or partnership in question.

9.   (1) Where a State has agreed in writing to submit a dispute which has arisen, or may arise, to arbitration, the State is not immune as respects proceedings in the courts of the United Kingdom which relate to the arbitration.

(2) This section has effect subject to any contrary provision in the arbitration agreement and does not apply to any arbitration agreement between States.

10.   (1) This section applies to:

(a) Admiralty proceedings; and

(b) proceedings on any claim which could be made the subject of Admiralty proceedings.

(2) A State is not immune as respects:

(a) an action in rem against a ship belonging to that State; or

(b) an action in personam for enforcing a claim in connection with such a ship,

if, at the time when the cause of action arose, the ship was in use or intended for use for commercial purposes.

(3) Where an action in rem is brought against a ship belonging to a State for enforcing a claim in connection with another ship belonging to that State, subsection (2)(a) above does not apply as respects the first-mentioned ship unless, at the time when the cause of action relating to the other ship arise, both ships were in use or intended for use for commercial purposes.

(4) A State is not immune as respects:

(a) an action in rem against a cargo belonging to that State if both the cargo and the ship carrying it were, at the time when the cause of action arose, in use or intended for use for commercial purposes; or

(b) an action in personam for enforcing a claim in connection with such a cargo if the ship carrying it was then in use or intended for use as aforesaid.

(5) In the foregoing provisions references to a ship or cargo belonging to a State include references to a ship or cargo in its possession or control or in which it claims an interest; and, subject to subsection (4) above, subsection (2) above applies to property other than a ship as it applies to a ship.

(6) Sections 3 to 5 above do not apply to proceedings of the kind described in subsection (1) above if the State in question is a party to the Brussels Convention and the claim relates to the operation of a ship owned or operated by that State, the carriage of cargo or passengers on any such ship or the carriage of cargo owned by that State on any other ship.

11. A State is not immune as respects proceedings relating to its liability for:

(a) value added tax, any duty of customs or excise or any agricultural levy; or

(b) rates in respect of premises occupied by it for commercial purposes.

Procedure

12. (1) Any writ or other document required to be served for instituting proceedings against a State shall be served by being transmitted through the Foreign and Commonwealth Office to the Ministry of Foreign Affairs of the State and service shall be deemed to have been effected when the writ or document is received at the Ministry.

(2) Any time for entering an appearance (whether prescribed by rules of court or otherwise) shall begin to run two months after the date on which the writ or document is received as aforesaid.

(3) A State which appears in proceedings cannot thereafter object that subsection (1) above has not been complied with in the case of those proceedings.

(4) No judgment in default of appearance shall be given against a State except on proof that subsection (1) above has been complied with and that the time for entering an appearance as extended by subsection (2) above has expired.

(5) A copy of any judgment given against a State in default of appearance shall be transmitted through the Foreign and Commonwealth Office to the Ministry of Foreign Affairs of that State and any time for applying to have the judgment set aside (whether prescribed by rules of court or otherwise) shall begin to run two months after the date on which the copy of the judgment is received at the Ministry.

(6) Subsection (1) above does not prevent the service of a writ or other document in any manner to which the State has agreed and subsections (2) and (4) above do not apply where service is effected in any such manner.

(7) This section shall not be construed as applying to proceedings against a State by way of counter-claim or to an action in rem; and subsection (1) above shall not be construed as affecting any rules of court whereby leave is required for the service of process outside the jurisdiction.

13. (1) No penalty by way of committal or fine shall be imposed in respect of any failure or refusal by or on behalf of a State to disclose or produce any document or other information for the purposes of proceedings to which it is a party.

(2) Subject to subsections (3) and (4) below:

(a) relief shall not be given against a State by way of injunction or order for specific performance or for the recovery of land or other property; and

(b) the property of a State shall not be subject to any process for the enforcement of a judgment or arbitration award or, in an action in rem, for its arrest, detention or sale.

(3) Subsection (2) above does not prevent the giving of any relief or the issue of any process with the written consent of the State concerned; and any such consent (which may be contained in a prior agreement) may be expressed so as to apply to a limited extent or generally; but a provision merely submitting to the jurisdiction of the courts is not to be regarded as a consent for the purposes of this subsection.

(4) Subsection (2)(b) above does not prevent the issue of any process in respect of property which is for the time being in use or intended for use for commercial purposes; but, in a case not falling within section 10 above, this subsection applies to property of a State party to the European Convention on State Immunity only if:

(a) the process is for enforcing a judgment which is final within the meaning of section 18(1)(b) below and the State has made a declaration under Article 24 of the Convention; or

(b) the process is for enforcing an arbitration award.

(5) The head of a State's diplomatic mission in the United Kingdom, or the person for the time being performing his functions, shall be deemed to have authority to give on behalf of the State any such consent as is mentioned in subsection (3) above and, for the purposes of subsection (4) above, his certificate to the effect that any property is not in use or intended for use by or on behalf of the State for commercial purposes shall be accepted as sufficient evidence of that fact unless the contrary is proved.

(6) In the application of this section to Scotland:

(a) the reference to "injunction" shall be construed as a reference to "interdict";

(b) for paragraph (b) of subsection (2) above there shall be substituted the following paragraph:

"(b) the property of a State shall not be subject to any diligence for enforcing a judgment or order of a court or a decree arbitral or, in an action in rem, to arrestment or sale"; and

(c) any reference to "process" shall be construed as a reference to "diligence", any reference to "the issue of any process" as a reference to "the doing of diligence" and the reference in subsection (4)(b) above to "an arbitration award" as a reference to "a decree arbitral".

Supplementary provisions

14.   (1) The immunities and privileges conferred by this Part of this Act apply to any foreign or commonwealth State other than the United Kingdom; and references to a State include references to:

(a) the sovereign or other head of that State in his public capacity;

(b) the government of that State; and

(c) any department of that government,

but not to any entity (hereafter referred to as a "separate entity") which is distinct from the executive organs of the government of the State and capable of suing or being sued.

(2) A separate entity is immune from the jurisdiction of the courts of the United Kingdom if, and only if:

(a) the proceedings relate to anything done by it in the exercise of sovereign authority; and

(b) the circumstances are such that a State (or, in the case of proceedings to which section 10 above applies, a State which is not a party to the Brussels Convention) would have been so immune.

(3) If a separate entity (not being a State's central bank or other monetary authority) submits to the jurisdiction in respect of proceedings in the case of which it is entitled to immunity by virtue of subsection (2)

above, subsections (1) to (4) of section 13 above shall apply to it in respect of those procedures as if references to a State were references to that entity.

(4) Property of a State's central bank or other monetary authority shall not be regarded for the purposes of subsection (4) of section 13 above as in use or intended for use for commercial purposes; and where any such bank or authority is a separate entity subsections (1) to (3) of that section shall apply to it as if references to a State were references to the bank or authority.

(5) Section 12 above applies to proceedings against the constituent territories of a federal State; and Her Majesty may by Order in Council provide for the other provisions of this Part of this Act to apply to any such constituent territory specified in the Order as they apply to a State.

(6) Where the provisions of this Part of this Act do not apply to a constituent territory by virtue of any such Order subsections (2) and (3) above shall apply to it as if it were a separate entity.

15. (1) If it appears to Her Majesty that the immunities and privileges conferred by this Part of this Act in relation to any State:

(a) exceed those accorded by the law of that State in relation to the United Kingdom; or

(b) are less than those required by any treaty, convention or other international agreement to which that State and the United Kingdom are parties,

Her Majesty may by Order in Council provide for restricting or, as the case may be, extending those immunities and privileges to such extent as appears to Her Majesty to be appropriate.

(2) Any statutory instrument containing an Order under this section shall be subject to annulment in pursuance of a resolution of either House of Parliament.

16. (1) This Part of this Act does not affect any immunity or privilege conferred by the Diplomatic Privileges Act 1964 or the Consular Relations Act 1968; and:

(a) section 4 above does not apply to proceedings concerning the employment of the members of a mission within the meaning of the Convention scheduled to the said Act of 1964 or of the members of a consular post within the meaning of the Convention scheduled to the said Act of 1968;

(b) section 6(1) above does not apply to proceedings concerning a State's title to or its possession of property used for the purposes of a diplomatic mission.

(2) This Part of this Act does not apply to proceedings relating to anything done by or in relation to the armed forces of a State while present in the United Kingdom and, in particular, has effect subject to the Visiting Forces Act 1952.

(3) This Part of this Act does not apply to proceedings to which section 17(6) of the Nuclear Installations Act 1965 applies.

(4) This Part of this Act does not apply to criminal proceedings.

(5) This Part of this Act does not apply to any proceedings relating to taxation other than those mentioned in section 11 above.

17.   (1) In this Part of this Act:

"the Brussels Convention" means the International Convention for the Unification of Certain Rules Concerning the Immunity of State-owned Ships, signed in Brussels on 10th April 1926;

"commercial purposes" means purposes of such transactions or activities as are mentioned in section 3(3) above;

"ship" includes hovercraft.

(2) In sections 2(2) and 13(3) above references to an agreement include references to a treaty, convention or other international agreement.

(3) For the purposes of sections 3 to 8 above the territory of the United Kingdom shall be deemed to include any dependent territory in respect of which the United Kingdom is a party to the European Convention on State Immunity.

(4) In sections 3(1), 4(1), 5 and 16(2) above references to the United Kingdom include references to its territorial waters and any area designated under section 1(7) of the Continental Shelf Act 1964.

(5) In relation to Scotland in this Part of this Act "action in rem" means such an action only in relation to Admiralty proceedings.

Part II

Judgments Against United Kingdom in Convention States

18.   (1) This section applies to any judgment given against the United Kingdom by a court in another State party to the European Convention on State Immunity, being a judgment:

(a) given in proceedings in which the United Kingdom was not entitled to immunity by virtue of provisions corresponding to those of sections 2 to 11 above; and

(b) which is final, that is to say, which is not or is no longer subject to appeal or, if given in default of appearance, liable to be set aside.

(2) Subject to section 19 below, a judgment to which this section applies shall be recognized in any court in the United Kingdom as conclusive between the parties thereto in all proceedings founded on the same cause of action and may be relied on by way of defence or counterclaim in such proceedings.

(3) Subsection (2) above (but not section 19 below) shall have effect also in relation to any settlement entered into by the United Kingdom

before a court in another State party to the Convention which under the law of that State is treated as equivalent to a judgment.

(4) In this section references to a court in a State party to the Convention include references to a court in any territory in respect of which it is a party.

19. (1) A court need not give effect to section 18 above in the case of a judgment:

(a) if to do so would be manifestly contrary to public policy or if any party to the proceedings in which the judgment was given had no adequate opportunity to present his case; or

(b) if the judgment was given without provisions corresponding to those of section 12 above having been complied with and the United Kingdom has not entered an appearance or applied to have the judgment set aside.

(2) A court need not give effect to section 18 above in the case of a judgment:

(a) if proceedings between the same parties, based on the same facts and having the same purpose:

(i) are pending before a court in the United Kingdom and were the first to be instituted; or

(ii) are pending before a court in another State party to the Convention, were the first to be instituted and may result in a judgment to which that section will apply; or

(b) if the result of the judgment is inconsistent with the result of another judgment given in proceedings between the same parties and:

(i) the other judgment is by a court in the United Kingdom and either those proceedings were the first to be instituted or the judgment of that court was given before the first-mentioned judgment became final within the meaning of subsection (1)(b) of section 18 above; or

(ii) the other judgment is by a court in another State party to the Convention and that section has already become applicable to it.

(3) Where the judgment was given against the United Kingdom in proceedings in respect of which the United Kingdom was not entitled to immunity by virtue of a provision corresponding to section 6(2) above, a court need not give effect to section 18 above in respect of the judgment if the court that gave the judgment:

(a) would not have had jurisdiction in the matter if it had applied rules of jurisdiction corresponding to those applicable to such matters in the United Kingdom; or

(b) applied a law other than that indicated by the United Kingdom rules of private international law and would have reached a different conclusion if it had applied the law so indicated.

(4) In subsection (2) above references to a court in the United Kingdom include references to a court in any dependent territory in respect of which the United Kingdom is a party to the Convention, and references to a court in another State party to the Convention include references to a court in any territory in respect of which it is a party.

Part III

MISCELLANEOUS AND SUPPLEMENTARY

20.   (1) Subject to the provisions of this section and to any necessary modifications, the Diplomatic Privileges Act 1964 shall apply to:

(a) a sovereign or other head of State;

(b) members of his family forming part of his household; and

(c) his private servants,

as it applies to the head of a diplomatic mission, to members of his family forming part of his household and to his private servants.

(2) The immunities and privileges conferred by virtue of subsection (1)(a) and (b) above shall not be subject to the restrictions by reference to nationality or residence mentioned in Article 37(1) or 38 in Schedule 1 to the said Act of 1964.

(3) Subject to any direction to the contrary by the Secretary of State, a person on whom immunities and privileges are conferred by virtue of subsection (1) above shall be entitled to the exemption conferred by section 8(3) of the Immigration Act 1971.

(4) Except as respects value added tax and duties of customs or excise, this section does not affect any question whether a person is exempt from, or immune as respects proceedings relating to, taxation.

(5) This section applies to the sovereign or other head of any State on which immunities and privileges are conferred by Part I of this Act and is without prejudice to the application of that Part to any such sovereign or head of State in his public capacity.

21.   A certificate by or on behalf of the Secretary of State shall be conclusive evidence on any question:

(a) whether any country is a State for the purposes of Part I of this Act, whether any territory is a constituent territory of a federal State for those purposes or as to the person or persons to be regarded for those purposes as the head or government of a State;

(b) whether a State is a party to the Brussels Convention mentioned in Part I of this Act;

(c) whether a State is a party to the European Convention on State Immunity, whether it had made a declaration under Article 24 of that Convention or as to the territories in respect of which the United Kingdom or any other State is a party;

(d) whether, and if so when, a document has been served or received as mentioned in section 12(1) or (5) above.

22. (1) In this Act "court" includes any tribunal or body exercising judicial functions; and references to the courts or law of the United Kingdom include references to the courts or law of any part of the United Kingdom.

(2) In this Act references to entry of appearance and judgments in default of appearance include references to any corresponding procedures.

(3) In this Act "the European Convention on State Immunity" means the Convention of that name signed in Basle on 16th May 1972.

(4) In this Act "dependent territory" means:

(a) any of the Channel Islands;

(b) the Isle of Man;

(c) any colony other than one for whose external relations a country other than the United Kingdom is responsible; or

(d) any country or territory outside Her Majesty's dominions in which Her Majesty has jurisdiction in right of the government of the United Kingdom.

(5) Any power conferred by this Act to make an Order in Council includes power to vary or revoke a previous Order.

23. (1) This Act may be cited as the State Immunity Act 1978.

(2) Section 13 of the Administration of Justice (Miscellaneous Provisions) Act 1938 and section 7 of the Law Reform (Miscellaneous Provisions) (Scotland) Act 1940 (which become unnecessary in consequence of Part I of this Act) are hereby repealed

(3) Subject to subsection (4) below, Parts I and II of this Act do not apply to proceedings in respect of matters that occurred before the date of the coming into force of this Act and, in particular:

(a) sections 2(2) and 13(3) do not apply to any prior agreement, and

(b) sections 3, 4 and 9 do not apply to any transaction, contract or arbitration agreement,

entered into before that date.

(4) Section 12 above applies to any proceedings instituted after the coming into force of this Act.

(5) This Act shall come into force on such date as may be specified by an order made by the Lord Chancellor by statutory instrument.

(6) This Act extends to Northern Ireland.

(7) Her Majesty may by Order in Council extend any of the provisions of this Act, with or without modification, to any dependent territory.

EUROPEAN CONVENTION ON STATE IMMUNITY AND ADDITIONAL PROTOCOL*

Preamble

The member States of the Council of Europe, signatory hereto,

Considering that the aim of the Council of Europe is to achieve a greater unity between its Members;

Taking into account the fact that there is in international law a tendency to restrict the cases in which a State may claim immunity before foreign courts;

Desiring to establish in their mutual relations common rules relating to the scope of the immunity of one State from the jurisdiction of the courts of another State, and designed to ensure compliance with judgments given against another State;

Considering that the adoption of such rules will tend to advance the work of harmonisation undertaken by the member States of the Council of Europe in the legal field,

Have agreed as follows:

Chapter I. Immunity from Jurisdiction

Article 1

1. A Contracting State which institutes or intervenes in proceedings before a court of another Contracting State submits, for the purpose of those proceedings, to the jurisdiction of the courts of that State.

2. Such a Contracting State cannot claim immunity from the jurisdiction of the courts of the other Contracting State in respect of any counterclaim:

(a) arising out of the legal relationship or the facts on which the principal claim is based;

(b) if, according to the provisions of this Convention, it would not have been entitled to invoke immunity in respect of that counterclaim had separate proceedings been brought against it in those courts.

3. A Contracting State which makes a counterclaim in proceedings before a court of another Contracting State submits to the jurisdiction of the courts of that State with respect not only to the counterclaim but also to the principal claim.

Article 2

A Contracting State cannot claim immunity from the jurisdiction of a court of another Contracting State if it has undertaken to submit to the jurisdiction of that court either:

* *Council of Europe,* No. 74 (1972).

(a) by international agreement;

(b) by an express term contained in a contract in writing; or

(c) by an express consent given after a dispute between the parties has arisen.

Article 3

1. A Contracting State cannot claim immunity from the jurisdiction of a court of another Contracting State if, before claiming immunity, it takes any step in the proceedings relating to the merits. However, if the State satisfies the court that it could not have acquired knowledge of facts on which a claim to immunity can be based until after it has taken such a step, it can claim immunity based on these facts if it does so at the earliest possible moment.

2. A Contracting State is not deemed to have waived immunity if it appears before a court of another Contracting State in order to assert immunity.

Article 4

1. Subject to the provisions of Article 5, a Contracting State cannot claim immunity from the jurisdiction of the courts of another Contracting State if the proceedings relate to an obligation of the State, which, by virtue of a contract, fails to be discharged in the territory of the State of the forum.

2. Paragraph 1 shall not apply:

(a) in the case of a contract concluded between States;

(b) if the parties to the contract have otherwise agreed in writing;

(c) if the State is party to a contract concluded on its territory and the obligation of the State is governed by its administrative law.

Article 5

1. A Contracting State cannot claim immunity from the jurisdiction of a court of another Contracting State if the proceedings relate to a contract of employment between the State and an individual where the work has to be performed on the territory of the State of the forum.

2. Paragraph 1 shall not apply where:

(a) the individual is a national of the employing State at the time when the proceedings are brought;

(b) at the time when the contract was entered into the individual was neither a national of the State of the forum nor habitually resident in that State; or

(c) the parties to the contract have otherwise agreed in writing, unless, in accordance with the law of the State of the forum, the courts of that State have exclusive jurisdiction by reason of the subject-matter.

3.   Where the work is done for an office, agency or other establishment referred to in Article 7, paragraphs 2(a) and (b) of the present Article apply only if, at the time the contract was entered into, the individual had his habitual residence in the Contracting State which employs him.

Article 6

1.   A Contracting State cannot claim immunity from the jurisdiction of a court of another Contracting State if it participates with one or more private persons in a company, association or other legal entity having its seat, registered office or principal place of business on the territory of the State of the forum, and the proceedings concern the relationship, in matters arising out of that participation, between the State on the one hand and the entity or any other participant on the other hand.

2.   Paragraph 1 shall not apply if it is otherwise agreed in writing.

Article 7

1.   A Contracting State cannot claim immunity from the jurisdiction of a court of another Contracting State if it has on the territory of the State of the forum an office, agency or other establishment through which it engages, in the same manner as a private person, in an industrial, commercial or financial activity, and the proceedings relate to that activity of the office, agency or establishment.

2.   Paragraph 1 shall not apply if all the parties to the dispute are States, or if the parties have otherwise agreed in writing.

Article 8

A Contracting State cannot claim immunity from the jurisdiction of a court of another Contracting State if the proceedings relate:

(a) to a patent, industrial design, trade-mark, service mark or other similar right which, in the State of the forum, has been applied for, registered or deposited or is otherwise protected, and in respect of which the State is the applicant or owner;

(b) to an alleged infringement by it, in the territory of the State of the forum, of such a right belonging to a third person and protected in that State;

(c) to an alleged infringement by it, in the territory of the State of the forum, of copyright belonging to a third person and protected in that State;

(d) to the right to use a trade name in the State of the forum.

Article 9

A Contracting State cannot claim immunity from the jurisdiction of a court of another Contracting State if the proceedings relate to:

> (a) its rights or interests in, or its use or possession of, immovable property;

or

> (b) its obligations arising out of its rights or interests in, or use or possession of, immovable property

and the property is situated in the territory of the State of the forum.

Article 10

A Contracting State cannot claim immunity from the jurisdiction of a court of another Contracting State if the proceedings relate to a right in movable or immovable property arising by way of succession, gift or bona vacantia.

Article 11

A Contracting State cannot claim immunity from the jurisdiction of a court of another Contracting State in proceedings which relate to redress for injury to the person or damage to tangible property, if the facts which occasioned the injury or damage occurred in the territory of the State of the forum, and if the author of the injury or damage was present in that territory at the time when those facts occurred.

Article 12

1. Where a Contracting State has agreed in writing to submit to arbitration a dispute which has arisen or may arise out of a civil or commercial matter, that State may not claim immunity from the jurisdiction of a court of another Contracting State on the territory or according to the law of which the arbitration has taken or will take place in respect of any proceedings relating to:

> (a) the validity or interpretation of the arbitration agreement;
>
> (b) the arbitration procedure;
>
> (c) the setting aside of the award,

unless the arbitration agreement otherwise provides.

2. Paragraph 1 shall not apply to an arbitration agreement between States.

Article 13

Paragraph 1 of Article 1 shall not apply where a Contracting State asserts, in proceedings pending before a court of another Contracting State to which it is not a party, that it has a right or interest in property which is the subject-matter of the proceedings, and the circumstances are such that it would have been entitled to immunity if the proceedings had been brought against it.

Article 14

Nothing in this Convention shall be interpreted as preventing a court of a Contracting State from administering or supervising or arranging for the administration of property, such as trust property or the estate of a bankrupt, solely on account of the fact that another Contracting State has a right or interest in the property.

Article 15

A Contracting State shall be entitled to immunity from the jurisdiction of the courts of another Contracting State if the proceedings do not fall within Articles 1 to 14; the court shall decline to entertain such proceedings even if the State does not appear.

Chapter II. Procedural Rules

Article 16

1.   In proceedings against a Contracting State in a court of another Contracting State, the following rules shall apply.

2.   The competent authorities of the State of the forum shall transmit

the original or a copy of the document by which the proceedings are instituted;

a copy of any judgment given by default against a State which was defendant in the proceedings,

through the diplomatic channel to the Ministry of Foreign Affairs of the defendant State, for onward transmission, where appropriate, to the competent authority. These documents shall be accompanied, if necessary, by a translation into the official language, or one of the official languages, of the defendant State.

3.   Service of the documents referred to in paragraph 2 is deemed to have been effected by their receipt by the Ministry of Foreign Affairs.

4.   The time-limits within which the State must enter an appearance or appeal against any judgment given by default shall begin to run two months after the date on which the document by which the proceedings were instituted or the copy of the judgment is received by the Ministry of Foreign Affairs.

5.   If it rests with the court to prescribe the time-limits for entering an appearance or for appealing against a judgment given by default, the court shall allow the State not less than two months after the date on which the document by which the proceedings are instituted or the copy of the judgment is received by the Ministry of Foreign Affairs.

6.   A Contracting State which appears in the proceedings is deemed to have waived any objection to the method of service.

7.   If the Contracting State has not appeared, judgment by default may be given against it only if it is established that the document by which the proceedings were instituted has been transmitted in conformi-

ty with paragraph 2, and that the time-limits for entering an appearance provided for in paragraphs 4 and 5 have been observed.

Article 17

No security, bond or deposit, however described, which could not have been required in the State of the forum of a national of that State or a person domiciled or resident there, shall be required of a Contracting State to guarantee the payment of judicial costs or expenses. A State which is a claimant in the courts of another Contracting State shall pay any judicial costs or expenses for which it may become liable.

Article 18

A Contracting State party to proceedings before a court of another Contracting State may not be subjected to any measure of coercion, or any penalty, by reason of its failure or refusal to disclose any documents or other evidence. However the court may draw any conclusion it thinks fit from such failure or refusal.

Article 19

1. A court before which proceedings to which a Contracting State is a party are instituted shall, at the request of one of the parties or, if its national law so permits, of its own motion, decline to proceed with the case or shall stay the proceedings if other proceedings between the same parties, based on the same facts and having the same purpose.

(a) are pending before a court of that Contracting State, and were the first to be instituted; or

(b) are pending before a court of any other Contracting State, were the first to be instituted and may result in a judgment to which the State party to the proceedings must give effect by virtue of Article 20 or Article 25.

2. Any Contracting State whose law gives the courts a discretion to decline to proceed with a case or to stay the proceedings in cases where proceedings between the same parties, based on the same facts and having the same purpose, are pending before a court of another Contracting State, may, by notification addressed to the Secretary General of the Council of Europe, declare that its courts shall not be bound by the provisions of paragraph 1.

Chapter III. Effect of Judgment

Article 20

1. A Contracting State shall give effect to a judgment given against it by a court of another Contracting State:

(a) if, in accordance with the provisions of Articles 1 to 13, the State could not claim immunity from jurisdiction; and

(b) if the judgment cannot or can no longer be set aside if obtained by default, or if it is not or is no longer subject to appeal or any other form of ordinary review or to annulment.

2. Nevertheless, a Contracting State is not obliged to give effect to such a judgment in any case:

(a) where it would be manifestly contrary to public policy in that State to do so, or where, in the circumstances, either party had no adequate opportunity fairly to present his case;

(b) where proceedings between the same parties, based on the same facts and having the same purpose:

(i) are pending before a court of that State and were the first to be instituted;

(ii) are pending before a court of another Contracting State, were the first to be instituted and may result in a judgment to which the State party to the proceedings must give effect under the terms of this Convention;

(c) where the result of the judgment is inconsistent with the result of another judgment given between the same parties:

(i) by a court of the Contracting State, if the proceedings before that court were the first to be instituted or if the other judgment has been given before the judgment satisfied the conditions specified in paragraph 1(b); or

(ii) by a court of another Contracting State where the other judgment is the first to satisfy the requirements laid down in the present Convention;

(d) where the provisions of Article 16 have not been observed and the State has not entered an appearance or has not appealed against a judgment by default.

3. In addition, in the cases provided for in Article 10, a Contracting State is not obliged to give effect to the judgment:

(a) if the courts of the State of the forum would not have been entitled to assume jurisdiction had they applied, *mutatis mutandis,* the rules of jurisdiction (other than those mentioned in the Annex to the present Convention) which operate in the State against which judgment is given; or

(b) if the court, by applying a law other than that which would have been applied in accordance with the rules of private international law of that State, has reached a result different from that which would have been reached by applying the law determined by those rules.

However, a Contracting State may not rely upon the grounds of refusal specified in sub-paragraphs (a) and (b) above if it is bound by an agreement with the State of the forum on the recognition and enforcement of judgments and the judgment fulfils the requirement of that agreement as regards jurisdiction and, where appropriate, the law applied.

Article 21

1. Where a judgment has been given against a Contracting State and that State does not give effect thereto, the party which seeks to invoke the judgment shall be entitled to have determined by the competent court of that State the question whether effect should be given to the judgment in accordance with Article 20. Proceedings may also be brought before this court by the State against which judgment has been given, if its law so permits.

2. Save in so far as may be necessary for the application of Article 20, the competent court of the State in question may not review the merits of the judgment.

3. Where proceedings are instituted before a court of a State in accordance with paragraph 1:

(a) the parties shall be given an opportunity to be heard in the proceedings;

(b) documents produced by the party seeking to invoke the judgment shall not be subject to legalisation or any other like formality;

(c) no security, bond or deposit, however described, shall be required of the party invoking the judgment by reason of his nationality, domicile or residence;

(d) the party invoking the judgment shall be entitled to legal aid under conditions no less favourable than those applicable to nationals of the State who are domiciled and resident therein.

4. Each Contracting State shall, when depositing its instrument of ratification, acceptance or accession, designate the court or courts referred to in paragraph 1, and inform the Secretary General of the Council of Europe thereof.

Article 22

1. A Contracting State shall give effect to a settlement to which it is a party and which has been made before a court of another Contracting State in the course of the proceedings; the provisions of Article 20 do not apply to such a settlement.

2. If the State does not give effect to the settlement, the procedure provided for in Article 21 may be used.

Article 23

No measures of execution or preventive measures against the property of a Contracting State may be taken in the territory of another Contracting State except where and to the extent that the State has expressly consented thereto in writing in any particular case.

Chapter IV. Optional Provisions

Article 24

1. Notwithstanding the provisions of Article 15, any State may, when signing this Convention or depositing its instrument of ratification, acceptance or accession, or at any later date, by notification addressed to the Secretary General of the Council of Europe, declare that, in cases not falling within Articles 1 to 13, its courts shall be entitled to entertain proceedings against another Contracting State to the extent that its courts are entitled to entertain proceedings against States not Party to the present Convention. Such a declaration shall be without prejudice to the immunity from jurisdiction which foreign States enjoy in respect of acts performed in the exercise of sovereign authority (*acta jure imperii*).

2. The courts of a State which has made the declaration provided for in paragraph 1 shall not however be entitled to entertain such proceedings against another Contracting State if their jurisdiction could have been based solely on one or more of the grounds mentioned in the Annex to the present Convention, unless that other Contracting State has taken a step in the proceedings relating to the merits without first challenging the jurisdiction of the court.

3. The provisions of Chapter II apply to proceedings instituted against a Contracting State in accordance with the present Article.

4. The declaration made under paragraph 1 may be withdrawn by notification addressed to the Secretary General of the Council of Europe. The withdrawal shall take effect three months after the date of its receipt, but this shall not affect proceedings instituted before the date on which the withdrawal becomes effective.

Article 25

1. Any Contracting State which has made a declaration under Article 24 shall, in cases not falling within Articles 1 to 13, give effect to a judgment given by a court of another Contracting State which has made a like declaration:

    (a) if the conditions prescribed in paragraph 1(b) of Article 20 have been fulfilled, and

    (b) if the court is considered to have jurisdiction in accordance with the following paragraphs.

2. However, the Contracting State is not obliged to give effect to such a judgment:

    (a) if there is a ground for refusal as provided for in paragraph 2 of Article 20; or

    (b) if the provisions of paragraph 2 of Article 24 have not been observed.

3. Subject to the provisions of paragraph 4, a court of a Contracting State shall be considered to have jurisdiction for the purpose of paragraph 1(b):

(a) if its jurisdiction is recognised in accordance with the provisions of an agreement to which the State of the forum and the other Contracting State are Parties;

(b) where there is no agreement between the two States concerning the recognition and enforcement of judgments in civil matters, if the courts of the State of the forum would have been entitled to assume jurisdiction had they applied, *mutatis mutandis,* the rules of jurisdiction (other than those mentioned in the Annex to the present Convention) which operate in the State against which the judgment was given. This provision does not apply to questions arising out of contracts.

4. The Contracting States having made the declaration provided for in Article 24 may, by means of a supplementary agreement to this Convention, determine the circumstances in which their courts shall be considered to have jurisdiction for the purposes of paragraph 1(b) of this Article.

5. If the Contracting State does not give effect to the judgment, the procedure provided for in Article 21 may be used.

Article 26

Notwithstanding the provisions of Article 23, a judgment rendered against a Contracting State in proceedings relating to an industrial or commercial activity, in which the State is engaged in the same manner as a private person, may be enforced in the State of the forum against property of the State against which judgment has been given, used exclusively in connection with such an activity, if

(a) both the State of the forum and the State against which the judgment has been given have made declarations under Article 24;

(b) the proceedings which resulted in the judgment fell within Articles 1 to 13 or were instituted in accordance with paragraphs 1 and 2 of Article 24; and

(c) the judgment satisfies the requirements laid down in paragraph 1(b) of Article 20.

Chapter V. General Provisions

Article 27

1. For the purposes of the present Convention, the expression "Contracting State" shall not include any legal entity of a Contracting State which is distinct therefrom and is capable of suing or being sued, even if that entity has been entrusted with public functions.

2. Proceedings may be instituted against any entity referred to in paragraph 1 before the courts of another Contracting State in the same

manner as against a private person; however, the courts may not entertain proceedings in respect of acts performed by the entity in the exercise of sovereign authority (*acta jure imperii*).

3. Proceedings may in any event be instituted against any such entity before those courts if, in corresponding circumstances, the courts would have had jurisdiction if the proceedings had been instituted against a Contracting State.

Article 28

1. Without prejudice to the provisions of Article 27, the constituent States of a Federal State do not enjoy immunity.

2. However, a Federal State Party to the present Convention, may, by notification addressed to the Secretary General of the Council of Europe, declare that its constituent States may invoke the provisions of the Convention applicable to Contracting States, and have the same obligations.

3. Where a Federal State has made a declaration in accordance with paragraph 2, service of documents on a constituent State of a Federation shall be made on the Ministry of Foreign Affairs of the Federal State, in conformity with Article 16.

4. The Federal State alone is competent to make the declarations, notifications and communications provided for in the present Convention, and the Federal State alone may be party to proceedings pursuant to Article 34.

Article 29

The present Convention shall not apply to proceedings concerning:

    (a) social security;

    (b) damage or injury in nuclear matters;

    (c) customs duties, taxes or penalties.

Article 30

The present Convention shall not apply to proceedings in respect of claims relating to the operation of seagoing vessels owned or operated by a Contracting State or to the carriage of cargoes and of passengers by such vessels or to the carriage of cargoes owned by a Contracting State and carried on board merchant vessels.

Article 31

Nothing in this Convention shall affect any immunities or privileges enjoyed by a Contracting State in respect of anything done or omitted to be done by, or in relation to, its armed forces when on the territory of another Contracting State.

Article 32

Nothing in the present Convention shall affect privileges and immunities relating to the exercise of the functions of diplomatic missions and consular posts and of persons connected with them.

Article 33

Nothing in the present Convention shall affect existing or future international agreements in special fields which relate to matters dealt with in the present Convention.

Article 34

1. Any dispute which might arise between two or more Contracting States concerning the interpretation or application of the present Convention shall be submitted to the International Court of Justice on the application of one of the parties to the dispute or by special agreement unless the parties agree on a different method of peaceful settlement of the dispute.

2. However, proceedings may not be instituted before the International Court of Justice which relate to:

(a) a dispute concerning a question arising in proceedings instituted against a Contracting State before a court of another Contracting State, before the court has given a judgment which fulfils the condition provided for in paragraph 1(b) of Article 20;

(b) a dispute concerning a question arising in proceedings instituted before a court of a Contracting State in accordance with paragraph 1 of Article 21, before the court has rendered a final decision in such proceedings.

Article 35

1. The present Convention shall apply only to proceedings introduced after its entry into force.

2. When a State has become Party to this Convention after it has entered into force, the Convention shall apply only to proceedings introduced after it has entered into force with respect to that State.

3. Nothing in this Convention shall apply to proceedings arising out of, or judgments based on, acts, omissions or facts prior to the date on which the present Convention is opened for signature.

Chapter VI. Final Provisions

Article 36

1. The present Convention shall be open to signature by the member States of the Council of Europe. It shall be subject to ratification or acceptance. Instruments of ratification or acceptance shall be deposited with the Secretary General of the Council of Europe.

2.   The Convention shall enter into force three months after the date of the deposit of the third instrument of ratification or acceptance.

3.   In respect of a signatory State ratifying or accepting subsequently, the Convention shall enter into force three months after the date of the deposit of its instrument of ratification or acceptance.

Article 37

1.   After the entry into force of the present Convention, the Committee of Ministers of the Council of Europe may, by a decision taken by a unanimous vote of the members casting a vote, invite any non-member State to accede thereto.

2.   Such accession shall be effected by depositing with the Secretary General of the Council of Europe an instrument of accession which shall take effect three months after the date of its deposit.

3.   However, if a State having already acceded to the Convention notifies the Secretary General of the Council of Europe of its objection to the accession of another non-member State, before the entry into force of this accession, the Convention shall not apply to the relations between these two States.

Article 38

1.   Any State may, at the time of signature or when depositing its instrument of ratification, acceptance or accession, specify the territory or territories to which the present Convention shall apply.

2.   Any State may, when depositing its instrument of ratification, acceptance or accession or at any later date, by declaration addressed to the Secretary General of the Council of Europe, extend this Convention to any other territory or territories specified in the declaration and for whose international relations it is responsible or on whose behalf it is authorised to give undertakings.

3.   Any declaration made in pursuance of the preceding paragraph may, in respect of any territory mentioned in such declaration, be withdrawn according to the procedure laid down in Article 40 of this Convention.

Article 39

No reservation is permitted to the present Convention.

Article 40

1.   Any Contracting State may, in so far as it is concerned, denounce this Convention by means of a notification addressed to the Secretary General of the Council of Europe.

2.   Such denunciation shall take effect six months after the date of receipt by the Secretary General of such notification. This Convention shall, however, continue to apply to proceedings introduced before the

date on which the denunciation takes effect, and to judgments given in such proceedings.

Article 41

The Secretary General of the Council of Europe shall notify the member States of the Council of Europe and any State which has acceded to this Convention of:

(a) any signature;

(b) any deposit of an instrument of ratification, acceptance or accession;

(c) any date of entry into force of this Convention in accordance with Articles 36 and 37 thereof;

(d) any notification received in pursuance of the provisions of paragraph 2 of Article 19;

(e) any communication received in pursuance of the provisions of paragraph 4 of Article 21;

(f) any notification received in pursuance of the provisions of paragraph 1 of Article 24;

(g) the withdrawal of any notification made in pursuance of the provisions of paragraph 4 of Article 24;

(h) any notification received in pursuance of the provisions of paragraph 2 of Article 28;

(i) any notification received in pursuance of the provisions of paragraph 3 of Article 37;

(j) any declaration received in pursuance of the provisions of Article 38;

(k) any notification received in pursuance of the provisions of Article 40 and the date on which denunciation takes effect.

Annex

The grounds of jurisdiction referred to in paragraph 3, sub-paragraph (a), of Article 20, paragraph 2 of Article 24 and paragraph 3, sub-paragraph (b), of Article 25 are the following:

(a) the presence in the territory of the State of the forum of property belonging to the defendant, or the seizure by the plaintiff of property situated there, unless

the action is brought to assert proprietary or possessory rights in that property, or arises from another issue relating to such property; or

the property constitutes the security for a debt which is the subject-matter of the action;

(b) the nationality of the plaintiff;

(c) the domicile, habitual residence or ordinary residence of the plaintiff within the territory of the State of the forum unless the assumption of jurisdiction on such a ground is permitted by way of an exception made on account of the particular subject-matter of a class of contracts;

(d) the fact that the defendant carried on business within the territory of the State of the forum, unless the action arises from that business;

(e) a unilateral specification of the forum by the plaintiff, particularly in an invoice.

A legal person shall be considered to have its domicile or habitual residence where it has its seat, registered office or principal place of business.

ADDITIONAL PROTOCOL TO THE EUROPEAN CONVENTION ON STATE IMMUNITY

The member States of the Council of Europe, signatory to the present Protocol,

Having taken note of the European Convention on State Immunity—hereinafter referred to as "the Convention"—and in particular Articles 21 and 34 thereof;

Desiring to develop the work of harmonisation in the field covered by the Convention by the addition of provisions concerning a European procedure for the settlement of disputes,

Have agreed as follows:

Part I

Article 1

1. Where a judgment has been given against a State Party to the Convention and that State does not give effect thereto, the party which seeks to invoke the judgment shall be entitled to have determined the question whether effect should be given to the judgment in conformity with Article 20 or Article 25 of the Convention, by instituting proceedings before either:

(a) the competent court of that State in application of Article 21 of the Convention; or

(b) the European Tribunal constituted in conformity with the provisions of Part III of the present Protocol, provided that that State is a Party to the present Protocol and has not made the declaration referred to in Part IV thereof.

The choice between these two possibilities shall be final.

2. If the State intends to institute proceedings before its court in accordance with the provisions of paragraph 1 of Article 21 of the Convention it must give notice of its intention to do so to the party in whose favour the judgment has been given; the State may thereafter

institute such proceedings before the European Tribunal. Once this period has elapsed, the party in whose favour the judgment has been given may no longer institute proceedings before the European Tribunal.

3. Save in so far as may be necessary for the application of Articles 20 and 25 of the Convention, the European Tribunal may not review the merits of the judgment.

Part II

Article 2

1. Any dispute which might arise between two or more States Parties to the present Protocol concerning the interpretation or application of the Convention shall be submitted, on the application of one of the parties to the dispute or by special agreement, to the European Tribunal constituted in conformity with the provisions of Part III of the present Protocol. The States Parties to the present Protocol undertake not to submit such a dispute to a different mode of settlement.

2. If the dispute concerns a question arising in proceedings instituted before a court of one State Party to the Convention against another State Party to the Convention, or a question arising in proceedings instituted before a court of a State Party to the Convention in accordance with Article 21 of the Convention, it may not be referred to the European Tribunal until the court has given a final decision in such proceedings.

3. Proceedings may not be instituted before the European Tribunal which relate to a dispute concerning a judgment which it has already determined or is required to determine by virtue of Part I of this Protocol.

Article 3

Nothing in the present Protocol shall be interpreted as preventing the European Tribunal from determining any dispute which might arise between two or more States Parties to the Convention concerning the interpretation or application thereof and which might be submitted to it by special agreement, even if these States, or any of them, are not Parties to the present Protocol.

Part III

Article 4

1. There shall be established a European Tribunal in matters of State Immunity to determine cases brought before it in conformity with the provisions of Parts I and II of the present Protocol.

2. The European Tribunal shall consist of the members of the European Court of Human Rights and, in respect of each non-member State of the Council of Europe which has acceded to the present Protocol, a person possessing the qualifications required of members of that Court designated, with the agreement of the Committee of Minis-

ters of the Council of Europe, by the government of that State for a period of nine years.

3. The President of the European Tribunal shall be the President of the European Court of Human Rights.

Article 5

1. Where proceedings are instituted before the European Tribunal in accordance with the provisions of Part I of the present Protocol, the European Tribunal shall consist of a Chamber composed of seven members. There shall sit as *ex officio* members of the Chamber the member of the European Tribunal who is a national of the State against which the judgment has been given and the member of the European Tribunal who is a national of the State of the forum, or, should there be no such member in one or the other case, a person designated by the government of the State concerned to sit in the capacity of a member of the Chamber. The names of the other five members shall be chosen by lot by the President of the European Tribunal in the presence of the Registrar.

2. Where proceedings are instituted before the European Tribunal in accordance with the provisions of Part II of the present Protocol, the Chamber shall be constituted in the manner provided for in the preceding paragraph. However, there shall sit as *ex officio* members of the Chamber the members of the European Tribunal who are nationals of the States parties to the dispute or, should there be no such member, a person designated by the government of the State concerned to sit in the capacity of a member of the Chamber.

3. Where a case pending before a Chamber raises a serious question affecting the interpretation of the Convention or of the present Protocol, the Chamber may, at any time, relinquish jurisdiction in favour of the European Tribunal meeting in plenary session. The relinquishment of jurisdiction shall be obligatory where the resolution of such question might have a result inconsistent with a judgment previously delivered by a Chamber or by the European Tribunal meeting in plenary session. The relinquishment of jurisdiction shall be final. Reasons need not be given for the decision to relinquish jurisdiction.

Article 6

1. The European Tribunal shall decide any disputes as to whether the Tribunal has jurisdiction.

2. The hearings of the European Tribunal shall be public unless the Tribunal in exceptional circumstances decides otherwise.

3. The judgments of the European Tribunal, taken by a majority of the members present, are to be delivered in public session. Reasons shall be given for the judgment of the European Tribunal. If the judgment does not represent in whole or in part the unanimous opinion of the European Tribunal, any member shall be entitled to deliver a separate opinion.

4.   The judgments of the European Tribunal shall be final and binding upon the parties.

Article 7

1.   The European Tribunal shall draw up its own rules and fix its own procedure.

2.   The Registry of the European Tribunal shall be provided by the Registrar of the European Court of Human Rights.

Article 8

1.   The operating costs of the European Tribunal shall be borne by the Council of Europe. States non-members of the Council of Europe having acceded to the present Protocol shall contribute thereto in a manner to be decided by the Committee of Ministers after agreement with these States.

2.   The members of the European Tribunal shall receive for each day of duty a compensation to be determined by the Committee of Ministers.

l'art IV

Article 9

1.   Any State may, by notification addressed to the Secretary General of the Council of Europe at the moment of its signature of the present Protocol, or of the deposit of its instrument of ratification, acceptance or accession thereto, declare that it will only be bound by Parts II to V of the present Protocol.

2.   Such a notification may be withdrawn at any time.

Part V

Article 10

1.   The present Protocol shall be open to signature by the member States of the Council of Europe which have signed the Convention. It shall be subject to ratification or acceptance. Instruments of ratification or acceptance shall be deposited with the Secretary General of the Council of Europe.

2.   The present Protocol shall enter into force three months after the date of the deposit of the fifth instrument of ratification or acceptance.

3.   In respect of a signatory State ratifying or accepting subsequently, the Protocol shall enter into force three months after the date of the deposit of its instrument of ratification or acceptance.

4.   A member State of the Council of Europe may not ratify or accept the present Protocol without having ratified or accepted the Convention.

Article 11

1. A State which has acceded to the Convention may accede to the present Protocol after the Protocol has entered into force.

2. Such accession shall be effected by depositing with the Secretary General of the Council of Europe an instrument of accession which shall take effect three months after the date of its deposit.

Article 12

No reservation is permitted to the present Protocol.

Article 13

1. Any Contracting State may, in so far as it is concerned, denounce the present Protocol by means of a notification addressed to the Secretary General of the Council of Europe.

2. Such denunciation shall take effect six months after the date of receipt by the Secretary General of such notification. The Protocol shall, however, continue to apply to proceedings introduced in conformity with the provisions of the Protocol before the date on which such denunciation takes effect.

3. Denunciation of the Convention shall automatically entail denunciation of the present Protocol.

Article 14

The Secretary General of the Council of Europe shall notify the member States of the Council and any State which has acceded to the Convention of:

(a) any signature of the present Protocol;

(b) any deposit of an instrument of ratification, acceptance or accession;

(c) any date of entry into force of the present Protocol in accordance with Articles 10 and 11 thereof;

(d) any notification received in pursuance of the provisions of Part IV and any withdrawal of any such notification;

(e) any notification received in pursuance of the provisions of Article 13 and the date on which such denunciation takes effect.

In witness whereof the undersigned, being duly authorised thereto, have signed the present Protocol.

Done at Basle, this 16th day of May 1972, in English and French, both texts being equally authoritative, in a single copy which shall remain deposited in the archives of the Council of Europe. The Secretary General of the Council of Europe shall transmit certified copies to each of the signatory and acceding States.

RESOLUTION (72) 2 OF THE COMMITTEE OF MINISTERS OF THE COUNCIL OF EUROPE CONCERNING THE EUROPEAN CONVENTION ON STATE IMMUNITY ADOPTED AT THE 206TH MEETING OF THE MINISTERS' DEPUTIES ON 18 JANUARY 1972

The Committee of Ministers of the Council of Europe,

Having taken note of the text of the European Convention on State Immunity;

Considering that one of the aims of this Convention is to ensure compliance with judgments given against a State,

Recommends the governments of those member States which shall become Parties to this Convention to establish, for the purpose of Article 21 of the Convention, a procedure which shall be as expeditious and simple as possible.

ALIEN TORT STATUTE

28 U.S.C. § 1350. Alien's action for tort

The district courts shall have original jurisdiction of any civil action by an alien for a tort only, committed in violation of the law of nations or a treaty of the United States.

TORTURE VICTIM PROTECTION ACT
(1992)

Section 1. Short Title.

This Act may be cited as the "Torture Victim Protection Act of 1991".

Section 2. Establishment of Civil Action.

(a) *Liability*.—An individual who, under actual or apparent authority, or color of law, of any foreign nation—

(1) subjects an individual to torture shall, in a civil action, be liable for damages to that individual; or

(2) subjects an individual to extrajudicial killing shall, in a civil action, be liable for damages to the individual's legal representative, or to any person who may be a claimant in an action for wrongful death.

(b) *Exhaustion of Remedies*.—A court shall decline to hear a claim under this section if the claimant has not exhausted adequate and available remedies in the place in which the conduct giving rise to the claim occurred.

(c) *Statute of Limitations*.—No action shall be maintained under this section unless it is commenced within 10 years after the cause of action arose.

Section 3. Definitions.

(a) *Extrajudicial Killing*.—For the purposes of this Act, the term "extrajudicial killing" means a deliberated killing not authorized by a previous judgment pronounced by a regularly constituted court affording all the judicial guarantees which are recognized as indispensable by civilized peoples. Such term, however, does not include any such killing that, under international law, is lawfully carried out under the authority of a foreign nation.

(b) *Torture*.—For the purposes of this Act—

(1) the term "torture" means any act, directed against an individual in the offender's custody or physical control, by which severe pain or suffering (other than pain or suffering arising only from or inherent in, or incidental to, lawful sanctions), whether physical or mental, is intentionally inflicted on that individual for such purposes as obtaining from that individual or a third person information or a confession, punishing that individual for an act that individual or a third person has commit-

ted or is suspected of having committed, intimidating or coercing that individual or a third person, or for any reason based on discrimination of any kind; and

(2) mental pain or suffering refers to prolonged mental harm caused by or resulting from—

(A) the intentional infliction or threatened infliction of severe physical pain or suffering;

(B) the administration or application, or threatened administration or application, of mind altering substances or other procedures calculated to disrupt profoundly the senses or the personality;

(C) the threat of imminent death; or

(D) the threat that another individual will imminently be subjected to death, severe physical pain or suffering, or the administration or application of mind altering substances or other procedures calculated to disrupt profoundly the senses or personality.

VICTIMS OF TRAFFICKING AND VIOLENCE PROTECTION ACT OF 2000

October 28, 2000

SEC. 2002.   PAYMENT OF CERTAIN ANTI–TERRORISM JUDGMENTS.

(a) PAYMENTS.—

(1) IN GENERAL.—Subject to subsections (b) and (c), the Secretary of the Treasury shall pay each person described in paragraph (2), at the person's election—

(A) 110 percent of compensatory damages awarded by judgment of a court on a claim or claims brought by the person under section 1605(a)(7) of title 28, United States Code, plus amounts necessary to pay post-judgment interest under section 1961 of such title, and, in the case of a claim or claims against Cuba, amounts awarded as sanctions by judicial order on April 18, 2000 (as corrected on June 2, 2000), subject to final appellate review of that order; or

(B) 100 percent of the compensatory damages awarded by judgment of a court on a claim or claims brought by the person under section 1605(a)(7) of title 28, United States Code, plus amounts necessary to pay post-judgment interest, as provided in section 1961 of such title, and, in the case of a claim or claims against Cuba, amounts awarded as sanctions by judicial order on April 18, 2000 (as corrected June 2, 2000), subject to final appellate review of that order. Payments under this subsection shall be made promptly upon request.

(2) PERSONS COVERED.—A person described in this paragraph is a person who—

(A)(i) as of July 20, 2000, held a final judgment for a claim or claims brought under section 1605(a)(7) of title 28, United States Code, against Iran or Cuba, or the right to payment of an amount awarded as a judicial sanction with respect to such claim or claims; or

(ii) filed a suit under such section 1605(a)(7) on February 17, 1999, December 13, 1999, January 28, 2000, March 15, 2000, or July 27, 2000;

(B) relinquishes all claims and rights to compensatory damages and amounts awarded as judicial sanctions under such judgments;

(C) in the case of payment under paragraph (1)(A), relinquishes all rights and claims to punitive damages awarded in connection with such claim or claims; and

(D) in the case of payment under paragraph (1)(B), relinquishes all rights to execute against or attach property that is at issue in claims against the United States before an international tribunal, that is the subject of awards rendered by such tribunal, or that is subject to section 1610(f)(1)(A) of title 28, United States Code.

(b) FUNDING OF AMOUNTS.—

(1) JUDGMENTS AGAINST CUBA.—For purposes of funding the payments under subsection (a) in the case of judgments and sanctions entered against the Government of Cuba or Cuban entities, the President shall vest and liquidate up to and not exceeding the amount of property of the Government of Cuba and sanctioned entities in the United States or any commonwealth, territory, or possession thereof that has been blocked pursuant to section 5(b) of the Trading with the Enemy Act (50 U.S.C. App. 5(b)), sections 202 and 203 of the International Emergency Economic Powers Act (50 U.S.C. 1701–1702), or any other proclamation, order, or regulation issued thereunder. For the purposes of paying amounts for judicial sanctions, payment shall be made from funds or accounts subject to sanctions as of April 18, 2000, or from blocked assets of the Government of Cuba.

(2) JUDGMENTS AGAINST IRAN.—For purposes of funding payments under subsection (a) in the case of judgments against Iran, the Secretary of the Treasury shall make such payments from amounts paid and liquidated from—

(A) rental proceeds accrued on the date of the enactment of this Act from Iranian diplomatic and consular property located in the United States; and

(B) funds not otherwise made available in an amount not to exceed the total of the amount in the Iran Foreign Military Sales Program account within the Foreign Military Sales Fund on the date of the enactment of this Act.

(c) SUBROGATION.—Upon payment under subsection (a) with respect to payments in connection with a Foreign Military Sales Program account, the United States shall be fully subrogated, to the extent of the payments, to all rights of the person paid under that subsection against the debtor foreign state. The President shall pursue these subrogated rights as claims or offsets of the United States in appropriate ways, including any negotiation process which precedes the normalization of relations between the foreign state designated as a state sponsor of terrorism and the United States, except that no funds shall be paid to Iran, or released to Iran, from property blocked under the International Emergency Economic Powers Act or from the Foreign Military Sales Fund, until such subrogated claims have been dealt with to the satisfaction of the United States.

(d) SENSE OF THE CONGRESS.—It is the sense of the Congress that the President should not normalize relations between the United States and Iran until the claims subrogated have been dealt with to the satisfaction of the United States.

(e) REAFFIRMATION OF AUTHORITY.—Congress reaffirms the President's statutory authority to manage and, where appropriate and consistent with the national interest, vest foreign assets located in the United States for the purposes, among other things, of assisting and, where appropriate, making payments to victims of terrorism.

(f) AMENDMENTS.—

(1) Section 1610(f) of title 28, United States Code, is amended—

(A) in paragraphs (2)(A) and (2)(B)(ii), by striking "shall" each place it appears and inserting "should make every effort to"; and

(B) by adding at the end the following new paragraph: "(3) WAIV-ER.—The President may waive any provision of paragraph (1) in the interest of national security."

(2) Subsections (b) and (d) of section 117 of the Treasury Department Appropriations Act, 1999 (as contained in section 101(h) of Public Law 105–277) are repealed.

VIENNA CONVENTION ON CONSULAR RELATIONS AND OPTIONAL PROTOCOL

Article 36

Communication and contact with nationals of the sending State

1. With a view to facilitating the exercise of consular functions relating to nationals of the sending State:

(a) consular officers shall be free to communicate with nationals of the sending State and to have access to them. Nationals of the sending State shall have the same freedom with respect to communication with and access to consular officers of the sending State;

(b) if he so requests, the competent authorities of the receiving State shall, without delay, inform the consular post of the sending State if, within its consular district, a national of that State is arrested or committed to prison or to custody pending trial or is detained in any other manner. Any communication addressed to the consular post by the person arrested, in prison, custody or detention shall also be forwarded by the said authorities without delay. The said authorities shall inform the person concerned without delay of his rights under this sub-paragraph;

(c) consular officers shall have the right to visit a national of the sending State who is in prison, custody or detention, to converse and correspond with him and to arrange for his legal representation. They shall also have the right to visit any national of the sending State who is in prison, custody or detention in their district in pursuance of a judgment. Nevertheless, consular officers shall refrain from taking action on behalf of a national who is in prison, custody or detention if he expressly opposes such action.

2. The rights referred to in paragraph 1 of this Article shall be exercised in conformity with the laws and regulations of the receiving State, subject to the proviso, however, that the said laws and regulations must enable full effect to be given to the purposes for which the rights accorded under this Article are intended.

OPTIONAL PROTOCOL CONCERNING THE COMPULSORY SETTLEMENT OF DISPUTES

The States Parties to the present Protocol and to the Vienna Convention on Consular Relations, hereinafter referred to as "the Convention", adopted by the United Nations Conference held at Vienna from 4 March to 22 April 1963,

Expressing their wish to resort in all matters concerning them in respect of any dispute arising out of the interpretation or application of the Convention to the compulsory jurisdiction of the International Court of Justice, unless some other form of settlement has been agreed upon by the parties within a reasonable period,

Have agreed as follows:

Article I

Disputes arising out of the interpretation or application of the Convention shall lie within the compulsory jurisdiction of the International Court of Justice and may accordingly be brought before the Court by an application made by any party to the dispute being a Party to the present Protocol.

Article II

The parties may agree, within a period of two months after one party has notified its opinion to the other that a dispute exists, to resort not to the International Court of Justice but to an arbitral tribunal. After the expiry of the said period, either party may bring the dispute before the Court by an application.

Article III

1. Within the same period of two months, the parties may agree to adopt a conciliation procedure before resorting to the International Court of Justice.

2. The conciliation commission shall make its recommendations within five months after its appointment. If its recommendations are not accepted by the parties to the dispute within two months after they have been delivered, either party may bring the dispute before the Court by an application.

Article IV

States Parties to the Convention, to the Optional Protocol concerning Acquisition of Nationality,[1] and to the present Protocol may at any time declare that they will extend the provisions of the present Protocol to disputes arising out of the interpretation or application of the Optional Protocol concerning Acquisition of Nationality. Such declarations shall be notified to the Secretary–General of the United Nations.

Article V

The present Protocol shall be open for signature by all States which may become Parties to the Convention as follows: until 31 October 1963 at the Federal Ministry for Foreign Affairs of the Republic of Austria and, subsequently, until 31 March 1964, at the United Nations Headquarters in New York.

Article VI

The present Protocol is subject to ratification. The instruments of ratification shall be deposited with the Secretary–General of the United Nations.

1. 596 UNTS 469.

Article VII

The present Protocol shall remain open for accession by all States which may become Parties to the Convention. The instruments of accession shall be deposited with the Secretary–General of the United Nations.

Article VIII

1.   The present Protocol shall enter into force on the same day as the Convention or on the thirtieth day following the date of deposit of the second instrument of ratification or accession to the Protocol with the Secretary–General of the United Nations, whichever date is the later.

2.   For each State ratifying or acceding to the present Protocol after its entry into force in accordance with paragraph 1 of this Article, the Protocol shall enter into force on the thirtieth day after deposit by such State of its instrument of ratification or accession.

Article IX

The Secretary–General of the United Nations shall inform all States which may become Parties to the Convention:

1.   (a) of signatures to the present Protocol and of the deposit of instruments of ratification or accession, in accordance with Articles V, VI and VII;

   (b) of declarations made in accordance with Article IV of the present Protocol;

   (c) of the date on which the present Protocol will enter into force, in accordance with Article VIII.

Article X

The original of the present Protocol, of which the Chinese, English, French, Russian and Spanish texts are equally authentic, shall be deposited with the Secretary–General [*172] of the United Nations, who shall send certified copies thereof to all States referred to in Article V.

IN WITNESS WHEREOF the undersigned plenipotentiaries, being duly authorised thereto by their respective Governments, have signed the present Protocol.

DONE AT VIENNA, this twenty-fourth day of April, one thousand nine hundred and sixty-three.

DISCOVERY AND FOREIGN GOVERNMENT COMPULSION: STATUTES AND TREATIES

FEDERAL RULES PERTAINING TO DISCOVERY

FEDERAL RULES OF CIVIL PROCEDURE

(as of 2003)

(Excerpts)

Rule 26. General Provisions Governing Discovery; Duty of Disclosure

(a) REQUIRED DISCLOSURES; METHODS TO DISCOVER ADDITIONAL MATTER.

(1) *Initial Disclosures*. Except in categories of proceedings specified in Rule 26(a)(1)(E), or to the extent otherwise stipulated or directed by order, a party must, without awaiting a discovery request, provide to other parties:

(A) the name and, if known, the address and telephone number of each individual likely to have discoverable information that the disclosing party may use to support its claims or defenses, unless solely for impeachment, identifying the subjects of the information;

(B) a copy of, or a description by category and location of, all documents, data compilations, and tangible things that are in the possession, custody, or control of the party and that the disclosing party may use to support its claims or defenses, unless solely for impeachment;

(C) a computation of any category of damages claimed by the disclosing party, making available for inspection and copying as under Rule 34 the documents or other evidentiary material, not privileged or protected from disclosure, on which such computation is based, including materials bearing on the nature and extent of injuries suffered; and

(D) for inspection and copying as under Rule 34 any insurance agreement under which any person carrying on an insurance business may be liable to satisfy part or all of a judgment which may be entered in the action or to indemnify or reimburse for payments made to satisfy the judgment.

(E) The following categories of proceedings are exempt from initial disclosure under Rule 26(a)(1):

(i) an action for review on an administrative record;

(ii) a petition for habeas corpus or other proceeding to challenge a criminal conviction or sentence;

(iii) an action brought without counsel by a person in custody of the United States, a state, or a state subdivision;

(iv) an action to enforce or quash an administrative summons or subpoena;

(v) an action by the United States to recover benefit payments;

(vi) an action by the United States to collect on a student loan guaranteed by the United States;

(vii) a proceeding ancillary to proceedings in other courts; and

(viii) an action to enforce an arbitration award.

These disclosures must be made at or within 14 days after the Rule 26(f) conference unless a different time is set by stipulation or court order, or unless a party objects during the conference that initial disclosures are not appropriate in the circumstances of the action and states the objection in the Rule 26(f) discovery plan. In ruling on the objection, the court must determine what disclosures—if any—are to be made, and set the time for disclosure. Any party first served or otherwise joined after the Rule 26(f) conference must make these disclosures within 30 days after being served or joined unless a different time is set by stipulation or court order. A party must make its initial disclosures based on the information then reasonably available to it and is not excused from making its disclosures because it has not fully completed its investigation of the case or because it challenges the sufficiency of another party's disclosures or because another party has not made its disclosures.

(2) *Disclosure of Expert Testimony.*

(A) In addition to the disclosures required by paragraph (1), a party shall disclose to other parties the identity of any person who may be used at trial to present evidence under Rules 702, 703, or 705 of the Federal Rules of Evidence.

(B) Except as otherwise stipulated or directed by the court, this disclosure shall, with respect to a witness who is retained or specially employed to provide expert testimony in the case or whose duties as an employee of the party regularly involve giving expert testimony, be accompanied by a written report prepared and signed by the witness. The report shall contain a complete statement of all opinions to be expressed and the basis and reasons therefor; the data or other information considered by the witness in forming the opinions; any exhibits to be used as a summary of or support for the opinions; the qualifications of the witness, including a list of all publications authored by the witness within the preceding ten years; the compensation to be paid for the study and testimony; and a listing of any other cases in which the witness has testified as an expert at trial or by deposition within the preceding four years.

(C) These disclosures shall be made at the times and in the sequence directed by the court. In the absence of other directions from the court or stipulation by the parties, the disclosures shall be made at least 90 days before the trial date or the date the case is to be ready for trial or, if the evidence is intended solely to contradict or rebut evidence on the same subject matter identified by another party under paragraph (2)(B), within 30 days after the disclosure made by the other party. The parties shall supplement these disclosures when required under subdivision (e)(1).

(3) *Pretrial Disclosures.* In addition to the disclosures required by Rule 26(a)(1) and (2), a party must provide to other parties and promptly file with the court the following information regarding the evidence that it may present at trial other than solely for impeachment:

(A) the name and, if not previously provided, the address and telephone number of each witness, separately identifying those whom the party expects to present and those whom the party may call if the need arises;

(B) the designation of those witnesses whose testimony is expected to be presented by means of a deposition and, if not taken stenographically, a transcript of the pertinent portions of the deposition testimony; and

(C) an appropriate identification of each document or other exhibit, including summaries of other evidence, separately identifying those which the party expects to offer and those which the party may offer if the need arises.

Unless otherwise directed by the court, these disclosures must be made at least 30 days before trial. Within 14 days thereafter, unless a different time is specified by the court, a party may serve and promptly file a list disclosing (i) any objections to the use under Rule 32(a) of a deposition designated by another party under Rule 26(a)(3)(B), and (ii) any objection, together with the grounds therefor, that may be made to the admissibility of materials identified under Rule 26(a)(3)(C). Objections not so disclosed, other than objections under Rules 402 and 403 of the

Federal Rules of Evidence, are waived unless excused by the court for good cause.

(4) *Form of Disclosures*. Unless the court orders otherwise, all disclosures under Rules 26(a)(1) through (3) must be made in writing, signed, and served.

(5) *Methods to Discover Additional Matter*. Parties may obtain discovery by one or more of the following methods: depositions upon oral examination or written questions; written interrogatories; production of documents or things or permission to enter upon land or other property under Rule 34 or 45(a)(1)(C), for inspection and other purposes; physical and mental examinations; and requests for admission.

(b) DISCOVERY SCOPE AND LIMITS. Unless otherwise limited by order of the court in accordance with these rules, the scope of discovery is as follows:

(1) *In General*. Parties may obtain discovery regarding any matter, not privileged, that is relevant to the claim or defense of any party, including the existence, description, nature, custody, condition, and location of any books, documents, or other tangible things and the identity and location of persons having knowledge of any discoverable matter. For good cause, the court may order discovery of any matter relevant to the subject matter involved in the action. Relevant information need not be admissible at the trial if the discovery appears reasonably calculated to lead to the discovery of admissible evidence. All discovery is subject to the limitations imposed by Rule 26(b)(2)(i), (ii), and (iii).

(2) *Limitations*. By order, the court may alter the limits in these rules on the number of depositions and interrogatories or the length of depositions under Rule 30. By order or local rule, the court may also limit the number of requests under Rule 36. The frequency or extent of use of the discovery methods otherwise permitted under these rules and by any local rule shall be limited by the court if it determines that: (i) the discovery sought is unreasonably cumulative or duplicative, or is obtainable from some other source that is more convenient, less burdensome, or less expensive; (ii) the party seeking discovery has had ample opportunity by discovery in the action to obtain the information sought; or (iii) the burden or expense of the proposed discovery outweighs its likely benefit, taking into account the needs of the case, the amount in controversy, the parties' resources, the importance of the issues at stake in the litigation, and the importance of the proposed discovery in resolving the issues. The court may act upon its own initiative after reasonable notice or pursuant to a motion under Rule 26(c).

(3) *Trial Preparation: Materials*. Subject to the provisions of subdivision (b)(4) of this rule, a party may obtain discovery of documents and tangible things otherwise discoverable under subdivision (b)(1) of this rule and prepared in anticipation of litigation or

for trial by or for another party or by or for that other party's representative (including the other party's attorney, consultant, surety, indemnitor, insurer, or agent) only upon a showing that the party seeking discovery has substantial need of the materials in the preparation of the party's case and that the party is unable without undue hardship to obtain the substantial equivalent of the materials by other means. In ordering discovery of such materials when the required showing has been made, the court shall protect against disclosure of the mental impressions, conclusions, opinions, or legal theories of an attorney or other representative of a party concerning the litigation.

A party may obtain without the required showing a statement concerning the action or its subject matter previously made by that party. Upon request, a person not a party may obtain without the required showing a statement concerning the action or its subject matter previously made by that person. If the request is refused, the person may move for a court order. The provisions of Rule 37(a)(4) apply to the award of expenses incurred in relation to the motion. For purposes of this paragraph, a statement previously made is (A) a written statement signed or otherwise adopted or approved by the person making it, or (B) a stenographic, mechanical, electrical, or other recording, or a transcription thereof, which is a substantially verbatim recital of an oral statement by the person making it and contemporaneously recorded.

(4) *Trial Preparation: Experts.*

(A) A party may depose any person who has been identified as an expert whose opinions may be presented at trial. If a report from the expert is required under subdivision (a)(2)(B), the deposition shall not be conducted until after the report is provided.

(B) A party may, through interrogatories or by deposition, discover facts known or opinions held by an expert who has been retained or specially employed by another party in anticipation of litigation or preparation for trial and who is not expected to be called as a witness at trial, only as provided in Rule 35(b) or upon a showing of exceptional circumstances under which it is impracticable for the party seeking discovery to obtain facts or opinions on the same subject by other means.

(C) Unless manifest injustice would result, (i) the court shall require that the party seeking discovery pay the expert a reasonable fee for time spent in responding to discovery under this subdivision; and (ii) with respect to discovery obtained under subdivision (b)(4)(B) of this rule the court shall require the party seeking discovery to pay the other party a fair portion of the fees and expenses reasonably incurred by the latter party in obtaining facts and opinions from the expert.

(5) *Claims of Privilege or Protection of Trial Preparation Materials.* When a party withholds information otherwise discoverable under these rules by claiming that it is privileged or subject to protection as trial preparation material, the party shall make the claim expressly and shall describe the nature of the documents, communications, or things not produced or disclosed in a manner that, without revealing information itself privileged or protected, will enable other parties to assess the applicability of the privilege or protection.

(c) PROTECTIVE ORDERS. Upon motion by a party or by the person from whom discovery is sought, accompanied by a certification that the movant has in good faith conferred or attempted to confer with other affected parties in an effort to resolve the dispute without court action, and for good cause shown, the court in which the action is pending or alternatively, on matters relating to a deposition, the court in the district where the deposition is to be taken may make any order which justice requires to protect a party or person from annoyance, embarrassment, oppression, or undue burden or expense, including one or more of the following:

(1) that the disclosure or discovery not be had;

(2) that the disclosure or discovery may be had only on specified terms and conditions, including a designation of the time or place;

(3) that the discovery may be had only by a method of discovery other than that selected by the party seeking discovery;

(4) that certain matters not be inquired into, or that the scope of the disclosure or discovery be limited to certain matters;

(5) that discovery be conducted with no one present except persons designated by the court;

(6) that a deposition, after being sealed, be opened only by order of the court;

(7) that a trade secret or other confidential research, development, or commercial information not be revealed or be revealed only in a designated way; and

(8) that the parties simultaneously file specified documents or information enclosed in sealed envelopes to be opened as directed by the court.

If the motion for a protective order is denied in whole or in part, the court may, on such terms and conditions as are just, order that any party or other person provide or permit discovery. The provisions of Rule 37(a)(4) apply to the award of expenses incurred in relation to the motion.

(d) TIMING AND SEQUENCE OF DISCOVERY. Except in categories of proceedings exempted from initial disclosure under Rule 26(a)(1)(E), or when authorized under these rules or by order or agreement of the parties, a party may not seek discovery from any source before the parties have conferred as required by Rule 26(f). Unless the court upon motion, for the convenience of parties and witnesses and in the interests of justice, orders otherwise, methods of discovery may be used in any sequence, and the fact that a party is conducting discovery, whether by deposition or otherwise, does not operate to delay any other party's discovery.

(e) SUPPLEMENTATION OF DISCLOSURES AND RESPONSES. A party who has made a disclosure under subdivision (a) or responded to a request for discovery with a disclosure or response is under a duty to supplement or correct the disclosure or response to include information thereafter acquired if ordered by the court or in the following circumstances:

(1) A party is under a duty to supplement at appropriate intervals its disclosures under subdivision (a) if the party learns that in some material respect the information disclosed is incomplete or incorrect and if the additional or corrective information has not otherwise been made known to the other parties during the discovery process or in writing. With respect to testimony of an expert from whom a report is required under subdivision (a)(2)(B) the duty extends both to information contained in the report and to information provided through a deposition of the expert, and any additions or other changes to this information shall be disclosed by the time the party's disclosures under Rule 26(a)(3) are due.

(2) A party is under a duty seasonably to amend a prior response to an interrogatory, request for production, or request for admission if the party learns that the response is in some material respect incomplete or incorrect and if the additional or corrective information has not otherwise been made known to the other parties during the discovery process or in writing.

(f) CONFERENCE OF PARTIES; PLANNING FOR DISCOVERY. Except in categories of proceedings exempted from initial disclosure under Rule 26(a)(1)(E) or when otherwise ordered, the parties must, as soon as practicable and in any event at least 21 days before a scheduling conference is held or a scheduling order is due under Rule 16(b), confer to consider the nature and basis of their claims and defenses and the possibilities for a prompt settlement or resolution of the case, to make or arrange for the disclosures required by Rule 26(a)(1), and to develop a proposed discovery plan that indicates the parties' views and proposals concerning:

(1) what changes should be made in the timing, form, or requirement for disclosures under Rule 26(a), including a statement as to when disclosures under Rule 26(a)(1) were made or will be made:

(2) the subjects on which discovery may be needed, when discovery should be completed, and whether discovery should be conducted in phases or be limited to or focused upon particular issues;

(3) what changes should be made in the limitations on discovery imposed under these rules or by local rule, and what other limitations should be imposed; and

(4) any other orders that should be entered by the court under Rule 26(c) or under Rule 16(b) and (c).

The attorneys of record and all unrepresented parties that have appeared in the case are jointly responsible for arranging the conference, for attempting in good faith to agree on the proposed discovery plan, and for submitting to the court within 14 days after the conference a written report outlining the plan. A court may order that the parties or attorneys attend the conference in person. If necessary to comply with its expedited schedule for Rule 16(b) conferences, a court may by local rule (i) require that the conference between the parties occur fewer than 21 days before the scheduling conference is held or a scheduling order is due under Rule 16(b), and (ii) require that the written report outlining the discovery plan be filed fewer than 14 days after the conference between the parties, or excuse the parties from submitting a written report and permit them to report orally on their discovery plan at the Rule 16(b) conference.

(g) Signing of Disclosures, Discovery Requests, Responses, and Objections.

(1) Every disclosure made pursuant to subdivision (a)(1) or subdivision (a)(3) shall be signed by at least one attorney of record in the attorney's individual name, whose address shall be stated. An unrepresented party shall sign the disclosure and state the party's address. The signature of the attorney or party constitutes a certification that to the best of the signer's knowledge, information, and belief, formed after a reasonable inquiry, the disclosure is complete and correct as of the time it is made.

(2) Every discovery request, response, or objection made by a party represented by an attorney shall be signed by at least one attorney of record in the attorney's individual name, whose address shall be stated. An unrepresented party shall sign the request, response, or objection and state the party's address. The signature of the attorney or party constitutes a certification that to the best of the signer's knowledge, information, and belief, formed after a reasonable inquiry, the request, response, or objection is:

(A) consistent with these rules and warranted by existing law or a good faith argument for the extension, modification, or reversal of existing law;

(B) not interposed for any improper purpose, such as to harass or to cause unnecessary delay or needless increase in the cost of litigation; and

(C) not unreasonable or unduly burdensome or expensive, given the needs of the case, the discovery already had in the case, the amount in controversy, and the importance of the issues at stake in the litigation.

If a request, response, or objection is not signed, it shall be stricken unless it is signed promptly after the omission is called to the attention of the party making the request, response, or objection, and a party shall not be obligated to take any action with respect to it until it is signed.

(3) If without substantial justification a certification is made in violation of the rule, the court, upon motion or upon its own initiative, shall impose upon the person who made the certification, the party on whose behalf the disclosure, request, response, or objection is made, or both, an appropriate sanction, which may include an order to pay the amount of the reasonable expenses incurred because of the violation, including a reasonable attorney's fee.

Rule 30. Depositions Upon Oral Examination

(a) When Depositions May Be Taken; When Leave Required.

(1) A party may take the testimony of any person, including a party, by deposition upon oral examination without leave of court except as provided in paragraph (2). The attendance of witnesses may be compelled by subpoena as provided in Rule 45.

(2) A party must obtain leave of court, which shall be granted to the extent consistent with the principles stated in rule 26(b)(2), if the person to be examined is confined in prison or if, without the written stipulation of the parties,

(A) a proposed deposition would result in more than ten depositions being taken under this rule or Rule 31 by the plaintiffs, or by the defendants, or by third-party defendants;

(B) the person to be examined already has been deposed in the case; or

(C) a party seeks to take a deposition before the time specified in Rule 26(d) unless the notice contains a certification, with supporting facts, that the person to be examined is expected to leave the United States and be unavailable for examination in this country unless deposed before that time.

(b) Notice of Examination: General Requirements; Method of Recording; Production of Documents and Things; Deposition of Organization; Deposition by Telephone.

(1) A party desiring to take the deposition of any person upon oral examination shall give reasonable notice in writing to every other party to the action. The notice shall state the time and place for taking the deposition and the name and address of each person to be examined, if known, and, if the name is not known, a general description sufficient to identify the person or the particular class or

group to which the person belongs. If a subpoena duces tecum is to be served on the person to be examined, the designation of the materials to be produced as set forth in the subpoena shall be attached to, or included in, the notice.

(2) The party taking the deposition shall state in the notice the method by which the testimony shall be recorded. Unless the court orders otherwise, it may be recorded by sound, sound-and-visual, or stenographic means, and the party taking the deposition shall bear the cost of the recording. Any party may arrange for a transcription to be made from the recording of a deposition taken by nonsteno-graphic means.

(3) With prior notice to the deponent and other parties, any party may designate another method to record the deponent's testimony in addition to the method specified by the person taking the deposition. The additional record or transcript shall be made at that party's expense unless the court otherwise orders.

(4) Unless otherwise agreed by the parties, a deposition shall be conducted before an officer appointed or designated under Rule 28 and shall begin with a statement on the record by the officer that includes (A) the officer's name and business address; (B) the date, time and place of the deposition; (C) the name of the deponent; (D) the administration of the oath or affirmation to the deponent; and (E) an identification of all persons present. If the deposition is recorded other than stenographically, the officer shall repeat items (A) through (C) at the beginning of each unit of recorded tape or other recording medium. The appearance or demeanor of deponents or attorneys shall not be distorted through camera or sound-recording techniques. At the end of the deposition, the officer shall state on the record that the deposition is complete and shall set forth any stipulations made by counsel concerning the custody of the transcript or recording and the exhibits, or concerning other pertinent matters.

(5) The notice to a party deponent may be accompanied by a request made in compliance with Rule 34 for the production of documents and tangible things at the taking of the deposition. The procedure of Rule 34 shall apply to the request.

(6) A party may in the party's notice and in a subpoena name as the deponent a public or private corporation or a partnership or association or governmental agency and describe with reasonable particularity the matters on which examination is requested. In that event, the organization so named shall designate one or more officers, directors, or managing agents, or other persons who consent to testify on its behalf, and may set forth, for each person designated, the matters on which the person will testify. A subpoena shall advise a non-party organization of its duty to make such a designation. The persons so designated shall testify as to matters known or reasonably available to the organization. This subdivision (b)(6) does

not preclude taking a deposition by any other procedure authorized in these rules.

(7) The parties may stipulate in writing or the court may upon motion order that a deposition be taken by telephone or other remote electronic means. For the purposes of this rule and Rules 28(a), 37(a)(1), and 37(b)(1), a deposition taken by such means is taken in the district and at the place where the deponent is to answer questions.

(c) Examination and Cross–Examination; Record of Examination; Oath; Objections. Examination and cross-examination of witnesses may proceed as permitted at the trial under the provisions of the Federal Rules of Evidence except Rules 103 and 615. The officer before whom the deposition is to be taken shall put the witness on oath or affirmation and shall personally, or by someone acting under the officer's direction and in the officer's presence, record the testimony of the witness. The testimony shall be taken stenographically or recorded by any other method authorized by subdivision (b)(2) of this rule. All objections made at the time of the examination to the qualifications of the officer taking the deposition, to the manner of taking it, to the evidence presented, to the conduct of any party, or to any other aspect of the proceedings shall be noted by the officer upon the record of the deposition; but the examination shall proceed, with the testimony being taken subject to the objections. In lieu of participating in the oral examination, parties may serve written questions in a sealed envelope on the party taking the deposition and the party taking the deposition shall transmit them to the officer, who shall propound them to the witness and record the answers verbatim.

(d) Schedule and Duration; Motion to Terminate or Limit Examination.

(1) Any objection during a deposition must be stated concisely and in a non-argumentative and non-suggestive manner. A person may instruct a deponent not to answer only when necessary to preserve a privilege, to enforce a limitation directed by the court, or to present a motion under Rule 30(d)(4).

(2) Unless otherwise authorized by the court or stipulated by the parties, a deposition is limited to one day of seven hours. The court must allow additional time consistent with Rule 26(b)(2) if needed for a fair examination of the deponent or if the deponent or another person, or other circumstance, impedes or delays the examination.

(3) If the court finds that any impediment, delay, or other conduct has frustrated the fair examination of the deponent, it may impose upon the persons responsible an appropriate sanction, including the reasonable costs and attorney's fees incurred by any parties as a result thereof.

(4) At any time during a deposition, on motion of a party or of the deponent and upon a showing that the examination is being conducted in bad faith or in such manner as unreasonably to annoy, embarrass, or oppress the deponent or party, the court in which the action is pending or the court in the district where the deposition is

being taken may order the officer conducting the examination to cease forthwith from taking the deposition, or may limit the scope and manner of the taking of the deposition as provided in Rule 26(c). If the order made terminates the examination, it may be resumed thereafter only upon the order of the court in which the action is pending. Upon demand of the objecting party or deponent, the taking of the deposition must be suspended for the time necessary to make a motion for an order. The provisions of Rule 37(a)(4) apply to the award of expenses incurred in relation to the motion.

(e) Review by Witness; Changes; Signing. If requested by the deponent or a party before completion of the deposition, the deponent shall have 30 days after being notified by the officer that the transcript or recording is available in which to review the transcript or recording and, if there are changes in form or substance, to sign a statement reciting such changes and the reasons given by the deponent for making them. The officer shall indicate in the certificate prescribed by subdivision (f)(1) whether any review was requested and, if so, shall append any changes made by the deponent during the period allowed.

(f) Certification and Delivery by Officer; Exhibits; Copies.

(1) The officer must certify that the witness was duly sworn by the officer and that the deposition is a true record of the testimony given by the witness. This certificate must be in writing and accompany the record of the deposition. Unless otherwise ordered by the court, the officer must securely seal the deposition in an envelope or package indorsed with the title of the action and marked "Deposition of [here insert name of witness]" and must promptly send it to the attorney who arranged for the transcript or recording, who must store it under conditions that will protect it against loss, destruction, tampering, or deterioration. Documents and things produced for inspection during the examination of the witness must, upon the request of a party, be marked for identification and annexed to the deposition and may be inspected and copied by any party, except that if the person producing the materials desires to retain them the person may (A) offer copies to be marked for identification and annexed to the deposition and to serve thereafter as originals if the person affords to all parties fair opportunity to verify the copies by comparison with the originals, or (B) offer the originals to be marked for identification, after giving to each party an opportunity to inspect and copy them, in which event the materials may then be used in the same manner as if annexed to the deposition. Any party may move for an order that the original be annexed to and returned with the deposition to the court, pending final disposition of the case.

(2) Unless otherwise ordered by the court or agreed by the parties, the officer shall retain stenographic notes of any deposition taken stenographically or a copy of the recording of any deposition taken by another method. Upon payment of reasonable charges therefor, the officer shall furnish a copy of the transcript or other recording of the deposition to any party or to the deponent.

(3) The party taking the deposition shall give prompt notice of its filing to all other parties.

(g) Failure to Attend or to Serve Subpoena; Expenses.

(1) If the party giving the notice of the taking of a deposition fails to attend and proceed therewith and another party attends in person or by attorney pursuant to the notice, the court may order the party giving the notice to pay to such other party the reasonable expenses incurred by that party and that party's attorney in attending, including reasonable attorney's fees.

(2) If the party giving the notice of the taking of a deposition of a witness fails to serve a subpoena upon the witness and the witness because of such failure does not attend, and if another party attends in person or by attorney because that party expects the deposition of that witness to be taken, the court may order the party giving the notice to pay to such other party the reasonable expenses incurred by that party and that party's attorney in attending, including reasonable attorney's fees.

[Amended 1963; 1970; 1971; 1975; 1980; 1987; 1993; 2000.]

Rule 34. Production of Documents and Things and Entry Upon Land for Inspection and Other Purposes

(a) Scope. Any party may serve on any other party a request (1) to produce and permit the party making the request, or someone acting on the requestor's behalf, to inspect and copy, any designated documents (including writings, drawings, graphs, charts, photographs, phonorecords, and other data compilations from which information can be obtained, translated, if necessary, by the respondent through detection devices into reasonably usable form), or to inspect and copy, test, or sample any tangible things which constitute or contain matters within the scope of Rule 26(b) and which are in the possession, custody or control of the party upon whom the request is served; or (2) to permit entry upon designated land or other property in the possession or control of the party upon whom the request is served for the purpose of inspection and measuring, surveying, photographing, testing, or sampling the property or any designated object or operation thereon, within the scope of Rule 26(b).

(b) Procedure. The request shall set forth, either by individual item or by category, the items to be inspected, and describe each with reasonable particularity. The request shall specify a reasonable time, place, and manner of making the inspection and performing the related acts. Without leave of court or written stipulation, a request may not be served before the time specified in Rule 26(d).

The party upon whom the request is served shall serve a written response within 30 days after the service of the request. A shorter or longer time may be directed by the court or, in the absence of such an order, agreed to in writing by the parties, subject to Rule 29. The response shall state, with respect to each item or category, that inspection and related activities will be permitted as requested, unless the request is objected to, in which event the reasons for the objection shall be stated. If objection is made to part of an item or category, the part shall be specified and inspection permitted of the remaining parts. The party submitting the request may move for an order under Rule 37(a) with respect to any objection to or other failure to respond to the request or any part thereof, or any failure to permit inspection as requested.

A party who produces documents for inspection shall produce them as they are kept in the usual course of business or shall organize and label them to correspond with the categories in the request.

(c) Persons Not Parties. A person not a party to the action may be compelled to produce documents and things or to submit to an inspection as provided in Rule 45.

[Amended 1948; 1970; 1980; 1987; 1991; 1993.]

Rule 37. Failure to Make Disclosure or Cooperate in Discovery: Sanctions

(a) Motion for Order Compelling Disclosure or Discovery. A party, upon reasonable notice to other parties and all persons affected thereby, may apply for an order compelling disclosure or discovery as follows:

(1) *Appropriate Court.* An application for an order to a party shall be made to the court in which the action is pending. An application for an order to a person who is not a party shall be made to the court in the district where the discovery is being, or is to be, taken.

(2) *Motion.*

(A) If a party fails to make a disclosure required by Rule 26(a), any other party may move to compel disclosure and for appropriate sanctions. The motion must include a certification that the movant has in good faith conferred or attempted to confer with the party not making the disclosure in an effort to secure the disclosure without court action.

(B) If a deponent fails to answer a question propounded or submitted under Rules 30 or 31, or a corporation or other entity fails to make a designation under Rule 30(b)(6) or 31(a), or a party fails to answer an interrogatory submitted under Rule 33, or if a party, in response to a request for inspection submitted under Rule 34, fails to respond that inspection will be permitted as requested or fails to permit inspection as requested, the discovering party may move for an order compelling an answer, or a designation, or an order compelling inspection in accordance with the request. The motion must include a certification that the movant has in good faith conferred or attempted to confer with the person or party failing to make the discovery in an effort to secure the information or material without court action. When taking a deposition on oral examination, the proponent of the question may complete or adjourn the examination before applying for an order.

(3) *Evasive or Incomplete Disclosure, Answer, or Response.* For purposes of this subdivision an evasive or incomplete disclosure,

answer, or response is to be treated as a failure to disclose, answer, or respond.

(4) *Expenses and Sanctions*.

(A) If the motion is granted or if the disclosure or requested discovery is provided after the motion was filed, the court shall, after affording an opportunity to be heard, require the party or deponent whose conduct necessitated the motion or the party or attorney advising such conduct or both of them to pay to the moving party the reasonable expenses incurred in making the motion, including attorney's fees, unless the court finds that the motion was filed without the movant's first making a good faith effort to obtain the disclosure or discovery without court action, or that the opposing party's nondisclosure, response, or objection was substantially justified, or that other circumstances make an award of expenses unjust.

(B) If the motion is denied, the court may enter any protective order authorized under Rule 26(c) and shall, after affording an opportunity to be heard, require the moving party or the attorney filing the motion or both of them to pay to the party or deponent who opposed the motion the reasonable expenses incurred in opposing the motion, including attorney's fees, unless the court finds that the making of the motion was substantially justified or that other circumstances make an award of expenses unjust.

(C) If the motion is granted in part and denied in part, the court may enter any protective order authorized under Rule 26(c) and may, after affording an opportunity to be heard, apportion the reasonable expenses incurred in relation to the motion among the parties and persons in a just manner.

(b) Failure to Comply with Order.

(1) *Sanctions by Court in District Where Deposition is Taken.* If a deponent fails to be sworn or to answer a question after being directed to do so by the court in the district in which the deposition is being taken, the failure may be considered a contempt of that court.

(2) *Sanctions by Court in Which Action is Pending.* If a party or an officer, director, or managing agent of a party or a person designated under Rule 30(b)(6) or 31(a) to testify on behalf of a party fails to obey an order to provide or permit discovery, including an order made under subdivision (a) of this rule or rule 35, or if a party fails to obey an order entered under Rule 26(f), the court in which the action is pending may make such orders in regard to the failure as are just, and among others the following:

(A) An order that the matters regarding which the order was made or any other designated facts shall be taken to be established for the purposes of the action in accordance with the claim of the party obtaining the order;

(B) An order refusing to allow the disobedient party to support or oppose designated claims or defenses, or prohibiting that party from introducing designated matters in evidence;

(C) An order striking out pleadings or parts thereof, or staying further proceedings until the order is obeyed, or dismissing the action or proceeding or any part thereof, or rendering a judgment by default against the disobedient party;

(D) In lieu of any of the foregoing orders or in addition thereto, an order treating as a contempt of court the failure to obey any orders except an order to submit to a physical or mental examination;

(E) Where a party has failed to comply with an order under Rule 35(a) requiring that party to produce another for examination, such orders as are listed in paragraphs (A), (B), and (C) of this subdivision, unless the party failing to comply shows that that party is unable to produce such person for examination.

In lieu of any of the foregoing orders or in addition thereto, the court shall require the party failing to obey the order or the attorney advising that party or both to pay the reasonable expenses, including attorney's fees, caused by the failure, unless the court finds that the failure was substantially justified or that other circumstances make an award of expenses unjust.

(o) Failure to Disclose; False or Misleading Disclosure; Refusal to Admit.

(1) A party that without substantial justification fails to disclose information required by Rule 26(a) or 26(e)(1) shall not, unless such failure is harmless, be permitted to use as evidence at a trial, at a hearing, or on a motion any witness or information not so disclosed. In addition to or in lieu of this sanction, the court, on motion and after affording an opportunity to be heard, may impose other appropriate sanctions. In addition to requiring payment of reasonable expenses, including attorney's fees, caused by the failure, these sanctions may include any of the actions authorized under subparagraphs (A), (B), and (C) of subdivision (b)(2) of this rule and may include informing the jury of the failure to make the disclosure.

(2) If a party fails to admit the genuineness of any document or the truth of any matter as requested under Rule 36, and if the party requesting the admissions thereafter proves the genuineness of the document or the truth of the matter, the requesting party may apply to the court for an order requiring the other party to pay the reasonable expenses incurred in making that proof, including reasonable attorney's fees. The court shall make the order unless it finds that

(A) the request was held objectionable pursuant to Rule 36(a), or

(B) the admission sought was of no substantial importance, or

(C) the party failing to admit had reasonable ground to believe that the party might prevail on the matter, or

(D) there was other good reason for the failure to admit.

(d) Failure of Party to Attend at Own Deposition or Serve Answers to Interrogatories or Respond to Request for Inspection. If a party or an officer, director, or managing agent of a party or a person designated under Rule 30(b)(6) or 31(a) to testify on behalf of a party fails

(1) to appear before the officer who is to take the deposition, after being served with a proper notice, or

(2) to serve answers or objections to interrogatories submitted under Rule 33, after proper service of the interrogatories, or

(3) to serve a written response to a request for inspection submitted under Rule 34, after proper service of the request, the court in which the action is pending on motion may make such orders in regard to the failure as are just, and among others it may take any action authorized under paragraphs (A), (B), and (C) of subdivision (b)(2) of this rule. Any motion specifying a failure under clause (2) or (3) of this subdivision shall include a certification that the movant has in good faith conferred or attempted to confer with the party failing to answer or respond in an effort to obtain such answer or response without court action. In lieu of any order or in addition thereto, the court shall require the party failing to act or the attorney advising that party or both to pay the reasonable expenses, including attorney's fees, caused by the failure, unless the court finds that the failure was substantially justified or that other circumstances make an award of expenses unjust.

The failure to act described in this subdivision may not be excused on the ground that the discovery sought is objectionable unless the party failing to act has a pending motion for a protective order as provided by Rule 26(c).

(e) Subpoena of Person in Foreign Country. [Abrogated eff. 1980]

(f) Expenses Against United States. [Repealed eff. 1981]

(g) Failure to Participate in the Framing of a Discovery Plan. If a party or a party's attorney fails to participate in good faith in the development and submission of a proposed discovery plan as required by Rule 26(f), the court may, after opportunity for hearing, require such party or attorney to pay to any other party the reasonable expenses, including attorney's fees, caused by the failure.

[As amended 1949; 1970; 1980; 1980; 1981; 1987; 1993.]

FEDERAL RULES OF CRIMINAL PROCEDURE
Rule 17. Subpoena

(a) Content. A subpoena must state the court's name and the title of the proceeding, include the seal of the court, and command the witness to attend and testify at the time and place the subpoena specifies. The clerk must issue a blank subpoena—signed and sealed—to the party requesting it, and that party must fill in the blanks before the subpoena is served.

(b) Defendant Unable to Pay. Upon a defendant's ex parte application, the court must order that a subpoena be issued for a named witness if the defendant shows an inability to pay the witness's fees and the necessity of the witness's presence for an adequate defense. If the court orders a subpoena to be issued, the process costs and witness fees will be paid in the same manner as those paid for witnesses the government subpoenas.

(c) Producing Documents and Objects.

(1) In General. A subpoena may order the witness to produce any books, papers, documents, data, or other objects the subpoena designates. The court may direct the witness to produce the designated items in court before trial or before they are to be offered in evidence. When the items arrive, the court may permit the parties and their attorneys to inspect all or part of them.

(2) Quashing or Modifying the Subpoena. On motion made promptly, the court may quash or modify the subpoena if compliance would be unreasonable or oppressive.

(d) Service. A marshal, a deputy marshal, or any nonparty who is at least 18 years old may serve a subpoena. The server must deliver a copy of the subpoena to the witness and must tender to the witness one day's witness-attendance fee and the legal mileage allowance. The server need not tender the attendance fee or mileage allowance when the United States, a federal officer, or a federal agency has requested the subpoena.

(e) Place of Service.

(1) In the United States. A subpoena requiring a witness to attend a hearing or trial may be served at any place within the United States.

(2) In a Foreign Country. If the witness is in a foreign country, 28 U.S.C. § 1783 governs the subpoena's service.

(f) Issuing a Deposition Subpoena.

(1) Issuance. A court order to take a deposition authorizes the clerk in the district where the deposition is to be taken to issue a subpoena for any witness named or described in the order.

(2) Place. After considering the convenience of the witness and the parties, the court may order—and the subpoena may require—the witness to appear anywhere the court designates.

(g) Contempt. The court (other than a magistrate judge) may hold in contempt a witness who, without adequate excuse, disobeys a subpoena issued by a federal court in that district. A magistrate judge may hold in contempt a witness who, without adequate excuse, disobeys a subpoena issued by that magistrate judge as provided in 28 U.S.C. § 636(e).

(h) Information Not Subject to a Subpoena. No party may subpoena a statement of a witness or of a prospective witness under this rule. Rule 26.2 governs the production of the statement.

(As amended 1949; 1966; 1972; 1975; 1975; 1980; 1987; 1993; 2002.)

U.S. STATUTES ON INTERNATIONAL JUDICIAL ASSISTANCE

28 U.S.C.

§ 1696.   Service in foreign and international litigation

(a) The district court of the district in which a person resides or is found may order service upon him of any document issued in connection with a proceeding in a foreign or international tribunal. The order may be made pursuant to a letter rogatory issued, or request made, by a foreign or international tribunal or upon application of any interested person and shall direct the manner of service. Service pursuant to this subsection does not, of itself, require the recognition or enforcement in the United States of a judgment, decree, or order rendered by a foreign or international tribunal.

(b) This section does not preclude service of such a document without an order of court.

§ 1781.   Transmittal of letter rogatory or request

(a) The Department of State has power, directly, or through suitable channels—

> (1) to receive a letter rogatory issued, or request made, by a foreign or international tribunal, to transmit it to the tribunal, officer, or agency in the United States to whom it is addressed, and to receive and return it after execution; and

> (2) to receive a letter rogatory issued, or request made, by a tribunal in the United States, to transmit it to the foreign or international tribunal, officer, or agency to whom it is addressed, and to receive and return it after execution.

(b) This section does not preclude—

> (1) the transmittal of a letter rogatory or request directly from a foreign or international tribunal to the tribunal, officer, or agency in the United States to whom it is addressed and its return in the same manner; or

> (2) the transmittal of a letter rogatory or request directly from a tribunal in the United States to the foreign or international tribunal, officer, or agency to whom it is addressed and its return in the same manner.

§ 1782.   Assistance to foreign and international tribunals and to litigants before such tribunals

(a) The district court of the district in which a person resides or is found may order him to give his testimony or statement or to produce a document or other thing for use in a proceeding in a foreign or international tribunal [, including criminal investigations conducted before formal accusation].* The order may be made pursuant to a letter rogatory issued, or request made, by a foreign or international tribunal or upon the application of any interested person and may direct that the testimony or statement be given, or the document or other thing be produced, before a person appointed by the court. By virtue of his appointment, the person appointed has power to administer any necessary oath and take the testimony or statement. The order may prescribe the practice and procedure, which may be in whole or part the practice and procedure of the foreign country or the international tribunal, for taking the testimony or statement or producing the document or other thing. To the extent that the order does not prescribe otherwise, the testimony or statement shall be taken, and the document or other thing produced, in accordance with the Federal Rules of Civil Procedure.

A person may not be compelled to give his testimony or statement or to produce a document or other thing in violation of any legally applicable privilege.

(b) This chapter does not preclude a person within the United States from voluntarily giving his testimony or statement, or producing a document or other thing, for use in a proceeding in a foreign or international tribunal before any person and in any manner acceptable to him.

§ 1783.   Subpoena of person in foreign country

(a) A court of the United States may order the issuance of a subpoena requiring the appearance as a witness before it, or before a person or body designated by it, of a national or resident of the United States who is in a foreign country, or requiring the production of a specified document or other thing by him, if the court finds that particular testimony or the production of the document or other thing by him is necessary in the interest of justice, and, in other than a criminal action or proceeding, if the court finds, in addition, that it is not possible to obtain his testimony in admissible form without his personal appearance or to obtain the production of the document or other thing in any other manner.

(b) The subpoena shall designate the time and place for the appearance or for the production of the document or other thing. Service of the subpoena and any order to show cause, rule, judgment, or decree authorized by this section or by section 1784 of this title shall be effected in accordance with the provisions of the Federal Rules of Civil Procedure relating to service of process on a person in a foreign country. The person serving the subpoena shall tender to the person to whom the subpoena is addressed his estimated necessary travel and attendance expenses, the amount of which shall be determined by the court and stated in the order directing the issuance of the subpoena.

* Bracketed language added in 1996.

§ 1784. Contempt

(a) The court of the United States which has issued a subpoena served in a foreign country may order the person who has failed to appear or who has failed to produce a document or other thing as directed therein to show cause before it at a designated time why he should not be punished for contempt.

(b) The court, in the order to show cause, may direct that any of the person's property within the United States be levied upon or seized, in the manner provided by law or court rules governing levy or seizure under execution, and held to satisfy any judgment that may be rendered against him pursuant to subsection (d) of this section if adequate security, in such amount as the court may direct in the order, be given for any damage that he might suffer should he not be found in contempt. Security under this subsection may not be required of the United States.

(c) A copy of the order to show cause shall be served on the person in accordance with section 1783(b) of this title.

(d) On the return day of the order to show cause or any later day to which the hearing may be continued, proof shall be taken. If the person is found in contempt, the court, notwithstanding any limitation upon its power generally to punish for contempt, may fine him not more than $100,000 and direct that the fine and costs of the proceedings be satisfied by a sale of the property levied upon or seized, conducted upon the notice required and in the manner provided for sales upon execution.

SWITZERLAND: BANKING AND BUSINESS SECRECY ACTS

Banking Act

(Excerpts)

Article 47

1. Whoever divulges a secret entrusted to him in his capacity as officer, employee, mandatory, liquidator or commissioner of a bank, as a representative of the Banking Commission, officer or employee of a recognized auditing company, or who has become aware of such a secret in this capacity, and whoever tries to induce others to violate professional secrecy, shall be punished by a prison term not to exceed six months or by a fine not exceeding 50,000 francs.

2. If the act has been committed by negligence, the penalty shall be a fine not exceeding 30,000 francs.

3. The violation of professional secrecy remains punishable even after termination of the official or employment relationship or the exercise of the profession.

4. Federal and cantonal regulations concerning the obligation to testify and to furnish information to a government authority shall remain reserved.

Penal Code

(Excerpt)

Article 273—Economic Espionage

Whoever attempts to obtain a trade or business secret in order to disclose it, or whoever discloses such a secret to a foreign official or private organization, or to a foreign business firm, or to their agents, shall be punished with imprisonment. . . . The judge may also levy a fine.

UNITED KINGDOM: SHIPPING CONTRACTS AND COMMERCIAL DOCUMENTS ACT 1964

An Act to secure Her Majesty's jurisdiction against encroachment by certain foreign requirements in respect of the carriage of goods or passengers by sea and in respect of the production of documents and furnishing of information.

BE IT ENACTED by the Queen's most Excellent Majesty, by and with the advice and consent of the Lords Spiritual and Temporal, and Commons, in this present Parliament assembled, and by the authority of the same, as follows:—

1. (1) If it appears to the Minister of Transport (in this section referred to as "the Minister")—

(a) that measures have been taken by or under the law of any foreign country for regulating or controlling the terms or conditions upon which goods or passengers may be carried by sea, or the terms or conditions of contracts or arrangements relating to such carriage; and

(b) that those measures, in so far as they apply to things done or to be done outside the territorial jurisdiction of that country by persons carrying on business in the United Kingdom, constitute an infringement of the jurisdiction which, under international law, belongs to the United Kingdom,

the Minister may by order direct that this section shall apply to those measures, either generally or in their application to such cases as may be specified in the order.

(2) Where an order is in force under subsection (1) of this section in relation to any measures—

(a) it shall be the duty of every person in the United Kingdom who carries on a business consisting of or comprising the carriage of goods or passengers by sea to give notice to the Minister of any requirement or prohibition imposed or threatened to be imposed on him pursuant to those measures so far as this section applies to them, including any requirement to submit any contract or other document for approval thereunder; and

(b) the Minister may give to any person in the United Kingdom who carries on such a business such directions for prohibiting compliance with any such requirement or prohibition as he considers proper for maintaining the jurisdiction of the United Kingdom.

(3) The power of the Minister to make orders under subsection (1) of this section shall include power to revoke an order by a subsequent order and shall be exercisable by statutory instrument; and any statutory instrument made by virtue of this section shall be subject to annulment in pursuance of a resolution of either House of Parliament.

(4) Any directions to be given by the Minister under subsection (2) of this section may be either general or special, and may prohibit compliance with any requirement or prohibition either absolutely or in such cases or subject to such conditions as to consent or otherwise as may be specified in the directions; and general directions given under that subsection shall be published in such manner as appears to the Minister to be appropriate.

2. (1) If it appears to any Minister of the Crown authorised to act under this section—

(a) that any person in the United Kingdom has been or may be required to produce or furnish to any court, tribunal or authority of a foreign country any commercial document which is not within the territorial jurisdiction of that country, or any commercial information to be compiled from documents not within that jurisdiction; and

(b) that the requirement constitutes or would constitute an infringement of the jurisdiction which, under international law, belongs to the United Kingdom,

that Minister may give directions to that person prohibiting him from complying with the requirement in question, or from complying with that requirement except to such extent or subject to such conditions as may be specified in the directions.

(2) The following Ministers are hereby authorised to act under this section, that is to say a Secretary of State, the President of the Board of Trade, the Minister of Aviation, the Minister of Power and the Minister of Transport.

(3) For the purposes of this section any request or demand for the supply of a document or information which, pursuant to the requirement of any court, tribunal or authority of a foreign country, is addressed to a person in the United Kingdom shall be treated as a requirement to produce or furnish that document or information to that court, tribunal or authority, and directions under this section may be given accordingly for prohibiting compliance therewith.

(4) In this section "commercial document" and "commercial information" mean respectively a document or information relating to a business of any description and "document" includes any record or device by means of which material is recorded or stored.

3. (1) Any person who wilfully fails to comply with section 1(2)(a) of this Act or contravenes any directions under this Act shall be liable on conviction on indictment to a fine which, in the case of an individual, shall not exceed £1,000.

(2) No proceedings for an offence punishable under this section shall be instituted in England and Wales or Northern Ireland except—

(a) in the case of a failure to comply with section 1(2)(a) of this Act, by the Minister of Transport; and

(b) in the case of a contravention of directions under this Act, by the Minister by whom those directions were given,

or in either case with the consent of the Attorney General or, as the case may be, the Attorney General for Northern Ireland.

(3) Proceedings against any person for an offence punishable under this section may be taken before the appropriate court in the United Kingdom having jurisdiction in the place where that person is for the time being.

4. (1) This Act may be cited as the Shipping Contracts and Commercial Documents Act 1964.

(2) It is hereby declared that this Act extends to Northern Ireland.

(3) Her Majesty may by Order in Council direct that this Act shall extend with such exceptions, adaptations and modifications, if any, as may be specified in the Order to any territory outside the United Kingdom, being a territory for the international relations of which Her Majesty's Government in the United Kingdom are responsible.

UNITED KINGDOM: PROTECTION OF TRADING INTERESTS ACT 1980

1. Overseas measures affecting United Kingdom trading interests

(1) If it appears to the Secretary of State—

(a) that measures have been or are proposed to be taken by or under the law of any overseas country for regulating or controlling international trade; and

(b) that those measures, in so far as they apply or would apply to things done or to be done outside the territorial jurisdiction of that country by persons carrying on business in the United Kingdom, are damaging or threaten to damage the trading interests of the United Kingdom,

the Secretary of State may by order direct that this section shall apply to those measures either generally or in their application to such cases as may be specified in the order.

(2) The Secretary of State may by order make provision for requiring, or enabling the Secretary of State to require, a person in the United Kingdom who carries on business there to give notice to the Secretary of State of any requirement or prohibition imposed or threatened to be imposed on that person pursuant to any measures in so far as this section applies to them by virtue of an order under subsection (1) above.

(3) The Secretary of State may give to any person in the United Kingdom who carries on business there such directions for prohibiting compliance with any such requirement or prohibition as aforesaid as he considers appropriate for avoiding damage to the trading interests of the United Kingdom.

(4) The power of the Secretary of State to make orders under subsection (1) or (2) above shall be exercisable by statutory instrument subject to annulment in pursuance of a resolution of either House of Parliament.

(5) Directions under subsection (3) above may be either general or special and may prohibit compliance with any requirement or prohibition either absolutely or in such cases or subject to such conditions as to consent or otherwise as may be specified in the directions; and general directions under that subsection shall be published in such manner as appears to the Secretary of State to be appropriate.

(6) In this section "trade" includes any activity carried on in the course of a business of any description and "trading interests" shall be construed accordingly.

2. Documents and information required by overseas courts and authorities

(1) If it appears to the Secretary of State—

(a) that a requirement has been or may be imposed on a person or persons in the United Kingdom to produce to any court, tribunal or authority of an overseas country any commercial document which is not within the territorial jurisdiction of that country or to furnish any commercial information to any such court, tribunal or authority; or

(b) that any such authority has imposed or may impose a requirement on a person or persons in the United Kingdom to publish any such document or information,

the Secretary of State may, if it appears to him that the requirement is inadmissible by virtue of subsection (2) or (3) below, give directions for prohibiting compliance with the requirement.

(2) A requirement such as is mentioned in subsection (1)(a) or (b) above is inadmissible—

(a) if it infringes the jurisdiction of the United Kingdom or is otherwise prejudicial to the sovereignty of the United Kingdom; or

(b) if compliance with the requirement would be prejudicial to the security of the United Kingdom or to the relations of the government of the United Kingdom with the government of any other country.

(3) A requirement such as is mentioned in subsection (1)(a) above is also inadmissible—

(a) if it is made otherwise than for the purposes of civil or criminal proceedings which have been instituted in the overseas country; or

(b) if it requires a person to state what documents relevant to any such proceedings are or have been in his possession, custody or power or to produce for the purposes of any such proceedings any documents other than particular documents specified in the requirement.

(4) Directions under subsection (1) above may be either general or special and may prohibit compliance with any requirement either absolutely or in such cases or subject to such conditions as to consent or otherwise as may be specified in the directions; and general directions under that subsection shall be published in such manner as appears to the Secretary of State to be appropriate.

(5) For the purposes of this section the making of a request or demand shall be treated as the imposition of a requirement if it is made in circumstances in which a requirement to the same effect could be or could have been imposed; and

(a) any request or demand for the supply of a document or information which, pursuant to the requirement of any court, tribunal or authority of an overseas country, is addressed to a person in the United Kingdom; or

(b) any requirement imposed by such a court, tribunal or authority to produce or furnish any document or information to a person specified in the requirement,

shall be treated as a requirement to produce or furnish that document or information to that court, tribunal or authority.

(6) In this section "commercial document" and "commercial information" mean respectively a document or information relating to a business of any description and "document" includes any record or device by means of which material is recorded or stored.

3.   Offences under §§ 1 and 2

(1) Subject to subsection (2) below, any person who without reasonable excuse fails to comply with any requirement imposed under subsection (2) of section 1 above or knowingly contravenes any directions given under subsection (3) of that section or section 2(1) above shall be guilty of an offence and liable—

(a) on conviction on indictment, to a fine;

(b) on summary conviction, to a fine not exceeding the statutory maximum.

(2) A person who is neither a citizen of the United Kingdom and Colonies nor a body corporate incorporated in the United Kingdom shall not be guilty of an offence under subsection (1) above by reason of anything done or omitted outside the United Kingdom in contravention of directions under section 1(3) or 2(1) above.

(3) No proceedings for an offence under subsection (1) above shall be instituted in England, Wales or Northern Ireland except by the Secretary of State or with the consent of the Attorney General or, as the case may be, the Attorney General for Northern Ireland.

(4) Proceedings against any person for an offence under this section may be taken before the appropriate court in the United Kingdom having jurisdiction in the place where that person is for the time being.

(5) In subsection (1) above "the statutory maximum" means—

(a) in England and Wales ... , the prescribed sum within the meaning of [section 32 of the Magistrates' Courts Act 1980] (at the passing of this Act £1,000);

(b) in Scotland, the prescribed sum within the meaning of section 289B of the Criminal Procedure (Scotland) Act 1975 (at the passing of this Act £1,000);

[(c) in Northern Ireland, the prescribed sum within the meaning of Article 4 of the Fines and Penalties (Northern Ireland) Order 1984].

4.   Restriction of Evidence (Proceedings in Other Jurisdictions) Act 1975

A court in the United Kingdom shall not make an order under section 2 of the Evidence (Proceedings in Other Jurisdictions) Act 1975 for giving effect to a request issued by or on behalf of a court or tribunal of an overseas country if it is shown that the request infringes the jurisdiction of the United Kingdom or is otherwise prejudicial to the sovereignty of the United Kingdom; and a certificate signed by or on behalf of the Secretary of State to the effect that it infringes that jurisdiction or is so prejudicial shall be conclusive evidence of that fact.

5. Restriction on enforcement of certain overseas judgments

(1) A judgment to which this section applies shall not be registered under Part II of the Administration of Justice Act 1920 or Part I of the Foreign Judgments (Reciprocal Enforcement) Act 1933 and no court in the United Kingdom shall entertain proceedings at common law for the recovery of any sum payable under such a judgment.

(2) This section applies to any judgment given by a court of an overseas country, being—

(a) a judgment for multiple damages within the meaning of subsection (3) below;

(b) a judgment based on a provision or rule of law specified or described in an order under subsection (4) below and given after the coming into force of the order; or

(c) a judgment on a claim for contribution in respect of damages awarded by a judgment falling within paragraph (a) or (b) above.

(3) In subsection (2)(a) above a judgment for multiple damages means a judgment for an amount arrived at by doubling, trebling or otherwise multiplying a sum assessed as compensation for the loss or damage sustained by the person in whose favour the judgment is given.

(4) The Secretary of State may for the purposes of subsection (2)(b) above make an order in respect of any provision or rule of law which appears to him to be concerned with the prohibition or regulation of agreements, arrangements or practices designed to restrain, distort or restrict competition in the carrying on of business of any description or to be otherwise concerned with the promotion of such competition as aforesaid.

(5) The power of the Secretary of State to make orders under subsection (4) above shall be exercisable by statutory instrument subject to annulment in pursuance of a resolution of either House of Parliament.

(6) Subsection (2)(a) above applies to a judgment given before the date of the passing of this Act as well as to a judgment given on or after that date but this section does not affect any judgment which has been registered before that date under the provisions mentioned in subsection (1) above or in respect of which such proceedings as are there mentioned have been finally determined before that date.

6. Recovery of awards of multiple damages

(1) This section applies where a court of an overseas country has given a judgment for multiple damages with the meaning of section 5(3) above against—

(a) a citizen of the United Kingdom and Colonies; or

(b) a body corporate incorporated in the United Kingdom or in a territory outside the United Kingdom for whose international relations Her Majesty's Government in the United Kingdom are responsible; or

(c) a person carrying on business in the United Kingdom,

(in this section referred to as a "qualifying defendant") and an amount on account of the damages has been paid by the qualifying defendant either to the party in whose favour the judgment was given or to another party who is entitled as against the qualifying defendant to contribution in respect of the damages.

(2) Subject to subsections (3) and (4) below, the qualifying defendant shall be entitled to recover from the party in whose favour the judgment was given so much of the amount referred to in subsection (1) above as exceeds the part attributable to compensation; and that part shall be taken to be such part of the amount as bears to the whole of it the same proportion as the sum assessed by the court that gave the judgment as compensation for the loss or damage sustained by that party bears to the whole of the damages awarded to that party.

(3) Subsection (2) above does not apply where the qualifying defendant is an individual who was ordinarily resident in the overseas country at the time when the proceedings in which the judgment was given were instituted or a body corporate which had its principal place of business there at that time.

(4) Subsection (2) above does not apply where the qualifying defendant carried on business in the overseas country and the proceedings in which the judgment was given were concerned with activities exclusively carried on in that country.

(5) A court in the United Kingdom may entertain proceedings on a claim under this section notwithstanding that the person against whom the proceedings are brought is not within the jurisdiction of the court.

(6) The reference in subsection (1) above to an amount paid by the qualifying defendant includes a reference to an amount obtained by execution against his property or against the property of a company which (directly or indirectly) is wholly owned by him; and references in that subsection and subsection (2) above to the party in whose favour the judgment was given or to a party entitled to contribution include references to any person in whom the rights of any such party have become vested by succession or assignment or otherwise.

(7) This section shall, with the necessary modifications, apply also in relation to any order which is made by a tribunal or authority of an overseas country and would, if that tribunal or authority were a court, be a judgment for multiple damages within the meaning of section 5(3) above.

(8) This section does not apply to any judgment given or order made before the passing of this Act.

7. Enforcement of overseas judgment under provision corresponding to § 6

(1) If it appears to Her Majesty that the law of an overseas country provides or will provide for the enforcement in that country of judgments given under section 6 above, Her Majesty may by Order in Council provide for the enforcement in the United Kingdom of [judgments of any description specified in the Order which are given under any provision of the law of that country relating to the recovery of sums paid or obtained pursuant to a judgment for multiple damages within the meaning of section 5(3) above, whether or not that provision corresponds to section 6 above].

[(1A) Such an Order in Council may, as respects judgments to which it relates—

    (a) make different provisions for different descriptions of judgment; and

    (b) impose conditions or restrictions on the enforcement of judgments of any description.]

(2) An Order under this section may apply, with or without modification, any of the provisions of the Foreign Judgments (Reciprocal Enforcement) Act 1933.

8. Short title, interpretation, repeals and extent

(1) This Act may be cited as the Protection of Trading Interests Act 1980.

(2) In this Act "overseas country" means any country or territory outside the United Kingdom other than one for whose international relations Her Majesty's Government in the United Kingdom are responsible.

(3) References in this Act to the law or a court, tribunal or authority of an overseas country include, in the case of a federal state, references to the law or a court, tribunal or authority of any constituent part of that country.

     .   .   .

FRANCE: LAW ON DOCUMENTS AND INFORMATION 1980*

Law relating to the Communication of Economic, Commercial, Industrial, Financial or Technical Documents or Information to Foreign Natural or Legal Persons

Article 1. Except when international treaties or agreements provide otherwise, no natural person of French nationality or habitually residing on French territory, nor any officer, representative, agent or employee of any legal entity having therein its principal office or an establishment, may in writing, orally or in any other form, transmit, no matter where, to foreign public authorities documents or information of an economic, commercial, industrial, financial or technical nature, the communication of which would threaten the sovereignty, security, or essential economic interests of France or public order, as defined by government authorities to the extent deemed necessary.

Article 1 *bis*. Except when international treaties or agreements and laws and regulations in force provide otherwise, no person may request, seek to obtain or transmit, in writing, orally or in any other form, documents or information of an economic, commercial, industrial, financial or technical nature, intended for the constitution of evidence in connection with pending or prospective foreign judicial or administrative proceedings.

Article 2. The persons referred to in Articles 1 and 1 *bis* are required to inform the relevant ministry immediately when they are asked to provide any such information.

Article 3. Without prejudice to any heavier penalties that may be provided by law, any violation of the provisions of Articles 1 and 1 *bis* of the present law shall be punished by imprisonment of from two to six months and a fine of from 10,000 to 120,000 francs or by one of these penalties.

* Law No. 80–538, [1980] J.O. 1799.

THE HAGUE EVIDENCE CONVENTION

CONVENTION ON THE TAKING OF EVIDENCE ABROAD IN CIVIL OR COMMERCIAL MATTERS

The States signatory to the present Convention,

Desiring to facilitate the transmission and execution of Letters of Request and to further the accommodation of the different methods which they use for this purpose,

Desiring to improve mutual judicial co-operation in civil or commercial matters,

Have resolved to conclude a Convention to this effect and have agreed upon the following provisions—

CHAPTER I—LETTERS OF REQUEST

Article 1

In civil or commercial matters a judicial authority of a Contracting State may, in accordance with the provisions of the law of that State, request the competent authority of another Contracting State, by means of a Letter of Request, to obtain evidence, or to perform some other judicial act.

A Letter shall not be used to obtain evidence which is not intended for use in judicial proceedings, commenced or contemplated.

The expression "other judicial act" does not cover the service of judicial documents or the issuance of any process by which judgments or orders are executed or enforced, or orders for provisional or protective measures.

Article 2

A Contracting State shall designate a Central Authority which will undertake to receive Letters of Request coming from a judicial authority of another Contracting State and to transmit them to the authority competent to execute them. Each State shall organize the Central Authority in accordance with its own law.

Letters shall be sent to the Central Authority of the State of execution without being transmitted through any other authority of that State.

Article 3

A Letter of Request shall specify—

(a) the authority requesting its execution and the authority requested to execute it, if known to the requesting authority;

(b) the names and addresses of the parties to the proceedings and their representatives, if any;

(c) the nature of the proceedings for which the evidence is required, giving all necessary information in regard thereto;

(d) the evidence to be obtained or other judicial act to be performed.

Where appropriate, the Letter shall specify, inter alia—

(e) the names and addresses of the persons to be examined;

(f) the questions to be put to the persons to be examined or a statement of the subject-matter about which they are to be examined;

(g) the documents or other property, real or personal, to be inspected;

(h) any requirement that the evidence is to be given on oath or affirmation, and any special form to be used;

(i) any special method or procedure to be followed under Article 9.

A Letter may also mention any information necessary for the application of Article 11. No legalization or other like formality may be required.

Article 4

A Letter of Request shall be in the language of the authority requested to execute it or be accompanied by a translation into that language.

Nevertheless, a Contracting State shall accept a Letter in either English or French, or a translation into one of these languages, unless it has made the reservation authorized by Article 33.

A Contracting State which has more than one official language and cannot, for reasons of internal law, accept Letters in one of these languages for the whole of its territory, shall, by declaration, specify the language in which the Letter or translation thereof shall be expressed for execution in the specified parts of its territory. In case of failure to comply with this declaration, without justifiable excuse, the costs of translation into the required language shall be borne by the State of origin.

A Contracting State may, by declaration, specify the language or languages other than those referred to in the preceding paragraphs, in which a Letter may be sent to its Central Authority.

Any translation accompanying a Letter shall be certified as correct, either by a diplomatic officer or consular agent or by a sworn translator or by any other person so authorized in either State.

Article 5

If the Central Authority considers that the request does not comply with the provisions of the present Convention, it shall promptly inform the authority of the State of origin which transmitted the Letter of Request, specifying the objections to the Letter.

Article 6

If the authority to whom a Letter of Request has been transmitted is not competent to execute it, the Letter shall be sent forthwith to the authority in the same State which is competent to execute it in accordance with the provisions of its own law.

Article 7

The requesting authority shall, if it so desires, be informed of the time when, and the place where, the proceedings will take place, in order that the parties concerned, and their representatives, if any, may be present. This information shall be sent directly to the parties or their representatives when the authority of the State of origin so requests.

Article 8

A Contracting State may declare that members of the judicial personnel of the requesting authority of another Contracting State may be present at the execution of a Letter of Request. Prior authorization by the competent authority designated by the declaring State may be required.

Article 9

The judicial authority which executes a Letter of Request shall apply its own law as to the methods and procedures to be followed.

However, it will follow a request of the requesting authority that a special method or procedure be followed, unless this is incompatible with the internal law of the State of execution or is impossible of performance by reason of its internal practice and procedure or by reason of practical difficulties.

A Letter of Request shall be executed expeditiously.

Article 10

In executing a Letter of Request the requested authority shall apply the appropriate measures of compulsion in the instances and to the same extent as are provided by its internal law for the execution of orders issued by the authorities of its own country or of requests made by parties in internal proceedings.

Article 11

In the execution of a Letter of Request the person concerned may refuse to give evidence in so far as he has a privilege or duty to refuse to give the evidence—

(a) under the law of the State of execution; or

(b) under the law of the State of origin, and the privilege or duty has been specified in the Letter, or, at the instance of the requested authority, has been otherwise confirmed to that authority by the requesting authority.

A Contracting State may declare that, in addition, it will respect privileges and duties existing under the law of States other than the State of origin and the State of execution, to the extent specified in that declaration.

Article 12

The execution of a Letter of Request may be refused only to the extent that—

(a) in the State of execution the execution of the Letter does not fall within the functions of the judiciary; or

(b) the State addressed considers that its sovereignty or security would be prejudiced thereby

Execution may not be refused solely on the ground that under its internal law the State of execution claims exclusive jurisdiction over the subject-matter of the action or that its internal law would not admit a right of action on it.

Article 13

The documents establishing the execution of the Letter of Request shall be sent by the requested authority to the requesting authority by the same channel which was used by the latter.

In every instance where the Letter is not executed in whole or in part, the requesting authority shall be informed immediately through the same channel and advised of the reasons.

Article 14

The execution of the Letter of Request shall not give rise to any reimbursement of taxes or costs of any nature.

Nevertheless, the State of execution has the right to require the State of origin to reimburse the fees paid to experts and interpreters and the costs occasioned by the use of a special procedure requested by the State of origin under Article 9, paragraph 2.

The requested authority whose law obliges the parties themselves to secure evidence, and which is not able itself to execute the Letter, may, after having obtained the consent of the requesting authority, appoint a suitable person to do so. When seeking this consent the requested authority shall indicate the approximate costs which would result from this procedure. If the requesting authority gives its consent it shall reimburse any costs incurred; without such consent the requesting authority shall not be liable for the costs.

CHAPTER II—TAKING OF EVIDENCE BY DIPLOMATIC OFFICERS, CONSULAR AGENTS AND COMMISSIONERS

Article 15

In a civil or commercial matter, a diplomatic officer or consular agent of a Contracting State may, in the territory of another Contracting

State and within the area where he exercises his functions, take the evidence without compulsion of nationals of a State which he represents in aid of proceedings commenced in the courts of a State which he represents.

A Contracting State may declare that evidence may be taken by a diplomatic officer or consular agent only if permission to that effect is given upon application made by him or on his behalf to the appropriate authority designated by the declaring State.

Article 16

A diplomatic officer or consular agent of a Contracting State may, in the territory of another Contracting State and within the area where he exercises his functions, also take the evidence, without compulsion, of nationals of the State in which he exercises his functions or of a third State, in aid of proceedings commenced in the courts of a State which he represents, if—

(a) a competent authority designated by the State in which he exercises his functions has given its permission either generally or in the particular case, and

(b) he complies with the conditions which the competent authority has specified in the permission.

A Contracting State may declare that evidence may be taken under this Article without its prior permission.

Article 17

In a civil or commercial matter, a person duly appointed as a commissioner for the purpose may, without compulsion, take evidence in the territory of a Contracting State in aid of proceedings commenced in the courts of another Contracting State if—

(a) a competent authority designated by the State where the evidence is to be taken has given its permission either generally or in the particular case; and

(b) he complies with the conditions which the competent authority has specified in the permission.

A Contracting State may declare that evidence may be taken under this Article without its prior permission.

Article 18

A Contracting State may declare that a diplomatic officer, consular agent or commissioner authorized to take evidence under Articles 15, 16 or 17, may apply to the competent authority designated by the declaring State for appropriate assistance to obtain the evidence by compulsion. The declaration may contain such conditions as the declaring State may see fit to impose.

If the authority grants the application it shall apply any measures of compulsion which are appropriate and are prescribed by its law for use in internal proceedings.

Article 19

The competent authority, in giving the permission referred to in Articles 15, 16 or 17, or in granting the application referred to in Article 18, may lay down such conditions as it deems fit, *inter alia,* as to the time and place of the taking of the evidence. Similarly it may require that it be given reasonable advance notice of the time, date and place of the taking of the evidence; in such a case a representative of the authority shall be entitled to be present at the taking of the evidence.

Article 20

In the taking of evidence under any Article of this Chapter persons concerned may be legally represented.

Article 21

Where a diplomatic officer, consular agent or commissioner is authorized under Articles 15, 16 or 17 to take evidence—

(a) he may take all kinds of evidence which are not incompatible with the law of the State where the evidence is taken or contrary to any permission granted pursuant to the above Articles, and shall have power within such limits to administer an oath or take an affirmation;

(b) a request to a person to appear or to give evidence shall, unless the recipient is a national of the State where the action is pending, be drawn up in the language of the place where the evidence is taken or be accompanied by a translation into such language;

(c) the request shall inform the person that he may be legally represented and, in any State that has not filed a declaration under Article 18, shall also inform him that he is not compelled to appear or to give evidence;

(d) the evidence may be taken in the manner provided by the law applicable to the court in which the action is pending provided that such manner is not forbidden by the law of the State where the evidence is taken;

(e) a person requested to give evidence may invoke the privileges and duties to refuse to give the evidence contained in Article 11.

Article 22

The fact that an attempt to take evidence under the procedure laid down in this Chapter has failed, owing to the refusal of a person to give evidence, shall not prevent an application being subsequently made to take the evidence in accordance with Chapter I.

CHAPTER III—GENERAL CLAUSES

Article 23

A Contracting State may at the time of signature, ratification or accession, declare that it will not execute Letters of Request issued for the purpose of obtaining pretrial discovery of documents as known in Common Law countries.

Article 24

A Contracting State may designate other authorities in addition to the Central Authority and shall determine the extent of their competence. However, Letters of Request may in all cases be sent to the Central Authority.

Federal States shall be free to designate more than one Central Authority.

Article 25

A Contracting State which has more than one legal system may designate the authorities of one of such systems, which shall have exclusive competence to execute Letters of Request pursuant to this Convention.

Article 26

A Contracting State, if required to do so because of constitutional limitations, may request the reimbursement by the State of origin of fees and costs, in connection with the execution of Letters of Request, for the service of process necessary to compel the appearance of a person to give evidence, the costs of attendance of such persons, and the cost of any transcript of the evidence.

Where a State has made a request pursuant to the above paragraph, any other Contracting State may request from that State the reimbursement of similar fees and costs.

Article 27

The provisions of the present Convention shall not prevent a Contracting State from—

(a) declaring that Letters of Request may be transmitted to its judicial authorities through channels other than those provided for in Article 2;

(b) permitting, by internal law or practice, any act provided for in this Convention to be performed upon less restrictive conditions;

(c) permitting, by internal law or practice, methods of taking evidence other than those provided for in this Convention.

Article 28

The present Convention shall not prevent an agreement between any two or more Contracting States to derogate from—

(a) the provisions of Article 2 with respect to methods of transmitting Letters of Request;

(b) the provisions of Article 4 with respect to the languages which may be used;

(c) the provisions of Article 8 with respect to the presence of judicial personnel at the execution of Letters;

(d) the provisions of Article 11 with respect to the privileges and duties of witnesses to refuse to give evidence;

(e) the provisions of Article 13 with respect to the methods of returning executed Letters to the requesting authority;

(f) the provisions of Article 14 with respect to fees and costs;

(g) the provisions of Chapter II.

Article 29

Between Parties to the present Convention who are also Parties to one or both of the Conventions on Civil Procedure signed at the Hague on the 17th of July 1905 [99 British Foreign and State Papers 990] and the 1st of March 1954 [286 UNTS 265], this Convention shall replace Articles 8–16 of the earlier Conventions.

Article 30

The present Convention shall not affect the application of Article 23 of the Convention of 1905, or of Article 24 of the Convention of 1954.

Article 31

Supplementary Agreements between Parties to the Conventions of 1905 and 1954 shall be considered as equally applicable to the present Convention unless the Parties have otherwise agreed.

Article 32

Without prejudice to the provisions of Articles 29 and 31, the present Convention shall not derogate from conventions containing provisions on the matters covered by this Convention to which the Contracting States are, or shall become Parties.

Article 33

A State may, at the time of signature, ratification or accession exclude, in whole or in part, the application of the provisions of paragraph 2 of Article 4 and of Chapter II. No other reservation shall be permitted.

Each Contracting State may at any time withdraw a reservation it has made; the reservation shall cease to have effect on the sixtieth day after notification of the withdrawal.

When a State has made a reservation, any other State affected thereby may apply the same rule against the reserving State.

Article 34

A State may at any time withdraw or modify a declaration.

Article 35

A Contracting State shall, at the time of the deposit of its instrument of ratification or accession, or at a later date, inform the Ministry of Foreign Affairs of the Netherlands of the designation of authorities, pursuant to Articles 2, 8, 24 and 25.

A Contracting State shall likewise inform the Ministry, where appropriate, of the following—

(a) The designation of the authorities to whom notice must be given, whose permission may be required, and whose assistance may be invoked in the taking of evidence by diplomatic officers and consular agents, pursuant to Articles 15, 16 and 18 respectively;

(b) the designation of the authorities whose permission may be required in the taking of evidence by commissioners pursuant to Article 17 and of those who may grant the assistance provided for in Article 18;

(c) declarations pursuant to Articles 4, 8, 11, 15, 16, 17, 18, 23 and 27;

(d) any withdrawal or modification of the above designations and declarations;

(e) the withdrawal of any reservation.

Article 36

Any difficulties which may arise between Contracting States in connection with the operation of this Convention shall be settled through diplomatic channels.

Article 37

The present Convention shall be open for signature by the States represented at the Eleventh Session of the Hague Conference on Private International Law.

It shall be ratified, and the instruments of ratification shall be deposited with the Ministry of Foreign Affairs of the Netherlands.

Article 38

The present Convention shall enter into force on the sixtieth day after the deposit of the third instrument of ratification referred to in the second paragraph of Article 37.

The Convention shall enter into force for each signatory State which ratifies subsequently on the sixtieth day after the deposit of its instrument of ratification.

Article 39

Any State not represented at the Eleventh Session of the Hague Conference on Private International Law which is a Member of this Conference or of the United Nations or of a specialized agency of that Organization, or a Party to the Statute of the International Court of Justice may accede to the present Convention after it has entered into force in accordance with the first paragraph of Article 38.

The instrument of accession shall be deposited with the Ministry of Foreign Affairs of the Netherlands.

The Convention shall enter into force for a State acceding to it on the sixtieth day after the deposit of its instrument of accession.

The accession will have effect only as regards the relations between the acceding State and such Contracting States as will have declared their acceptance of the accession. Such declaration shall be deposited at the Ministry of Foreign Affairs of the Netherlands; this Ministry shall forward, through diplomatic channels, a certified copy to each of the Contracting States.

The Convention will enter into force as between the acceding State and the State that has declared its acceptance of the accession on the sixtieth day after the deposit of the declaration of acceptance.

Article 40

Any State may, at the time of signature, ratification or accession, declare that the present Convention shall extend to all the territories for the international relations of which it is responsible, or to one or more of them. Such a declaration shall take effect on the date of entry into force of the Convention for the State concerned. At any time thereafter, such extensions shall be notified to the Ministry of Foreign Affairs of the Netherlands.

The Convention shall enter into force for the territories mentioned in such an extension on the sixtieth day after the notification indicated in the preceding paragraph.

Article 41

The present Convention shall remain in force for five years from the date of its entry into force in accordance with the first paragraph of Article 38, even for States which have ratified it or acceded to it subsequently.

If there has been no denunciation, it shall be renewed tacitly every five years.

Any denunciation shall be notified to the Ministry of Foreign Affairs of the Netherlands at least six months before the end of the five year period.

It may be limited to certain of the territories to which the Convention applies.

The denunciation shall have effect only as regards the State which has notified it. The Convention shall remain in force for the other Contracting States.

Article 42

The Ministry of Foreign Affairs of the Netherlands shall give notice to the States referred to in Article 37, and to the States which have acceded in accordance with Article 39, of the following—

(a) the signatures and ratifications referred to in Article 37;

(b) the date on which the present Convention enters into force in accordance with the first paragraph of Article 38;

(c) the accessions referred to in Article 39 and the dates on which they take effect;

(d) the extensions referred to in Article 40 and the dates on which they take effect;

(e) the designations, reservations and declarations referred to in Articles 33 and 35;

(f) the denunciations referred to in the third paragraph of Article 41.

IN WITNESS WHEREOF the undersigned, being duly authorised thereto, have signed the present Convention.

DONE at The Hague, on the 18th day of March 1970, in the English and French languages, both texts being equally authentic, in a single copy which shall be deposited in the archives of the Government of the Netherlands, and of which a certified copy shall be sent, through the diplomatic channel, to each of the States represented at the Eleventh Session of the Hague Conference on Private International Law.

Done at The Hague March 18, 1970; entered into force for the United States October 7, 1972.

MODEL FOR LETTERS OF REQUEST RECOMMENDED FOR USE IN APPLYING THE HAGUE CONVENTION OF 18 MARCH 1970 ON THE TAKING OF EVIDENCE ABROAD IN CIVIL OR COMMERCIAL MATTERS

Request for International Judicial Assistance Pursuant to the Hague Convention of 18 March 1970 on the Taking of Evidence in Civil or Commercial Matters

N.B. Under the first paragraph of article 4, the Letter of Request shall be in the language of the authority requested to execute it or be accompanied by a 05translation into that language. However, the provisions of the second and third paragraphs may permit use of other languages.

———

In order to avoid confusion, please spell out the name of the month in each date.

———

I.   *(Items to be included in all Letters of Request.)*

    1. Sender   ____*(identity and address)*____

    2. Central Authority of the Requested State   ____*(identity and address)*____

    3. Person to whom the executed request is to be returned   ____*(identity and address)*____

II. *(Items to be included in all Letters of Request.)*

    4. In conformity with article 3 of the Convention, the undersigned applicant has the honour to submit the following request:

    5. a. Requesting judicial authority (article 3, a)   ____*(identity and address)*____

        b. To the competent authority of (article 3, a)   ____*(the requested State)*____

6. Names and addresses of the parties and their representatives (article 3, b)
    a. Plaintiff

    _____
    _____
    _____

    b. Defendant

    _____
    _____
    _____

    c. Other parties

    _____
    _____
    _____
    _____

7. Nature and purpose of the proceedings and summary of the facts (article 3, c)

    _____
    _____
    _____

8. Evidence to be obtained or other judicial act to be performed (article 3, d)

    _____
    _____
    _____

III. *(Items to be completed where applicable.)*

9. Identity and address of any person to be examined (article 3, e)

    _____
    _____
    _____

10. Questions to be put to the persons to be examined or statement of the subject-matter about which they are to be examined (article 3, f)

    _____
    ____*(or see attached list)*____
    _____
    _____

11. Documents or other property to be inspected (article 3, g)

    _____
    ____*(specify whether it is to be produced, copied, valued, etc.)*

12. Any requirement that the evidence be given on oath or affirmation and any special form to be used (article 3, h)

    _____
    _____
    ____*(In the event that the evidence cannot be taken in the manner requested, specify whether it is to be taken in such manner as provided by local law for the formal taking of evidence.)*_____

13. Special methods or procedure to be followed (articles 3, i and 9)

    _____
    _____

14. Request for notification of the time and place for the execution of the Request and identity and address of any person to be notified (article 7)

    _____
    _____
    _____
    _____

15. Request for attendance or participation of judicial personnel of the requesting authority at the execution of the letter of Request   _____

16. Specification of privilege or duty to refuse to give evidence under the law of the State of origin (article 11, b)   _____

17. The fees and costs incurred which are reimbursable under the second paragraph of article 14 or under article 26 of the Convention will be borne by   *____(identity and address)____*

IV. *(Items to be included in all Letters of Request.)*

18. Date of request   _____

19. Signature and seal of the requesting authority   _____

HAGUE EVIDENCE CONVENTION
DECLARATIONS PURSUANT TO ARTICLE 23

Standard Declaration (made by all states except the United States, Czechoslovakia, and Israel, and those states following the British example):

[The Federal Republic of Germany] declares in pursuance of Article 23 of the Convention that it will not, in its territory, execute Letters of Request issued for the purpose of obtaining pre-trial discovery of documents as known in Common Law countries.

British Declaration (made by the United Kingdom and Singapore):

In accordance with Article 23 Her Majesty's Government declare that the United Kingdom will not execute Letters of Request issued for the purpose of obtaining pre-trial discovery of documents. Her Majesty's Government further declare that Her Majesty's Government understand "Letters of Request issued for the purpose of obtaining pre-trial discovery of documents" for the purposes of the foregoing Declaration as including any Letter of Request which requires a person:—

> a. to state what documents relevant to the proceedings to which the Letter of Request relates are, or have been, in his possession, custody, or power; or

> b. to produce any documents other than particular documents specified in the Letter of Request as being documents appearing to the requesting court to be, or to be likely to be, in his possession, custody or power.

Modified French Declaration Under Article 23
(January 19, 1987)

. . .

The declaration made by the French Republic in accordance with Article 23 relating to Letters of Request issued for the purpose of obtaining pre-trial discovery of documents does not apply when the requested documents are enumerated limitatively in the Letter of Request and have a direct and precise link with the object of the procedure.

Letter from Ministry of Justice Federal Republic of Germany
(October 16, 1990)

. . . With reference to the issuance of an order concerning discovery of documents pursuant to Section 14(2) of the German Law for the Implementation of the Hague Evidence Convention of 1970, I hereby inform you that there is hardly any prospect for the issuance of such an order. It can only be suggested to counsel for German firms which are supposed to produce documents to apply to the American court for appointment of a commissioner, so that the document production in Germany may take place in accordance with the rules of the judicial administration of the respective states ...

Switzerland Declaration

In accordance with Article 23, Switzerland declares that Letters of Request issued for the purpose of obtaining pre-trial discovery of documents will not be executed if:

a) the request has no direct and necessary link with the proceedings in question; or

b) a person is required to indicate what documents relating to the case are or were in his/her possession or keeping or at his/her disposal; or

c) a person is required to produce documents other than those mentioned in the request for legal assistance, which are probably in his/her possession or keeping or at his/her disposal; or

d) interests worthy of protection of the concerned persons are endangered.

Parties to the Convention

(as of 2004)

Argentina
Australia
Barbados
Belarus
Bulgaria
China (People's Republic of)
Cyprus
Czech Republic
Denmark
Estonia
Finland
France
Germany
Hungary
Israel
Italy
Kuwait
Latvia
Lithuania
Luxembourg
Mexico
Monaco

Netherlands
Norway
Poland
Portugal
Romania
Russian Federation
Seychelles
Singapore
Slovak Republic
Slovenia
South Africa
Spain
Sri Lanka
Sweden
Switzerland
Turkey
Ukraine
United Kingdom of Great Britain and Northern Ireland
United States of America
Venezuela

†